T0384657

THE VANISHED SETTLERS
OF GREENLAND

For 400 years Norse settlers battled to make southern Greenland a new, sustainable home. They strove against gales and winter cold, food shortages, and, in the end, a shifting climate. The remnants they left behind speak of their determination to wrest an existence at the foot of this vast, icy, and challenging wilderness. Yet finally, seemingly suddenly, they vanished and their mysterious disappearance in the fifteenth century has posed a riddle to scholars ever since. What happened to the lost Viking colonists? For centuries people assumed their descendants could still be living, so expeditions went to find them, to no avail. Robert W. Rix tells the gripping story of the missing pioneers, placing their poignant history in the context of cultural discourse and imperial politics. Ranging across fiction, poetry, navigation, reception, and tales of exploration, he expertly delves into one of the most contested questions in the annals of colonisation.

Robert W. Rix is Associate Professor and Director of Research at the University of Copenhagen. He is widely known for his prolific publication profile in eighteenth- and nineteenth-century studies, covering areas such as politics, religion, language, nationalism, and print culture. He is author of *William Blake and the Cultures of Radical Christianity* (2007) and *The Barbarian North in Medieval Imagination Ethnicity, Legend, and Literature* (2014).

THE VANISHED SETTLERS OF GREENLAND

IN SEARCH OF A LEGEND AND ITS LEGACY

ROBERT W. RIX

University of Copenhagen

CAMBRIDGE
UNIVERSITY PRESS

CAMBRIDGE
UNIVERSITY PRESS

Shaftesbury Road, Cambridge CB2 8EA, United Kingdom

One Liberty Plaza, 20th Floor, New York, NY 10006, USA

477 Williamstown Road, Port Melbourne, VIC 3207, Australia

314–321, 3rd Floor, Plot 3, Splendor Forum, Jasola District Centre, New Delhi – 110025, India

103 Penang Road, #05–06/07, Visioncrest Commercial, Singapore 238467

Cambridge University Press is part of Cambridge University Press & Assessment, a department of the University of Cambridge.

We share the University's mission to contribute to society through the pursuit of education, learning and research at the highest international levels of excellence.

www.cambridge.org
Information on this title: www.cambridge.org/9781009359474
DOI: 10.1017/9781009359450

First published 2023
(version 2, August 2023)

Printed in Great Britain by CPI Group (UK) Ltd, Croydon CR0 4YY

A catalogue record for this publication is available from the British Library.

ISBN 978-1-009-35947-4 Hardback

CONTENTS

v

FIGURES

ACKNOWLEDGEMENTS

Research towards this book was supported by a generous grant from the Carlsberg Foundation, which enabled me to spend a glorious twelve months to complete the monograph. During the time it took to write the book, several people provided moral support. I am thankful for the opportunity to acknowledge them. I especially thank Line, David, my mother, and Cian Duffy. I appreciate the invaluable feedback I received from Robert Rintoull and Kevin Kroh, as well as from Naja Trondhjem on Kalaallisut issues. Moreover, I benefitted from the two readers' comments, which have helped to make this a better book. The work on James Hogg's *Surpassing Adventures* was first undertaken as the result of a kind invitation from Marcus Poetzsch and Cassandra Falke to contribute to *Wild Romanticism* (2021), but the article that ended up in that collection bears little resemblance to the analysis included in Chapter 6. For the images, I would like to thank Nemi Nødskov, who put her digital skills to good use in making the Greenland map, Helle Brünnich Pedersen at the Danish Royal Library and Hanne Kirkegaard at Nuuk Art Museum. Fortunately, this book landed in the expert hands of Cambridge University Press, where Bethany Thomas has been an excellent editor. Needless to say, errors and inadequacies are my responsibility.

INTRODUCTION

Greenland is the world's largest island. Its mainland extends from Cape Farewell (Nunap Isua) in the south to Odak Island (Oodaap Qeqertaa) in the north. Around 94 per cent of the island is covered by ice, and only the fjords in the coastal areas are suitable for human habitation. Greenland is geologically as well as geographically part of North America but belongs politically to Denmark. Since 2008 the island has been a self-governing overseas administrative division within the Danish realm. The modern European colonisation of Greenland began in 1721, when the Dano-Norwegian missionary Hans Egede landed in Greenland. This was a significant step towards cementing Greenland's political affiliation with Denmark, which had long claimed the island without having a physical presence there. The inhabitants of Greenland at the time were Inuit, but the argument consistently put forward for Danish possession contended that a colony had settled on the island in the mid-980s (primarily Icelandic farmers) and that this colony had later come under Danish suzerainty. The Greenland settlements formed a northern outpost of European civilisation and Christianity until all contact with Greenland was lost soon after 1410. The fate of the colonists remained a mystery, and the circumstances surrounding their disappearance have still not been fully explained. Archaeology has shown that the colonists vanished from Greenland in the course of the fifteenth century. For centuries, it was thought that their descendants still inhabited the land. The enigma of the colony's survival was compounded by an erroneous interpretation of what is referred to in old texts as the 'Eastern Settlement'. Although the settlement was located on Greenland's west coast, the name led to the belief that it was placed on the east coast. As the eastern shore of Greenland is inaccessible because of pack ice, what was hidden there could only be guessed at, and many presumed that the colonists were still living on their farms, tilling their fields.

The present book does not purport to be a history of Greenland as it exists in real space and time. I distinguish between Greenland, its actual local culture and heritage, and the Western European and North American cultural constructions of it. This study seeks to understand how Greenland's vanished settlers became a cultural memory, augmented and amplified in a large number of texts over time. In the centuries when there was no empirical knowledge about most of the landmass, Greenland became a 'myth' in the sense coined by Claude Lévi-Strauss – that is, not a complete fiction but what may best be described as a multifaceted cultural and ideological construct.[1] Enduring narratives of Greenland were established based on a mélange of garbled facts, misunderstandings, and sometimes runaway imagination. When it came to conceptions of precious resources, Greenland and its settlements found a place in the discourse of Western imperialism which warrants more attention than it has received.

Studies of why the European colonists vanished from Greenland are not in short supply, but it is not among my aims to proffer yet another revisionary explanation for their demise. Rather, the focus in the present book is on how the 'lost colony' lived on in the Western imagination, how the colony attained an extensive narrative afterlife. *The Vanished Settlers of Greenland: In Search of a Legend and Its Legacy* is the first study to examine how the memory of Greenland's 'lost colony' was transmitted, interpreted, and negotiated from the late sixteenth century to the early twentieth. The vanished settlers became a central reference in a series of both connected and diverse discourses. One of the earliest uses of the history of Greenland's colonisation was that it made legible a hope of conquering the Arctic. The 'lost colony' was a myth that memorialised a colonial past, yet it also configured the forward flow of history by providing schemas for imperialist politics. However, as Europeans settled in areas yet more remote from the centre, the vanished settlers also became a mirror reflecting the fears associated with Europe's two expansionist movements, colonialism and Christian mission. For much of the timespan covered in this book, the Greenland colonists were thought to still be alive, but the inability to find them meant that they were believed to suffer under total isolation from the civilised world. This spoke to the danger of colonising remote lands and the fear of losing one's Christian identity in foreign climes. Yet, in other representations, the colony, isolated behind a wall of ice allowing no ingress, was hailed as a safe haven from the corruption of modern life. This book studies the multifaceted and shifting functions that the myth of the vanished settlers assumed.

Greenland was imagined in texts long before it was explored. Even after the west coast was comprehensively surveyed by Europeans, writers kept guessing at what secrets may lie beyond the unmapped horizon in the east. When new information was brought back from Greenland, it further stirred the imagination, thus creating a loop, rendering it relevant to study textual and actual exploration as part of the same nexus. To understand how the signifier of the 'lost colony' developed and transmuted into legend in Western discourse, I shall on several occasions refer to the workings of print culture, since texts and translations of those texts enabled information about Greenland to travel across time and language. The myth of Greenland's vanished settlers was created through intertextuality.

The examination of how Greenland became part of the West's discourse begins in the late sixteenth century and concludes in the late 1920s. The termination point is chosen because, at this time, the extensive exploration of the Arctic finally extinguished all hope of finding a 'lost colony' hidden somewhere in the vast Arctic Sea. This left even writers of adventure fiction bereft of a legitimate space for the imagination. If *The Vanished Settlers of Greenland* ranges far in its temporal scope, each chapter fits a jigsaw piece into our understanding of how Greenland's colonial past became a centuries-long narrative that gained renewed significance in step with shifting political needs and national discourses, first in Europe, then in North America. It is from the longitudinal study of the West's imagining of Greenland's vanished settlers that one can draw conclusions about historical trends and patterns that would not otherwise be visible. Giving priority to long-term historical structures allows me to trace recurring tropes and observe evolving frameworks of representation across time.

When I first spoke to colleagues about Greenland's vanished settlers as a subject for a monograph, several of them compared Greenland to the Roanoke colony in what is now North Carolina. Roanoke was the first British attempt at colonisation on mainland North America, but by 1590 some 112 to 120 colonists had mysteriously vanished. The Roanoke colony's narrative afterlife in the United States is vast and often tinged with various degrees of mystery-solving, nostalgia, and white entitlement to the land. Unlike the extensive scholarship that has accumulated around this incident of American history, researchers have made no matching effort to investigate Greenland's 'lost colony'. Several excellent studies of Greenland have focused on Denmark's modern colonial role, but my thesis is that a history of Greenland's past cannot be examined solely from a mono-national perspective. The present study includes not only Danish, but also British, German, French, Dutch, Italian, and American sources. This is because the settlements in Greenland came to be seen as part of a shared Western history. Especially British interest in Greenland warrants critical study. As Duncan Depledge reminds us: for a period of 400 years, Britain was an 'Arctic state' with its polar explorations, holdings in Arctic North America, and industrial whaling operations on Spitsbergen (Svalbard).[2] The engagement with the 'lost colony' in British texts, not least in literary writing, has not previously been the subject of comprehensive inquiry.

As will become clear, it is also in relation to literary and fictional texts about Greenland's lost European colony that we find a critical lacuna, which it is my ambition to fill. In this respect, it is useful here at the outset to give an example of how Greenland's unsolved mystery intrigued a nineteenth-century literary writer. As a twenty-year-old medical student Arthur Conan Doyle enlisted as a surgeon on board a Greenland whaler which would sail to the ice-clogged waters between Greenland and Spitsbergen. Service aboard whalers was relatively common among medical students, lured by both money and the experience, and Conan Doyle would subsequently draw upon his experiences in several articles. In one of these articles, entitled 'The Glamour of the Arctic' (1892), he speculates about the potential that the 'ancient city' of Greenland, imprisoned behind sea ice, holds for the imagination.[3] Conan Doyle wonders if the Norse colonists are 'still singing and drinking and fighting', have been 'destroyed by the hated Skraelings [the Inuit]', or have intermarried to produce 'a race of tow-headed, large-limbed Esquimaux?'.[4] As we shall see, the possibilities that Conan Doyle mentions were all suggested and sometimes vigorously pursued by several others. In his article, Conan Doyle decides that the fate of the colonists is 'one of those interesting historical questions' better left 'unsolved' because it is among the last remaining mysteries and mystery is what makes speculation so enticing. Hence, he decides not to attempt to answer the questions about the colonists in the article, since '[t]here is nothing so artistic as a haze'.[5]

When Conan Doyle came to write his novel *The Lost World* (1912) he decided to set it in the Amazon basin of South America. The unsolved enigma of Greenland's vanished settlers, however, spurred numerous writers of fiction. Several adventure fiction stories imagined an encounter with a colony in the Arctic – if not descendants of the Greenland colonists themselves, then at least a community of Vikings. It is the cultural significance and political symbolism of such fiction which will be examined in the chapters of this book. The Norse people who settled in Greenland were the same as the Viking forefathers who came to English shores to first raid and then settle. Hence, the imagined discovery of a lost Viking colony functioned as a proxy for reconnecting with an Anglo-American past, and it was in Anglophone fiction that the imagination of a 'lost colony' found its most fertile ground.

The Structure of the Book

The book is organised thematically but unfolds roughly chronologically. The first three chapters are concerned with how Greenland was constructed in European texts until the end of the eighteenth century, as I examine the rhetorical strategies and textual practices of the period's key writings. From Chapter 4, the book shifts focus primarily to British and American material, taking its starting point in the important year of 1818. There are also other transitions. In the first part of the nineteenth century literary writers began to take an interest in the vanished settlers. Literary imaginings reached their peak towards the end of the century. These literary adventure tales consciously mimicked the style and genre of the Arctic exploration account as it had been written for centuries. In this way they made the yearned-for discovery of the 'lost colony' come true, if only imaginatively. Literary works were in many ways a continuation of the political and scientific imaginings of previous centuries.

That literary fantasy was entangled with exploratory and imperialist ambition is no more transparent than in the Arctic explorer Fitzhugh Green's novel, *ZR Wins* (1924), discussed in Chapter 7. Green published the novel with the specific purpose of shaping public perceptions to support Arctic exploration, which included a search for Greenland's vanished settlers. If the texts analysed in the early and the late chapters are certainly different genres, the gap may not be so wide in other respects.

As we move into the late nineteenth century we see the imagined 'lost colony' relocated beyond Greenland. As an effect of Western exploration, the great island was gradually deprived of its mystery as *terra incognita*. This did not mean that hope of finding the vanished settlers was given up: its possible location was only pushed further beyond the horizon. The hypothesis was that the colonists had fled their misery in Greenland to migrate to a new location in the Arctic. Sometimes their new habitat is imagined to be the North Pole, which was hypothesised to have a temperate climate. Thus the Western dream that Europeans had conquered the Arctic remained intact – the light that the colony had lit in the high north had not been extinguished: it had only moved out of sight. Building on a mix of historiographical, ethnological, and geological speculations, popular novels responded by imagining new locations to where the vanished settlers had migrated. While the sources discussed in this book range far and wide across centuries, genres, and imagined Arctic locations, they are all grounded in same enduring belief that European ancestors were alive and could be recovered. The permutations of this belief within various national, political, and cultural frameworks make a coherent study of its manifestations both compelling and necessary.

The following is a summary of how the chapters are organised. In the Prologue, I give an overview of the historical knowledge we have of the Norse colony in Greenland. The purpose is to outline the factual backdrop against which tales about the vanished settlers were told. Chapter 1 takes its beginning in the period up until the mid-seventeenth century. During this time Greenland existed primarily as a discursively produced memory. The chapter discusses the central texts that came to establish what we may call Greenland's discursive terrain. Two major themes are identified: *wealth* and *violence*. I examine how this dualistic perception of Greenland came to dominate European representations. The chapter also includes a discussion of Inuit legends that contained a memory of the European colony. It is important that the Indigenous Greenlanders themselves would produce stories about the European colony. Yet missionaries not only solicited and wrote down the legends, they also disseminated them in print, so that the Indigenous tales became part of the West's repertoire.

Chapter 2 examines the language of imperialism in the period leading up to the Danish recolonisation of Greenland in 1721 (and its immediate aftermath). The chapter provides an analysis of how the conspicuous gathering, organisation, and publication of knowledge about Greenland and its 'lost colony' of people – who were arguably Danish subjects – marked a symbolic form of possession. Chapter 3 trains the lens on post-1721 developments, analysing the Dano-Norwegian missionary Hans Egede's struggle to fit observations made in

Greenland into the framework of established ideas promoted in the texts he had read before his arrival. One
of these ideas was the mistaken conception that the
Eastern Settlement was located on the east coast, which
compelled numerous expeditions there. Rather than dis-
miss these attempts out of hand as irrelevant to the colonial project, I argue that the search for the settlers and
their resource-rich lands is significant for understanding
Denmark's political, religious, and commercial ambitions
in Greenland.

British interest in exploring the Arctic after the
Napoleonic Wars is well documented, but the specific
interest in Greenland is a critical road less travelled. In
Chapter 4, I discuss how Britain's new-found confidence
in Arctic exploration encouraged literary writers to speculate on the fate of the vanished settlers. The aim of
the chapter is to pull together diverse texts and genres
to draw a picture of the role Greenland played among
British travellers and commentators.

Chapter 5 examines a series of significant themes in
eighteenth- and early nineteenth-century literary representations of the Christian mission in Greenland. As
the old colonists had been Christian and new missions
were now making progress, a 'fall-and-restoration' structure became embedded in several texts – most notably in
the British poet James Montgomery's *Greenland* (1819),
a somewhat neglected text that was very popular in the
Romantic period, for which reason critical attention is
long overdue.

Chapter 6 examines one of the most intriguing fiction stories about Greenland: the Scottish author James

Hogg's *The Surpassing Adventures of Allan Gordon* (1837). This novella is the first of many nineteenth-century stories imagining an encounter with the vanished settlers. This text is important for a central argument in my book because it shows how the 'lost colony' could function as a mirror for the writer's own culture and its concerns. Through the analysis of Hogg's adventure tale, I therefore introduce a theme that resonates in the final two chapters.

Critical studies of adventure fiction written for the nineteenth- and twentieth-century popular market have tended to focus on novels about forays into Africa. However, Chapter 7 shows that the Arctic provided an alternative arena for such stories. I delineate a category of 'lost colony' stories in which writers draw on contemporary environmental and geophysical theories to imagine the survival of Europeans in the Arctic. In some of these tales the ideas of imperialism and exploitation of the Arctic become pronounced, thereby returning us to the fantasies discussed in the early chapters. Chapter 8 offers an analysis of an understudied episode in British and American fiction. Inspired by Greenland's vanished settlers, a number of tales imagine isolation as a means to preserve the virtues and primordial purity of a white, ancestral past. I examine these stories as compensatory fantasies that offset contemporary concerns about cultural and racial decay for a culture under stress. The last part of the chapter unravels the story of a press sensation that disrupted the idea of ring-fenced whiteness. This was the discovery of the so-called Blond Eskimos, purportedly the result of the old European colonists intermixing with the Inuit. I conclude with an examination of how this late imagining of the fate of Greenland's vanished settlers also impacted the writing of adventure tales.

A Note on Terminology

It would be prudent here at the outset to include a few notes on the terminology used to describe Greenland and its inhabitants. The knowledge that Greenland is an island only became accepted as a fact relatively late in the material covered in this book. To give an example, the American adventurer and author William Joseph Snelling begins his section on Greenland in his comprehensive study *The Polar Regions of the Western Continent Explored* (1831) with the statement that there is 'no means to ascertain whether Greenland is joined with America, or is an island, or a part of a polar continent'.[6] Uncertainty persisted until 1891 when the American explorer Robert Peary reached Independence Fjord and proved conclusively that Greenland is surrounded by water. Yet the denomination of Greenland as a 'country' is first of all a European geographical – and later political – concept. The conception of Greenland as a country – a coherent island space seen as a political unity – came late. Greenland's territory was confirmed as a single country when an international tribunal of 1933 decided that Norway could not occupy part of the east coast but that the whole island belonged to the Danish crown. This may dislocate somewhat the circumpolar experience of the Inuit by separating the history of Greenland from that of Arctic Canada. Nicole Waller has called for a recognition of this wider region as a connective space which the Inuit united in their imagination of a homeland extending across wider archipelagic lands, ice, and water.[7]

In this connection a note should be added on Greenland's peoples, past and present. The Indigenous Greenlanders call themselves 'Kalaallit', but I will refer to this group under the recognised term 'Inuit', which was decided upon as the preferred designation for Indigenous Arctic peoples at the 1977 Inuit Circumpolar Conference. However, I shall sometimes use the names of the source texts, such as 'Skraeling' or 'Eskimo'. The former was most definitely always derogatory and the latter is today generally considered to carry pejorative connotations. I refer to these as historical terms which are essential for scholarly precision, to avoid guessing at what modern terms they might be translated into and because within them lies a clue to how a group of people were perceived by outsiders.

Finally, how should we speak of the colonists who lived in Greenland for more than 400 years? They were primarily settlers who came from Iceland, but presumably settlers also came from Norway and there were connections to the rest of Scandinavia. Thus I shall refer to them as the 'Norse Greenlanders' to indicate that they were a community of people from medieval Scandinavia. For many of the commentators and historians I discuss in the pages to follow, the colonists were seen as first and foremost 'Europeans' in distinction from the Indigenous people. In other words, they were not only perceived as Scandinavians; in Europe and later America there was an ideological assimilation of the colonists into a shared European history of colonial achievement.

To reflect this fact, it is often useful to refer to them as the 'European colony'.

The colonists can be called 'Vikings' only insofar that they came to Greenland as a seafaring people and because they later ventured out to reach the coast of America in their ships. Their main occupation was not, as the stereotype dictates, raiding and pillaging; they were farmers who took unoccupied land. Thus, 'Vikings' is not the most useful term to use about the original 'European colony'. However, in the adventure stories of the late nineteenth century, they are clearly depicted as 'Vikings', sea rovers and often belligerent men, as this had become the dominant perception of the Scandinavians of old, so the term does play a part in the study of reception history for this later period.

All translations are my own, except where specifically noted.

Prologue

The Medieval Settlements in Greenland

To understand the background for the narratives, legends, and, not least, the political claims related to Greenland's history, it is useful to first provide a survey of what is factually known about the medieval settlers. Most important to the history of reception examined in this book is the mystery of their disappearance. We may begin by noting that the European colonisation of Greenland predates what the historian and philosopher Enrique Dussel has discussed as 'colonial modernity' – that is, the appearance of a global centre–periphery system in which European states, beginning with Spain in 1492, sought domination and exploitation of a colonised periphery.[1] The Norse settlements of south-western Greenland began as a westward relocation of Icelandic farmers. It was a 'colony' in the original sense of the word (from Latin *colere*, 'cultivate'), indicating a settlement shooting off from larger communities to cultivate new lands. This was not to dominate or exploit another people, as south-western Greenland was not inhabited when the Norse people arrived. For at least 425 years, the island became part of what Judith Jesch has called the 'Viking diaspora', one of the many places the Norse people settled outside of Scandinavia.[2]

The colony in Greenland is mentioned in sagas and other Icelandic texts, for example *Saga of Erik the Red* (thirteenth century), *Saga of the Greenlanders* (thirteenth century), included in the manuscripts *Hauksbók* (fourteenth century), *Flateyjarbók* (fourteenth century). In these accounts a key figure is the temperamental Erik the Red, who grew up in Norway in the latter half of the tenth century. When Erik was charged with murder he left for Iceland, a colony first settled by Norwegians in the 870s. In Iceland Erik became embroiled in further controversy, and around 982 he was sentenced to banishment for three years. Heading for a land to the west, which one Gunnbjörn Úlfsson had spotted about a century earlier, Erik explored Greenland's coast and found it had good pastureland. When he returned to Iceland, he canvassed farmers about settling the new land. The two oldest records about the new settlements are *Book of Icelanders* and *Book of Settlements*. The main parts of both these accounts have been attributed to the twelfth-century priest Ari Thorgilsson, Iceland's most prominent medieval chronicler, who mentions that Erik called the land 'Greenland' because he believed that a good name would make people eager to go there. Greenland's southwest coast was settled from either 985 or 986 (the sources disagree).[3] The Greenland colony was based on farming, and in the Icelandic sagas the Greenland settlers are named *landnámsmenn* – that is, 'land takers'. They would place their farms near the sheltered fjord systems in south-west Greenland. According to modern estimates, the population in Norse Greenland would have counted as many as 2,000 to 3,000 people at its peak.[4]

When discussing the Norse 'discovery' of Greenland, we may ask a question like the one Edmundo O'Gorman posed about America six decades ago: whether the idea that America was 'discovered' is 'acceptable as a satisfactory way of explaining its appearance on the historical scene of Western culture'.[5] In fact, Paleo-Eskimos had first come to Greenland from North America between 2500 and 2000 BC. The *Book of Icelanders* seems to refer to the traces of another people. Quoting the authority of his uncle, Thorkel Gellison, who was an early visitor to Greenland, Ari Thorgilsson tells us that the first Norse settlers found remnants of 'human habitation, both in the Eastern and Western parts of the country, and fragments of skin-boats and stone implements'.[6] These would have been the remains of a people known as the Dorset, who were also in Arctic Canada. Around AD 1300, the ancestors of the Inuit, known as the Thule, migrated into north-western Greenland, supplanting the Dorset. It was the Thule people who would come into contact with the Norse settlers.

The Greenland fjords were ecological pockets, and the Norse people used them for keeping imported livestock, primarily sheep and cattle, as well as for limited agriculture. Archaeologists have identified the ruins of hundreds of farms and fourteen main churches.[7] The written records mention two major settlements. The largest was the Eastern Settlement (Eystribyggð) on the lower west coast, situated around 61°, covering areas of the present-day municipalities of Nanortalik, Qaqortoq, and Narsaq. The designation of 'eastern' caused much confusion in the centuries after communication with Greenland was cut off. Although the Eastern Settlement was placed on the western side, it was mistakenly believed that it was on the east coast because of its name. It was so named because Greenland's west coast veers east as it runs south;

FIGURE 0.1 The location of the Eastern and Western Settlements in Greenland. Graphic design by Nemi Nødskov.

thus, in relative terms, the Eastern Settlement was to the east of the smaller Western Settlement (Vestribyggð), located about 240 miles to the north, at 65°, near the present-day municipality of Nuuk.

Certain political developments are important for understanding Denmark's later territorial claim to Greenland. In 1261 King Håkon Håkonsson of Norway made the settlements a protectorate, which meant that the Norse Greenlanders were liable to annual tribute (what the sagas refer to as *skattgildi*).[8] The agreement struck with the Norwegian crown concerning tax collection has not been preserved, but it was probably similar to the agreement made with the major chiefs of Iceland in 1262–4. Here, one benefit of becoming a tributary land was that a regular shipping route from Norway was upheld, which was crucial for a remote colony's ability to trade. It may be that the Norwegian king also threatened to impose an embargo on Greenland unless its people swore allegiance to him.[9] In 1380 Norway and its North Atlantic dependencies (Iceland, Faroes, Shetland, Orkney, and Greenland) entered into a personal union with the Danish crown (the Kalmar Union), and, from 1397, the two countries shared the same monarch, who was from the Danish line. This shifted political power southwards in Scandinavia, making Norway peripheral in a new Scandinavian power structure, which probably resulted in a decline in Norwegian shipping contact with Iceland and Greenland.

Christianity was an important part of medieval politics. We are told in the Icelandic *Saga of Erik the Red* that Greenland converted to Christianity in the late tenth century, when Leif Eriksson (son of Erik the Red) returned from Norway to preach the Gospel. In 1124 the Roman Church appointed the first bishop of Greenland, Arnaldur. The last bishop to reside in Greenland, Álfr, died in 1378. It says something about the infrequent communication at this time that the news of Álfr's death did not reach Norway until six years later.[10] After this time bishops of Greenland were still appointed, although 'bishop' was now only a nominal title with no expectation that appointees would actually reside in Greenland.

The End

When it comes to information about the end of Norse Greenland, the sagas and other older texts are silent. The last written record of the Norse Greenlanders is the wedding of Sigrid Björnsdóttir and Thorstein Olafsson at Hvalsey in the Eastern Settlement. This event is mentioned in three letters written between 1409 and 1424 and subsequently recorded for posterity by Icelandic scribes. The last documented ship sailed from Greenland to Norway in 1410, after which we have no further records of contact with the Norse Greenlanders.[11] It is usually assumed that the colony must have come to an end no later than 1450, but studies of pollen in the area of colonisation suggest a conceivable termination date towards the end of the century.[12]

What happened to the Norse Greenlanders became a question that gave rise to much speculation throughout the centuries, and it is what constitutes the subject matter of the present book. Some entrenched ideas were based on misunderstandings or simply wild guesswork. Even with the scientific methods and historical acumen available today, it has not been possible to establish with certainty why the Norse settlements did not survive. Most likely, several factors contributed to the unsustainability of the European colony in Greenland. Some of these will be taken up here.

One factor may be the colony's remoteness and inability to protect itself. In 1769 the Danish missionary Niels Egede wrote down an interesting Inuit tale taken from an account by an *angakkoq* (shaman) from the southern Uunartoq Fjord. This informant relayed a traditional tale of his forefathers. The Inuit wanted to settle near the Norse farmsteads. However, the Norse people rejected this proposal – yet they were willing to trade. While a trade agreement was in place, raiders descended upon the coast. After the Norse people had fended off the first attack, albeit with many losses, the Inuit forefathers gave promises to help if 'something evil' should happen again. The narrative continues:

A year later, the evil pirates returned and, when we [the Inuit] saw them again, we took flight, taking some of the Norse women and children along with us to the fjord, leaving others in the lurch. When we returned in the autumn to find some of them again, we learned to our horror that everything had been pillaged, houses and farms burnt and destroyed. Upon this sight, we took some Norse women and children with us and fled far into the fjord. And there they remained in peace for many years, taking the Norse women into marriage.[13]

This story speaks of European pirates and the major upset they caused in the social structure of south-western Greenland. However, although early twentieth-century scholarship would lean towards the theory that mass destruction of Norse Greenland had taken place, this has not been upheld in critical studies after the 1970s. Archaeologists have extensively examined Norse ruins and found no sign of large-scale ruination by violence or fire.[14] Attacks from the sea may therefore not be the sole reason for the end of Norse Greenland, but repeated attacks on an inadequately defended colony would undoubtedly have contributed to its dissolution.

The storyteller who relayed the tale to Niels Egede adds that an 'English' ship came back sometime after the attacks, this time only to trade. It is certainly possible that English or other European ships raided Greenland's coast for slaves on a small scale. The historians Finn Gad and Kirsten Seaver both give credence to this possibility since English plunderers are known to have raided the coasts of Norway, Iceland, and the Faroe Islands.[15] In 1425 sailors forcibly carried the governor of Iceland, Hannes Pálsson, to England. From prison, he wrote a letter to the king of England listing the crimes committed by English fishermen over the prior five years, which included the raiding of farms, the murder of farmers, the looting of churches, and, not least, kidnappings. This did not put an end to the raids, however: we know eight Icelandic children were offered for sale as slaves in Norfolk in 1429.[16]

The English were able to fish in such far-off locations as a result of building larger vessels that made transport of Icelandic stockfish a prosperous business. Archives of trade licences and customs accounts in England show that, already in 1408–9, an extensive and direct contact was in place between England and Iceland concerning fish (as well as trade).[17] There can be little doubt that English vessels also fished in Greenlandic waters, and they may have had contact with the colony there. In the second part of the fifteenth century Basque whalers may have begun to follow the whales migrating north from their wintering grounds near Labrador, giving the mariners the opportunity to land on the west coast of Greenland for trade or raids. Garments found in digs at Herjolfsnæs (in the Eastern Settlement), of which the youngest item is radiocarbon-dated to the mid-1430s, show that middle-class Greenlanders adopted a clothing fashion known from the mercantile class of Western Europe (with no compelling comparisons in Scandinavia). This indicates that unrecorded sailings and trade connections with Europe were upheld in the late stages of the colony.[18]

The fact that colonists were following European fashion may be another clue to explain the unsustainability of the remote settlements. At least some historians have ascribed the downfall to the Eurocentrism of the settlers and their inability to adapt. The most influential iteration of this argument is provided by the American geographer and historian Jared Diamond. He explains Eurocentrism as a problem among a nexus of other cumulative factors (some of which will be mentioned in the following).[19] One problem the colonists faced was a colder climate. What is known as the Medieval Warm Period (lasting from c.950 to c.1250) was followed by a cooler period in the North Atlantic, which meant a lowering of hay production in Greenland (the Norse used hay for animal feed), and ship lanes became more frequently clogged with sea ice.[20] In fact, ice floes had increased to such an extent that a Norwegian text, *Konungs skuggsjá* [*King's Mirror*], from circa 1250, reports that the old sailing course had to be abandoned.[21] This was a problem because the settlements in Greenland were not self-sufficient. According to *Konungs skuggsjá*, the settlements imported iron and timber for house construction as these resources were not available in Greenland. Some researchers see the deteriorating climate as a factor that put an inflexible Eurocentric culture to the test and contributed to the colony's demise.[22] Yet recent archaeological studies have shown that the colonists were not completely dependent on farming and European imports; for example, they seem to have adjusted to subarctic conditions through adopting a marine-based diet.[23]

Earlier historians also ascribed the disappearance of the Norse population to ethnic violence or even genocide by a people known in the Icelandic sources as Skrælíngjar (I will henceforth use this term in its anglicised form: Skraelings), a catch-all term used for various Eskimo communities whom the Norse met, first on the American coast and later in Greenland. The etymology of the name is uncertain, but E. V. Gordon notes that modern Scandinavian languages use the term *skræling* to refer to a weakling or a churl.[24] The name was clearly derogative for a people who were perhaps of smaller stature than the Norse. These Skraelings migrated from hunting grounds in the north of Greenland, reaching close to the European settlements in the course of the fourteenth century.

Some sources describe skirmishes between the Norse and the Skraelings. There is a note in *Historia Norwegiae* (late twelfth century) of an encounter in the north when a Norse weapon hit the enemy and the wounds became white. When they died their bleeding did not stop. This account smacks of the monsterisation that the West often applied to other people in distant lands, going back to the first-century Roman natural historian Pliny the Elder. Other descriptions do not embellish in the same way, but simply note violent encounters. In the Icelandic Annals for 1379 an incident is described when eighteen Norsemen were killed and two boys captured.[25] This is perhaps an indication that relationships between the Norse and Indigenous people deteriorated towards the end of the fourteenth century. Yet drawing sweeping historical conclusions from such textual fragments is methodologically problematic. Clashes may have happened, but archaeology also tells another story of the thirteenth and fourteenth centuries. Norse objects found in remains of Inuit settlements and Inuit artifacts in Norse ruins indicate that there may also have been good trading relations – although the provenance of objects cannot be determined with certainty; some of them may be finds from abandoned camps or taken on raids.[26]

To return to the European orientation of the Norse Greenlanders, one factor may have significantly furthered the demise of the colony: the failing fortunes in trading with the continent. Shipping to and from Greenland primarily went through Bergen, the major harbour and trading station in Norway. The most important source of income for the Norse Greenlanders was the export of walrus ivory, a commodity in high demand throughout Europe. Supplying elites with ivory crucifixes, knife handles, and chess pieces was a lucrative business. New studies show that Greenland had become the major supplier of ivory to much of Europe by 1100.[27] However, prices for walrus teeth may have fallen after 1350 as Asian and East African markets were sourced for elephant tusks, whose whiteness is superior to that of walrus ivory and hence were seen as more prestigious. This was problematic for the colony since trade with Europe would have grown in importance as farming became progressively more difficult due to climatic changes. There is today increasing support for an explanatory model that sees trade as a major cause for the colony's collapse.[28]

Interestingly, the Inuit may have participated in upholding the Norse colony during its final phase of existence. Researchers have detected a shift in European use of ivory around the thirteenth century towards animals with DNA most prevalent in the waters around Baffin Bay. This means that hunting would have taken the Norse further north-west, probably as the catch around Disko Bay was overexploited. The younger ivory specimens that circulated in Europe were also from mainly smaller, often female animals. Since the Inuit of the region favoured female walruses when hunting, this could imply that Norse exports towards the end relied on a growing trade with the Inuit for supplies.[29]

When we weigh up all the evidence discussed here, the colony's depopulation is still not entirely understood. Yet one must view Diamond's 2003 statement that 'every one of them [the Norse colonists] ended up dead' as misrepresenting what most likely happened.[30] It is more plausible that the dwindling possibilities in Greenland, aggravated by pirate raids and other factors, drove a constant emigration back to Iceland and Norway. Niels Lynnerup, a physical anthropologist, has applied population and historical models to debunk the 'spectacularity' of Norse Greenland's demise. At the turn of the fifteenth century, when climate change would have stressed the Norse Greenlanders, there was a general decrease in the Scandinavian population due to a plague epidemic. The result was that better land became available in larger settler communities in Iceland. Many Norse settlers probably left Greenland of their own volition, possibly invoking old family claims to land, back in their country of origin.[31] This would have brought the settlements to a relatively peaceful close without colonists starving to death or being massacred by the Inuit. Robert McGhee suggests that opportunities to leave could have presented themselves in the form of English fishing or trading vessels that may have called on Greenland's shores.[32]

If the colony of Europeans disappeared in the course of the fifteenth century, the mystery of its end continues to this day. The concept positing that descendants of the colonists had survived in Greenland came to have an enduring hold on the Western imagination well into the twentieth century. These assumptions, speculations, and imaginings will be traced and analysed in the chapters of this book.

I

Land of Wealth and Violence
Early Representations of Greenland

~

– fine mundi sita in terra Gronlandie

(Pope Alexander VI)

This first chapter examines how Greenland was represented in the centuries after contact with the Norse settlements was lost. When we look at European texts that deal with Greenland's history, it is possible to identify two central themes that recur with consistency – *wealth* and *violence*. Focusing on these two themes is not to write a reductive account. The perception of Greenland was certainly multifaceted, but I argue that *wealth* and *violence* were the two most central tropes dominating European discourse as well as directing political actions.

A foundational text in which the themes of wealth and violence are first clearly present is the mid-fourteenth-century report by the church official Ívar Bárdarson. The report is concerned primarily with the Eastern Settlement, which Ívar describes as a prosperous community in possession of many riches and resources. With early European readers retaining only a limited amount of knowledge of Greenland, it was generally believed that the Eastern Settlement was still standing. Thus, Ívar's report was instrumental in making Greenland a land surveyed by Europe's imperial gaze (in ways similar to other New

World settings). The first part of the chapter will examine texts published in Denmark and England which mapped avenues for future profit while staking claims to land.

The second part of the chapter will concentrate on Ívar's account of the Western Settlement. Here, he introduces the theme of native violence – a peril which often attended early imperialism. The alleged attack on the Western Settlement impacted imperial discourses in Europe, but the theme of violence was also reflected in Inuit legend. In the final section of the chapter I will discuss Indigenous accounts of violence against the Norse colonists, as they give us a perspective from the other side of the conflict. However, if these narratives point to potential genocide of Norse inhabitants, the legends were to a large extent solicited by missionaries. I shall therefore argue, in line with some earlier studies, that Inuit oral stories were selected and reconstructed to fit European conceptual frameworks once they were circulated as written texts. As we shall see, the legends would affirm preconceived ideas about Greenland's history (derived from Ívar and other sources) and may have in part helped to justify Christian missionising.

Ívar Bárdarson's Report

Because Ívar Bárdarson's text is central to the discourses discussed in this chapter, it makes sense to begin with a short note on what is known about it and why it came to be such a principal reference. Ívar Bárdarson was a Norwegian clergyman first dispatched to Greenland in 1341 to serve as *officialis* to Bishop Árni of Gardar.[1] He was probably sent to register church property and claim rights and tithes for the Norwegian king.[2] Ívar spent about twenty years in Greenland and probably delivered his famous report upon his return to Norway. Records tell us he was back in Bergen in 1364, but the report may have been given on a previous return trip. The text gives the impression that it contains information taken down from Ívar's oral communication ('All this that has been said here was told to us by Ívar Bárdarson'). Added to Ívar's report are the words of an interpolator – that is, commentary written either by the one who transcribed the oral report or by a later copyist. The original transcript of the oral report is lost, but we have copies from the sixteenth and seventeenth centuries.[3]

Ívar lists what he considers of value (perhaps taxable) in the Eastern Settlement, including church buildings and other property, bays for catching whales, fishing lakes, polar bears, reindeer, ivory, and hot springs with healing properties. The interpolated voice goes on to speak about fruitful vegetation in Greenland and the settlers growing wheat. It is also mentioned that Greenland has many mountains that contain silver ore.[4] The section adds a fantastical element to the report, but it would also significantly have increased the appeal of Greenland as an imperial land.

The textual transmission of Ívar's report is indicative of its importance in early European reception. The Old Norwegian text exists in several manuscripts. Notably, it is also found in a number of Low German translations.[5] With the introduction of printing, it was further translated (in full, excerpted, or summarised) several times: in Dutch (trans. Barents, 1594), Danish (trans. Claussøn,

1596), German (1679), and Latin (trans. Torfæus, 1707). An English translation appeared in *Hakluytus Posthumus or, Purchas His Pilgrimes* (1625), and the preface to this translation reveals the text's circuitous route of transmission: '[T]ranslated out of the Norsh Language into High Dutch, in the yeere 1560. And after out of High Dutch into Low Dutch, by William Barentson of Amsterdam ... And this was translated ... by Master William Stere, Marchant, in the yeere 1608 for the use of me Henrie Hudson.'[6]

What are we to make of the fact that the text was actively reproduced and circulated around Europe? The many translations show us that Ívar's account of the Greenland colony was considered relevant not only to the Norwegian church authorities to which he presumably reported. One should here consider that the languages into which the text was translated were those spoken in countries engaged in fishing or perhaps trading in the North Atlantic. Thus, readers of the translations could be expected to have an interest in Ívar's information, perhaps not least the navigation instructions given at the beginning of the report. Knowledge about sailing routes to Greenland suffered a regression in the course of the fifteenth century, as regular trading routes were no longer upheld. That a 'marchant' (merchant) was asked to translate the text into English at the behest of Henry Hudson (who sailed under both English and Dutch flags to open up North America for colonial settlements and advance trade by locating the Northwest Passage) is testament to the mercantile interest in the report. Ívar's report became constitutive in making Greenland part of transnational 'collective memory', as this has been discussed within the field of memory studies.[7] In this case, Greenland was remembered as a place with ample resources and profitable trade.

Imagining Greenland's Wealth

The focus of Ívar's report is the abundance of resources available in and near the fjords of the Eastern Settlement. Ívar emphasises Bærefiord as particularly good for fishing and whaling, but for which (as he does not fail to note) one needs the bishop's permission.[8] The focus on regulating what is caught shows that the report is very much a public record of Greenland as a colonial economy. In this context, it should be remembered that the waters surrounding Iceland, Spitsbergen, Greenland, and Newfoundland played an important role for European nations which has not always been sufficiently emphasised. As D. B. Quinn notes, it was the colourful descriptions of extracting bullion from Mexico and Peru that caught the imagination of European writers and explorers, although the produce caught in the northern seas was of equal if not greater worth to Europe.[9] This point can be made specifically about the fishing colony of Newfoundland. Although it was the land of the Indigenous Beothuk, it was claimed as England's first overseas colony in 1583 under the Royal Charter of Queen Elizabeth I. If fish and whales caught off the coast contributed significantly to England's prosperity, Mary C. Fuller notes, it was too drab a subject to write about for poets and authors of promotional literature. Thus, Newfoundland did not receive the same 'lyrical abundance' as more southern English colonies in North America.[10] When we scan writings about

Greenland from the sixteenth to the eighteenth centuries, we may also get the impression that fishing did not matter, but it was precisely because of fishing and whaling in the North Atlantic that Europe never lost sight of Greenland. We know that fishing and trade vessels travelled from Bristol to Iceland (and perhaps also further west) in the fifteenth century.[11] It was a dispute over trading and fishing rights that caused the sea war between England and Denmark from 1468 to 1473, and Christian I of Denmark threatened to confiscate English vessels on their way to Iceland and northern waters.

Greenland was part of an imperial geography long before it came to be of interest as a cultural and ethnographic space. Thus, early knowledge-gathering about Greenland focused on its resources. Archbishop Erik Valkendorf, who was installed at the Norwegian Nidaros Cathedral, Trondheim, in 1510, collected all available knowledge about Greenland. One of the texts was, of course, Ívar's report, and he appears to have annotated a transcript of the text.[12] Valkendorf knew that Greenland was previously a tributary country under the Norwegian king, for which reason he obtained a papal indulgence for sailing to Greenland in 1514. The immediate purpose would have been to resume the collection of tithes for the church, but he seems also to have hoped for personal profit since he offered to pay for the expedition himself.[13] Among Valkendorf's notes, we find an itemised list of commodities that could be claimed in taxes or traded with the Norse Greenlanders. This includes what can be caught in the sea (salmon, whale blubber, and walrus ivory), as well as what can be found on land, such as furs and hides (fox, wolf, sable, deer, and marten) and white falcons (i.e. gyrfalcons used for hunting by European courtiers), but silver and gold ores are also mentioned.[14] In fact, sable and marten had never lived in Greenland, so Valkendorf probably confused these items with what was traded from other northern locations like the Finnmark (on which Valkendorf would later write a manuscript in 1522). Nor were precious metals to be found. Valkendorf's mistakes show us how Greenland, 100 years after communication was discontinued, had become an amalgam of historical information, inaccurate knowledge, and tall tales. Valkendorf's Greenland expedition never went ahead, as he fell out with King Christian II, on whom he relied for ships and men.[15]

Another extant work that considers Greenland as an attractive land for exploitation is the manuscript *Gronlandia* (1606), written by Arngrímur Jónsson, a priest at Hólar, the northern episcopal see of Iceland. Arngrímur was at the forefront of an antiquarian movement that sought to collect information about Iceland and to commit information from the oral sagas to the permanence of print. *Gronlandia* contains several references to the old Greenland colony from Icelandic manuscripts and other sources.[16] However, as Arngrímur extrapolates information about Greenland from a number of sources, he makes several erroneous inferences. For instance, he replicates the sixteenth-century Spanish historian Francisco López de Gómara's geographical misconception that the northern part of mainland India is connected with Greenland.[17] This was a widespread misapprehension. On the Ruysch map of 1508, for example, Greenland is depicted as a peninsula connected to the Indian continent. Beyond its own resources, interest in Greenland was stimulated by the belief that it was a bridgehead to the East and thereby could open up a road to even more profitable trade.

Arngrímur wrote *Gronlandia* at the same time as the Danish king Christian IV was sending out expeditions to rediscover Greenland. The three journeys undertaken between 1605 and 1607 galvanised a new optimism in Copenhagen and were seen throughout Europe as a major achievement. The expeditions were comprehensively celebrated by the clergyman Claus Christoffersen Lyschander in the 5,281-line poem *Den Gronlandske Chronica* [*The Greenland Chronicle*] (1608). This early key text introduces a compendium of information about Greenland that was later repeated as stock knowledge in European texts. Despite its significance for the reception of Greenland – through the intermediary of a French summary (to be discussed in what follows) – Lyschander's poem has received practically no exposure in Anglophone scholarship. Therefore, I will discuss this text in some detail here and in the next chapter.

The *Chronica* was self-financed and published in a small octavo for the general public. Lyschander's motive for publishing was probably a direct response to the royal historiographer Jon Jakobsen Venusin's sudden passing on 30 January 1608 and had the purpose of showing that Lyschander was a worthy successor to this post (however, Lyschander had to wait until September 1616 before the office was conferred on him). This context is important for understanding the motivation for writing a panegyric to Christian IV and his expeditions: the poem talks up the possibilities of exploiting Greenland's many supposed resources and thereby also justifies the significant costs of the expeditions, which had been financed through levying a tax.

The *Chronica* is divided into two parts. The first is a chronology of the history of the medieval colony in Greenland; the second focuses on Christian IV's three expeditions. Many of the lines are dedicated to the riches of Greenland. Lyschander mentions furs and hides from foxes and bears, as well as the ivory of the unicorn (i.e. the narwhal), prized for its magical and medical properties (ll. 2809–11, 3358–60, 3621–33). Greenland is clearly represented as an imperial space and its colonists as subjects of the Danish king. In this respect, the purpose is to raise the prospect of reward to Denmark by seeking to re-establish connections with the Greenland colony. Lyschander tells his readers that the Norse settlers who first landed in Greenland found the ground shining with silver and red gold (ll. 286–8). In fact, Lyschander's quill is enamoured with the topic of precious metals, returning to it time and time again. At the time of writing, the trope of precious metals would often overshadow trade as a source for imperial wealth in colonial texts, as I will now examine.

Arctic Gold Rush

The myth of precious metals in the Arctic came to the fore in the second half of the sixteenth century in connection with the English privateer Martin Frobisher's three voyages (1576, 1577, and 1578). Although Frobisher's crew mined a location in present-day Canada, the geographical confusion that characterised reporting at the time makes it relevant to discuss Frobisher's endeavours in relation to the reception of Greenland. The purpose of the first voyage was to discover the Northwest Passage, a navigable sea route northwest of Greenland, which would allow ships to sail to the Orient for trade without the disruption caused by the Spanish and the Portuguese via the normal route.[18] From his first journey, Frobisher brought back a specimen of black rock found in the place referred to as 'Meta Incognita' (the Baffin Island location also known as Kodlunarn Island, situated in the now Canadian region of Nunavut). An early test indicated that it contained a precious metal. Therefore, Frobisher and his financial backer, Michael Lok, focused the two subsequent expeditions on mining the ground there. Attempts at extracting valuable metals proved unsuccessful, however.

Historians do not usually explain Frobisher's interest in collecting rocks on the first voyage, but certain texts he knew and read had raised expectations of riches in the Arctic. We know that Frobisher sailed following the instructions on a map published in 1558 by Nicolò Zeno the Younger. This was an account of travels purportedly made by his ancestors Nicolò and Antonio Zeno but is now known to be a fraud. The text, *De I Commentarii del Viaggio*, contains a long passage on Antonio, who claimed to have landed on the northern island of 'Frislanda' (either a cartographic approximation of Iceland or the southern part of Greenland) around 1380. It is claimed that Antonio met a group of fishermen who told him that they had once been blown westward by a storm to a place called 'Estotiland' (which would geographically be the American coast). The people in 'Estotiland' traded with 'Engroenelandt' (most certainly a reference to the Norse settlement in Greenland), from where they received furs, brimstone, and pitch. The Estotilanders also knew of metal ores in the south of their own country which abounded with gold.[19] The Zeno text, with its vague and often imaginary geography, helped to foster expectations of wondrous treasures in the North Atlantic.

The hope of finding precious metals was intrinsically connected with the ongoing competition among European powers. Spain had consolidated its status as the leading European nation by means of the so-called treasure fleet that since the 1560s had systematised the transportation of bullion and other resources from the Americas to the Spanish mainland. Thus, Frobisher's auspicious find of ore on his first expedition threatened to change the balance of power. This worried the newly appointed Spanish ambassador to England, Don Bernardino de Mendoza, enough to plant a spy on the second expedition.[20]

In 1577 and 1578 Frobisher's men chiselled out several tons of ore, which they carried back to England. But the material turned out to be valueless iron pyrite, leaving Frobisher's reputation in tatters and bankrupting the Cathay Company.[21] The news that the many tons of rock that Frobisher had brought back were worthless was generally known by 1579. Yet, the year before, George Best, who travelled as a lieutenant on the second voyage and as a captain on the third, had published a report of the expeditions in which he declared that a 'greate store of golde, and all other mettals' could be found 'in the supposed hard and congealed frosen Lands, almost vnder the Poles'.[22] Such grandiloquent statements seemed to have had more resonance than news of the disappointing result, and the hope of finding valuable ore still played a significant role in Christian IV's expeditions to Greenland a quarter of a century later.

In his poem about Greenland Lyschander mentions Frobisher's discovery of metal-bearing ore and includes in this connection a long passage about the precious metals that Greenland purportedly holds (ll. 3944–74). The confusing geography in accounts of Frobisher's travels led Lyschander, and others at the time, to believe that the find-spot was in Greenland (ll. 2697–9). Did Lyschander fail to note that Frobisher's many tons of rock had been declared valueless? It is not an easy question to answer, but it is likely that he thought the hope of treasure was intact, even if he knew about the disappointing result. We know Lyschander read a Latin translation of Dionise Settle's report of Frobisher's journeys (published 1580), in which it is recounted that Frobisher's men, while digging on Kodlunarn Island, came into contact with natives who made 'signes of certaine people that weare bright plates of gold in their foreheads, and other places of their bodies'.[23] When Lyschander adapts Settle's passage for inclusion in *Chronica*, he introduces it with a promise that golden treasures are there for those who can find them (l. 3074).

Furthermore, Christian IV's 1605 expedition seems to have raised its own expectations. Lyschander mentions that 36 *lod* (*c.*540 g or 19 oz) of silver was brought back (l. 3949). This was probably from samples of the 'earth and stones' that James Hall, an Englishman who served as pilot on all the Danish voyages, had collected just above 66° on the west coast.[24] At some point (perhaps after publication of the poem) the sample must have been re-assayed and found worthless. The hope was apparently still alive in 1606, when Christian IV sent out five ships to Greenland and quantities of rock were mined without yielding any results.

Christian IV's letters of instruction for the 1605 and 1606 expeditions have not survived, but correspondence relating to the 1607 voyage makes it very clear that the aim this time was not the west coast. The purpose was to land between 60° and 61° on the east coast of Greenland (where the Eastern Settlement was thought to be located). The instructions advise to look not just for mountains with silver mines (*sölffbierge*), but also to search for church buildings.[25] The logic appears to be that the inhabitants of the settlement (churches would be salient landmarks to look out for) could assist in leading the way to underground ores. However, the 1607 expedition was a complete failure as ice prevented the expedition from landing.

James Hall did not lay the hope of treasure to rest. No longer in Danish service, he returned to the west coast of Greenland in 1612, having persuaded four London merchants to help finance an expedition with a silversmith on board to assay what was found. We know from the report of the journey that Hall returned to the 'silver mine' he had previously visited at Itilleq Fjord on the west coast.[26] Yet nothing valuable was discovered and Hall was speared to death by Inuit when he reached Amerdloq Fjord.

If discoverers failed to plot mines of precious ore on maps of the Arctic, dreams of gold and silver were firmly lodged in the imperial imagination. When speaking of Greenland, Lyschander mobilises a recognisable mythological and classical vocabulary: its metals are a gift from Pluto, the god of wealth, and the land holds Saturni treasures (ll. 3024, 3964, and 3967). The latter is a reference to the Templum Saturni where Rome's reserves of gold and silver were stored. This classical framing of treasures in the Arctic was not unique to Lyschander's writing. Nearly thirty years earlier, the sailor Thomas Ellis had also used classical references in a celebratory poem attached to the report he wrote about the Frobisher expedition of 1577. Ellis casts Frobisher as a modern Jason leading his Argonauts, as well as a Hercules taking Zeus' golden apples: 'A Fleece in value that exceeds, / the Fleece of Colchis ground, / Or golden fruite of Hesperis land, / Which Hercules out found.'[27] We find the unmistakable ideology of *translatio imperii* ('transfer of empire') embedded in Ellis' lines. The prospect of finding gold leads him to proclaim: 'Give place, therefore, you Graecians now, and to me geve assent.'[28]

The notion that modern European powers would take the place of the ancient empires was frequently found in the context of bringing back spoils from New World conquests.[29] Although no expeditions to the Arctic succeeded in extracting gold or silver, hope often burned stronger than disappointed experiences. V. S. Naipul summarises imperial fantasies: 'The legend of El Dorado, narrative within narrative, witness within witness, had become like the finest fiction, indistinguishable from truth.'[30]

The Popularisation of Greenland's 'Lost Settlements'

Lyschander's *Chronica* came to influence the narrative about Greenland. The poem was never translated into other European languages (except for two separate Icelandic prose translations which remained in manuscript).[31] Nevertheless, Lyschander's information on

Greenland reached a wide European audience, indirectly, as it was extensively summarised in Isaac La Peyrère's popular *Relation du Groenland* [*Account of Greenland*], published in Paris in 1647. It is to this work I will now turn.

The popularity of the text is owed to the sensational claims Peyrère makes (or repeats). Its format would also have helped. The first edition measures only 17.5 × 10.5 cm and became a neat acquisition that appealed to the educated middle classes. The book achieved Europe-wide circulation during the seventeenth and eighteenth centuries. It was reprinted in 1663, 1715, and 1731, published in German in 1674 and 1679, translated into Dutch in 1678, and English editions appeared in 1732, 1744, and 1752. There was also a Danish translation from 1732. But the transmission of La Peyrère's writing cannot be assessed only by the number of standalone editions, since several sections of his text were excerpted in various collections.[32]

Relation du Groenland takes the form of a letter to La Peyrère's friend, François de La Mothe Le Vayer, a member of the Académie Française and supporter of scepticism. Le Vayer had called for a programme of books about foreign places that could increase the French nation's knowledge bank. He also thought the French king would benefit from having his diplomats write about Northern Europe to gain political leverage with the countries there.[33] La Peyrère's book on Greenland accords with Le Vayer's geopolitical concerns and the investigation into Greenland's history and its resources should be seen as partly a diplomatic exercise of mutual benefit to both France and Denmark.

The account of the Norse colony takes up a substantial part of La Peyrère's book (pp. 10–52), and the main source for this, Lyschander's *Chronica*, is referred to throughout as 'la Chronique Danoise' ['the Danish chronicle']. If Lyschander had spoken rather uncritically about Greenland's many wonders, La Peyrère comes to the subject with a new Enlightenment sensibility. At the outset, La Peyrère demonstratively declares that he will distance himself from Lyschander's recourse to 'fables and ancient customs'.[34] La Peyrère wanted to write a history based on principles of rational assessment, which could guide those who wanted to sail to Greenland and explore the land. In a playful metaphor La Peyrère notes that there are 'perils' to be found when 'navigating' the material, for which reason he feels it is incumbent upon him to find the right 'route'.[35]

La Peyrère is intent on assessing the claims made about Greenland with an open mind. For instance, he repeatedly discusses the interpolated section of Ívar's report, which mentions 'fruits as big as apples and good to eat' (*olden saa sore som nogle æble och gode at æde*) as well as the Greenlanders' ability to harvest 'the best wheat that can be' (*bese huede som vere maa*).[36] This is spurious as apples cannot grow in Greenland's climate, and it would not have been possible for wheat to ripen. For this reason, the modern editor of Ívar's text, Derek Mathers, assesses the report as nothing but 'pure fantasy'.[37] Yet, if we look at the word *olden*, it essentially means the mast or samaras of trees, which could perhaps grow in Greenland's few groves of mountain birch and mountain ash trees. These 'fruits' were traditionally used for animal feed. However, the size stated in the text is not realistic. Wheat for human consumption would not have been possible, even in the hot periods of Greenland's history, but it was possible to grow hay for animals. In any case, La Peyrère does not reject Ívar's report offhand. Rather he thinks that fertile soil may be found in Greenland at certain latitudes.[38] In addition to this he conveys the familiar expectations that precious metals may be found.

For much of his information, La Peyrère relied on Danish antiquaries. The same was the case for his *Relation de l'Islande* [*Account of Iceland*], the publication of which was delayed until 1663. In fact, the research for both books was carried out during 1644–6 when La Peyrère was on a diplomatic mission to Scandinavia, including a stint as secretary to the French ambassador in Copenhagen.[39] For translation and explanation of the Nordic sources, La Peyrère enlisted the assistance of the Danish nobleman 'M. Rets' (whom I have identified as the diplomat and later chancellor Peder Reedtz).[40] La Peyrère also discussed many matters with the Danish polymath Ole Worm, who is mentioned several times in *Relation du Groenland*.[41] In the spirit of the Enlightenment, Worm was helpful in debunking some long-standing myths about Greenland. For instance, he showed La Peyrère a narwhal cranium with the tusk attached. This was evidence that these spectacular 'horns', which were also known in France and other European countries, were in fact from a 'fish' that lived in Greenland waters, not from a four-legged creature.[42] However, without the possibility of comparing all textual sources with similar empirical evidence, the only way La Peyrère could live up to his own requirement of accuracy was sometimes by copying old documents as meticulously as he could. This is precisely what he says he does in connection with Ívar's account of Greenland's riches.[43] Thus, the myths of precious metals and a fertile Greenland were allowed to survive into the age of a sceptical Enlightenment.

It was the imaginary land of plenty that attracted attention around Europe. In the 1679 German translation of La Peyrère's book the original bare map of Greenland, which was enclosed with the original 1647 French edition, is here adorned with added details of archers shooting game, and (below the map) four panels are inserted, showing scenes of hunting and fishing (Figure 1.1).[44]

European texts also hailed Greenland as a productive place for livestock farming. The mid-thirteenth century *Konungs skuggsjá* [*King's Mirror*], written as an educational text for the future Magnus VI of Norway, mentioned that cattle and sheep produced butter and cheese in great quantities. The Bavarian humanist Jacob Ziegler picked up this information and included it in his well-known treatise *Schondia*, published in Strasbourg in 1532.[45] Greenland's potential as an agrarian country was discussed in several publications, such as the Dutch text *Drie voyagien gedaen na Groenlandt* (1663?), which lists the country's many wondrous assets.[46]

When such ideas circulated in European texts, it was no surprise that Greenland was made an object of colonial attention. The year after the Scot John Ogilby became royal cosmographer to Charles II, he published *America* (1671), a survey of this continent's colonial potential. The book also included a substantial section on North Atlantic lands, including Greenland (because it was believed that Greenland and America were connected via a land bridge). Relying on information from La Peyrère, Ogilby declares that Greenland is 'a Countrey not unfertile of

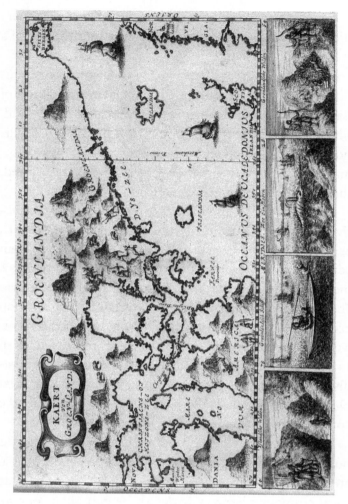

FIGURE I.I 'Kaert von Groen-Land', from a 1679 German edition of La Peyrère's work on Greenland. The Royal Danish Library.

Corn, and other Productions of the Earth; and in respect of its verdant Aspect at some Seasons of the Year, above the rest of those *Septentrional* Regions'.[47] Ogilby also

46

provides what was by now a standard list of Greenland resources: apple-sized acorns, rich fishing grounds, and silver mines.

Ogilby's credulous collection of legends about Greenland's riches speaks to the desire for imperial gains and may have piqued Charles II's interest because Scotland had recently raised its stakes in the Arctic with the establishment of the 'Glasgow Soaperie' (1667) to procure whale oil at Spitsbergen. In this connection it is worth noting that Ogilby gives attention to La Peyrère's statement that the Norse settlements made up only 'a small part of all the extensive northern land [Greenland]'.[48] However, Ogilby reformulates this statement to further diminish the Danish claims to the land; it is now asserted that only 'the hundredth part of Groenland is possess'd by the Norwegians', to which he adds that the land is now inhabited by 'several different sorts of People, of different Fashions and Governments, altogether unknown to the Norwegians'.[49] The question of rights to Greenland will be discussed in the next chapter, but here I will turn to the Norse people's relationship with others in Greenland to investigate the trope of violence, which was ubiquitous in the early perception of Greenland.

Violence in the Western Settlement

One explanation for the disappearance of the Norse Greenlanders took its cue from Ívar's report: clashes with the Skraelings had caused the European colonists' downfall. The passage in question concerns the journey Ívar undertook by sea with volunteers from the Eastern

Settlement (which he had surveyed in much detail) to the Western Settlement. In tantalisingly brief lines, Ívar tells us that he went on this journey because he had been informed that Skraelings had now all of the Western Settlement in their possession (*nu haffue Skrelinge all Vesterbijgden vdt*).[50] When Ívar's company arrived the Western Settlement appeared abandoned, and he found neither Christian nor pagan there, only 'straying horses, goats, cattle, and sheep'.[51] This brief narrative is followed by an interpolated passage providing the additional information that Ívar and his men ate some of the livestock and carried as many animals with them as their ships could hold.[52]

The account of the abandoned Western Settlement has been widely debated in later historical criticism, but it is not a passage that easily lends itself to analysis. The circumstances Ívar describes defy clear-cut and logical explanation. Sheep could be kept out all year, but cattle and horses would not survive a winter. Had the settlement been abandoned very recently? If the Skraelings had usurped the Western Settlement, why had they not slaughtered or taken the animals? That there were animals but no people to be found led one nineteenth-century commentator to conclude that 'the savages' (Inuit) were probably still there, but at the sight of Ívar's vessel they 'took to flight and concealed themselves in the woods and rocks'.[53] The modern historian Kirsten Seaver has offered a reading that reverses this interpretation: it was the Norse inhabitants who were hiding in the knowledge that Ívar came to register what tithes and taxes could be collected for church and crown.[54] This is a provocative possibility, but if Ívar came to survey the Western

Settlement, why has he nothing to say about it, apart from noting a church building named Stensnes? Perhaps his silence makes sense insofar as king and church needed people to hand over a part of their annual produce; if the settlement was empty, there was no reason for Ívar to record anything in his tax ledger.

Hidden from the inquisitive gaze of both past and present is the exact reason for the abandonment of the Western Settlement. The vacated farms constitute textual *Leerstelle* ('blanks' or 'places of indeterminacy') in the history of Norse Greenland. In older historiography, these blanks were traditionally filled with a narrative of racial violence. The idea that savages would attack and massacre peaceful European settlers is found soon after communication with Greenland was lost. Tales of aggression were already in circulation in the late 1420s, when the Danish scholar Claudius Clavus promoted the story that the Christian colony in Greenland was under perennial attack by pagans. Claudius lived in Rome and was friends with a cardinal, Giordano Orsini, and the pope's secretary, Gian Francesco Poggio Bracciolini, who were working on updating old Roman cartography. In this context Claudius drew a map displaying territory from Greenland to the Baltic, noting that '*caroli infideles quotidie cum exercitu in Gronlandiam* [infidel *caroli* frequently descend upon Greenland in great armies]' and that these pagan hordes came from below the North Pole.[55] This is usually interpreted as a reference to the Karelians, a Baltic-Finnic ethnic group which could be believed to ravish Greenland if one takes into account the faulty geography at the time that connected Greenland with Scandinavia. However, Fridtjof

Nansen's assumption that the ethnonym Claudius uses here is a corruption of the name 'Skraelings' is not unreasonable.[56] More recently, Robert Petersen has added that Poul Egede's dictionary of the Greenlandic language from 1750 includes *karálek* as a term for Inuit (more precisely, it was the name the Inuit remembered the Norse people gave them).[57] Whomever Claudius was referring to, it is important to understand the statement in light of the fact that he had close connections to papal circles. Janus Møller has pointed to several fifteenth-century Scandinavians and Icelanders who wrote letters, circulating in Rome, which represented the northern part of Christendom as under constant threat of attack from heathens looming at its borders.[58] This makes it relevant to place the reports of heathen attacks on Greenland within a political context, so that we are, perhaps, to understand Claudius' objective as an attempt to solicit support and funding from Rome to keep Christian frontier lands safe from pagan incursions.

A letter supposedly written at the behest of Pope Nicholas V in 1448 to the bishops of Iceland calls for help to the Eastern Settlement, which had reportedly been sacked by pirates. The pirates allegedly carried a large number of the inhabitants away and burned their houses, leaving only nine remote parish churches standing.[59] In assessing this information, Kirsten Seaver suggests that the reference to 'heathens' (*barbari*) must be to European pirates, who could reasonably be considered beyond the pale of Christian morality.[60] Yet the specification in the letter that these heathens came from 'neighbouring pagan shores' (*ex finitimis littorinus paganorum*) seems rather to point to an Inuit attack.[61] Such an attack from the sea would not be unprecedented. *Saga of the Greenlanders*, for example, tells of 'a great swarm of skin-boats' attacking the Norsemen's camp on the American coast.[62] In any case, the information in the letter is spurious. It clearly plays on the familiar fears of Christian communities coming under attack in border areas. The information in the 1448 letter may have been cooked up by Marcellus de Niveriis, a German Franciscan and adventurer. Marcellus committed numerous crimes and frauds for which he was arrested (and escaped) prior to his appearance in Rome in 1447. Here he managed to convince Nicholas V to appoint him, on 15 April 1448, as the twenty-sixth bishop of Skálholt, Iceland. This was a lucrative job as it allowed him to collect papal revenues throughout Scandinavia. It has been suggested that Marcellus could have concocted the story of Greenland settlers needing help as part of a ploy to extend his power.[63]

Greenland had undoubtedly great symbolic importance for Rome, not least because a Christian colony in a far-off corner of the world highlighted the might and reach of the church. In a letter of 1492, Pope Alexander VI mentions the church at Gardar as lying *fine mundi sita in terra Gronlandie* (at the world's end in Greenland).[64] This seems to allude to Christ's instruction to his disciples that they should spread the gospel to all corners of the world (the most quoted version of which is found in Matthew 28:16–20). The statement is made in connection with the appointment of Matthias Knutsson, a Danish monk of the Benedictine Order, as the bishop of Greenland. The letter speaks of the colonists having allegedly 'renounced the holy sacrament of baptism' and mentions that no ship had made landfall on Greenland's coast for eighty years (which corresponds with the last recorded sailing from Greenland in 1410).[65] The information of a failing Greenland colony would have been conveyed to Pope Alexander VI by clerics from the northern sees, who likely wanted to paint a bleak picture of Greenland to appeal to Rome for increased funding. Thus, political savvy may be behind the story of settlers abandoning the faith, rather than any fresh first-hand accounts.

When considering the notion of violent adversaries pushing against the northern frontier of Christendom, the exiled Swedish Catholic priest Olaus Magnus' map of Scandinavia and the North Atlantic is of interest. Olaus was in Rome when he drew *Carta Marina* (1539). In the upper left-hand border of the map, Olaus depicts the southern part of Greenland as a *lieu dangereux*: two men are threatening each other with spears. This image seems apposite considering the stories that circulated about violence in the North Atlantic.[66] The small man is perhaps a representation of native Greenlanders, inspired by the claim he read in Clavus' text that there were *Pigmei maritime* (coastal pygmies) in Greenland.[67] It is probable that this is a garbled representation of the idea that Skraelings were diminutive men. The image was enlarged as a separate illustration in Olaus Magnus' *Historia de Gentibus Septentrionalibus* (*History of the Northern Nations*) (Rome, 1555) (Figure 1.2).

This image evidently was made before any idea of Indigenous clothing had impacted European pictorial art. Indigenous people were sometimes depicted on maps because they were targets of Christianisation (or taxation). Olaus Magnus' representation of battle at the

DE MIRA NAT. RERVM SEP.

De Pygmæis Gruntlandiæ, & rupe Huitfark.

CAP.   XI.

FIGURE I.2   Detail from Olaus Magnus' *Historia de Gentibus Septentrionalibus* (1555). The Royal Danish Library.

periphery of Christendom may again have served the purpose of arguing that the northern sees needed attention from Rome as they were in danger of being lost to irreligion (perhaps, at this time, also to Protestant agitators who would destabilise the Catholic Church).

Adding to such accounts was Ívar's story of Skraelings taking over a Christian outpost. This story was repeated in print with such regularity over the centuries that it may be akin to what Dagmar Freist has identified as a 'memoryscape' – that is, usually tales of religious deaths or massacres which garnered transnational interest in early modern Europe.[68] The attack on a Christian community in Greenland would similarly have appealed to Catholics across Europe as a symbolic event at the end of the world that would strengthen Christian resolve against the threat of heathenism. Later, the

53

eighteenth-century Lutheran missionary Hans Egede, who in 1721 was the first European to settle in Greenland since communication was lost, insisted that the loss of the Western Settlement was the result of a conscious attack on Christianity. In a book with the English title *A Description of Greenland* (1741), he reflects that 'the Norway Christians' were 'destroyed' and 'Christianity rooted out by the savage Heathens'.[69] Thus, Ívar's journey to the Western Settlement is interpreted explicitly as the Christian church sending 'assistance ... to expel the barbarous nation of the Schrellings, who were fallen upon the Christians'.[70]

The idea of losing a Christianity settlement could be spun to suit various agendas. Late nineteenth-century Catholic writers, for instance, sought to cultivate the understanding that the loss of Christian Greenland was caused by the Reformation. As one writer notes, the reformative changes that swept over Norway had the effect that 'silence and oblivion fell upon Catholic Greenland', which meant that it was neglected.[71] Another writer claims that the Reformation left the Catholic Greenlanders without support, thus allowing 'the Skraellings in greater force than before' to raid their settlements.[72]

When it comes to modern assessments of violence in medieval Greenland, archaeologists and historians generally reject genocide as an explanation for the Norse abandonment of Greenland.[73] There are, however, dissenting voices. The Norwegian historian Arnved Nedkvitne has criticised what he sees as the tendency to gloss over past ethnic conflict for the benefit of a harmonious relationship between Danes and Inuit today.[74] Some of the stories from Inuit tradition to which he gives credence will be discussed next, but without reaching the same conclusion.

Inuit Accounts of Violence

In this section I will draw on examples of Inuit oral records to gain as wide-angled a view as possible on the history of the Norse people. To introduce 'plural voices into the account', as the historian Natalie Zemon Davis formulates it, has been practised in connection with the history of Arctic peoples.[75] In the case of Greenland, however, it is fraught with difficulty. Of particular concern is the fact that the early records of Inuit tradition were written down by missionaries, which means they may have been coloured by Western preconceptions. A useful term when discussing colonial places is Mary Louise Pratt's concept of the contact zone, which she describes as 'the space in which peoples geographically and historically separated come into contact with each other and establish ongoing relations'.[76] The early eighteenth-century Danish mission established such a contact zone, and we may in this connection expand the concept to include also the mixing of discourses and mythologies as the newcomers sought to record the Indigenous people's stories, beliefs, and history – but also to interpret them.

In 1737 the Greenland missionary Poul Egede recorded an Indigenous legend from his time in Christianshaab (Qasigiannguit). The legend tells of an Inuk who was out hunting when his dart missed a sea fowl. A Norseman saw this and challenged the Inuk to shoot at him in the belief that the Inuk would miss again. This time the dart hit its mark. The killing caused strife between the two peoples with the result that the Inuit overthrew the 'Kablunæt' (Norse people) and eventually 'destroyed them all'.[77] Poul Egede concludes the retelling of the story in his diary by noting that this 'accords' with the European story of the Norse colonists' destruction. Poul Egede is surely thinking of Ívar's account of the empty Western Settlement.

Poul's father, Hans Egede, repeats the story, practically verbatim, in his published work from 1741 and thereby made the legend available to generations of European readers.[78] At this time, Hans Egede seems to have become convinced that the Inuit had indeed 'destroyed' the Norse, even though he earlier had come across contradictory information. In 1723, only two years after his arrival in Greenland, Hans Egede had asked the Inuit if their forefathers had destroyed the church that was now only a ruin at Ujaragssuit (which Egede knew to be in the old Western Settlement). To this, they had answered that 'the Norwegians themselves did it when they left the country'.[79] Jette Arneborg, Birgitte Sonne, and Kirsten Thisted have all discussed how Egede's earliest diary entries about interviews with the Inuit show that genocide was not the only explanation offered for the Norse people's disappearance. When Egede first interviewed the Inuit, they gave different explanations for the disappearance of the Norse, including the possibility that they had left of their own accord.[80] But, later, he seems more intent on confirming genocide. For instance, Egede recounts that he had asked a number of native Greenlanders about the Norse population and found that 'the savages did absolutely not deny, when we have said to them that they were the children of the erstwhile Norwegians'.[81] How are we to understand Egede's rather peculiar formulation here? Did his questioning about violence compel the Inuit to equivocate out of politeness? If anything, the idea that Christians had been exterminated would have strengthened his own self-understanding about the mission as bringing redemption to Greenland, converting not only people who did not know Christianity but also the pagan sinners who had once attacked it.

In *A Description of Greenland* Hans Egede declares unequivocally that the Norse people were 'destroyed by the barbarity of the savage Schrellingers'.[82] In a published book meant for the European book market, the focus on the atrocity of native violence could have a propagandistic appeal. The historian H. C. Porter has shown that the news of the 1622 Indian massacre of Christian colonists in Virginia compelled contemporary writers to speak more fervidly of Englishmen's natural right to settle and inhabit the land because an injustice had been done to them.[83] By propagating the idea of a 'well established Norwegian colony' on the west coast, which was brought to 'ruin and total destruction' by Skraeling incursions, Egede may similarly be seen to justify Dano-Norwegian recolonisation.[84]

It is a fact that the Inuit legends about the Norse inhabitants written down by missionaries tend to corroborate the story of Inuit attacks on Norse settlers, which we have seen was already established in Europe before the eighteenth century. Jette Arneborg, who has collected the most extensive selection of Inuit stories about violent conflict with the Norse, proposes that stories of extermination may have been 'planted' in the process of questioning the Inuit about this possibility.[85] She notes, for instance, that Poul Egede's diary sometimes gives the impression that he puts words into the mouth of the Inuit he interviews. One place where this may be the case is a situation from 1727 when Poul Egede tells us that an Inuk sold him a piece of melted metal. Poul Egede had seen what he thinks must be a Norse church building at Hvalsey and therefore deduces that this metal must be a piece from a broken church bell. The passage is as follows:

When I said that it was a big bell, which had been melted down at the time their countrymen destroyed our ancestors, a fright got into him. He said that it was the evil ancestors, who had done it, and that those who now live were good-natured, as we knew them to be. When I confessed that this was correct, he was pleased.[86]

The Inuk appears to respond to the history that Poul Egede imposes upon him. There is further the indication that Poul makes the Inuk feel guilty about his ancestors' evil deeds – and perhaps also frightened of retaliation, as feuding was a still-existing cultural practice in Inuit society.

We may also consider the conclusion that Hans Egede reached after he had interviewed several Inuit about what had happened to the Norse colony. He writes that 'they affirm [*stadfæste*] what the ancient histories tell us, that their ancestors made war with them, and destroyed them'.[87] The formulation here signals that the narrative of genocide was one Egede knew from European sources before he solicited stories from the Inuit. Precisely what the Inuit informers said at the time is hard to know, as their words are filtered through Egede's interpretation. Elizabeth Tonkin usefully reminds us that the communication of oral genres is often actively 'dialogic': it is a social interaction between teller and listener.[88] Did Egede steer his storytellers to provide a history that fitted his preconception of historical events? Evidently, the missionaries gave incentives for the Greenland Inuit to look for traces of Norse history. For example, J. F. Jørgensen, the priest in Qaqortoq, offered a rifle to anyone who could find a rune stone supposedly located in a nearby islet (the stone was never recovered, even though several Greenlanders searched for it).[89]

A central question, of course, is if it is at all possible that any real memory of the Norse was preserved in Inuit oral tales. In relation to oral national legends in Europe, the historian Walter Goffart has used anecdotal evidence to claim that 'memory rarely carries back more than three generations'.[90] Wolf Libeschuertz has provided a counterclaim to this, pointing to examples of multi-generational memory in connection with both the *Iliad* and Maori tradition.[91] Robert Comeau, a modern Inuk from Iqaluit, writes that the knowledge of the Elders and 'the understanding of their lived experience and survival is something that we have to admire and replicate if we are to keep our culture strong'.[92] Studies in contemporary Inuit traditions support this statement.[93] Passing down to future generations knowledge about foreigners, and what contact with them would entail, may have been considered an essential function of oral culture.

In a book translated from Danish into English as *Tales and Traditions of the Eskimo* (1875), the administrator in Greenland, Hinrich Rink, draws attention to the fact that the Indigenous population of Labrador had tales reaching back several centuries. For instance, there was the tradition that their ancestors once lived together with a people known in Greenland as the Tunit, but that this people had fled after violent clashes and moved north to what is now Cape Chidley.[94] It is generally believed that the Tunit were the Dorset Eskimo culture, a population group which became extinct between AD 1000 and 1500.[95]

Rink was specifically interested in Greenland legends. Encouraged by the Greenlander Samuel Kleinschmidt, Rink sent out handbills in 1858 soliciting legends and drawings for the printing press he had set up in Greenland. Between 1859 and 1861, Rink published four illustrated volumes with Inuit legends (Figure 1.3). One of the most active respondents was the seal-hunter and storyteller Aron (1822–69), brought up in Kangeq, near present-day Nuuk, at the mission station of the German-speaking Moravian Brethren.[96] Aron provided no fewer than fifty-six stories and numerous drawings. This was a way to supplement his failing income as Aron suffered from tuberculosis and was unable to fish and hunt. Aron was the son of Kristian Hendrik, who had trained as a catechist, so Aron was literate and part of a 'new' Greenland which had been significantly impacted by colonial and Christian culture. Thus, we must understand Aron as a figure who straddled two cultures; he was able to collect his people's traditions but poured them into a new mould of written discourse, woodcuts, and watercolours – arts the missionaries had introduced to Greenland. Thus, the tales were a (Westernised) modified form of the original tales, whose original oral telling would have had a very different presentation with gestures and dramatic performance, as was the norm in Kalaallisut storytelling.

FIGURE 1.3   Aron of Kangeq, woodcut (1859) illustrating the
Inuit legend of Qasapi killing the Norse chief Uunngortoq.
Nuuk Art Museum.

The tales Aron collected about the Norse are primarily
concerned with hostilities. The general story arc has the
Inuit and the Norse people living in peaceful coexistence,
only to be disrupted by misunderstandings that later lead
to hostilities. In one tale the Inuit and the Norse are so
close that they could understand each other's languages,
and a Norse family took in an Inuit maid servant (*kif-
faq*); however, she causes a rift between the two peoples.[97]
This legend of a maidservant causing division between
two peoples living in peace is a motif known from stories over large parts of Canada, only here she goes to live
with other Indigenous people and incites them against
the Inuit.[98] Inge Kleivan notes that Aron concludes the
tales he solicited about the Norse by expressing suspicion
about their truth value. In a letter he sent on 20 February
1859, featuring a tale about the Greenlanders' first meeting with the Norse, he wraps it up by stating that little

was known about the Norse people's disappearance, so his informers may likely have 'either reported wrongly or embellished it with a number of additions'.[99]

The problem with the narratives involving the Inuit forefathers' skirmishes with the Norse is that very similar storylines appear in other tales about the relationship with other strangers. Kirsten Thisted has shown that several of the stories about the Norse are adapted from what is best described as an archive of Inuit legends.[100] In particular, there may be overlap with legends about the fights with the Tunit. A recycling of narrative material about strife with strangers was already apparent to Rink.[101] It is therefore possible that Inuit storytellers adapted traditional storylines to fit the request for stories about the Norse.

Why would Aron question older community members about such legends in the first place? I suggest Aron was very much part of the aforementioned contact zone established in nineteenth-century Greenland. Educated by missionaries, he knew what they found interesting and was ready to placate this interest. Nonetheless, the assertion of the Greenland Inuit being victorious in their feuding against the Norse is important. It shows us that the *lieux de mémoire* Aron helped to commit to paper may have provided a 'remembering back' against the colonisers, just as many native texts in other parts of the colonised world would later 'write back' against the empire.[102]

This chapter has examined how Greenland became mythologised and grew in importance after communication with the Norse colony was cut off in the early fifteenth century. Failure to uphold shipping routes gradually made Greenland an unknown territory. The Dano-Norwegian crown saw Greenland as an old colonial land that had once been subject to taxation, and stories of wealth circulated in European texts. Thus, there was interest in finding the old colonists and re-establishing trade with them. Yet Greenland was also cast, like other places in the New World, as a land brimming with precious metals. This made Greenland and the North Atlantic the object of a European scramble for possessions. The last two Frobisher expeditions of the late sixteenth century and Christian IV's three expeditions of the early seventeenth century were essentially hunting expeditions for global resources in the Arctic. The dreams that took European powers into the Arctic in the late sixteenth century have continued into our own time, if for different resources, as John F. Richards has pointed out in his illuminating study *The Unending Frontier*.[103] The exploratory drive that compelled Europeans to seek out the North Atlantic was intrinsically bound up with the hope that it would help the respective nations to gain leverage in the European balance of power. The reports of finding precious ore would all prove false, and it was the fishing and whaling grounds (if less glamorous to write about) were where real profits could be made.

Myths of rich settlements and treasure were not the only images of Greenland that circulated, however. Ívar's report of the Western Settlement compelled a cultural narrative of a Christian colony overrun by pagans. Although no violence is directly mentioned in the report, European writers universally assumed it. We have seen that various political interests and the need for increased papal funding could have been behind the promotion of stories of pagan attacks at the borders of Christendom.

Since history writing is marked by power asymmetries, it is important to also listen to Indigenous voices and not just European accounts. However, this is not such a simple thing to do, as the early records of oral sources may have been contaminated by the European transcribers. When Inuit storytellers were asked what they knew about the Norse people's disappearance, they drew on genuine traditions while also extrapolating material from a broader tradition about encounters with foreigners. The Inuit production of oral stories about battles with the Norse settlers in the eighteenth and nineteenth centuries was undoubtedly encouraged by what the Europeans told them. In broad terms this bricolage of various elements is not entirely dissimilar from how European antiquarians, prior to the recolonisation of 1721, had constructed a memory of Greenland and its settlers from scraps of real knowledge, to which was added tales of rich fields and myths of treasure.

2

Greenland and Discourses of Possession

~

This chapter examines the rhetoric of imperialism in the period leading up to the Danish recolonisation of Greenland in 1721 and its immediate aftermath. It was the English privateer Martin Frobisher's expeditions in the late sixteenth century that first gave impetus to ambition concerning potential rich lands in the Arctic. The slew of texts published in the wake of the expeditions provided the nation with a sense of courageous Englishmen establishing claims to lands in the North Atlantic. The examination here will focus on English examples that allude to Greenland in ways that constitute claims to land. Danish expeditions began in the early seventeenth century and were also documented in print. I aim to show how Danish endeavours can be seen partly as a response to English activity. The discussion in the chapter will be an inquiry into how Danish writers attempted to ascertain Greenland as a land belonging to the Dano-Norwegian crown.

The many self-conscious travel accounts as well as the poetic effusions about land in the North Atlantic were intended to excite audiences with new knowledge about an expanding world while signalling the nation's place in it. Thus, print culture did more than just broaden intellectual culture. The discussion will show how historiography became a politicised tool, and that writing the history of the 'lost colony' came to play a significant role. In the final part of the chapter I will give attention to an English and a Dutch text, respectively, which were remonstrations against Danish historiography. To my knowledge, neither of these texts has previously been the object of scrutiny, but they will help to shed new light on the extent to which the writing of Greenland's history became a matter of contention in Europe.

English Representations of Greenland

The first new detailed travel accounts of Greenland and nearby lands were published in connection with Frobisher's three expeditions that took place between 1576 and 1578. These journeys have long been seen as a dead-end insofar as they failed to achieve their immediate objectives. Nonetheless, they made a lasting impression in print. In fact, few other expeditions have left such a range of narratives (Best, Hall, Fenton, Ellis, Settle, Lok, and others). As I will argue, the published accounts were important in what became a competition between England and Denmark for possessions in the North Atlantic. I will begin with an examination of how reports from Frobisher's journeys were intended to both legitimise and galvanise English political ambition.

It makes sense to first clarify the role Greenland played in the accounts related to Frobisher's expeditions, since this is not often addressed in the otherwise vast amount of critical literature published about them. On 1 July 1576, the first Frobisher expedition caught sight of south-eastern Greenland. Because Frobisher made use of the Zeno map (printed in Venice in 1558), which depicted the fictitious fourteenth-century travels of the Zeno brothers, he misidentified Greenland as the imaginary island of 'Freeseland' (sometimes written as 'Friesland').[1] On this occasion Frobisher was prevented from reaching the coast due to adverse weather conditions. However, on the expedition of 1578, the crew went ashore on 20 June. Although mostly privately financed, Frobisher's expeditions were undertaken in the spirit of imperialism. George Best, Frobisher's lieutenant on the second expedition and captain on the third, writes that the crew were 'the fyrste knowen Christians that we havue true notice of, that euer set foote vpon that ground', and by that action 'toke possession thereof to the vse of our Soueraigne Lady the Quéenes Maiestie'.[2] Best also notes that Frobisher referred to 'Freeseland' as 'Weast [West] *England*'.[3] The statements accord with an axiom often marshalled in political rhetoric: undiscovered land was *terra nullius* and the nation first to set foot on new land gained right of ownership. The definition of first 'Christians' is important because the assertion of rights would discount the Indigenous Inuit.

Publishing expedition reports was an essential epilogue to any European exploration. Best's report was published in London in late 1578 (prefaced with a dedication to Queen Elizabeth I). One intention was clearly to publicise English achievements and claims to the newly discovered land. Best does not define the place where they made landfall as Greenland (which it was). This was partly because of Frobisher's use of faulty maps, which displaced the landing to 'Freeseland'. Furthermore, the Privy Council demanded the suppression of all accurate navigational information; hence it would not be immediately clear to the Danes that a rival claim to Greenland had been made. Yet Best adds the geographical speculation that 'Weaste Englande' may be 'firme lande ... with Groenlande'.[4] He also speculates that the natives could 'trade with some ciuill people'.[5] In abandoned tents the crew found a box of small nails, earrings, boards of well-cut fir wood, and other artificially wrought artifacts. These objects probably derived from trading with European whaling ships – but did some contemporary readers believe that traders had made contact with the Norse colonists (as has indeed been proposed in more recent times)?[6]

Whether landfall was believed to be in Greenland or close to it, the English success in exploring and claiming lands in the Arctic would have been uncomfortable reading in Copenhagen. The Danish king Frederik II clearly felt that Frobisher had made incursions into his imperial domain. Hence, Frederik II decided to fit out two ships for an expedition to Greenland. He commissioned the English navigator James Alday (who appears to have sailed with Frobisher in 1576) to lead the ships. Alday's royal orders survive in a document signed 21 May 1579: it states in no uncertain terms that Greenland belongs 'under our kingdom Norway' and that the aim is once again to bring the 'common people' (*mennige allmue*) – that is, the Norse settlers, under the law and protection of the crown as well as convert them to the true faith.[7] Frederik II would never know whether these aims were achievable. Because of a delay in departure, Alday did not reach Greenland until late in the year and was unable to make landfall due to the blockage of ice.

Another Danish expedition, led by the Faroese captain Mogens Heinesen in 1581, also failed to reach Greenland due to coastal ice. These disappointing attempts were probably why Frobisher was invited to Copenhagen in 1582. Frederik II wrote a letter to Queen Elizabeth, asking permission to make use of his services for one or two years.[8] Whether Elizabeth was reluctant to have her star navigator explore the same latitudes where he had earlier claimed land for her or other practical reasons stood in the way of accepting the proposal is not known, but nothing came of the request.

If Frobisher's expeditions were privately funded, the English court was following developments closely and sought historical justifications for land-taking in the Arctic. In the manuscript collection *Brytanici Imperii Limites* (*The Borders of British Empire*), Queen Elizabeth's court advisor and astrologer John Dee put forward that the English crown was justified in laying claim to all coasts and islands near Terra Florida unto 'Atlantis' (i.e. America), Greenland, and beyond. This was, Dee asserts, by dint of the earlier discoveries made by King Arthur, Prince Madoc, and St Brendan the Navigator.[9] The journeys mentioned here were all the stuff of legend or outright fabrication. Dee's claims may appear incredulous today, but Blaire Zeiders has recently shown that Dee expected his historical research to be taken seriously and justify political action.[10] In fact, the part of the manuscript in which Dee invokes these 'English' discoveries is dated 4 May 1578, when Frobisher was still planning his 1578 voyage. Dee and the court he represented evidently felt that the imperialism that drove the expeditions needed the backup of antiquarian scholarship. Since the Danes had not yet sent out expeditions to Greenland, Dee's history of English possession of American lands must be seen against the backdrop of Spain's success in occupying large parts of the American continent. Greenland also remained a land of interest, however. Already around the time of Frobisher's first voyage, Dee made clear to Queen Elizabeth, who came to visit him at his home, that she had the 'title to Greenland, Estetiland and Friseland'.[11]

Among the legends Dee promotes, the story of Madoc is particularly interesting with respect to Greenland as it concerns a Welsh prince who had allegedly crossed the Atlantic in 1170 and established communities in both Greenland and North America.[12] The legend about Madoc in Greenland was later included in the third chapter of George Peckham's *A True Reporte of the Late Discoveries of Newfound Land* (1583), in which it is argued that England has an obligation to bring to fruition the seed of religion that Madoc had planted in the New World. The geographer Richard Hakluyt, noted for his indefatigable promotion of Elizabethan overseas expansion, also turned to Madoc's travels in his 1584 *Discourse of Western Planting* with the express purpose of challenging Spanish claims to the Americas and persuading Queen Elizabeth (as well as English merchants) to support Walter Raleigh's colonisation schemes.[13]

After these late sixteenth-century assertions, official declarations of English rights to Greenland all but faded from imperial rhetoric. This was perhaps because no new empirical evidence was brought forward that could keep the legend alive, whereas the idea of a Welsh legacy in North America continued to amass interest based on circumstantial evidence provided by travellers among the American Indians (fair skin, Welsh-sounding words, etc.).[14] However, as late as the mid-eighteenth century, the German antiquarian Johann Friedrich Schröter reasoned that Madoc probably did reach Greenland but was unlikely to have sailed all the way to Florida, Virginia, or Mexico, as some sources claimed.[15]

If Greenland was not officially claimed by England, it was a different story with the adjacent island of Spitsbergen, known under the name 'New Greenland'. Capitalising on Denmark's weakened attention to the Arctic during the Kalmar War with Sweden (1611–13), the London-based Muscovy Company began sending ships to Spitsbergen whaling grounds in 1611, while the Dutch parliament granted the Noordsche Compagnie a charter to fish and trade between Nova Zembla and the Davis Strait in 1614. Whale oil, obtained by melting blubber, was a valuable commodity in Europe used for lamp oil, soap, and lubrication. It made the waters around Spitsbergen and Greenland the equivalent of a modern-day oil field. In 1614 King James I granted the Muscovy Company permission to annex Spitsbergen, as several English whalers had set up tryworks on the coast to process whale blubber. If the Royal Charter did not refer to medieval legend for justification, it was issued on another false presumption, which was that the Arctic explorer Hugh Willoughby had discovered the land in 1553 (in the service of Henry VIII). In response to James I's annexation, Christian IV of Denmark dispatched a warship in 1615 to protect Danish whaling near Spitsbergen, which it was his ambition to name 'Christiansbergen'. In the following year he further tried to assert Danish claims over the island through diplomatic missions to European courts but failed to receive a positive hearing.[16] The hope of securing Spitsbergen for

Denmark was eventually given up, while claims to 'Old Greenland' were amplified in the course of the seventeenth century.

We must here return to the importance of Frobisher's navigation through the Arctic. Crucially, if the journeys were unsuccessful in both locating the Northwest Passage and precious metals, they could upset the status quo and leave a long-lasting impact on Arctic politics. Adriana Craciun has noted that the textual vagueness and confusion that characterises the publications describing Frobisher's journeys led to garbled representations when projecting English achievements onto the concrete medium of maps. On geographical charts and globes that began to appear some twenty years after the last expedition, the 'Meta Incognita' (which Frobisher claimed for England) was placed on the southern shores of Greenland – although its actual location was in south-east Baffin Island.[17]

I have not been able to assess whether any of these maps were known in Copenhagen, but Christian IV moved to reassert what he believed to be his inherited rights over Greenland by financing three expeditions, in 1605, 1606, and 1607. These were launched with the purpose of filling the crown's coffers through collecting taxes from the Norse settlers and income from an expected lucrative trade. However, the expeditions were also very public performances, as Christian IV wanted to display his political will to reach Greenland; continued neglect of the territory would be tantamount to forfeiting the right to it.

Even if the Danish expeditions reached Greenland, it was with the help of the Scottish explorer John Cunningham, who was enlisted as chief commander and captain, and the experienced Englishman James Hall, who piloted all three expeditions. Navigational knowledge of the Arctic clearly resided with English and Scottish seamen. This fact was not missed in the competition over the Arctic that played out in print. That an Englishman had piloted the Danish expeditions was not lost on Samuel Purchas when he included accounts of them in the third volume of *Hakluytus Posthumus, or Purchas His Pilgrimes* (1625). It should be remembered here that the overall design of the third volume of this work is to document English discoveries in the Arctic (as well as other areas of the world). So, by including his compatriot Hall's reports, Purchas implies that the exploration of Greenland is an English achievement. Purchas transcribes Hall's official reports to Christian IV from the 1605 and 1606 expeditions. However, with respect to the third voyage of 1607, Purchas inserts the following note:

I have also Master Hall's voyage of the next yeere 1607 ... written, and with representations of Land-sights, curiously delineated by Josias Hubert of Hull, but the Danes (envious perhaps that the glory of the discovery would be attributed to the English pilot), after the land saluted, mutinied, and in fine forced the ship to returne to Island [Iceland]. For which cause I have omitted the whole.[18]

It is odd, of course, that Hall would not write the report on the 1607 expedition, as he had done on the two earlier occasions. Given the fact that the expedition was a non-event (it was a failure as the Danish ships did not reach Greenland's coast), the task may have been left to a junior member of the crew. Although Purchas generally leaves out travel accounts that he finds dull, his wording in the quoted passage appears to exonerate his compatriot from blame. The omitted report is made to stand as a testament to what should have been another English success and aspersions about the failure are cast squarely on the Danish crew. The historian Mary C. Fuller has provided a useful framework for understanding selective representations. She notes that the English 'heroic Age of Discovery' was a construction based upon on 'a number of deliberate and specific omissions' in printed accounts.[19] Indeed, Purchas' management of information can be seen to serve a national agenda, and it is an example of how print culture was immersed in imperialist power dynamics.

The question remains, however, whether the Danes were so averse to let an Englishman discover Greenland that they would mutiny. Let us weigh up the evidence. There is the record of an earlier incident on the 1605 voyage, when Hall had separated from the two other ships and sailed further north, because he relied on maps different from those used by the companion ships. When C. C. Lyschander writes about this event in *Den Gronlandske Chronica*, he valorises Danish navigational knowledge as superior to that of the Englishman.[20] Danish patriots could use Hall's nationality against him. Yet, on his detour, Hall had proved his loyalty to Denmark by naming the locations of Anne's Cape and Sophia's Cape after the queen and the queen mother, respectively.[21] Hall also had drawn a map of what he named 'Kinge Christianus His Ford' (Itilleq), in reference to the Danish monarch, and the map features a huge *C4* monogram (for Christian IV).[22] Given the trust that Christian IV put in Hall, it seems unlikely that a Dano-Norwegian crew decided to mutiny out of fear that Hall should claim discoveries as 'English', as Purchas suggests.

Josias Hubert's report of the 1607 expedition has not survived elsewhere, and there is no other eyewitness account of what happened. However, in his patriotic poem on Christian IV's expeditions, Lyschander gives us an account that does not square with Purchas' representation of events. Lyschander points to bad weather conditions and vast ice shoals near the coast as the main reasons Captain Carsten Richardson and James Hall did not land on the east coast. (The east coast is less accessible than the west coast because a current draws ice down from the Pole.) Here also, propaganda is introduced into the account. Lyschander glosses over the failure by invoking the master narrative of Israel in Canaan, which Paul Stevens has shown was a strategy employed by many colonial texts of the early modern period.[23] In Lyschander's poem, the two men would 'gaze like Moses into the land of Canaan / And could yet not enter' (ll. 4831–2). With this biblical analogy the Danes (and Hall is here allowed to be a loyal subject of the Danish monarch) are only temporarily exiled from the crown land. The propagandistic notion of the need to reunite Greenland with the Danish realm became a recurrent feature in the rhetoric of the seventeenth century, as will now be examined.

Recovering the Greenlanders for the Danish Realm

What can be discerned from early seventeenth-century Danish texts is that the Norse Greenlanders were seen as an old tributary people who had once accepted the king as their suzerain. Thus, it was expected this loyalty could be revived. Arngrímur Jónsson, whose *Gronlandia* (1606) was discussed in Chapter 1, makes the Danish claims to the former colony crystal clear: 'Greenland was once governed by, and paid taxes to, Norway, and subsequently to the Danish kings, when the Norwegian realm was ceded to Denmark.'[24] He hastens to add that recovery of the lost land and its people is 'not just for the Danish kingdom, but also for God': Greenland should be reconnected 'with the body of the Nordic church'.[25] It was assumed that the Norse inhabitants were still there, but that they, after 200 years of isolation, had grown ignorant of their king and knew not of the Lutheran state church. Denmark–Norway had become Protestant, but the Reformation was believed to have bypassed the Greenland colonists. The notion of reasserting Dano-Norwegian suzerainty in Greenland was almost invariably joined with religious/missionary concerns.

Only some thirty years after Lutheranism was made the official religion in areas under the Danish crown, the Norwegian clergyman Absalon Pedersön Beyer, in his *Om Norgis Rige* (*On the Norwegian Realm*) (1567), held out the hope that one would 'seek out the lost sheep' and 'let the prodigal son return to his father's house'.[26] With an optimism characteristic of the Renaissance, Lyschander argues in the prefatory poem to *Chronica* that rediscovering Greenland has the twin benefits of extending both 'God's kingdom and our Danish Realm ... to the end of the world' (ll. 77–8).[27] Temporal and religious rule are also enfolded within each other in the official documents given to the commanders of the three ships participating in the 1605 expedition to Greenland. The objectives are to locate good harbours and provide the long-neglected settlements with instructions in religion, law, and order.[28] In the case of Greenland, converting the colonists to the state religion was a crucial motivation for establishing good trade relations and keeping order. We may see how this was later expressed in connection with the Danish recolonisation of the early eighteenth century. One of the Bergen Company directors, Jens Andersen Refdal, makes it clear in a letter to King Frederik IV that the conversion of the eastern colonists and gaining access to the resources they possessed were integrated aims.[29] That religious and commercial ambitions were interlocked can also be seen in the advertisement to attract capital investments, issued by the Bergen Company in March 1723. The advertisement requests funding for a mission among the former Christians (falsely assumed to reside the east coast) as 'the pact of baptism' will aid 'the future beneficial trade for the fatherland'.[30]

If it was hoped that loyalty to the Danish crown could be re-established over time, a present major concern was how Danish rights to Greenland could be upheld against other European nations. In this respect, purely historical claims had little actual potency. If Dano-Norwegian subjects could be found living in Greenland, it would help the crown gain juridico-political leverage and the territory could be claimed as a protectorate that it had the right to defend. We see this notion reflected in Lyschander's poetry. He writes: 'foreign realms and lands / Can ask and be told / That Greenland has been in the hands and possession / Under Norway since the beginning', to which he adds the important argument, 'the Greenlander is kin of our Norwegians [*Grønlændder er' voris Baggers Æth*] / And the land their property and province' (ll. 33–8). The legal claim to Greenland is here connected with an ethnic argument that sees the Dano-Norwegian people as united with the Norse Greenlanders. It should not be forgotten that Lyschander's framework for writing these lines is Frobisher's declaration that he worked on behalf of Elizabeth I to 'expand her realm' (l. 2530) to territories near Greenland, which is a focus in the poem.

The immediate problem for the Danes was that no one knew if the Norse settlers remained. Territory would have to be occupied, or in a legal phrase, 'put to use', for a legal claim to be recognised. Finding the 'lost colony' was therefore of considerable importance to the Danish crown. To understand the political mechanisms behind this focus on continual habitation, we may briefly turn to French philosopher Michel Foucault, who has noted a change in the way government began relating to territory from around the mid-sixteenth century. The importance of the people in the territory was increasingly emphasised and, as a result, imperium was seen as something held over people rather than over barren territory: 'One never governs a state, a territory, or a political structure', but 'people, individuals, or groups.'[31] As Stuart Elden points out, biopolitics and geopolitics became entwined and enfolded in multiple ways at this time.[32] With respect to developments in America, the historian Patricia Seed notes that cultivating and building on the land reinforced claims to territories as opposed to merely being first discoverers or having performed symbolic gestures to take possession of land.[33] If imperialist rights were made manifest in Danish claims that settlers subject to the Danish crown had made 'use of the land', no similar logic was applied to Indigenous people. They were not entitled to any rights according to European principles of land possession. However, in later centuries, Danish colonial officials began prolonged negotiations with the Inuit that at least partly respected their traditional modes of living.[34]

Unlike Ívar Bárdarson's account of the Western Settlement, no texts spoke of the Eastern Settlement as having come to an end. Thus, the hope was that it was still standing. What was hidden from view became a space for speculation and mythmaking. The rumour of a surviving Christian community in Greenland was bolstered by several anecdotal stories that circulated in print. One oft-repeated story had its origin in the German preacher Dithmar Blefken's Latin book about Iceland from 1607. Blefken describes spending the winter of 1563 in Iceland, where he met a monk who told him he had trained in Greenland at the monastery of St Thomas.[35] Finn Gad, a twentieth-century historian of Greenland, writes that the story of a functioning monastery, more than a century and a half after communication with Greenland was discontinued, 'had lost any claim to be considered seriously'.[36] If this is a sound evaluation from a modern perspective, it fails to acknowledge the willingness to believe the story when it was published. Indeed, Blefken's book gained traction around Europe with a Dutch translation in 1607 and a German version in 1608, both with subsequent editions. The story of the monastery was also given attention in Rudolph Capel's popular *Norden, Oder zu Wasser und Lande im Eise und Snee* (*The North, or About Water and Land in Ice and Snow*) (1678).[37] Excerpts of Blefken's chapters appeared in learned journals, and both major eighteenth-century writers concerned with Greenland – Hans Egede and David Crantz – felt compelled to include the anecdote in their histories.[38]

There was intermittent Danish activity throughout the seventeenth century. In 1636 a Danish expedition with two ships was launched under the auspices of the newly established Greenland Trade Company with the purpose of initiating trade with the Greenlanders. At this time Denmark had entered the scramble for colonial possessions beyond the North Atlantic. An agreement had been negotiated with the Hindu kingdom of Thanjavur on the south-east Indian Coromandel coast, allowing the Danish East India Company to establish a trading post by the village of Tharangambadi, later known as Tranquebar (held between 1620 and 1845). A similar trading post was intended for Greenland, but nothing came of it. King Frederik III later gave permission to the merchant Henrik Müller to trade in Greenland, which resulted in three expeditions between 1652 and 1654, led by the Dutch-born captain David Danell. Trade with the Inuit population took place, but four Inuit were also kidnapped.

These Danish trade expeditions were belated; other nations had already made landings on the west coast. Especially the Dutch would often supplement their whale hunts with income from trading with the Inuit. When Danell went to Itivdleq Fjord (now Itilleq), the Inuit were already familiar with foreigners and came out in boats to sell wares they knew were popular.[39] The Inuit needed iron for hunting and fishing tools and for utensils like knives and axes; in return the Dutch got whale products, seal meat, skins, and narwhal ivory. Dutch whalers increasingly systematised this trade, thus robbing Denmark of potential profits.

In response to these developments, Frederik III had a royal seal manufactured in which a polar bear represented possession of Greenland, alongside images of stockfish (Iceland) and sheep (Faroe Islands). The skin of a polar bear was a high-end commodity at the time, and live animals were traded in Europe in the seventeenth century.[40] In 1669, Frederik III also had a two-rixdollar minted, emblazoned with a coat of arms that included a polar bear.[41] Both seal and coin were circulatory 'texts' intended to signal Danish sovereignty over Greenland. This is akin to twenty-first-century nation states printing stamps with Arctic images to display their political interest in the North Atlantic.[42]

Throughout most of the seventeenth century the Danish crown considered Greenland an old tributary land, inhabited by what was in principle an independent people. Therefore, the Danish expeditions were not undertaken with the purpose of colonising Greenland – for all they knew, there was already a settled colony. However, we read in the entry on 'Greenland' in *Border Disputes: A Global Encyclopedia* that there were 'efforts to establish settlements in 1605'.[43] This is certainly mistaken. Although we do have the report from James Hall that two people were left in Greenland in connection with Christian IV's first expedition, these men ('both being Malefactors') were abandoned on shore with 'things necessarie, as victuall and other things' as a punishment, probably the result of a commuted death sentence.[44] Thus, if we are to characterise official Danish policy throughout the seventeenth century according to Nancy Shoemaker's typology of various forms of colonialism, the aim was *trade* and *extractive* colonialism, not *settler* colonialism.[45]

Danish imperial gesturing with insignia and symbols did not prevent other European ships from entering the waters in the part of the North Atlantic to which the Danes wanted to lay claim. From the middle of the seventeenth century Spitsbergen whale hunters saw new interlopers from Hamburg and Bremen in the area, competing with the Dutch. On average 50 ships sailed from 'German' ports every year, and Dutch traffic numbered 126 ships that set sail to fish near Spitsbergen.[46] High hunting pressure on the whales in the eighteenth century led the European whaling fleet to explore resources in the Davis Strait off Greenland's west coast, focusing on the Disko Bay, and whalers made contact with the Inuit population. In 1719 Dutch whaling vessels increased their presence in waters off west Greenland.[47] It became increasingly clear that the Danish claim to Greenland could not rely solely on a colony of Dano-Norwegian subjects who once had or may still inhabit the land: a new colonial presence was imperative.

The rhetorical build-up to the recolonisation of Greenland in 1721 has not received the attention it warrants, although it is an important chapter in how political perspectives gradually changed. One example of a change in argumentation towards more robust Danish action is found in the historian Peder Hansen Resen's *Groenlandia* (which was meant for publication but remained in manuscript at his passing in 1688).[48] Resen believes in the continued existence of the old Norse colony. He describes the colonists as a people of the 'same blood as us' who are enjoying Danish hospitality as 'guests' on land owned by the crown.[49] Resen's approach to Greenland may best be defined as irredentist – that is to say, he highlights the crown's right to reclaim an unredeemed territory (an irredenta).

In addition to invoking a sense of moral duty to reclaim old land, Resen encourages a colonial desire for Greenland which could be 'calculated in mercantilist terms', as Jean-François Lyotard would put it.[50] Working from a number of older sources related to the Norse colony, Resen presents Greenland as a fertile land, and his sixth chapter includes an extensive list of precious metals. He notes in the ninth chapter that Greenland fishing offers many opportunities, from which Denmark sadly did not sufficiently profit. In chapter twenty Resen argues that Greenland's waters would be better controlled if a recolonisation took place, using Icelanders and Norwegians for the resettlement.[51] Presumably, the logic is that men from these parts of the Danish realm were inured to the cold and therefore well suited to life in Greenland. The new colonists should be protected by a fort armed with cannons, and the men posted in this remote part of the world should be rewarded with honours and gifts upon their return home.[52]

The Danish colonial administration had erected citadels on the Gold Coast in present-day Ghana. These installations served a dual function as trading stations (including slaves) and military fortifications (usually armed with cannons and other guns) protecting the coast. In the case of Greenland, such a measure would not only be a bulwark against foreign ships, but also be politically expedient as an actual presence on land was better than claiming possession from across the Atlantic. The historian Ken MacMillan has noted that, in the late seventeenth century, Richard Whitbourne and William Vaughan advocated strongly for reinforcing the English colony in Newfoundland to strengthen England's legal sovereignty over the island against French and Dutch whaling and fishing ships.[53] Resen was thinking in similar terms.

Another argument for resettling Greenland was put forward by the Icelandic historian Arngrímur Thorkelsson Vídalín in the treatise *De veri et nova Grönlandia diatribe* (*New and True Discussion of Greenland*) (1704). The two first parts recycle a standard history of the old colony, but in the third section (written in Danish) Vídalín makes several proposals for political actions. Greenland is represented as a theatre of colonial fantasies – that is, a chance for Denmark to gain possession of a land that may match the rich imperial targets of other European nations. Vídalín argues that a mission should be sent out to rescue the Norse settlers because one could not but expect that they would welcome Frederik IV taking 'possession of the land again'.[54] He also proposes the establishment of several new colonial settlements.[55]

Interestingly, the Inuit play a relatively large role in this recolonisation scheme. Vídalín may see the Inuit as usurpers of land, for which reason there is 'no injustice in chasing away the Greenland barbarians from the settlements where they have either driven our colony to flight, or … done them great harm'.[56] Yet, as manpower was often a scarce resource in fledgling colonies, Vídalín suggests that the most agreeable of the savages could be employed

84

to help the farmers, fishermen, and even the soldiers.[57] Such integrationist strategies were not unknown. In the French colonisation of Canada in the early 1600s, for example, Samuel de Champlain, the founder of Quebec, would make intermarriage with the Hurons and Ottawas a goal for the purpose of consolidating the colony.[58] If Vídalín does not go this far, he does argue that Denmark, as a rising imperial power, could improve its international standing if it invested in converting the savages to Christianity, just like the Portuguese, the Dutch, and the English had done in their colonies, while, he notes, the Spanish are universally shamed for their brutality against the American Indians.[59] Spain's policies and practices were frequently taken up for discussion by participants in the colonial fray as a detestable standard against which one could measure one's own moral compass.[60]

Dutch whaling and fishing near Greenland also impinged on the mind of Thormod Torfæus, an Icelander appointed to the office of Danish royal historiographer in 1682. Not long after his appointment, Torfæus wrote a letter to Christian V, dated 18 January 1683, in which he places emphasis on the economic gains to be made in Greenland (referencing the 1679 German translation of La Peyrère's text as evidence of Greenland's many resources). Torfæus advocates that the king pursue an active colonial policy legitimated by Greenland's historical attachment to Denmark-Norway. He promotes measures to bring back the Norse colonists under Danish control, but also that new settlements should be established. To this end, Torfæus proposes that the surplus workforce of Icelanders be drafted to build a fort on the west coast.[61] Danish forts in Africa held slaves, but Torfæus explicitly warns against kidnapping Greenlanders because he believes this would lead to great resentment among the native population. On 3 March, the king passed Torfæus' letter on to Kommercekollegiet (The Board of Trade), set up in 1668 to compete with the Dutch in international trade.[62] Nothing came of Torfæus' proposal for recolonisation, however.

The fact that a royal historiographer would occupy himself with such an overt political proposal makes it relevant to consider the nature of historiography at the time. When Torfæus applied to Christian V for the post of royal historiographer in September 1682, part of his assignment was to prove that the Danish king descended from the Norwegian royal family and therefore held a natural right to Norway and its old dependencies (of which Greenland was one).[63] Torfæus continued along these lines in his work *Orcades* (1697), a history of the Orkney Islands. This book is an interesting case study of how history writing and politics intermingled. The islands had formally belonged to Scotland since 1468 when the impoverished Christian I of Denmark pawned them off to James III. In his study Torfæus details the former Norwegian sovereignty over the islands and includes the letters exchanged in negotiating the handover. Torfæus submitted his manuscript to the censor as early as 1690, but complications arose as it was feared the publication could be construed as official remonstrance to the political settlement. It was 1696 before a royal decree was issued in Torfæus' favour and *Orcades* was passed by the censors for publication.[64]

These wrangles prepare us for considering Torfæus' *Gronlandia Antiqua* (*Old Greenland*), which was published in Latin for an international readership in 1706, but also translated by Torfæus himself into Danish in the same year. This dual publication strategy indicates that Torfæus deemed it important both to garner domestic support for colonial action and to communicate the Danish will to possess Greenland to a European audience. Torfæus wanted *Gronlandia Antiqua* (which he dedicates to Frederik IV) to be the authoritative history of Greenland, collecting all available knowledge about the settlements, the climate, and eyewitness accounts of the possible survival of the colonists. In this respect historiography had a performative function. The ability to show superior knowledge about a territory – that is, to 'occupy' it in the intellectual world, signposted the nation's will to possess.

Torfæus' small octavo is primarily concerned with the history of the medieval settlements. Already in the 'Preface to the Reader', however, a plan for recolonisation is suggested. Torfæus proposes that the Danish king send at least fifty soldiers to search out the east coast and force back the Skraelings, who may have destroyed Norse settlements. Yet, like Vídalín, Torfæus is not intent on all-out war with the natives; rather he sees that trade with them could help to pay for the expenses of recolonisation.[65]

When assessing Torfæus' work relating to Greenland, we should ignore his arguments for further 'reconquests' in the New World. In the letter Torfæus wrote to the king in 1683, he mentions the unspecified North American locations Helluland, Markland, and Vinland as old discoveries, areas in what is now north-eastern Canada. The Norse Greenlanders' landing on the American continent was known from both the Icelandic sagas and Book IV of Adam of Bremen's *Gesta Hammaburgensis ecclesiae pontificum (History of the Archbishops of Hamburg-Bremen)* (1072).

Torfæus proposes that Denmark should reclaim these lands alongside Greenland because they were supposedly brimming with sable and salmon and had an ample supply of wood that could be exported to timber-poor Iceland (a Danish dependency). Torfæus devised a plan for the circulation of goods in a Danish-dominated North Atlantic with Greenland having strategic geopolitical significance as a port of call where ships could put in for supplies before venturing further west. Torfæus may have been emboldened by the example of Sweden, another Baltic naval power, which had managed to establish colonies in the Americas in the seventeenth century, including New Sweden (1638–55) on the Delaware River.

In 1705 Torfæus published the treatise *Vinlandia Antiqua* (*Old Vinland*), in which he collects the historical evidence for the Greenlanders taking possession of a part of North America (in present-day Canada). Before publication Torfæus wrote a letter to the governor-general of Norway, Ditlev Vibe, in which he stresses that the Danish kings had a claim to the land as 'its first discoverers'. He makes clear that his book of history is intended to promote this assertion:

When my *Vinlandia* sees the light of day, it will be realised what injustice has been made, as that which the French, the Dutch, and the English, and in some respect also the Spanish have now taken as their possession in North America, and the possible finds of gold in Peru, we could have had long before Christopher Columbus was born.[66]

Had the Danish king taken steps to occupy parts of northeast Canada, it would undoubtedly have caused a reaction from the English, who had built several defensive military installations there between the 1660s and 1680, including Fort Charles, Fort Albany, Fort Nelson, and Fort Severn. Propaganda ran ahead of what was realisable and with limited resources the Danes would focus on Greenland.

The Norse Settlements: Contention and Remonstrance

If Torfæus nurtured future grand ambitions in the North Atlantic, Greenland was clearly the unredeemed territory over which Denmark had the strongest claim, insofar as it had held suzerainty over the settlers there. Remaining was the vexatious question about the size of the area the Danes could claim. Denmark's historical rights to territory (land and sea) was attenuated by La Peyrère's statement that the Norse settlements made up only 'a small part of all the extensive northern land [Greenland]'.[67] I will address this print-culture debate over rights in the remainder of the chapter.

La Peyrère's remark was exploited in some English texts to cast doubt on the legitimacy of Danish claims. For example, in *The English Atlas* (1680), it is stated that 'what the *Norwegians* conquered, or possessed in this Country [Greenland], was an inconsiderable corner of that large Continent'.[68] This conclusion was deemed so politically expedient that it was repeated almost verbatim in the hugely popular *An Account of Several Late Voyages & Discoveries ... towards Nova Zembla, Greenland or Spitsberg, Groynland or Engrondland* (1694), a book in which England's Arctic efforts are weighed up positively against those of other nations.[69]

Torfæus was aware that the size and location of the Norse settlements was a contentious issue. Therefore, he dedicated a significant part of his historiographical research to the printing of maps that documented the extent of historical occupation. In *Gronlandia Antiqua*, he appends no fewer than five maps of Greenland. The first four are reprinted from earlier sources. The oldest specimen is Sigurdus Stephanius' map from 1570, followed by the Icelandic Bishop Gudbrand Torlakson's map from 1606, then another Icelander Jonas Gudmund's map from 1640, and there is a representation of the North Atlantic by Theodor Thorlacius from 1668. Three of these maps erroneously place the Eastern Settlement on the east coast. Torfæus uses the cartographical outlines as political signposting, legitimising present political claims to large swathes of Greenland's territory. By freezing historical settlements in time, re-inking old maps for new publication, the idea of occupation is extended into the present.

The fifth map of 'Old Greenland' (Figure 2.1) was drawn up especially for Torfæus' book with the help of his collaborator, Jacob Rasch, who aided in the printing of several of Torfæus' texts. On this new map, large letters indicating the placement of the *'Vester bÿgd'* and the *'Oster bÿgd'* are superimposed on the landmass, giving the impression that the land under Norse control was expansive. In relation to the Eastern Settlement, the nineteenth-century Scottish antiquarian John Pinkerton acerbically observes: 'it would seem that the colony extended over about 200 miles in the SE extremity'.[70]

No European had at this time examined Greenland's ruins, so the map was not, of course, based on any land

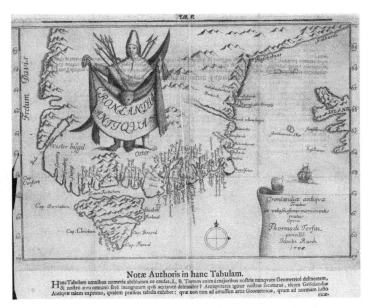

FIGURE 2.1 Torfæus' map of Greenland: *Gronlandiæ Antiqvæ Tractus ex Vetustissimis Monumentis Erutus. Opera Thormodi Torfæi penicillo Jacobi Rasch 1706.* The Royal Danish Library.

surveys. However, Torfæus explains that he has painstakingly traced out the list of churches in the colony (from Ívar Bárdarson's report) and used the old maps at his disposal, which he then amalgamated with the reports of the Arctic explorers Martin Frobisher and Jens Munk.[71] If Torfæus willingly concedes that the procedure of collating and synthesising is problematic, it is clearly justified by the aim, which is to show the ability and determination to systematise knowledge about Greenland on behalf of the Danish crown.

It is not always easy to assess the political efficacy of interventions such as the publication of Torfæus' historical research. We are fortunate, however, to have the record of one important reader. On the eve of the actual recolonisation of Greenland, in 1720, Hans Egede wrote to King Frederik IV to advocate a royal ban against foreign traffic near Greenland. Egede was concerned about the viability of the newly established Bergen Company, in which he was an investor. Even if the king had ensured that the company was exempt from customs and duties, once it began sailing to Greenland, Egede thought it would be difficult to generate a stable revenue stream if foreign nations were not effectively prevented from trading with the natives on the west coast.[72] To convince the king that he was justified, on historical grounds, to issue a ban against other European nations, Egede points to Torfæus' recently published map, which 'placed the old Norwegian colony, called the Western Settlement, under 64 degrees on the west side of Greenland, which is now called the Davis Strait'.[73] Torfæus' map was invoked as evidence of land rights by virtue of the old settlements it depicted.

It is pertinent to extend the discussion of historiography's political dimension, which Egede confirms here, by focusing on two previously unexamined published documents from the early eighteenth century. Both challenged Denmark's rights to Greenlandic waters. The first of these texts was published in 1710 by Joducus Crull, a member of the Royal Society in London. The book he wrote was intended to make up for the omissions in Samuel von Pufendorf's *Continuirte Einleitung zu der Historie der vornehmsten Reiche und Staaten von Europa* (which Crull had translated into English as *An Introduction to the History of the Principal Kingdoms and States of Europe*). Crull's *A Supplement to Mr. Samuel Puffendorf's Introduction to the*

History of Europe contains a twenty-four-page survey of the establishment and demise of the Norse settlements in Greenland. Interestingly, one of Crull's earlier works was *Denmark Vindicated* (1694), written to denounce the diplomat Robert Molesworth's fierce attack on the Danish state in *An Account of Denmark, As It Was in the Year 1692* (1694). Crull's purpose with the previous text was to prevent a diplomatic crisis as connections between the Danish and English royal houses were close at the time. Having acquainted himself with Danish politics, Crull now turned against Denmark in favour of England in the section on Greenland in the *Supplement*.

Crull accuses Danish kings of seeking to recover Greenland at such *'prodigious Expences'* only to *'challenge* [those who could rightfully claim] *the Honour of being the first Discoverers of* New Greenland, *so much frequented by most of the* European Nations *in our time'.*[74] 'New Greenland' here refers to Spitsbergen, a harbour for Dutch and English whalers. The immediate goal of Crull's intervention is to challenge the Danish policy of *mare clausum* (the doctrine of restricting maritime access). The principle that some parts of sea were international waters, free for all nations to use, had been proposed by Hugo Grotius, a legal scholar working for the Dutch East India Trading Company, whose treatise *Mare liberium (The Free Seas)* (1609) provided ideological justification for the principle.

Crull also spends considerable time discussing Frobisher's landing on Greenland (here asserting this as a geographical fact), as well as the Danish king's reliance on English seamen, 'having sent for a Captain and Pilot very well acquainted with those Seas out of England', for his early seventeenth-century expeditions.[75] Apart from the English patriotism, Crull also digs deep in the historical sources available to him to reach the conclusion that the inhabitants of Old Greenland 'inhabited but a very small Tract of Land in Greenland', which was not much larger than 'a third Part of a Bishoprick [*sic*] in Denmark' or what is but a 'hundredth part of Greenland'.[76]

This leads Crull to weigh in on a suggestion originally made by La Peyrère that two native Greenlanders shipped to Copenhagen in 1605 had been found to be descendants of the old colonists. Crull rejects this assertion as pro-Danish propaganda. The kidnapped men could not possibly be 'the Ancient Norwegian Inhabitants of Greenland', he argues, because a people who had 'for so considerable a time been train'd up and confirm'd in the Christian Religion' would not completely abandon the remnants of their religion, especially not 'when they saw themselves transported into a Christian Country'.[77] Evidently Crull was keen to disprove the possibility of 'Danish' subjects still inhabiting the west coast of Greenland. For the argument over access to the waters off Greenland, it was important to contain Danish claims, as rich whaling banks were found in the Davis Strait.

Crull illustrates how historians could use their craft to serve various political agendas.[78] The section on Greenland is written in the context of an English push to expand whaling near Greenland. Later, in 1724, an act of Parliament stipulated that Greenland fishery should be encouraged by repealing the duty on whale fins, oil, and blubber (10 *Geo. I c.* 16), and freedom from all custom was extended to the Davis Strait for any produce of seals or fish (12 *Geo. I c.* 26). The national importance for Britain of fishing near Greenland was most vocally argued by the whaler Henry Elkin. In a pamphlet, he urged the South Sea Company to send ships to Greenland waters since 'Neglect of this Fishery may be counted a dead Loss to the Nation' and would prevent Britain from 'growing in Power and Riches'.[79]

Before we reach the second publication offering remonstrance to Danish claims, a short historical preamble is necessary. In 1734, Christian VI of Denmark granted the merchant Jacob Severin full monopoly rights to trade in Greenland, which had previously been withheld from the Bergen Company for fear of antagonising the Dutch. Severin was instrumental in establishing the northern settlements of Christianshaab (1734), Jakobshavn (1741), and Frederikshaab (1742), thus expanding Danish presence on the west coast. With the royal grant followed naval support to fend off foreign ships fishing in this area. In 1739, the Danes fought four Dutch ships at Disko Bay over rights to fish in these waters. Three Danish galiots defeated a four-ship Dutch flotilla. The struggle lasted about an hour before the Dutch surrendered. This was the first and only naval battle fought over rights to Greenland (if we discount the whalers who often got into minor fracases).

It is in connection with the skirmish at Disko Bay that Jan Jacob Mauricius published *Naleesing over Groenland voor de historie van den Noorweeschen Erik* (*Rereading Greenland's History concerning the Norwegian Erik*) (early 1740s?).[80] Mauricius was a prolific lawyer, poet, and historian who in his diplomatic career served the States of Holland and West-Friesland as minister in Hamburg.

Mauricius was interested in Dutch colonial matters and was appointed governor of Suriname in 1742, an office he held for nine years. The overarching purpose of *Naleesing over Groenland* is to 're-read' historical sources to show that Denmark's 'pretension of ownership of Greenland ... is entirely groundless'.[81] Mauricius' opens with a tirade against historians who have written about Greenland's past, including Lyschander, La Peyrère, and Egede, whom he accuses of having propagated misinformation in the service of the Danish nation.[82] He goes on to challenge these allegedly Danish-friendly historians with the following questions: Was Erik really the first to discover Greenland? Could one not also give a fair hearing to the British twelfth-century historiographer Geoffrey of Monmouth, who reports the tradition of King Arthur having brought 'the vast North under his territory, especially Greenland' at the beginning of the sixth century?[83] Mauricius sees no reason why one nation's legend of having discovered Greenland should be taken more seriously than that of another – after all, legends were not historical truths.

Mauricius launches a particularly fierce attack on Torfæus, whom he accuses of being a hireling of the Danish king, paid from the royal coffers to collect all manner of fabulous tales (*wonderfabelen*).[84] Mauricius especially targets Torfæus' depiction of churches and other buildings on his map of Greenland. Since their existence is not authenticated by any eyewitness accounts, Torfæus' cartography is deemed to have no more merit than 'the beautiful maps we have of the moon'.[85] Mauricius takes the Icelandic historian to task for regurgitating saga material not corroborated by more reliable sources.[86] In short, Torfæus is accused of writing political propaganda, which makes him a bad historian.

Torfæus was indeed receiving patronage from the Danish king, but not all the 'errors' that Mauricius lists can be assigned to political skulduggery. Torfæus' technique is often to let the sources speak for themselves, adding little or no critical commentary. It was not a case of evaluating the truth value of sources, rather to compile them as if they were a collection of *scriptores*. Torfæus' handling of source material would be too uncritical for a modern historian, but Lars Boje Mortensen reminds us that what today may appear to be 'historical naivety' was perfectly acceptable at the time.[87]

Even though not all of Mauricius' conclusions are correct, he skilfully demonstrates how history writing and mapmaking are instrumentalised as political tools. For instance, he notes that Torfæus places the Eastern Settlement at too high a latitude on his map – a location that does not square with the accounts of the settlers growing crops. In this way, Mauricius makes clear that Torfæus' intent is to manufacture a claim to a larger part of the land than was ever occupied. In general, Mauricius questions how much of Greenland's area was actually settled by the Norse colonists in order to challenge contemporary Danish claims over the Davis Strait, where Dutch fishing companies had long had commercial interests. He holds that the historical settlements did not reach all the way to northern Greenland where fishing-rich grounds were located off the coast. To debunk the Danish claim to all of Greenland, Mauricius compares their medieval settlement with the Danish occupation of the town of Tranquebar in India. Although the Danish king can claim possession of this tiny corner of the Indian coast, it would be ludicrous to maintain that he ruled all of the Indian subcontinent.[88]

The argument for allowing Dutch fishing in the Davis Strait had been made earlier in another Dutch publication, which should be briefly mentioned here. The book is titled *Beschryving van de straat Davids, benevens des zelven inwooners, zede, gestalte, en gewoonte, misgaders hunne visvangst, en andere handelingen* (*Description of the Davis Strait and Its Inhabitants, Their Customs, Stature, Habits, and Their Fisheries and Other Activities*) (1720), by Lourens Feykes Haan, a pilot for the Dutch shipping company Jakob Wynkoop en Zoon. Haan looks back at his experiences of trading with the people on Greenland's west coast. He begins the book with a short notice on Erik the Red's settlement of Greenland, but notes that the Danes had not sailed to Greenland since 1636 (Haan is seemingly unaware of his compatriot David Danell's voyages of 1652–4 in Danish service).[89] In another, more veiled attack on Danish claims to Greenland, Haan makes a note of the fact that the present inhabitants near the fishing grounds of the Davis Strait are not of European extraction, evidenced by the fact that they speak a throaty language unlike any he has heard.[90] Mauricius also indirectly questions that descendants of the Norse colony would still live in Greenland. For instance, he makes much of the fact that the natives near Disko Bay (whom, he stresses, the Danes derogatively refer to as 'savages' or 'barbarians') are clearly not related to the medieval inhabitants. For this reason, the Danes' claims to the northern reaches of Greenland are void and cannot be used to exclude other nations from operating in the Davis Strait.[91]

The overall point Mauricius wants to drive home is that Danish historiography is supercharged with political motives. Based on the discussion in this chapter, it is difficult not to sympathise with the accusations. However, not all the historians to whom Mauricius assigns guilt were as complicit in statecraft as he thinks. Some of the historians' findings were simply an uncritical acceptance of saga material and a simple misunderstanding of the sources. It should also be added that modern archaeology has verified some of the Icelandic storytelling about Greenland's settlement. Similarly, the saga legends of the Norse discovering 'Vinland' has been confirmed by the find of a camp at L'Anse aux Meadows in Newfoundland.[92]

For all Mauricius' strident protestations against Danish historiography, it should be noted that he essentially confirms the unwritten principle that past occupation is a legitimate reason for contemporary land claims, and this was the logic in which Danish historians placed their confidence. Mauricius rails against the claim that the Danes have a right to invoke the principle in relation to *all* of Greenland, since they likely never occupied more than a small corner of this vast land. Like Crull, Mauricius wants to challenge the Danish assertion of *mare clausum* (which had been the cause of the skirmish between Dutch and Danish ships at Disko Bay) and defend Dutch rights to fish in the waters surrounding Greenland. He therefore refers to Hugo Grotius' treatise *Mare liberium*.[93] I have not been able to find any Danish publications that directly confronted Mauricius' publication. In any case, the Dutch continued their whaling activities in the Davis Strait until the late 1770s, after which profits tailed off.

This chapter has shown that interest in Greenland is best considered within the framework of European competition for resources. The Artic was seen as a place where an easy route to Asian markets could be found. In the wake of Frobisher's expeditions, a new interest in possession became part of the imperial rhetoric. When it came to Greenland, both first discovery and hereditary right based on legends were invoked. In England, the legend of Madoc was given some attention in relation to North Atlantic lands, but it was trumped by Danish historians who could refer to a centuries-long history of Norse settlements to consolidate their claims to Greenland. But for both England and Denmark, publications about North Atlantic lands, whether it be histories or travel accounts, were important vehicles for staking claims to possessions. In this respect, it is useful to conclude the examination of land rights discourse with a reference to Carol Rose's discussion of the legal process known as *adverse possession*. According to this principle, the relinquishing of property occurs when owners allow trespassers to use it over an extended period of time without voicing objections. In this way, 'property looks like a kind of speech, with the audience composed of all others who might be interested in claiming the object in question'. The law 'requires the acquirer to *keep on* speaking' if the right to property is not to be lost through the doctrine of adverse possession.[94] Writers loyal to the Danish crown certainly continued to voice the claim of Greenland as an ancestral country, on whose land it was assumed that Danish subjects were still to be found. The shoring up of historical sources that told of the existence of the old tributary colony in several publications functioned as quasi-legal assertions of rights to land.

However, the search throughout the seventeenth century to find descendants of the old Greenlanders – a discovery that would significantly buttress Danish entitlement to Greenland – was unsuccessful. With other nations' increasing incursions into Greenland waters, colonisation became a pressing issue. This entailed a shift in the conception of Greenland from that of a tributary but essentially independent country to a land that should be under direct Danish control. In this chapter I have therefore analysed the rhetoric textual procedures that historians deployed to embolden more assertive colonial action in the late seventeenth and early eighteenth centuries. Writers continued to represent Greenland through the familiar trope of wealth, which was traced in the previous chapter. This clearly galvanised colonial desire, but a new consideration of containing the Inuit now made its appearance in writing as a practical problem that needed a solution.

The argument that underpins my examination in this chapter is that history writing at the time was not simply a reproduction of facts about the past, rather it aimed to construct a collective memory of Greenland (and its surrounding waters) that would serve a national agenda. For Danish historians, political leverage lay not only in the physical discovery of Greenland, the public study of its history and geography had significance in itself. Printing, publishing, and inscribing legends on a map had impact beyond the semantic meaning of the words; the production of historiographical works and accompanying maps framed a symbolic discourse of empire. Making public textual and visual representations of Greenland's past was not only about writing history; it also formed a political index of possession. Before Danish presence in Greenland became a reality, the land was already considered reconquered on the page. However, this was not a one-sided debate and it has been my aim to lay the critical groundwork for a new analysis that shows how Greenland's historiography was a contested topic in Europe. To this, the attempts by English and Dutch historians to undermine the Danish narrative are clear examples.

3

Beyond the Horizon

Greenland in Eighteenth-Century Perspectives

∼

The Inuit who resided near present-day Nuuk observed three ships approach the island of Kangeq on 3 July 1721. This time the ships came not just to barter; they carried the Dano-Norwegian missionary Hans Egede, who sought to establish a combined mission and trading station. This marked the beginning of the modern European colonisation of Greenland. Egede's missionary work on the west coast has been the subject of considerable critical attention, and excellent studies of Danish colonialism have been published.[1] This chapter also deals with the colonisation but asks different questions. My central inquiry is not primarily concerned with how the colonial/missionary project progressed in the eighteenth century; rather the interest is in how Greenland and its people were first perceived, and how it was *assumed* (from what was known at the time) that the colonial/missionary project would develop. I propose that the new knowledge produced in the encounter with the land was filtered through Old World texts and traditions about the first European settlement. The transition from reading about Greenland in books to observing it *in situ* led to a crisis of representation as the archive of knowledge stored up over the centuries became difficult to reconcile with experience.

The chapter begins with an assessment of Egede's perception of the Inuit. Whenever the history of the 1721 colonisation is told, it is invariably mentioned that Egede was expecting to find Norse colonists in Greenland. Yet how he dealt with his disappointment is rarely, if ever, part of the inquiry that follows. To address this lacuna, it is the purpose here to examine Egede's ethnic speculations about the Inuit and how he tried to reconcile his expectations with reality. Shifting the attention from people to landscapes, I turn the attention to the maps Egede drew of Greenland, as they are visual records of how traditional perceptions could be merged with new empirical data.

Modern studies of eighteenth-century colonial Greenland tend to ignore the mistaken fantasies about a still-standing Eastern Settlement to focus on the actual missionary work on the west coast, but this narrow lens produces a blind spot to the considerable financial and intellectual investment that went into finding the eastern settlers. We now know that the attempts to reach them on the east coast were wild goose chases, yet this chapter will shine a new light on them as costly mistakes that illustrate how important the recovery of the presumed Eastern Settlement was to eighteenth-century colonial ambition.

The Norse Inuit?

Since this chapter deals with how eighteenth-century factual accounts of Greenland adopted elements of imagination, it is interesting to start with a work that is essentially the reverse: an imaginative text that draws on factual knowledge about Greenland. On the eve of Egede's landing in Greenland, a strange story was published about another man of religion on a Greenland-bound journey. This was an early French novel entitled *La vie, les aventures, & les voyage de Groenland du Révérend Père Cordelier Pierre de Mésange (The Life, the Adventures, and the Journey to Greenland of the Franciscan Father Pierre de Mésange)* (1720) written by Simon Tyssot de Patot, a writer from the Huguenot diaspora who had sought exile in Holland.[2] In the early eighteenth century Dutch ships dominated whaling in Greenland waters, and this provides a starting point for the narrative about the Franciscan monk Rev. Mésange, who leaves France aboard a Dutch vessel in 1679. In the story storms force the ship off course and it narrowly passes icebergs to the north of Greenland and Spitsbergen, where the crew are caught up in pack ice.[3] Pierre and a few others are saved and led to the shores of an unknown island. They enter the underground kingdom of Rufsal, a land inside the hollow shell of the earth's crust. The Rufsal community has elements of utopia, as there is neither class nor privilege and women are considered equal to men. The Rufsal people are colonists who had come from elsewhere to finally settle in the Arctic – an idea that likely draws some inspiration from the European settlement of Greenland. In their isolated community the Rufsal develop a new social and civil society blissfully disconnected from the mores of the Old World. Tyssot de Patot relies on speculative geophysical theory for the location of Rufsal. The hollow-earth concept is based on the theory that the globe contained a substantial interior cavity as the English astronomer Edmond Halley had proposed in 1692. Critical readings have also long established that the world imagined in the novel borrows substantially from La Peyrère's *Relation du Groenland*: there are the descriptions of the harsh climate, the lack of sun throughout much of the year, the landscape, and the wildlife.[4] To the existing criticism on the novel, I will add that the references to large forests and oaks bearing fruits the size of hen's eggs clearly allude to the account of Greenland's natural wealth in Ívar Bárdarson's text.[5]

I begin with Tyssot de Patot's novel because it illustrates how the Arctic was overwritten with perceptions and speculations based on European textual tradition before it was discovered. The information taken from La Peyrère's book on Greenland helps to create a believable setting for an unbelievable story. Nonetheless, a transposition of bookish knowledge to new geography is also found in travel accounts written by Europeans, who would struggle to give perceptual form to the lands and people they encountered. This epistemological paradigm has been discussed from different angles by J. H. Elliott, Donald Lach, D. B. Quinn, and others in relation to Europe's discovery of the New World.[6] I contend that Egede's representation of Greenland was also an attempt to fit his new first-hand observations into a referential framework established in old texts.

In the diary covering his years in Greenland from 1721 to 1736 (published as a book in 1738) Egede recounts how he received information about Greenland's eastern side being inhabited by his countrymen, the Norwegians. He explains that he subsequently developed a strong impulse to find the 'old Northern Christians' and provide them with the religious instruction they had been lacking for so many years in isolation.[7] Thus, on his journey to Greenland, Egede brought with him a list of words with Norse terms that he believed could come in handy. The only people he found inhabiting the west coast, however, were the Inuit, a non-European people. This made Egede change his plans. He decided to spread the gospel among these natives, for which reason he painstakingly learned their language and studied their religious ideas. Yet, as we shall see in this section, Egede's understanding of the Inuit was based on the assumption that he had landed in the area of the old Western Settlement. This was indeed the case, and Norse ruins were located not far from the new colony of Godthaab where Egede built a house with a small chapel in 1728.

Egede's ethnological speculations on the Inuit were published in *Det gamle Grønlands nye Perlustration* (*A New Survey of Old Greenland*) (1741). The book enjoyed much popularity and was translated into several European languages (English in 1745, Dutch in 1746, French in 1763, and German in 1763). The English translation was given the title *A Description of Greenland* and was reissued in a second edition of 1818.[8] Egede's claim to provide a 'new survey' must be understood in relation to previous 'armchair' studies of Greenland, such as publications by Lyschander, La Peyrère, and Torfæus. Among other things, Egede gives a detailed eyewitness account of the Inuit, providing much new information about their culture, manners, and religion, which had not previously been available in European books. Egede's survey catered to a public craving for information about so-called primitive peoples, an interest stirred by the popular *Moeurs des Sauvages Amériquains compareées aux moeurs des premiers temps* (*Customs of the American Savages Compared to the Customs of the First Ages*) (1724) by Joseph-François Lafitau, a Jesuit missionary to the Canadian Iroquois.

A Description of Greenland is haunted by the ghosts of the Norse colony. For instance, Egede describes the ruins of old stone buildings he had come across when exploring the west coast (some of which – unbeknown to him – were the remains of the Eastern Settlement).[9] He also believed that he could see vestiges of the Norse people in the human population on the west coast. In the book he makes a statement about the Inuit that scholars usually pass over: they are 'some mixture ... of the ancient Norway colonies that formerly dwelled in the country, who in length of time were blended and naturalised among the natives'.[10] The framework for this statement is Ívar Bárdarson's report of the Western Settlement having fallen to the Skraelings. Egede continues by noting that 'some remains of them [the inhabitants of the Western Settlement] joined with the natives and became all one nation', and it was people of mixed background that could therefore be found in the native communities on the west coast.[11]

Egede does not make clear how he would discern Norse heritage in the Inuit. The only telltale sign he mentions is their use of 'Norway words'.[12] When Egede writes about the language of the Inuit (i.e. Kalaallisut, or what would have been an older form of West Greenlandic), he notes that some words show Norse provenance.[13] In his diary he records several supposed Norse as well as Latin loanwords, which suggest to him that an assimilation of the Norse population had taken place.[14] In a modern linguistic re-assessment of Egede's material, it is apparent that some of the words listed are false equivalents, while others may reflect contact through trade with European whalers. However, some words could be traces of Norse, for which reason modern linguists take them up for re-examination from time to time.[15]

Egede became convinced that he found himself among a mixed-blood population not long after he arrived in Greenland. We know this from his diary entry for 17 February 1723 (i.e. after having lived in Greenland for a little more than a year and a half), he first proposes the theory that the Norse population were 'naturalized and mixed in' with their old enemies, the Skraelings.[16] In *A Description of Greenland*, Egede further tells us that he actively looked for traces of Christian knowledge among the Inuit. However, this inquiry yielded no results, and he had come to the conclusion that the natives had no idea of a divine creator and did not acknowledge God's invisible being through the works of nature.[17] In the copious outpouring of eighteenth- and nineteenth-century texts providing views on the comparative history of religions, specific principles of belief were often used as benchmarks to determine the origin of a people. A hundred years after Egede, the German mineralogist Carl Ludwig Giesecke (who spent eight years in Greenland) claimed to have found a link between Inuit religion and the Norse settlers. He proposed that the Inuit sky god, Toornaarsuk, was cognate with the Norse god Thor. Unlike Egede, he did not ascribe this (almost certainly mistaken) supposition to ethnic intermixing, but to a past in which 'the Greenlanders were in intimate connection with the old Icelanders' so that 'they adopted some of their religious principles'.[18] Giesecke's spurious claim presupposes an early contact that predated the Norse people's conversion to Christianity).

Despite not finding traces of Christianity in Inuit religion, Egede used his scriptural knowledge in adopting a theory already circulated in Western books. He became convinced that he could recognise elements of Jewish tradition in the Inuit's religious practices, such as throwing away clothes worn after touching a deceased person, bewailing the loss of virginity, and making marks on the skin. Based on such examples, he proposes that the west coast Inuit could be descendants of one of the lost 'ten tribes of Israel', who, according to the Old Testament, were 'led into captivity, and afterwards dispersed into unknown countries'.[19] Egede refers to 'the opinion of a certain famous writer concerning the Americans among whom as he found sundry Jewish rites and ceremonies' – without naming this author.[20]

However, several writers had ascribed Jewish provenance to the Indians on the American continent since the mid-seventeenth century.[21] The idea had first been proposed by Spanish and Portuguese travellers, and later advocates were Thomas Thorowgood, Cotton Mather, Elias Boudinot, and William Penn. That Egede would assign a similar ethnic provenance for the Inuit is not surprising given the ethnographical conjecture he proposes in *A Description of Greenland*. Here, he lends support to the notion that the northern part of Greenland is separated from the American continent only by a narrow strait, for which reason the Inuit's ancestors, the Skraelings, were 'originally descended from the Americans'.[22] With this theory of migration in place Egede can interpret Inuit customs as congruent with what he has read about the ancient Hebrews in the Bible and subsequently apply the recent diaspora theory about the American Indians to the Greenland Inuit. At stake here is book-learning being piled upon book-learning to guide Egede in his perception of a people among whom he now found himself.

Egede was not alone in 'reading' the Inuit in the light of Greenland's medieval history. In 1724 two Inuit hunters, Pooq and Qiperoq, were persuaded to travel to Copenhagen. They purportedly were the first Inuit to visit Europe of their own free will. The purpose was twofold: they were to be exhibited in Copenhagen to garner support for Egede's mission, and they were expected to return home with good stories about Denmark. The well-renowned Dano-Norwegian dramatist Ludvig Holberg saw the two Inuit display their kayaking skills on the Copenhagen canals and wrote enthusiastically about it. In a published piece, he expresses the belief that Pooq and Qiperoq were descendants of Skraelings intermixing with (what he calls) 'the first inhabitants' – that is, the Norse population. Holberg lamented that the Christian faith can evidently be lost in a people in the course of just a few hundred years. Yet he has confidence in the Greenlanders' propensity for relearning the belief in the one God, for which reason he pledges support among his readers for the mission in Greenland.[23] Holberg's rationale shows us an important supposition to which I shall return: if the current population on the west coast were partly descended from the Norse people, there was a missionary obligation to restore Christianity in Greenland.

The Inuit were not just objects of observations; they were also themselves observing agents. Most interesting in this respect is the account given by Pooq because it shows that interpretation of a new world went both ways. Upon his return Pooq composed a song about his experiences. In the song, which was written down and distributed in Greenland, he details his impression of Norway (to which he had first arrived) as 'the land of the long-bearded men', and Copenhagen is described as swarming with people as if they were mosquitos.[24] Pooq's description (translated into Latin, Danish, and German in the eighteenth century) could benefit from analysis that takes into account how it reflects Inuit perspectives and beliefs. Coll Thrush has demonstrated how this would work in relation to Inuit travellers' impressions of eighteenth-century London, and Karen Routledge has incorporated it more broadly as a method of writing history.[25] In the following the focus will, however, be on how Europeans attempted to link the Inuit to the history of the Norse colony.

Ethnic Speculations

The first instance of interpreting the Inuit as Norse descendants is found in connection with two men kidnapped and carried off to Copenhagen in 1605. This incident warrants attention not only as background for Egede's theories but also because it reveals a history of seeing Greenlanders through the lens of European history. We may begin with a little-known poem entitled *Om Grønland* (*On Greenland*) by Jens Bielke, later Lord High Chancellor of Norway, which was completed in 1606 and given in a fine manuscript version as a gift to Christian IV.[26] In the fifth book of this 1,902-line poem, Bielke presents his observations of these two males.[27] His detailed description makes clear that the Greenlanders were expected to be descendants of the Norse colonists. For instance, we learn that an Icelandic interpreter was called upon in Copenhagen to translate the two men's language (because Icelandic is known to have preserved more of Old Norse than Danish). However, the interpreter failed to understand the 'grating' sounds the men uttered (ll. 813–20). Reading between the lines, we are left with the impression that the failure to use language as an identifier does not quite settle the matter for Bielke.

Bielke does not hide the fact that he views the two men as visibly different from modern Danes, even unsavoury, with their black hair, brown skin, small limbs, big heads, and sparse facial hair (ll. 798–809). Yet we should be careful not to transpose rigid racial categorisations anachronistically. In the seventeenth century, physical differences were often thought to stem from external influence, such as climate and diet, which affected the four bodily humours. This meant that transporting a people from one environment to another could change their bodies over time. This theory finds a particularly clear expression in the Dutch scholar Hugo Grotius' *De Origine Gentium Americanarum Dissertatio* (*Dissertation on the Origin of the American People*) (1642), in which it is theorised that the tribes north of Yucatan were descendants of the Norse Greenlanders who had migrated to America. Grotius accounts for the Indians' dark skin by pointing to their exposure to climatic influences and backs this up with the somewhat unconvincing assertion that many words in American Indian languages bear relation to Norwegian and that the Indians preserve customs derived from Scandinavia. By claiming that the

American Indians were actually Norse migrants from Greenland, Grotius could preserve the veracity of scriptural history insofar as he could explain how a people who lived on the American continent were unknown to the writers of the Bible.[28] Although Bielke and others who saw the two men in 1605 would not, of course, have known Grotius' later theory, they would have been familiar with the logic that underpins his analysis: it was possible to conceive of 'darker' races as climatically changed Europeans.

In relation to the history of Greenland, Grotius was not seriously challenged until the publication of Isaac La Peyrère's *Relation du Groenland* (1647), in which Grotius' theories come under critical scrutiny. On the basis of Icelandic records that relate how the Europeans encountered Skraelings when they sailed to Vinland (the American continent), La Peyrère puts forward the counter-theory that the Skraelings in America had migrated to Greenland centuries before Erik the Red arrived.[29] Hence, La Peyrère became the first writer to offer a systematic defence of separate human origins, and his interest in Greenland is likely to have originated in the desire to find evidence against Grotius' monogenetic history writing.[30]

What we also find in La Peyrère's book is another claim with respect to the two Greenlanders kidnapped in 1605. The notion that they were descendants of the Norse colonists appears to have been perpetuated in Danish circles. Based on conversations with eyewitnesses who had seen the two abductees in Copenhagen thirty years earlier, La Peyrère declares himself willing to believe that they were descendants of Scandinavians.[31]

A similar suggestion is floated in relation to the Inuit forcibly brought to Europe by David Danell in 1654. In a book translated into several European languages, the German geographer Adam Olearius describes three Inuit women who had been kidnapped and transported to Schleswig, where King Frederik III was temporarily staying because of an outbreak of plague in Copenhagen. Regarding the woman named Kabelau, Olearius notes that she was 'not so black as the two others', had 'more wit, subtlety, and compliance', and would not (unlike the other two) eat meats considered unclean in Europe. For this reason, '[w]e conceived she might be descended of those antient Christians, who some time lived in Groenland'.[32] It is notable here that interpreting Kabelau as a descendant of the Norse relied on observations of characteristics, customs, and manners – criteria evidently deemed important for determining origins, and perhaps as important (if not more) than skin colour and other exterior features.

De-texualising Greenland

Egede came to the conclusion that traces of the Norse could be detected in the ethnic makeup of the Inuit and thereby confirmed Ívar Bárdarson's report of the defeated Western Settlement. The narrative that could be spun out of this was that the vanquished settlers had been co-opted into Inuit culture. It was more difficult for Egede to square the Greenland landscapes with the texts about a Greenland dotted with once-prosperous farms. As he explored Greenland's west coast, it became apparent to him that tales about Greenland's fertility did not tally with the harsh climate and dearth of resources he observed at first hand. In Stephen Greenblatt's seminal text about European discovery and imperialism, 'wonder' is the operative term, designating the emotional response engendered in the travel accounts of early modern explorers to the New World in response to what they found radically different.[33] The European conception of Greenland also contains moments of 'wonder', but what I will examine here is a crisis of interpretation I shall call the *de-textualisation* of Greenland. This crisis registers in Egede's writing, as he was forced to qualify considerably the textual knowledge he had accrued in the years prior to his departure.

In *A Description of Greenland*, Egede provides much new information about the air, plants, animals, and, not least, Inuit culture. The ghost of Greenland's history is felt throughout the survey, however, and the long second chapter is a scholarly summary of the information available in older texts. Today it is scarcely realised that many of Egede's own observations in chapter three are actually responses to what he had read in European books. Thus, Egede's factual report of Greenland's soil, vegetation, and minerals is drawn up as an implicit comparison with the conventional lists of riches included in texts about medieval Greenland. Egede does not name his textual sources, but the chapter begins tellingly with a notice of its referentiality: 'we are informed by ancient histories'.[34] If chapter three is often passed over in the critical literature, it is because it is spectacularly unexciting and may best be described as a checklist of negatives. For example, we are told that modern Greenland has no cattle, no cultivated farmland, and no forests negations relevant for readers familiar with the descriptions of Norse Greenland. For the same reason, Egede also declares that there is 'little or nothing to say' about (precious) minerals or metals.[35] What we can read out of his somewhat disillusioned account can be paralleled with Anthony Grafton's descriptions of European travellers to the Americas. These were observers who often found themselves in a situation where their discoveries 'gradually stripped the books [of authority] of their aura of completeness as repositories of information and their appearance of utility as tools for interpretation'.[36]

Not long after the publication of Egede's *A Description of Greenland*, a more sceptical de-textualisation of Greenland can be found in the other key eighteenth-century text about Greenland: the German historian David Crantz' *Historie von Grönland* (*History of Greenland*) (1765).[37] This account was translated into several languages: Dutch in 1767, Swedish in 1765–9, English in 1767 (and an entirely new translation in 1820), and French in 1779. Like Egede, Crantz mentions that Frobisher brought home several tons of gold ore from Greenland and they met a native king named Cakiunge who was bedecked with gold pieces and precious stones (at the time of writing it was not yet realised that the place Frobisher had come to was in present-day Canada, the territory of Nunavut). However, drawing on his experience in Greenland during 1761–2, Crantz can reject such stories. He comments that either Frobisher's crew are accommodating their story to 'the prevalent tales of the times, which require in every voyage of discovery a large proportion of gold and silver mountains, rich palaces, magnificent courts, and above all a whole shower of impossible adventures', or else 'his editors embellished his unadorned narrative from the ballads and romances then in vogue'.[38]

Running contrary to the de-textualisation of Greenland was an attempt to preserve the archive of knowledge that had circulated in books. Egede is evidently reluctant to reject information from older surveys of Greenland as long as his own experiences do not conclusively prove them wrong. The sections that deal with Greenland's nature and fauna consist of his own observations, where he will even actively add information culled from anti-quarian texts. For example, Egede includes references to animals whose furs were valuable commodities (such as sables, martens, and wolves) because 'ancient historians tell us [they] are found in Greenland', although he must concede he has never seen them himself.[39] Similarly, Egede maintains that the finds of precious metals reported in connection with both Frobisher's journeys as well as the 1636 Danish expedition could be repeated elsewhere in the vast country of Greenland, thus raising prospects for future success. However, his own attempts at extracting gold from the sand he sampled on the west coast yielded only negative results.[40]

Egede's confidence in old texts becomes more pro-nounced when he speaks of the regions he has not yet seen. Since he himself only managed to survey a limited swathe of the west coast during his stay in Greenland, he allows for earlier accounts to hold authority unless they can be proved false or are patently absurd. In this way, Egede places Greenland's marvels just beyond the discovered horizon. This dynamic contains within it a willingness to believe in an enchanting hinterland.

For a parallel, we may turn to the travel account of the Hungarian poet Stephen Parmenius, who accompanied the English explorer Humphrey Gilbert on his expedition to North America. In a letter to Richard Hakluyt, written after having reached St John's Harbour in Newfoundland in 1583, Parmenius declares: 'I see nothing but desolation.'[41] Yet he is so convinced of what he has been told about the new land that he does not give up his optimism. 'The more that is reported about the regions we are making for, the greater will our expectations be from day to day.'[42]

Similarly, Egede seizes on clues given about the undiscovered parts of Greenland as evidence that the old texts could speak the truth. To give a concrete example of this, Egede recounts an anecdote about an Inuk who visited the Egede family from 'the most southern part of the country'. The Inuk saw the lemons that the family had received from Europe, which he noted were very like the fruits growing on trees in his part of the country, although not quite the same size. Egede takes this as confirmation of Ívar Bárdarson's report, which speaks of trees that grow produce the size of apples.[43] We shall probably never know what the native Greenlander was actually referring to, but no trees matching his description are known to have existed in Greenland in the eighteenth century. The episode illustrates how Egede's reading in old texts guided his understanding of Greenland. As John Sutton Lutz notes about Europeans who came to the New World: they 'did not see their "new worlds" with fresh eyes; they saw them through the lenses of their ancient stories'.[44]

The Eastern Settlement As a Model
for a New Greenland

The greatest allure for Europeans who came to the west coast was the Eastern Settlement, which both texts and maps erroneously placed across the ice cap on the inaccessible east coast. For example, Egede tells his readers in *A Description of the Greenland* that he 'cannot conceive' that the Eastern Settlement was 'destroyed and laid waste', given that it is known to have 'contained twelve large parishes, and one hundred and ninety villages, besides one bishop's see and two convents'.[45] So, what did Egede expect to find on the east coast? He repeats information from the mid-thirteenth-century Norwegian text *King's Mirror* about green and cultivated fields with cattle providing the colonists with 'milk, butter, and cheese in such abundance, that a great quantity thereof was brought over to Norway, and for its prime and particular goodness was set apart for the King's kitchen'.[46] Egede also invokes Ívar Bárdarson's report, which refers to 'the choicest wheat corn', game, and fish – resources that were the basis for 'considerable trade and commerce' among the old colonists.[47] There are clearly good reasons for seeking out the Eastern Settlement.

His descriptions stand in stark contrast to what was found on the west coast, which does not show 'the same plenty and richness'. Nevertheless, Egede expresses confidence that it can regain the former 'plenty and fruitfulness' it would have had in the time of the Norse farms.[48] Even when he recounts his own failed attempt at sowing barley (night frost nipped it before it could reach maturity), he suggests in the same breath that the wheat grown in Norway, where the climate is not dissimilar from that of the Greenland fjords, could be imported to once again make all of Greenland a land of cornfields.[49] Climate changes had, however, made crop growing difficult. By drilling into the ice core, scientific research shows that the Norse habitation of Greenland began at the end of a mild period with a higher average temperature, while depopulation took place during a cold period which reached its lowest point around 1350.[50] The Norse Greenlanders had grown barley, but primarily focused on hay for animal husbandry.[51] When Egede arrived in the eighteenth century, average temperatures had risen again, but extensive agriculture could not be revived. Whereas cattle farming was introduced in the 1780s, agricultural farming proved difficult beyond the cultivation of chervil, cress, lettuce, radishes, parsley, leek, turnips, and the like.

If we are to understand Egede's apparent willingness to promote the truth of old texts and legends about the not-yet-recovered Eastern Settlement, it is important to remember that *A Description of Greenland* served a promotional purpose, which was to secure backing for and capital investment in the mission. Hence, as Sarah Moss comments, Egede needed 'to lend weight to the idea of the Arctic utopia'.[52] Historians of colonialism have shown us that settler colonialism was often about the 'settling' of plants as much as people. The image and metaphor of gardening was central to Europeans' understanding of their own ability to tame the wild. Conquest of space was never enough if dominion over the environment was not accomplished as well. Michael Bravo has written on the importance of gardens at mission stations, not least those maintained by Moravian missionaries. One of these was the station in Greenland, which was established with permission from the Danish king in 1733. The Moravians' sheltered garden at New Hernnhutt had symbolic significance far beyond its low quantity of produce, as the domestication of plants within the mission station contrasted with the nomadic hunting and fishing culture of the Inuit in a way that would speak to the Moravians' assumptions about the superiority of Christian agrarianism.[53]

The Moravians also tried to grow barley, but, like Egede, they failed because of the short growth season. However, for early eighteenth-century colonists, the revival of extensive farming was a persistent theme. We see this in the writings of Major Claus Enevold Paars, who arrived in 1728 with the title of Governor of Greenland bestowed on him by Frederik IV of Denmark. Paars was accompanied by a Danish man-of-war, supply ships, soldiers, horses, and a group of convicts set to work in the fledging colony. In the report Paars sent back to the king in July 1729, he gives a positive account of the area that had once been part of the Western Settlement. Paars notes visible signs of past farming activity, including what he believes to be plough furrows and the remains of manmade fishponds.[54] These remains of the former colony hold more than just an archaeological interest for Paars; he examines the soil and finds it suitable for modern livestock farming, which leads him to propose a plan for future colonisation. Paars recommends that landed gentry who have fallen on hard times at home (having committed a crime or suffered a loss of honour) should be offered land packages in this region of Greenland.[55] In this way, Paars imagines, a new colonial economy could be built – literally – on the ruins of Erik the Red's empire. In his hope to attract gentry, Paars was perhaps inspired by the seventeenth-century British practice of awarding baronetcies in Nova Scotia in order to encourage settlement of this far-off province. However, Paars' plans for Danish settlers did not receive government backing.

In *A Description of Greenland* Egede similarly holds out a hope of renewing 'the old dwelling places, formerly inhabited by the ancient Norway colonies', which he suggests may 'recover their former fertility, if they were again peopled with men and cattle'.[56] Therefore, Egede promotes 'settlements and manuring' of the land, so that it can 'recover its former fertility', after which Greenland may again become a 'good and profitable country'.[57] Farming the land was necessary to increase food supplies for the colony. Unlike Paars, Egede was not expecting to lure Europeans to Greenland, but believed this could be done with native labour. For Egede, the imagined remaking of Greenland is connected, both literally and metaphorically, with the ambition to Christianise the Inuit. Egede knew that he needed to persuade the Inuit to settle down 'where the ground is fit for tillage and pasturage' if they were to become farmers.[58] At the time the Inuit lived primarily as nomadic hunters, and it was necessary for them to stay long enough in one place for the missionaries to attend to 'their growth and advancement in the Christian faith and virtues, which would ripen to the full harvest of eternal happiness'.[59] For this to happen, one must 'advance the growth of piety and devotion' and 'grub up an untilled ground, where a new church is to be planted'.[60] The metaphors are not coincidental, but shows how Egede joins material pragmatism to missionary ambitions in the hope of reviving Greenland as a colonial land. The image of planting a church on land not currently cultivated is an apt one, insofar as it looks forward to a time when Greenland will again be peopled with inhabitants of the true religion who till the country as farmland. Egede's rhetoric here chimes with ideas promoted by Puritans in America, for whom planting and subduing the wilderness was an exalted calling. In turn, this provided them with a reservoir of biblical metaphors about farming and cultivating that would echo in much later American writing.[61]

The old textual descriptions of Norse Greenland as an agricultural community would continue to rub up against contemporary reality. For example, in the summer of 1869, when the American explorer Isaac Israel Hayes arrived at Tunulliarfik (called Eriksfjord in the time of the Norse settlements), it was with the knowledge that the 'old Northmen' had 'cultivated barley', but found that 'severe frosts' now only allowed 'ordinary garden vegetables' to be cultivated.[62] This was the reason he decided to entitle his 1871 book about the visit *The Land of Desolation*, noting this name 'suits the country much better than Eric [the Red's] "Greenland"'.[63] However, at Igaliku, a settlement not far from the Norse ruins of Gardar, Hayes describes a journey up the coast in an *umiaq*, when the landscape seems to resonate with a memory of its green and lush past, which can be activated by the imagination:

The shores, though destitute of human life, were yet rich in historical association. As we passed along, it was hard to realise that voices were not calling to us from the shore; and where miles of rich meadow-land stretched before us, girdling the cliffs with green, the fancy, now catching the lowing of cattle and the bleating of sheep, would sometimes detect the shouts of herdsmen; while again we seemed to hear.[64]

Hayes' imaginative vision illustrates well how the reading of old texts could enhance what was observed in the present with a textual memory of the past. The hope for remaking a pastoral Eden in Greenland underpinned colonial hopes and ambitions in the early days of Danish re-colonisation. At the time Hayes visited Greenland, however, commercial farming existed only as a nostalgic glance at the Norse past. Between 1721 and the early twentieth century, only two places in Greenland saw farming activity: Igaliku (near the Norse ruins of Gardar) where the retired administrator Anders Olsen and his Greenlandic wife, Tuperna, established a farm with livestock in 1783, and at Narsaq/Narssaq, where cattle farming was taken up in the 1880s. However, in the 1930s industrious Inuit began establishing farms and reclaiming Norse fields, leading to farming opportunities today, helped by an increasingly warmer climate.

Egede's Maps

On the west coast of Greenland, Egede did not find the fertile fields he had hoped for, and only faint (albeit imagined) traces of the Norse colonists in the Inuit population. Yet he never gave up hope that the Eastern Settlement would still be standing with farmland and 'descendants of pure Norwegians' (*puure Norske Folchis Extraction*) – that is, an unmixed colony of his ancestors.[65] Egede, like others at the time, was mistaken in the belief that the Eastern Settlement had been placed on the east coast.

This belief had significant impact on how he viewed Greenland's colonial potential in the future.

In *A Description of Greenland*, Egede includes a number of apocryphal stories from various printed sources about alleged sightings of Norse Greenlanders, as late as the year 1625. If these were to be believed (and Egede seems to include them because he does not want to rule them out), the continued existence of a pure Norse community could be traced to within a century of Egede's arrival.[66] With the ambition of locating the Eastern Settlement, Egede tried to reach the east coast on two expeditions. He first set out from Hope Island with two boats on 9 August 1723. At that time, both La Peyère's and Torfæus' maps mistakenly depicted a water passage, known as the Frobisher Strait, intersecting Greenland at about 61–62°. Egede therefore hoped that it was possible to travel to the east coast through this channel. When he discovered that no inland waterway was to be found, he changed tack and attempted to round the southern tip of Greenland to reach the east coast. However, storms and drift ice prevented Egede from rounding Cape Farewell and he was forced to turn back on 26 August. On the return trip, Egede discovered the relatively well-preserved remains of Hvalsey Church, at around 60°, in Qaquortoq Fjord, which he took to have belonged to the Western Settlement, although it was, in fact, one of the churches of the Eastern Settlement. He returned in disappointment to Hope Island on 13 September. Egede would try for the Eastern Settlement again in late February 1724. This time the strategy was to cross from west to east by sailing with two boats, inland, by the long Kangerlussuaq Fjord in central-western Greenland.

Weather conditions forced him to return on 16 March without having reached very far.

The maps Egede drew of Greenland are of much interest for interpreting the eighteenth-century European imaginings of Greenland, which combine observed reality with wishful thinking. The first of three maps is dated 4 January 1737 and covers latitudes 60–67°.[67] The map offers correctives to the geographical outlines found on earlier maps. Most significantly, Egede writes a note on the map, stating that the Frobisher Strait did not exist. This is a clear example of de-textualising Greenland by dint of observation. Nonetheless, Egede repeats other errors from books as his map shows the east coast dotted with buildings and vegetation in the form of stylised trees.[68] Exactly how we are to understand the map is uncertain. The trees (indicating forests?), buildings, and churches on the east coast may be how they looked at the time of the medieval settlements, but this does not tally with Egede introducing his own empirical observations of the west coast on the map. For instance, he informs us in a note placed around 66° that the lodge of the Danish mission and trading post at Nipisat (which he had helped establish in 1724) had been burned down by the Dutch.[69] Thus, for all intents and purposes, the map gives the impression that the Eastern Settlement is still standing.

The dating of the map is interesting because it coincides with Egede submitting a comprehensive proposal to the authorities for a reconnaissance of the east coast in early January 1737 (he had returned to Copenhagen the year before), offering his services on the expedition. Egede's written proposal is now lost, but we know that it was passed on to the Royal Mission College in

Copenhagen, which funded missions under royal patronage.[70] If the map was indeed drawn in connection with the proposal, it would seem that it was calculated to appeal to the authorities as a spur for them to take an interest in the Eastern Settlement. However, the expedition was not awarded the funding to go ahead.

Around 1739, Egede made another hand-drawn map with many similar details, but covering a slightly larger area, 60–69°. Again, the Eastern Settlement is given detailed representation. The most interesting of the maps is, however, the engraved version, entitled *Grønlandia Antiqva* (*Old Greenland*) (Figure 3.1), which Egede published in *A Description of Greenland* (1741). The map contains many of the same features as the other maps,

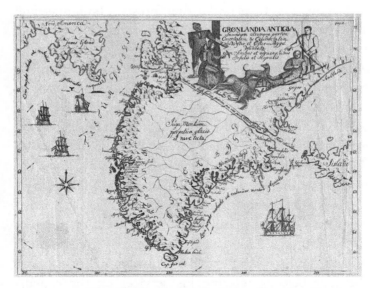

FIGURE 3.1 Hans Egede, *Grønlandia Antiqva Secundum Utramque Partem Orientalem & Occidentalem seu Wester et Øster-Bygd Delineata* (1741). The Royal Danish Library.

but it is the most wide-ranging, delineating a latitudinal range from 60° to 71°. The map was regarded as the most authoritative representation at the time and was copied in 1747 by Emanuel Bowen, a well-known printer of maps in London.[71]

As on the previous maps Egede had drawn, information from books (about the east) mixes indiscriminately with what was actually surveyed in the west. Evidently it is no obstacle for Egede to combine epistemologically different types of information within the same cartographical space. On the west coast Egede shows his new colony, 'Got Haab' (Good Hope), and indicates other place names that relate to his expeditions during 1723–4, when he travelled from 60° to 67°. Among these are several names derived from Kalaallisut for inlets and places (Amaralik [Amerelik], Nepisene [Nipisat], Kanersuit, Agluitsot, etc.), which Egede had learned from the Indigenous population (some of these place names would later be replaced with Danish designations, such as Kvanefjeld for Kuannersuit). At this early stage, Egede is simply trying to record as much as possible and is using the names available. The outline of the Eastern Settlement on the eastern shoreline, however, is a representation with no correspondence to any observed reality. Egede imagines that the settlement was placed as high as 63°, so this is where he places *Eriksfjord* – that is, the landing place where Erik the Red was said to have erected the first colonial farm (in fact, Erik had landed at Tunulliarfik on the west coast). All the place names on the east coast are copied from Torfæus' map. Egede explains this mixing of diverse information by telling the reader that the map shows 'the contiguity of the East and the West

Greenland, agreeably to other new charts by Thormoder [Torfæus] and others, which I follow, as far as I find they do not contradict the description of the ancients and to my own experience'.[72] Again we see that Egede's approach is to assume the validity of antiquarian knowledge unless directly disproved by observation. This representation suits Egede's belief that the Eastern Settlement was still standing, and in *A Description of Greenland* he proposes that the east coast should be resettled.[73]

Modern critical studies have examined Egede's map in relation to earlier and later cartography to assess its geographical accuracy.[74] My discussion here has a different goal: I aim to discuss Egede's representation with respect to political discourse. One strategy behind drawing a map that folds in separate temporalities (new surveys of the west coast and antiquarian ideas of what the east coast looked like in the past) is to expand Danish claims to a much wider area of Greenland than was currently under control. Here, it is useful to remind ourselves of Jeffers Lennox' analysis of how cartography could be used as a colonial instrument: cartography was often pressed into service as a signalling strategy whereby accuracy was sometimes less important than the contribution the very existence of a map made to imperial discourse.[75] Egede's 1741 map, which includes markings of sea currents (the stylised arrows), is proof of an ambition to document and show superior knowledge of a territory over which Denmark claimed sovereignty, but of which it had not yet taken physical possession, let alone fully surveyed.

Egede's map in *A Description of Greenland* substantially increases the level of detail compared with his 1737 and

1739 efforts. In this connection, it should not be overlooked that this map was published in the aftermath of the minor Dutch–Danish skirmish over fishing rights near Disko Bay. As we saw in the previous chapter, the Dutch diplomat Mauricius published his critical discourses in its aftermath, refuting Denmark's historical rights to the north-western parts of Greenland. Egede's meticulous naming of west coast bays and fjords, I contend, must be seen partly as a response to this conflict. For example, Egede places a ship patrolling Disko Bay, which may reflect the fact that the merchant Jacob Severin was supported in 1738 by a royal fund (substantially increased in 1740) to carry ammunition for the protection of Danish trade. On the map, several oversized Danish ships can be seen in the Davis Strait and in the waters between Iceland and Greenland. These are trading or whaling vessels as well as warships (recognisable by the swallow-tailed flag). Ships on maps was a convention used to communicate power since the Renaissance, and Egede clearly wants to signal Danish sovereignty over the area and the ability to defend it by naval presence.[76]

Positing knowledge onto representations of space was a way to inscribe possession of the land. Yet Egede's map lists a number of names connected to Greenland's coastal geography provided by Dutch whalers, such as 'Swarte Vogel Bay', 'Rodebay', 'Wejde Fiord', 'Hundeejland', 'Rodebay', and 'Staten Huck'. Thus, Egede's aim to convey a message of Danish dominance (past and present) is partly undermined by his recourse to nomenclature (including Kalaallisut names) that reveals Greenland as a multiplicity of national histories. So, as Egede attempts to assert Danish dominance over Greenland, the map is ultimately a palimpsest of both Inuit and several European narratives.

Expeditions to the Eastern Settlement

Egede's eighteenth-century mission and the colonial activities on the west coast changed the course of Greenland's history. This legacy has had a huge impact on modern Greenland and its consequences on society are much discussed today. Historians usually take a teleological approach, focusing on present conditions such as the result of Egede's missionary work on the west coast. This approach makes sense, of course, but it neglects the many failed expeditions to reach the (non-existent) Eastern Settlement in the east. These attempts, I will argue, need to be rescued from the rubbish heap of history as their political and commercial subtexts are key to understanding eighteenth-century Denmark's colonial interest in Greenland. Thus, the remainder of the chapter will focus on the planned, attempted, and failed eighteenth-century expeditions to the east coast. Working from letters and records, I will present a brief chronological survey that shows how much investment went into reaching the East Settlement. It is historically significant that these expeditions were undertaken on the basis of sources that spoke of good farmland and riches in the Eastern Settlement, because it tells us something about the sustained influence old texts, such as Ívar Bárdarson's report, held over the modern colonisation of Greenland.

As mentioned, Egede began planning an expedition to the east coast not long after he arrived in Greenland. Egede's hope was to convert the 'pure' descendants of the Norse people to Lutheranism. Yet as an investor in the Bergen Company, which financially underwrote the mission, he also believed that a rediscovery of the Eastern Settlement would yield commercial benefits. A letter signed 19 April 1723 by the company directors laid out plans for exploring the east coast. Old texts spoke of forests there, so the acquisition of wood (sorely needed for building houses and as fuel for fire) was among the expected boons from discovering this uncharted part of Greenland. The company offered 20 rixdollars to those of its men who could locate these forests. Another reward, between 10 and 100 rixdollars, was offered to those who could discover silver or gold.[77]

Captain Berent Hansen Wegner and Officer Selgen Dahl, who worked for the Bergen Company, set out from Bergen on 7 June 1723 with two ships for a combined whaling and trading expedition. The smaller vessel, *Printz Friederick*, was navigated inshore along the east coast to look for the Eastern Settlement when the ship went down in a storm near Cape Farewell on 22 July, leaving no survivors.[78] Egede's decision just a few months later in 1723 to stay close to the coast when rounding the southern tip of Greenland in his attempt to reach the east coast was hence a judicious way to proceed, as an approach from the sea was clearly dangerous.

On 13 May 1724, the Bergen Company's vessel *Egte Sophia* arrived in Greenland and cruised for around three months along the east coast between 60° and 66°. Captain Hans Fæster's order was to search for descendants of the old colonists and assess the language they spoke, for which reason the expedition was given a dictionary with Old Norse words.[79] After the Bergen Company folded in 1726, and the Greenland project came under administration of the Danish crown, the hopes of finding the Eastern Settlement continued to be a priority. Frederik IV gave his appointed governor of Greenland, Claus Paars, orders to cross the inland ice sheet to seek out the Eastern Settlement and assess its present state, which included the inhabitants' language, manners, and religion. Factors of commercial utility were also to be examined, such as the fertility of their lands, existence of horses and livestock, and access to valuable minerals.[80] Paars was furthermore instructed to look for good, ice-free harbours.

Eleven horses were carried on the ship from Denmark for the purpose of crossing the ice from west to east, but five died in transit and the rest perished during the first winter and spring. On 25 April 1729, Paars therefore decided to make the journey on foot with two assistants and five 'common men'.[81] They failed to make headway past the long inland-going Ameralik Fjord, near Nuuk, and were forced to return on 7 May. However, Paars did not give up hope of reaching the Eastern Settlement. He proposed that a station be established near Cape Farewell, from which one could then sail up close to the coast for the Eastern Settlement. He suggested this eastbound push could be financed by capturing wild cannibals said to roam in the east and selling them to the Dutch. This proposal was not plucked out of the air, as we know that a Dutch sailor had offered him 1,000 ducats for two Inuit children he had in his care, of which the boy was of a very small stature.[82] The offer was made with the intention of exhibiting the captured natives in Holland for profit, especially if the natives turned out to be pygmies. Ironically, if Paars was stationed in Greenland to curtail Dutch trade dominance, some of his plans apparently depended on trading with the competitors.

After helping Paars move the Danish colony from Hope Island to Godthaab (now Nuuk) on the mainland in 1728–9, Lieutenant Jesper Hansen Reichard tried to reach the east coast with the ship *West Vlieland* on his homebound journey. Leaving on 3 June 1729, he wanted to look for the Eastern Settlement, but he was prevented from reaching the coast due to ice.[83]

In 1733 the royal investigator Mathias Jochimsen had just served a term in Iceland to write a report on the economic benefits of this Danish dependency. He was subsequently reassigned to a post in Greenland with orders to search for the Eastern Settlement. Jochimsen set out from Godthaab on 20 April but did not make progress beyond 61° on the east coast (no further than Egede had reached ten years earlier) due to ice-clogged waters.[84] The eastward push to locate the Norse settlers was partly a response to the fact that trade on the west coast was not taking off. In a long passage, Jochimsen vocally laments Danish inefficiency when it comes to trading with the Inuit, which had led to significant financial losses. He believes the Danish trading failure was caused by Satan's 'wily hocus pocus', which had confused traders' otherwise good sense and commercial pragmatism.[85] Jochimsen's comments illustrate the conceptual connection between Christianity and commercial success at the time.

Egede was also cognisant of the fact that funding for continuing the mission depended on profits from trade.

He was not the only missionary who saw the necessity of Christian missions piggybacking on mercantile interests. The prolific English Methodist John Wesley, for example, also advocated for such an alliance in his sermon 'On the Spread of the Gospel' (1783). Here, he speaks of how the Word of God may spread to 'distant nations with whom the Christians trade' and he goes on to mention as examples the heathens who have benefitted from the alliance between trade and Christian mission in 'Norway, Finland, and Lapland'.[86] Wesley emphasises, however, that missionaries travelling with commercial agents were able to impart to new trading partners 'what is of infinitely more value than earthly pearls, or gold and silver'.[87]

The problem for the Danes was that the Inuit had become so accustomed to Dutch traders that they craved their wares and only expressed moderate interest in what the Danes had to offer.[88] This testifies to the fact that Danes could not ignore the agency of the people they saw as colonial subjects. As Chris Gosden has argued, all actors involved in colonial encounters could act and react.[89] The Danes recognised that the lack of Inuit interest in Danish goods also meant that it would be difficult to maintain their interest in the Danish mission, as there was no incentive to keep up regular contact.

The interest in expanding trade in Greenland drove a continued interest in the fabled Eastern Settlement. In a letter dated November 1747, the Greenland merchant Niels Rasch put forward a long and detailed proposal for trading in Greenland, which he sent to the Royal Mission College. This included a suggestion for discovering the eastern part of Greenland 'which is thought to be the best and most fertile part of the land'.[90] Logistically, this was to be achieved either by sailing up near the coast or by approaching it at the right time of year from the west side of Iceland. On board each ship should be two Inuit and an Icelander, since one would need to communicate either with natives or the descendants of the Norse colonists.[91] To support the theory that Norse descendants could be found, Rasch cites an account by Poul Egede (Hans Egede's son) about a native Greenlander who had told Poul that he had been near the east coast and seen people with pointed (*spitse*) faces. Rasch reasons that this could not be native Greenlanders, as their faces are usually flat, and that it therefore indicated the existence of European descendants.[92]

No action was taken on Rasch's proposal. However, in 1751, the Greenland Trading Company commissioned Peder Olsen Walløe, who had come to Greenland as a craftsman, to look for the Eastern Settlement. Walløe departed from Godthaab in August and rounded Cape Farewell using a Greenlandic *umiaq* but reached no further than 60°. Nonetheless, he managed to make contact with the inhabitants on the east coast, whom he discovered to be Inuit.[93] At this time, the Dutch still seemed to have the leading edge; Egede mentions that they had managed to travel and trade with eastern Greenlanders, as high as 62°, during the ice-free season.[94] The Danes remained on the back foot in this respect.

In 1785 Poul Egede persuaded the crown prince that a mission to find the lost colonists in the east would be a great achievement and a grant of 12,000 rixdollars was awarded towards an 'attempt at discovering the east coast'.[95] A year later the Danish naval officer Christian Thestrup Egede and the cartographer Poul Lövenörn undertook an expedition to this end, but they were unable to approach the east coast because of pack ice. They launched another expedition in 1787 but with the same disappointing result.[96]

As we reach the end of the century, the long-standing assumption that placed the Eastern Settlement on the east coast was cast into doubt, partly due to intensified examinations of the ruins on the west coast. In 1777 the recently established Royal Greenland Trade Company sent the Norwegian explorer Aron Arctander to assess the possibility of agriculture and cattle breeding near Julianehaab (Qaqortoq), on the west coast. During his time in Greenland, Arctander spent considerable time scrutinising the remains of what he believed to be the Western Settlement (which was, in fact, the Eastern Settlement) and produced several maps. In Denmark the geographer Heinrich Peter von Eggers used Arctander's notes to write a gold-medal dissertation at the University of Copenhagen, in which he proposed that the Eastern Settlement was placed on the west coast. Eggers deduced that the most southerly series of ruins on the west coast were therefore the remains of the Eastern Settlement. He reasoned (correctly) that the term 'eastern' was misleading and only indicated that this settlement was placed in an eastern direction from the Western Settlement higher up on the coast.[97]

The theory met with a positive response and Egger's dissertation was translated into German in 1794. However, the Danish explorer Morten Wormskiold and the historian H. F. J. Estrup vocally contested this revisionary interpretation. A dispute ensued, which was reported in the international press. In the course of the early nineteenth century, Egger's theory slowly gained acceptance in European scientific circles.[98] Even so, speculations that descendants of the old colonists still inhabited remote parts of Greenland, or that they migrated to other parts of the Arctic, were not silenced, and this is a topic to which we shall return in the following chapters.

To conclude, we have seen that the encounter with Greenland confused and confounded European expectations. Central to the analysis is the attempt among observers to salvage old textual knowledge about Greenland even after being confronted with the extra-textual world of experienced data. The many attempts to reach the east coast show us that the promises of riches preserved in the faded print of old books were taken seriously by the Danes and sought out at great expense. The enduring hope of recovering the Eastern Settlement throughout the eighteenth century has been overlooked in criticism, although – as I hope to have shown – it was an important driving force underpinning colonial interest and investment in Greenland. Prominent in the colonial rhetoric was the ambition to convert the lost colonists to Lutheranism. One of the findings is the difficulty of drawing absolute lines of demarcation between missionary aims and commercial interests: the two objectives formed an alliance in many respects. The religious concern for the Norse colonists was undoubtedly heartfelt, but the conversion of people in colonial settings was simultaneously a conduit for successful trade.

The hoped-for existence of a settlement of 'pure' Norse people and the expectations of rich lands are inscribed on the maps Egede drew. If these maps gave new geographical accuracy to the west coast, they also perpetuated the mistake that the Eastern Settlement was to be found on the east coast. In this way, past and present are telescoped into an artificial simultaneity. While place names on the map are evidence of how much the Danes learned from the Inuit about the land, through friendly interaction, the map also elides native claims to that land. Cartographical representation such as this is first and foremost a mapping of colonial assertion directed at other European nations; it commoditises a yet undiscovered space and signals an imperial command over territory.

If this was colonial signalling, resettlement of Greenland and the meeting with its inhabitants also compelled a genuine conceptual reassessment. Egede debunks many antiquarian conventions in *A Description of Greenland,* offering a measured appraisal of the people and the resources he found on the west coast. The disillusion did not mean a total renunciation of antiquarian learning, however, and we see with Egede an attempt to integrate knowledge inherited from books together with new observations. Thus, he interprets the Inuit he interacted with on the west coast as stamped with Greenland's Norse past. At the same time, he did not jettison the hope of finding the fertile lands and 'pure' Norse inhabitants, which he had read about prior to his arrival, on the undiscovered east coast. What emerges from Egede's account of Greenland is an incoherent picture: the meagre conditions on the west coast are counterbalanced by the promise of abundance beyond the horizon. In this particular case, the horizon was the prohibitive ice sheet that made the eastern shores impenetrable and thus allowed for promises to be deferred rather than annulled. Both in terms of understanding the rediscovered land and possessing it, eighteenth-century Greenland was a space under negotiation.

4

1818

British Greenland

~

In Britain, interest in exploring the Arctic received a significant boost after the Napoleonic Wars (1799–1815). Whalers and fur traders had never ceased operating in the Arctic, but in the public eye, the Admiralty's two expeditions navigating either side of Greenland made an impact. The main impetus for launching these explorations was reports of vanishing ice. This phenomenon was erroneously believed to herald a sweeping climate change that would make the Arctic navigable for discovery. Because sea ice was thought to have hemmed in the Eastern Settlement on Greenland's east coast, hopes were raised that the Admiralty's Arctic programme would lead to a recovery of the 'lost colony'. The cultural and literal response to the expectations that the new and highly publicised investment in the Arctic elicited will be examined in this chapter.

Several studies have dealt with Britain's early nineteenth-century Arctic ambitions, but the role Greenland played in these discourses has not received much attention. I will show that a variety of text genres – ranging from scientific writing to poetry – included Greenland as part of British imperial imaginary. One focus is on how the possible rescue of the European colony, believed to have been trapped behind an ice sheet on Greenland's east coast, was an anticipated national achievement for

Britain. The hope of recovering the colony inspired an outpouring of philanthropic sentiments of beneficent intent towards the supposedly struggling Greenlanders. For example, ideas of helping their agriculture prosper can be traced in poetic works published at the time. Yet the sense of duty towards the Greenlanders could shade into imperialist thinking. In other cases, the new-found confidence in British abilities would lead to statements that challenged Denmark's long-standing claims to the land. The chapter will also reveal that a number of voices explicitly urged colonial action. By collecting and juxtaposing diverse sources, the chapter attempts to produce a picture of Greenland's role in British imperial thinking. The texts to be examined formed part of a discursive nexus, in which reports of ice-free waters, compassion for the Norse settlers, and a new buoyant faith in Britain as a conqueror of the Arctic were essential constituents. British plans for Greenland were never officially mandated by the Admiralty but found expression in the writings of non-state actors (who, however, often desired to speak on behalf of the government and serve British interests). These plans ranged from the idea that Britain (because of its superior sea power) had both a moral and philanthropic obligation to rescue the 'lost colony' languishing in Greenland to more blunt schemes for land grabs.

Climate Change and New Possibilities

In the nineteenth century a very popular explanation for the loss of communication with the colony in Greenland was that a change in temperature had cut off lines of communication with Norway and the rest of Europe. An entry in the *Edinburgh Encyclopaedia* gives a common early nineteenth-century rationale for the ice on the east coast: polar ice 'descended so as completely to embargo the whole of the colonized districts of Greenland', enveloping the old habitations.[1] However, around 1817, ice appeared to be disappearing. On a whaling trip off the east coast of Greenland, the prolific English whaler and explorer William Scoresby Jr observed that large ice floes, which only two years prior had been limited to the near-shore waters off east Greenland, were now becoming detached and drifting south. Other navigators also confirmed the phenomenon.

This new information was picked up by John Barrow, the important second secretary to the Admiralty, who was appointed in 1804 and held the post for nearly forty years. Barrow was instrumental in renewing the public's engagement with northern latitudes. He wrote nearly 200 pieces of unsigned articles and reviews for the *Quarterly Review*, at least 18 of which dealt with Arctic subjects.[2] An article he published in the *Quarterly Review* in February 1818 was, for all intents and purposes, the Admiralty's Arctic manifesto. Barrow describes how Britain may profit from Arctic discovery in terms of both glory and trade. The issue of the *Quarterly Review* in which the piece was published sold 12,071 copies on the first day.[3] The announcement of a new era of British interest in the Arctic was partly self-serving publicity. In fact, there was already much activity in the Arctic. In the northern Canadian wilderness the Hudson's Bay Company and the Montreal-based North West Company competed over fur trade (but merged in 1821), and Scoresby Sr's whaling ship had reached latitude 81°, north of Spitsbergen, in 1806. Nonetheless, in terms of attracting public attention and eliciting national pride, Barrow's article made a splash.

Barrow quotes a letter from Scoresby Jr to the president of the Royal Society, Sir Joseph Banks, in which it is related that, in 1817, Scoresby had seen 'about two thousand square leagues (18,000 square miles) of the surface of the Greenland seas, included between the parallels 74° and 80°, perfectly void of ice, all of which has disappeared within the last two years'.[4] Barrow saw this change as a spur to revive attempts at finding the hoped-for Northwest Passage that would provide a route from Northern Europe to Eastern markets. This route remained the holy grail of exploration and had most recently been attempted in 1773 by Captain Phipps (who had reached no further than 80° before the expedition was stopped by ice). However, naval resources were freed up after the British victory over Napoleon, and Barrow also saw the resumption of Arctic exploration as pragmatic, insofar as a whole generation of naval captains were now on half-pay; this exploration would be useful employment for them.

One of the expeditions the Admiralty sent out in search of the Northwest Passage was led by Captain David Buchan. He was given instructions to examine the sailing conditions in the Greenland Sea, which Barrow believed was now navigable. The purpose was to locate a passage into the Pacific Ocean cutting across the Pole. Reaching Spitsbergen in June, Buchan's expedition became ice-bound at Magdalena Bay for a few weeks. They managed to continue to around 80° 34' N, but had to return after being jammed in sea ice for three weeks. The other expedition was led by Captain John Ross, who commanded HMS *Isabella* and HMS *Alexander* along the west coast of Greenland. Ross' expedition entered Lancaster Sound at the north end but then turned around, as Ross was misled by a mirage: he thought that mountains (which he named 'Crocker Hills') were blocking the end of the strait. An indication of how much was riding on the expedition is the way in which Ross was turned into a national scapegoat, ridiculed by Barrow and lampooned by caricaturists.[5] Finding a navigable route across the Arctic ultimately proved unsuccessful and, over the next fifty years, it was a costly ambition in terms of resources and the loss of lives, with the fatal conclusion to the Franklin Expedition of 1845, which became a national trauma.

Despite Ross' misfortune, the expedition did result in an interesting cultural encounter, which was significant for raising the hopes of recovering other peoples in the Arctic. The crew made contact with the Inughuit in the northern region of Prince Regent's Bay, at Qaanaaq (also known as Thule). It was possible to communicate with this isolated group because the expedition included an Inuit interpreter from the Disko Island area, John Sacheuse (sometimes called Sackhouse), who had travelled to Scotland two years earlier aboard a whaler and learned English. Sacheuse made a now-famous drawing of the meeting with this secluded people, who had probably never seen Europeans. Perceptions of the 'other' always went both ways and, as Michael Bravo has observed, the drawing and the accompanying account of the meeting are unique in providing an insight into how the Inughuit saw the strange people who came to them.[6]

According to eyewitness accounts, Sacheuse did not see the Inughuit as only an alien people but apparently exclaimed: 'These are *right* Eskimaux, these are *our* fathers!'⁷ He believed the Inughuit were an original colony of his ancestors from which a contingent had migrated from the north to settle in south-west Greenland. The theory of the Inughuit as a remnant of the southern Greenlanders' forefathers who had preserved their original culture and manners was propounded in many articles throughout the nineteenth century. The discovery of this 'ancestral' tribe was a poor compensation for failing to find a navigable trade route, but it raised expectations that European ancestors, believed to be iced in on the east coast of Greenland, could be recovered. In 1818 and the following years, there was an acute sense that old mysteries of the Arctic would be solved.

To promote public interest in Arctic discovery – a course for British glory – Barrow published *A Chronological History of Voyages into the Arctic Regions* (1818). This was a book written for the popular market, printed in no fewer than 1,500 copies.⁸ Here, Barrow declares that 'the discovery of a north-west passage to India and China has always been considered as an object peculiarly British' and avers that Britain should therefore not be a passive bystander while 'another nation' accomplished what was considered 'almost the only interesting discovery that remains to be made in geography'.⁹ Barrow mentions Greenland around eighty times in the text, making it clear that it is a geography that falls within the British sphere of interest. Among the several scientific aims for Arctic explorers was to investigate the fate of the European colony in Greenland. This aim Barrow calls an 'object of rational curiosity'.[10] But he could well have written 'national curiosity' as Britain had emerged victorious from the sea battles of the Napoleonic Wars, and British ships were the most likely candidates to recover the 'lost colony'.

The Admiralty's two expeditions of 1818 and, later, Scoresby's published accounts awakened British interest in Greenland. We see this, for example, in the English translation of Egede's *A Description of Greenland*, which had first appeared in 1745, but was reissued in 1818 with a new 'Historical Introduction'. The anonymous writer of the new introduction explains that a new edition was needed since Greenland had recently 'attracted a more than usual interest'.[11] The recovery of the 'lost colony' was a prize of national prestige Britain should grasp before its European competitors:

May we hope that the execution of this project [saving the Greenland colonists], which is prompted, not only by curiosity but by philanthropy, is reserved for the present era, and that it will be finally accomplished by the nautical skill and enterprise of this country![12]

There was an enduring interest in the European Greenlanders, and sensational stories emerged from time to time in the British press. On 30 November 1750, for example, *The Royal Magazine* announced that missionaries in Greenland had discovered, to the north of mountains on the west coast, 'a numerous colony, that appear to be Christians, and, by their frequent use of the cross, prove, that they are descendants of persons settled there before *Luther's* Reformation'.[13] This short notice is all the information given about this sensational discovery at the time. As it was false or mistaken news, no further announcements related to this community seem to have been made.

Curiosity about what Greenland's east coast would hide intrigued scientific communities around Europe. For example, the Dano-French writer and geographer Conrad Malte-Brun speculates in an 1818 article that the disappearance of ice from Greenland's coast may reveal a 'mummy of a nation', a 'frozen Herculaneum', where the people may have 'preserved the language, the manners, and the catholicism [*sic*] of the North, as they were in the fifteenth century'.[14] Malte-Brun was writing from his exile in France and would have known that Britain, which emerged as the principal naval power after the Napoleonic Wars, was clearly poised to make such a discovery. However, the dream of thawing a part of world history which had been covered in ice for centuries remained unfulfilled. The reduction in the ice near the east coast of Greenland was only temporary: colder conditions would return in the years that followed.

'Our kindred hearts have shelter'd been!'

European settlers, perhaps still active behind the prohibitive coastal ice shoals on the east coast of Greenland, were seen as a branch of the Northern European people who had populated British shores over the centuries – first in the form of fifth-century Germanic invaders and later as Vikings. This section will examine this hope that British ships would discover a community of kinspeople as it was expressed in literary texts. The novelty of the following discussion is twofold: some of the texts are well known, but criticism has ignored how these texts refer to the Greenland settlers as part of their sentimental discourse, while other texts have not previously been discussed at all.

One poet who took up the theme of the lost Greenland colony was Anna Jane Vardill. She is today best known for writing a sequel to S. T. Coleridge's *Christabel* but she also published several literary pieces in the *European Magazine* using the signature 'V'.[15] In 'The Arctic Navigator's Prayer' (1818) Vardill expresses optimism about what the new expeditions may achieve, especially the possible discovery of 'some bright cove, where long unseen / Our kindred hearts have shelter'd been!'[16] Vardill and others used the expectation that British ships would come to the rescue of Europe's ancestors to express national pride. One significant way was through emphasising the danger to which British sailors exposed themselves. She renders in verse a familiar legend which was included in La Peyrère's *Relation de Groenland*. It is the story of the archbishop of Trondheim, who in 1406 sent the prelate Andrew (Andreas) to take up the see of Gardar in Greenland. It is believed that Andrew's ship never reached Greenland as no records survive of him ever having filled the post. As Vardill explains in a note to the poem, Andrew's ship most likely succumbed to the 'prodigious barrier of ice'.[17] This is expressed in the following lines: 'Like the lost race which home again / Norwegia's pastor call'd in vain, / When savage Greenland's giant shore / They tempted and returned no more.'[18] In the poem the loss of Andrew becomes a symbol of how nature can take back what humankind has cultivated and extinguish the Christian light that had once burned so bright in the far-northern outpost of Greenland.

The hope of recovering and offering relief to the 'lost' Greenlanders as a kindred people was raised in the British press in connection with the Admiralty's Artic expeditions. The *Edinburgh Philosophical Journal*, for example, declared that the 'change of temperature', which had 'effected an opening through the frozen ridge', gave impetus to the 'romantic enterprize of releasing the lost colony of Eastern Greenland, whom the accumulated ice was supposed to have for ever separated from the rest of the world'.[19]

Vardill fictionalised a romance tale of discovery in a three-part prose adventure which was serialised in the *European Magazine* during 1818. The story concerns a hidden colony in a land near Spitzbergen (i.e. where the British expedition led by David Buchan would pass en route to the North Pole). Although the dominant mode of the story is satire, Vardill entertains the notion that the Arctic belonged to the English. In the episode entitled 'Extracts from an Arctic Navigator's Journal', Vardill tells the story of explorers who discover 'fair-haired inhabitants' with 'kindred countenances' living in an ice valley.[20] It is subsequently revealed that they were '*ab origine* English', which is explained by reference to 'the Welsh tradition of Prince Madoc's emigration to North America'.[21] The legend once used to advise Queen Elizabeth about her political right to Arctic territory is here deflated as satire. One should not, however, discount the fact that imagining an English colony still speaks to the notion that Englishmen were the true inheritors of the Arctic, having been among its first explorers. In one of Vardill's episodes, we learn that the Elf-King of the North, who reigns over this settlement, has vowed that 'none but the sons of Engelland shall unveil his throne, since none but a woman of Engelland was found worthy to share it'.[22] If the pseudo-Elizabethan spelling here places English claims to the Arctic in the past rather than in the present (i.e. it belongs to the fancy of John Dee more than the ambition of John Barrow), there is a patriotic sense of British influence and dominance in Vardill's other writing that cannot be mistaken. We see the argument for British prosperity on the world stage in, for example, 'Epitaph Designed for William Franklin, Esq. Late Governor of New Jersey' (1813), 'The Progress of British Sculpture' (1813), and 'English versus French' (1817).

British naval power had long been hailed as superior to that of other European countries. The anonymous poet of the 'The Patriot' (1804), for example, would proclaim that 'British power is felt' far and wide, and 'British fame' made nations tremble in fear near the waters of China, at the shores of the 'mighty Ganges' as well as 'O'er Greenland's bleak inhospitable shore'.[23] If the control over northern reaches was meant metaphorically in this poem, then the expeditions sent out in 1818 gave new substance to patriotic claims. In a poem published that year, Archibald Johnston celebrates how 'By naval glory wak'd and trump of fame, / Britannia rises from the dark blue main … Her daring sons the wat'ry waste explore / And wave their flag round Greenland's ice-girt shore'.[24] If we find no direct calls for taking possession of Greenland in the poetry of the time, British writers saw opportunity in their nation's expeditions, which put Denmark on the back foot.

A sense of future national achievement underpins Barrow's discussion of the 'lost colony' in *Chronological History*. Here, he raises the hope that one may 'ascertain the fate of the unhappy colonists' now that 'the recent disruption of the ice from that coast may afford the opportunity of examining into the fate of the wretched inhabitants'.[25] The emphasis on the Greenland settlers' presumed destitution functions as an enabling discourse insofar as imperialist desires were often propped up by philanthropic claims that posited the 'West' as a rescuer to the 'rest'.[26] Barrow frames the discovery of the 'lost colony' as a national competition: 'it would be a reproach to the Danish government' if they did not seek out the people they claimed to be their subjects.[27] However, this is not so much a plea as a slight on Denmark, whose past failures to reach the east coast of Greenland are elaborated in the book. Barrow was also perfectly aware of the difficulty Denmark had in initiating such ventures since much of its fleet had been comprehensively bombed by the British fleet in 1807 (during the Napoleonic Wars), and the rebuilding of the Danish fleet was only slowly beginning in 1818.

National prestige and imperialist aspirations are given free rein in the English cleric and poet [Charles] Pleydell [Neale] Wilton's poem 'Polar Ice: Written at the Time of the Sailing of the Northern Expedition' (1818). Britain is here celebrated for its Arctic ambition: 'Ride on ye barks and bear ye wide unfurl'd / The British colours to a Polar sky / And proudly tell it to a Northern world / How Britons learn to conquer or to die.'[28] Such rhetoric also includes the ambition that a British mission may save the lost Europeans caught behind Greenland's wall of ice since 'the loosen'd fetters' (i.e. icebergs becoming detached and drifting away from the coast) now make it possible 'in the British name ... the long lost region to explore / And bid the sons of pity doubt no more'.[29] Wilton evidently sees Britain as delivering the isolated settlers from their long, involuntary imprisonment behind a wall of ice, and he quotes Barrow's buoyant belief in British accomplishment (from the 'Polar Ice' article in the *Quarterly Review*): 'It has fallen to the lot of the present age to have opportunity ... of instituting an enquiry into the fate of these unfortunate colonies.'[30] Wilton would never see British expeditions liberate any colony in Greenland, but he later came to care – spiritually – for another type of colonist. He was appointed chaplain in 1826 for New South Wales, Australia, where he also oversaw convict labourers.[31]

The notion that Britain could offer relief to the 'lost colony' also inspired the poet Eleanor Anne Porden (who would marry the Arctic explorer John Franklin in 1823 following his return from the Coppermine Expedition). In 1818 she published the poem *The Arctic Expeditions* in a small octavo containing just over 200 lines and several supplementary notes. Before this eulogy to the Admiralty's expeditions is discussed, it is important to make the connection with Vardill. Porden and her father hosted the Attic Chest literary circle, a group of friends who met at the Pordens' house in London's Berners Street. Vardill was among the key members. The theme of British Arctic expeditions was evidently of interest to the circle, as can be seen in one of the contributions to the Grecian cedar wood chest in which the society members stored their poetic manuscripts. Vardill wrote a contribution dated 12 April 1818, just a week after Buchan's

ships had left London to sail a route that went east of
Greenland to reach near Spitsbergen. Vardill regards
Porden's *The Arctic Expeditions* (and, by extension, her
poetry in general) as offering deliverance to an emotionally iced-up readership in Britain, by comparing her
verses to the climatic change that was believed to effect
the release of the colonists languishing on Greenland's
frozen east coast.

Come, then! – with bland and genial sway
The icy barriers melt away,
From long oblivious frost release
Of wand'ring thoughts whole colonies
That all in search of gems and flow'rs
Stray'd far from safe domestic bow'rs
As pilgrims rov'd to Greenland's shore
And prison'd there, return'd no more.[32]

The poetic conceit makes sense because Porden focuses
on the 'lost colony' in *The Arctic Expeditions*. I will argue
that it also enables Vardill to establish a sense of female
empowerment for Porden. Vardill posits her companion
poet as a partaker in a patriotic project of sentimentalism,
in which women were leading by dint of stereotypical
natural virtue and morality. If the male explorers could
physically travel towards new discoveries (and potentially
come to the aid of the colonists) now that the barrier of
ice was lifted, Porden's poetic effusions are explorations
into the territory of the Arctic as well as the territory of
sentimentalism: she will thaw Britain's hardened minds
and help them in their capacity to feel compassion. In
this way, Vardill sees Porden's poetry as benefitting the
nation by promoting philanthropic improvement that
could bolster national identity.

In fact, the public appeal that Porden's *The Arctic Expeditions* was intended to have cannot be in doubt. The publisher was John Murray, who was Barrow's regular bookseller, so the verses should be seen as part of a promotional campaign for the Admiralty's Arctic expeditions (Murray would later publish Franklin's accounts of his Arctic expeditions). Indeed, an ideology of *translatio imperii* is embedded in Porden's poem, as she implies Britain will take the place of Rome. Britain stands to become a new centre from which conquests of northern regions will venture out. Thus, the 'Muse of all that hymn'd Saturnian Jove' found on 'Pindus top or in Hæmonia's grove' is no longer what will 'inspire the arduous lay' of the poet; she has been replaced by the North Star pursued by Britain's brave explorers (ll. 9–11). Despite not selling in great numbers, Porden's poetry did receive a positive reception for its patriotism when reviewed in the politically conservative *Anti-Jacobin Review*. It is here noted that Porden 'strikes the strings of her harp with a Druid's boldness and encourages the enterprize [of Arctic conquest] with the most ardent hopes of success'.[33]

In *The Arctic Expeditions* Porden emphasises that a significant prize of the expedition into the Greenland Sea (Porden's sweetheart, John Franklin, sailed on the HMS *Trent*) would be the recovery of the lost colonists, described as 'long sever'd from his kind' (l. 6).[34] In the foreword Porden describes the background for her verses:

The doubtful fate of the Colony believed to have been once established on the Eastern Coast of Greenland, and the possibility of a passage to the Pole, are subjects on which for some years my mind has dwelt with peculiar interest; this feeling was again excited when I heard of the great revolution in the Polar Seas, which made it probable that the one might be reached, and the fate of the other ascertained.[35]

Porden offers up the familiar tale of how Greenland was once a verdant land, which she claims sustained a thriving settlement of Christians to the number of 20,000 (it may have done so over the ages, but never at one time).[36] When the climate grew gradually colder the colonists saw 'their scantier herbage fail' year after year (l. 40). With respect to the fate of the Greenlanders, Jen Hill has analysed *The Arctic Expeditions* as an example of 'feminine domestic sympathy' in relation to the hope of saving the distressed colonists, which shows her interest in Arctic exploration, even if she could not herself be physically involved in it.[37] This is a helpful observation for our understanding of how female perspectives could shape patriotic outpourings and how Porden's poetry can be viewed through the critical study of feminist geopolitics, which shifts the focus from the operation of elite agents to the gendered political subjects in everyday political practice.[38] In this respect Sarah Richardson has shown how early nineteenth-century women used arguments of charity and compassion in relation to the debate on the slave trade or when encouraging a more empathetic, reflective, and compassionate view of the so-called savages in Ireland.[39] Porden can be seen to argue for a 'Greater Britain', whose dominance is measured not only in terms of its geographical expanse but also through its philanthropic outreach.

The warming of the Arctic, which today is viewed as both an omen and a driver for the climate crisis, was something Porden wholeheartedly embraced. In the *Quarterly Review* article Barrow puts forward the theory that the disappearance of ice near Greenland was a harbinger of a permanent climate change in the northern hemisphere.[40] Porden subscribes to this theory and expresses the hope that Britain might benefit from the warming climate; it would bring improved agricultural possibilities: 'hail returning Summer's prime; / Its ruddy grapes shall lavish Autumn bring, / And all Sicilia's sweets adorn the Spring' (ll. 73–6).[41] Her foremost concern is what a warmer climate would mean for the beleaguered colonists in Greenland. She sees the climate shift as a providential gift from 'th'Almighty hand' that 'Showers blessings e'en on that secluded land, / That fortitude can warm that frozen air / And clothe in flowers that region of despair' (ll. 51–4). Porden sketches how the old colonists 'Again their light canoes shall sail, again' and how 'milder Summers' may 'rear their golden grain … long by frosts opprest' (ll. 71–3). That this leads her to speculate on how Britain could help the settlers take advantage of this new situation, and once again thrive in a greening Greenland, is an unexamined aspect of *The Arctic Expeditions*, which I will discuss here.

Porden sees the British explorers as emissaries from a country on which Providence had smiled benignly. Her ambition is that the British can '[t]each them [the colonists] again to till the barren sod / And praise once more a long neglected God' (ll. 69–70). I contend that this vision of Britain helping the Greenlanders is undergirded by imperialistic notions, if ever so subtly. The reference to Britain offering the Greenlanders instruction on how to grow crops under adverse conditions chimes with what we know about Porden's general interest in agricultural improvement. In the 1790s a series of crop failures had led to the popularisation of the English horticulturist Thomas Andrew Knight's programme for improving British yield. If Britain would focus on cultivating new varieties of crops better suited to a northern climate, bad harvests could become a thing of the past. Porden was introduced to Knight's ideas through the lectures of Humphry Davy and the botanist James Edward-Smith, and she championed Knight, who was made president of the London Horticultural Society in 1811, as a national hero in her poem *The Veils* (1815).[42] Porden's idea in *The Arctic Expeditions* is that Britain can 'teach' the Greenland farmers to cultivate plants suitable for the climate, perhaps based on Knight's theories of agrarian transformation – that is, growing northern crops in northern climates – which she had celebrated as a discovery of great benefit.

We may view Porden's suggestion of exporting agricultural knowledge to the beleaguered Greenland colonists in the light of what Michael Bravo has called the 'global and imperial maritime dimensions of Britain's agricultural wealth'.[43] He discusses how gardeners and botanists travelled across Britain's overseas empire in an effort to transplant crops from one location to another with the purpose of increasing yield. Improvement of botanical knowledge was essential for maintaining the empire. The main purpose of this was to sustain the supply of food, but, in turn, nineteenth-century scientific advances in botany were also worked into a compelling argument for Britain's expansion abroad. As the model developed, British expertise allied with capital would sometimes outcompete native farmers in favour of introducing plantation-based industries under British control. One may therefore ask whether the agricultural improvement Porden imagines Britain could facilitate on Greenland's distressed coast would be limited to a form of charity, or whether Britain was expected to create a system of dependence that would entwine peasant farmers into a colonial economy?

The historian Richard Drayton has argued that British colonialism evolved in close association with botany, in particular so that 'imperialism of improvement' held out the promise that 'people and things might be administered, in the cosmopolitan interest, by those who understood nature's laws'.[44] Porden further mentions that the British should teach the long-isolated colonists about the Word of God, which indicates a long-term missionary commitment in eastern Greenland that might parallel the Danish missionary-colonial efforts on the west coast.

If *The Arctic Expeditions* does not concretise how British help to the Greenlanders would translate into Arctic politics, Porden does not shy away from using imperialistic vocabulary in her verses. Britain's trident will be planted 'in seas unknown' (l. 4) and Britain's heroes will be 'conquerors' of the Arctic Sea (l. 130) who will set themselves up as 'sovereigns of that awful zone' (l. 144). Porden's philanthropic concern for the well-being of the European settlers is intrinsically connected with the fact that she sees Greenland as falling within Britain's new sphere of political interest.

Overtures to Arctic Imperialism

Because Greenland became a target for British exploration in the early nineteenth century, several published
texts reflected on Greenland as a colonial possession.
The prerequisite for colonial thinking is that new land
could benefit the growth of the metropolitan economy
at home. In this respect it should be noted that the standard tropes about Arctic plenty were still promulgated
in the early nineteenth century. Barrow's *A Chronological
History of Voyages into the Arctic Regions*, for example, contains several references to silver and gold mines purportedly waiting to be discovered. Rumours of Greenland's
rich underground resources could be found in the mid-
thirteenth-century Norwegian text *Konungs skuggsjá* (*The
King's Mirror*), which had been made available in a Latin
translation of 1765. It was translated into English in 1817
(i.e. in the lead-up to the Admiralty's highly publicised
Arctic expeditions) as a fifteen-page pamphlet entitled
Extracts from the Kongs-Skugg-Sio; or, Speculum Regale.
The translation exclusively selects passages from the original text relating to Greenland, including the oft-quoted
passage on the existence of 'marble ... of various colours
red, blue, and green'.[45]

The historian Francis Palgrave repeated the claim of
Greenland's 'costly marble' in an 1818 review published
in the *Quarterly Review*.[46] The Danes had indeed found
marble on the west coast, on the basis of which Palgrave
jumps to the conclusion that deposits must abound in
even greater amounts on the undiscovered east coast.[47]
Palgrave further compels colonial interest in Greenland
by reasoning that it was likely 'precious ores' were hidden

underground awaiting extraction since some 'beds of pit coal' had been found, and that old 'tales of gold and silver' could not be completely unfounded because rich specimens of copper ore had recently been sent to Denmark.[48] Whether the fabled east coast contained valuable metals was put to the test only a few years later in 1822, when Scoresby landed at several locations along the shore and collected rock samples. These were later analysed by his patron, the Edinburgh professor of mineralogy Robert Jameson, but yielded no positive results.[49]

For an example of the excitement British exploration raised, we may turn to Bernard O'Reilly's *Greenland, the Adjacent Seas, and the North-West Passage to the Pacific Ocean* (1818). O'Reilly was an Irishman who had taken employment as a ship's surgeon on a Davis Strait whaler. O'Reilly intends to tap into the British public's interest in exploration of northern latitudes, and he advertises himself as a voyager who speaks with authority on Greenland and the Arctic.[50] The book is a handsome quarto with several full-page illustrations, and an American edition was published the same year. To my knowledge, the imperialist designs on Greenland that O'Reilly promotes in this book have received only very scant attention.[51] O'Reilly published the book outside of the control that Barrow would usually exert on publications related to the Admiralty's programme, for which reason he could say things that were not in line with official British policy.[52]

O'Reilly has a long discussion about finding the Northwest Passage, describing this project as a 'matter of the weightiest interest to the trade and general commerce of Great Britain'.[53] In this connection, he mentions the potential for acquiring colonial possessions, such as 'numerous islands not hitherto discovered', which could 'receive the advantages of European commerce, and British constitutional laws!'.[54] O'Reilly also makes an imperialist recommendation about Greenland (which he was well aware Denmark considered its sovereign territory):

I would at once propose that the British government should get possession of the island of Disko, and all the lands adjacent to south east. The present wretched state of that colony renders it of little value to Denmark; but in the hands of Great Britain it would be rendered of great importance in many points of view.[55]

The Danish settlement on Disko Island (Qeqertarsuaq) was founded in 1773 under the name of Godhavn but was clearly a poor and neglected outpost at the time O'Reilly visited. The claims of improving the conditions of peoples and making them colonial subjects were often two sides of the same coin. As a result of being on the losing side in the Napoleonic Wars, Denmark faced state bankruptcy in 1813 and was forced to cede Norway the next year. O'Reilly sees this as an opportunity. As the Danes are 'crippled by the late naval wars', he argues, their inability to finance and maintain this outpost makes it likely that they would only be glad to transfer the settlement for a small recompense.[56]

Whaling was hailed as an industry of importance to British national prosperity and O'Reilly understood that the British could see tangible profits if they could control an important bay on the west coast. O'Reilly furthermore imagines that British hold over this part of Greenland would be of 'great importance' for its strategic value in case the Northwest Passage was discovered. It would not only be a convenient layover, but, as traffic was expected to increase in the area, a fort there could 'be at hand for the protection of British commerce in case of any future misunderstanding with other states'.[57]

Whaling interests and possessions in Greenland also converge in the writings of George William Manby, a captain of the militia who joined William Scoresby Jr on a whaling expedition in 1821.[58] The expedition sailed first to Spitsbergen, then along the east coast of Greenland, rounding Iceland before returning home. The purpose of Manby's presence on the *Baffin* was to test a new harpoon design he had invented. He believed that upgraded technology could help Britain's ailing whale oil industry, which was facing competition from coal gas as a cheap and easily available source for lighting. Scoresby's success in navigating Greenland's previously prohibitive east coast showed that it was possible to gain new whaling grounds for Britain. What warrants our interest here is how this navigational success at sea would translate into colonial speculations.

At the time the *Baffin* was approaching the east coast at around 73°, Manby wrote a letter, signed 14 July, in which he reveals that 'it is Capt Scoresby's intention not only to survey it [the east coast], but to take possession of that long lost continent of West Greenland [i.e. Greenland proper, as opposed to Spitsbergen, which was to the east]'.[59] Exactly what 'possession' would entail for Scoresby is not revealed. However, it is likely that he had a whaling station in mind, and this, in turn, could develop into a more substantive occupation. At least whaling and colonisation were intrinsically connected in Australia where the whaling industry had helped Britain's fledgling Botany Bay (established in 1787) to survive. When ships unloaded their human cargo from Britain, some went whaling to bring back valuable blubber. This colonial industry flourished until a downturn in the 1850s, when the overharvesting of many species of whale made the practice less profitable.

The Australian model of whaling and penal colony evidently appealed to Manby. In a letter signed 4 September (i.e. on the return trip to Britain) he expresses the wish to discover whether the Norse colonists on Greenland's east coast were still alive. This is not just for 'the gratification of common curiosity', but 'to take possession' of the colony 'in the name of my King', and by reaching this part of the island, he would pave the way for 'British dominion of Greenland'.[60] He follows this proposal by calculations of how much British expeditions to the east coast would cost. Should the climate prove not to be 'inimical to existence' (the survival of the Norse colonists would show whether this was the case), then, Manby suggests, the east coast of Greenland could serve as a British penal colony producing goods to be sent to Britain. Thus, if convicts' 'comfort, health & morals' could be secured in a settlement on the east coast, they might 'become useful members of society & probably contribute to the benefit of this country [Britain] from the production of the colony'.[61]

Manby published an account of his journey, entitled *Journal of a Voyage to Greenland, in the Year 1821* (1822). Like O'Reilly's publication, the book was furnished with numerous illustrations and aimed at the popular market. Manby shows much fascination with Greenland's east coast. Although colonial rhetoric is toned down, he never-theless sees it as his duty to propose to the British author-ities that further investigations of east coast resources must be made 'in the confident expectation that much valuable information would be derived, beneficial to mankind, and honourable to the fame of England'.[62]

In 1829 Manby returned to his idea of a penal col-ony in the pamphlet *Reflections and Observations upon the Probability of Recovering Lost Greenland* (1829). Here he suggests that eking out an existence in the inclement cli-mate of Greenland would function as more of a deter-rent for would-be criminals than transportation to New South Wales. The reason for this is that the 'delightful temperature' in the Antipodes and the fertility of the Australian soil are 'so readily and abundantly productive' that it 'scarcely will require labour' and therefore not make the convicts 'feel the weight of their misdeeds'.[63] With this opinion, Manby joined the chorus of critics sceptical of transporting British convicts to Australia. One of these voices was Jeremy Bentham, who also felt the antipodean colonies failed to live up to the neces-sary requirements for punishment. Among other things, Bentham did not believe that the easy life in a warm cli-mate would compel personal reform and it thus lacked the effect of deterrence.[64] In fact, Manby proposes the establishment of two distinct convict colonies on the east coast of Greenland: one at a northern location 'for those in the full vigour of youth and health', and a south-ern site 'for those who are in a certain degree enfeebled by age or constitutional impurity'.[65] Another complaint detractors raised was the enormous cost of transporting convicts to Australia. In his pamphlet, Manby therefore emphasises that transportation to Greenland was a much smaller financial burden to the British state than crossing the Pacific.[66]

The purifying effects on criminals in taking responsibility for their own life and being spiritually reborn through hard labour was an idea welcomed even among radicals in Britain. The political philosopher William Godwin discusses transportation in his *Political Justice* (1793) as something positive in removing criminals from the environment that created crimes. He sees far-off locales as unnecessarily cruel, however, and recommends that 'banishment to the Hebrides would appear as effectual as banishment to the Antipodes'.[67] If the rough climate of the Hebrides could make criminals appreciate their own hard work as rewarding, it was difficult to make Arctic locations productive penal colonies. In the 1630s the mariner Edward Pelham recounted how the English Muscovy Company, in an attempt to safeguard its whaling stations on Spitsbergen, persuaded prisoners facing death sentences to spend the winter there by promising them both life and wages. However, when the prisoners arrived and saw 'the desolatenesse of the place' they 'conceived such a horrour and inward feare in their hearts' that they begged to be taken home to face death in England rather than overwinter.[68]

Manby's plans for British occupation of Greenland did not go unnoticed; he was recognised in the press for his ambitious proposal of opening up the east coast 'to commercial adventure' and claiming the Arctic for Britain.[69] Manby did not represent the Admiralty and official policy, but this did not mean that he shied away from trying to win over the government to his cause. In

1831 he published an open letter to Charles Earl Grey, First Lord of the Treasury, entitled *Hints for Improving the Criminal Law ... with Suggestions for the Settlement of a New Convict Colony*. In the letter, Manby again criticises the use of Australia as a convict colony and suggests east Greenland as an alternative destination. In this connection, Manby explains that the Norse population 'has occupied my thoughts day and night for many years', as he regards their fate as 'a subject of the most intense importance, both to the moralist and the philosopher'.[70] The reason for this is that the historical Norse colony proved that survival on the east coast was possible (here Manby perpetuates the erroneous location of the medieval settlement). Because 'Eric's Norwegians' had settled and survived in eastern Greenland, he argues, it would be 'an appropriate spot' to which convicts could be banished and where they could start a new life.[71] The advantage of 'these dreary frigid regions' is that the miscreant can 'be made to feel some of the miseries he may have entailed on his fellow creatures' by having to support himself on sparse resources, and yet the coast is 'sufficiently ample for the wants of existence, both in the articles of food and raiment'.[72] Indeed, Greenland is ideal for establishing a British penal colony in which men should be reformed, Manby advises, because manners 'retain, and even increase ferocity' in a hot climate like that of Australia while it is 'a well known physical fact, that, in the arctic regions, the hot and furious passions lose their energy'.[73]

Manby was apparently unaware of the fact that the Danes had tried transporting convicts to Greenland a century earlier. Travelling on Governor Claus Paars' ships in 1728 to the west coast were twelve male convicts accompanied by twelve young women from a correctional facility in Copenhagen. The men and women were forcibly wed so that they could 'copulate' (as King Frederik IV formulates it in one of his missives) and thereby help the fledgling Danish colony.[74] The couples were provided with clothing and food, and the men were paid a salary to serve as soldiers. However, during the first winter in Greenland, about half of them died from scurvy and other diseases.[75]

Even if this had been known to Manby, he (like so many others) laboured under the illusion that the climate on the east coast (the alleged location of the rich Eastern Settlement) was better than the conditions on the west coast. In the pamphlet *Hints for Improving the Criminal Law*, Manby tells us that he, in 1828, had approached the Danish general-consul as well as the Swedish minister resident in London, Count Magnus Björnstjerna, offering his services in recovering the lost European colony in Greenland, but received no reply from either. Yet Manby surmises that his proposal was probably what spurred the Danes to send an expedition to the east coast later in 1828.[76] In the years that followed Manby continued to insist on the validity of his colonial plans.

In the early 1850s Lord Chief Justice John Campbell would again take up the question of whether Greenland should be considered as a potential British penal colony. At this time, however, exploration had provided better information about the actual conditions on Greenland's east coast, and opponents of the scheme raised the objection that the climate was too inhospitable to make it a workable solution.[77] The idea of a convict colony in

Greenland was raised again in 1867 when US secretary of state William H. Seward looked into extending the negotiations with Denmark for the purchase of the Danish West Indian islands of St Thomas and St John to also include the requisition of Greenland and Iceland. The report he commissioned highlights the benefit of having prisoners manning US stations in the Arctic.[78] This would not only be practical solution, as it would probably be hard to find volunteers for this duty, but it would also be salutary for the convicts. This is because Greenland's climate has 'the means of developing man in any way physically or mentally'.[79] However, there is more to pique American interest, the author of the report, Benjamin Mills Peirce, argues. Greenland has 'a vast interior, which is perfectly unknown, and a far north and west, which has only been guessed at', thus, in addition to the 'kryolite and other ores' that were known, 'we have every reason to believe that there is a warmer climate, a richer fauna, and a more favorable aspect than in any of the known portions of the island'.[80] Evidently the age-old legends of Greenland's riches beyond the horizon died hard.

Reaching the East Coast

One myth that came under much pressure in the course of the 1820s and early 1830s was the long-standing belief that the fabled Eastern Settlement had been placed on the east coast. As we have seen in Chapter 3, the geographer Heinrich Peter von Eggers had already punctured this myth in the 1790s, but new geographical knowledge provided the final nail in its coffin, although not everyone was ready to accept this fact. The competing

British and Danish explorations of the east coast and the responses they elicited are the focus in the remainder of the chapter.

Manby, who had sailed with Scoresby's expedition along Greenland's east coast in 1821, could only guess at what was inland as the *Baffin* was prevented from approaching the shore because of heavy sea ice. When Scoresby returned to the east coast on a new expedition in 1822, he was, however, successful in making several landfalls. The British press widely praised his *Journal of a Voyage to the Northern Whale-Fishery* (1823) as a great national accomplishment. On the voyage Scoresby came ashore at places he named Cape Swainson (Nuua), Cape Stewart (Sermersooq), and Cape Hope (Noorajik Kangitteq). Scoresby found remnants of recent human activity, including a hamlet of nine or ten winter huts and traces of two summer dwellings. In the huts he discovered tusks with drill holes, which he believed could not be of Inuit origin. At Cape Hope he also found a wooden coffin in a grave. This led Scoresby to claim that he had come upon the remnants of a people that were 'an admixture with some other nation – doubtless the ancient colonies planted by the Icelanders'.[81] Scoresby had no archaeological training and his conclusions about the existence of a mixed Norse–Inuit population in east Greenland were mistaken.

Scoresby was the first European to chart around 400 miles of the east coast between 69° and Cape Parry, a headland at 72° on the north side of Mountnorris Fjord, a coastline previously deemed inaccessible because of pack ice. Although he does not make any statements in *Journal of a Voyage to the Northern Whale-Fishery* that directly contest Danish sovereignty, the publication was clearly a snub to the Danes. Scoresby boasted that his navigational skills should be evaluated against 'the singular and total failure of the many attempts of the Danes to reach this coast for the recovery of the ancient colonies'.[82] The *North British Review* summarised what was at stake in what was clearly construed as a national competition:

The published opinion of Captain Scoresby was, in fact, a challenge and a reproach to the Danish government in the eyes of the scientific world. Here was a Whitby captain exploring and laying down their own coast for them in his merchant vessel, and doing in a week or two what they had been talking of doing for two hundred years.[83]

What is expressed in this passage is an ideology that equates discovery with moral right to territory. Scoresby's scientific and exploratory forays into the North Atlantic fit a model proposed by the historian Daniel A. Baugh in relation to how discovery was handmaiden to sea power in the Pacific from the late 1760s. Gaining geographical knowledge of new areas functioned as what is best defined as defensive maritime imperialism – that is, it was believed that that one could pre-empt other nations' claims to land through the entitlement of first discoverers.[84] After Scoresby's successful landing on Greenland's east coast in 1822, Douglas Clavering would go on to map the east coast on an Admiralty-sponsored expedition the next year, extending Scoresby's observations up to 74°, naming Pendulum Islands, Shannon Island, and Loch Fyne.

British proactivity in Greenland irked Denmark, and in 1823 the Danish minister of state consulted the

Greenland expert Morten Wormskjold about the possibility of Britain adducing their discoveries as rights to occupy the east coast.[85] A committee was set up to prepare a Danish expedition. However, departure was delayed and the brig *Hvalfisken* did not leave Copenhagen until 1828. Royal orders were for mapping the coast and to make scientific investigations, but this was to be combined with a search for traces of the Norse colonists.[86] Lieutenant Wilhelm August Graah sailed from Copenhagen on 31 March 1828 and did not return until 1831. On his voyage he reached 65° – that is, some 550 km (or 332 miles) up the east coast. Part of the journey took place in a skin-covered *umiaq*, in recognition of the fact that Indigenous means of transport were the most efficient and nimble for exploration. Graah had orders to explore as far as 69°. Although Graah did not reach this goal, he named several locations after historical Danish heroes (similar practices were well-rehearsed imperialist strategies). To stress how discovery was tantamount to land claims, Graah named the whole extent of the shoreline he examined 'King Frederik VI Coast'.

The title of Graah's published account, *Undersøgelsesrejse til Østkysten af Grønland, efter kongelig Befaling udført i Aarene 1828–31* (*Exploration of the East Coast of Greenland, by Royal Order Executed in the Years 1828–31*) (1832), points up the national-political importance of the expedition. Not unexpectedly, Graah aims to undermine Scoresby's previous discoveries. He writes that Scoresby's voyage, 'which some years ago attracted so much notice', had landed 'at a much higher latitude than where the ancient colonies were to be looked for'.[87] Graah therefore holds that he is the first to truly grapple with the mystery of the 'lost colony' and concludes that no living European colony could be found south of Dannebrog Island (65° 18'N).

Graah's negative conclusions on the survival of the Eastern Settlement may in part have contributed to a shift in Danish policy. At least the government would soon afterwards intensify its missionary efforts on the west coast. Only sixteen days after his return in 1831, Graah was appointed director of the Greenland and Faroese Trading Company, which goes to show how closely entwined were the projects of exploration and colonisation. As a member of the Greenland Commission (established 1835), Graah supported the improvement of housing, better health service, and an expanded school system for the Indigenous population.

Before Graah published his official account, which confirmed Egger's more than forty-year-old theory that the Norse people had never been on the east coast, the press was eagerly reporting his progress, sometimes with a little too much enthusiasm. In 1829 the *Indicateur de Calais* precipitously announced that Graah had found the long-lost colonists, who still professed Christianity, and spoken to a Norwegian of the tenth century. I have not seen this article, but the report was picked up by several journals, such as the *Archives du Christianisme au XIXe siècle*, the German *Dinglers Polytechnisches Journal*, and *Edinburgh Philosophical Magazine*.[88] A longer notice about the sensational discovery appeared in the *Journal of the Royal Institution of Great Britain*, where it was announced that Graah had discovered a people 'from a remote age' who had been 'deprived of all communication with Europe'. Allegedly the colonists 'retained some vestiges of the

Christian religion'.[89] The news was momentous enough to be repeated in the entry on 'Greenland' included in the 1849 edition of the *Encyclopaedia Americana*.[90] This was despite the fact that Graah, in his published account of the expedition, had explicitly denied that the Indigenous peoples he had come across were of European descent, even if their appearance seemed to differ somewhat from that of the common Eskimo.[91] The *Foreign Quarterly Review* gave an accurate and pithy summary of the Danish explorer's account: 'The results of Captain Graah's expedition may be stated in a few words. He found no trace whatever of European colonisation any where along the east coast.'[92] The ease with which false news would race ahead of Graah's return to Europe in international publications is a reminder of how promiscuously entangled Arctic discovery was with the increasing commercialisation of the book market and the need for selling press sensations, as Janice Cavell and others have shown.[93]

As the translation scholar Susan Pickford notes, English translations of travel writing were 'potentially a prime site for ideologically motivated textual manipulation, with translators historically engaging in practices such as abridgements and paratextual commentary to adapt the text to the prevailing ideologies of the new publishing and reading context'.[94] I will argue that in the English translation of Graah's travel account about exploration of east Greenland (which was an area for which Scoresby had previously been held as the 'discoverer'), the text was deracinated.

The Royal Geographical Society of London assigned an English translation of Graah's travel account to George Gordon MacDougall, who was employed as Keeper of the Classen Library in Copenhagen. MacDougall adds his own notes to the translated text, occasionally offering reservations or even contradictory arguments to Graah's conclusions. For instance, MacDougall includes a long note in which he suggests that a European colony may be located on the east coast, which the Danish explorer could have discovered had he only 'penetrated into the interior of the country, instead of confining himself to a mere coasting voyage'.[95] Hence, it appears that MacDougall wanted to keep alive the hope of discovery that Scoresby had raised with his findings.

Due to MacDougall's premature death from drowning, the publication of the English translation was delayed until 1837. In the version that was finally published the British Royal Navy officer and Arctic explorer James Clarke Ross adds additional notes to the work, 'which cannot fail to enhance its value'.[96] Hence, the English version of Graah's journal resembles a palimpsest in which the Danish author is robbed of his status as the final authority on Greenland. Indeed, pride in British achievements was stressed when the *Foreign Quarterly Review* reviewed the translation. Graah's account is appreciated, but only for being 'no unworthy companion to the narratives of the various expeditions of our own distinguished navigators to the Polar seas, and particularly to that of Scoresby'.[97] In short, Graah's pioneering discoveries were depreciated as no more than an adjunct to previous British exploration and achievement. In the decades that followed a few Anglophone scholars continued to question Graah's conclusions, claiming that the east side of Greenland was still the most likely place to find it.[98]

It should be noted that the debate about the Eastern Settlement not only took place in the western capitals of Copenhagen and London. Inuit legend spoke of strange peoples in remote regions of Greenland, but the notion of a European settlement on the east coast was created in Europe. In fact, Inuit could read a debunking of the theory that the Eastern Settlement had been placed on the east coast in the magazine *Atuagagdliutit* (i.e. 'distributed reading material') which began publication in 1861. The third volume featured a translation into Kalaallisut of an article by the Danish historian Carl Christian Rafn, including a map of the old Eastern Settlement clearly located on the west coast.[99]

Despite the general de-mythologisation of the east coast, which was revealed to have no ancient settlement and hold no immediately recoverable riches, English mercantile interest in East Greenland was not laid to rest. In 1863 the Danish government gave the prolific J. W. Tayler (who fronted the English Antony Gibbs & Sons trading company) a charter to establish 'stations for the purpose of trading with the natives, hunting, fishing, or working any metalliferous or other mineral-bearing mines there discovered, or engaging in any other business which he may consider to his advantage' in east Greenland for a thirty-year period. This was on the condition that Tayler would give 5 per cent of the turnover to the Danish state.[100] The strategy was likely an attempt to develop the east coast at a time when the government lacked resources to do so themselves. However, Tayler was unable to establish any stations. On neither of his two expeditions to the east coast in 1863 and 1864 did he manage to penetrate the sea ice and land on the shore. It appears that Tayler was attracted to the project with an interest in more than just trading with the Inuit. From one of the crew who sailed on the failed expeditions, we learn that Tayler's reading of Icelandic saga literature had led him to believe that the lost Norse colonists, could they be found, would enable him to establish a flourishing trade station on the east coast.[101] British dreams of making a profit in Greenland's eastern reaches and the intransigent myth of the Eastern Settlement were not easily abandoned.

This chapter has examined discourses encouraged by the purported climate change in the Greenland Sea. Studies of the efflorescence of British works that followed in the wake of the 1818 expeditions into the Arctic have not been lacking, but the purpose of this chapter has been to highlight speculations about Britain's use of Greenland which have not generally received the scholarly attention they warrant. Since the Danes had colonised the west coast for nearly a century, it was primarily the east coast which commanded British colonial interest. The Admiralty never officially announced a claim to East Greenland, but the superior maritime and naval might of the British fleet made it possible, if not natural, for independent explorers and commentators to entertain the thought that Britain could take hold of this territory.

Porden's poetry is an important case study in understanding how the belief in a surviving European colony both motivated and focused British interest in Greenland. By sentimentalising the presumed plight of the colonists, she manages to simultaneously express concern for a destitute people and propose that only British intervention would bring them relief. Porden envisions a re-greening of the now ice-free east coast, which was to take place through the export of hardy plants cultivated in Britain. The history of colonialism shows that botanical knowledge was often wielded as an instrument of power in the establishment of plantations and other institutions that created an imbalance between a technologically superior giver and a poor recipient. If Porden's suggestion of help to the Greenland settlers may seem more solicitous than oppressive, it would be an intervention that could easily lend itself to colonialism over time.

Others were more manifestly colonial in their proposals. Manby also believed the east coast could be utilised for the benefit of Britain. Rather than exporting plants, he wanted to transport miscreants, whom he believed would grow to become better people from the adversity they would encounter on the east coast. Also, in this case, philanthropy connects with a hope for British expansion into the Arctic. Importantly, the penal scheme was an idea conceived on the basis of the misunderstanding that Europeans had once populated the east coast.

Previous chapters of the present book have analysed how superior information about a territory could be claimed as a substitute for actual ownership of land, when physical possession had not yet been achieved. In this chapter we have seen how a war of intelligence was also carried out in the early nineteenth century. Signalling authoritative knowledge about the east coast became imperative. Graah's state-commissioned exploration of the east coast was a response to British activity (not least Scoresby's popular report of exploration). The national rivalry never led to a British colonial grab, but it can be discerned in the English translation of Graah's *Narrative of an Expedition to the East Coast of Greenland,* in which the geopolitical struggle for superior knowledge was continued, by proxy, through the introduction of competing statements into an already occupied textual space.

Britain's newfound confidence in Arctic discovery and possession, from 1818 and the following years, was buoyed not only by the sense of its own sea power, but also by reports that the prohibitive wall of ice had been lifted. A new imperial space had opened up. However, perhaps because it was realised that the east coast of Greenland would be difficult to manage in terms of regular commercial and naval traffic, it never became subject to the same intense colonial machinations as areas of Africa. When it became clear that the disappearance of ice was not permanent, the most immediate enthusiasm for occupation also cooled.

5
Greenland's Fall and Restoration

~

Tropes related to the Arctic have received critical attention in several studies. These are tropes primarily connected with the landscape, such as icebergs, infinite whiteness, or the terrible cold.[1] Tropes of climate and landscape are also important to the narrative constructions examined in this chapter, but my focus is specially on how these tropes were integrated with the cultural memory of the 'lost colony' in nineteenth-century texts. After the Christian missions arrived a dominant cultural narrative developed about Greenland of *fall* and *restoration*. The chapter begins with an examination of how European Greenland was imagined to have come to its end. In this respect, it is my argument that the loss of the Christian colony became a prism through which it was possible to reflect on the two globalising European projects of the nineteenth century: colonialism and Christian mission. The 'lost colony' in Greenland came to function as a mirror for contemporary anxieties about the danger of settling in the wilderness far from European metropoles. As we shall see, what focused this fear more than anything was anecdotal evidence that the European Greenlanders had descended into savagery.

The second part of the chapter will turn to the theme of restoration. In several representations, the new Christian mission to Greenland is seen to remedy the fall. As one nineteenth-century church historian formulated it, the missionising of the Inuit would 'win back this legendary country to the fellowship of European and Christian society'.[2] The theme of restoration was encoded in various ways in nineteenth-century texts. One version was that the Inuit were reawakened to the Christian faith, which had lain dormant in them since the time of the medieval European colonisation. In other texts, emphasis is on the working of God's redemptive grace in human history. The fall of the European colony is here interpreted as part of a larger *Heilsgeschichte*. In the final section of the chapter James Montgomery's best-selling *Greenland* (1819) will be examined as a poem exemplifying this interpretation.

Colonists-cum-Cannibals

There was much conjecture concerning the fate of the European settlers. It is the cultural anxieties associated with the settlers' presumed loss of faith and the fate of 'going native' I want to contextualise in this section. Adriana Craciun has expertly documented how forays into the Arctic were bound up with apprehensions of pending disaster and national disgrace.[3] What needs to be brought to attention is the fact that the loss of Christian Greenland also became a focal point for raising general concerns about venturing out. More than anything, it was evidence of the perils involved in establishing far-flung colonies around the world. In modern criticism is a growing body of work that questions the idea of European imperialism as strong, confident, and indomitable. Instead, what is examined are the moments when colonialists display signs of fallibility, frailty, and fear of failure. Doubts were fundamental to the colonial project. 'Going native' haunted the Western imaginary, as Marianna Torgovnick has analysed it in her wide-ranging *Gone Native: Savage Intellects, Modern Lives*; and Linda Colley and Mark Condos have shown it to be an underlying concern in colonial settings.[4] To these studies, I propose to add the 'lost colony' of Greenland, as this was singled out as an example of colonial failure in several influential texts of the nineteenth century.

The fate of the Greenland settlers was used as a metonymy for the dangers of colonialism at large, allowing writers to voice general apprehensions about settling colonies in remote regions. We see this in John Howison's monumental *European Colonies, in Various Parts of the World* (1834), in which extensive passages on erstwhile European Greenland are included alongside his survey of contemporary (and primarily British) colonial possessions. Howison was widely travelled and had observed many colonial settlements on his visits to Canada, India, Africa, and the Arctic. In his work, he turns to the fate of the Greenland colonists as an illustration of how a disruption of commerce and communication could spell disaster for a colonial outpost. In a long narrative section, Howison imagines how pack ice bore down on the east coast of Greenland one winter, imposing a 'frozen barrier' that led to 'imprisonment', leaving the settlers to interact only with the native Greenlanders.[5] Howison speculates that the anticipation of famine in Greenland would 'take undivided possession of every mind', the consequence of which was that 'the impulse of self-preservation would set the colonists in array against one another'.[6] Howison suggests that one should seek out the Norse settlers to learn colonial lessons from them – either by finding accounts in their abandoned libraries of how the crisis evolved, or by questioning survivors about how they had managed 'to remedy the evils that first attended their separation from the rest of the world'.[7] The fundamental question Howison extracts from the fateful history of European Greenland is existential: 'Can any community in a state of civilization, be it high or low, continue to make progression in that state without foreign aid or intercourse?'[8] A little later he provides the reader with the answer: 'No community ... possesses within itself the means of social improvement; this originating almost altogether in the frequency of its external collision with its neighbours, or with the inhabitants of remote parts of the world.'[9] Greenland's loss of communication with Europe is an admonishment to colonialists at large: one should take all possible measures to avoid isolation, as this inexorably leads to stagnation or decline.

The tragic fate of the Norse colony was a lesson for modern colonial powers. Events at the beginning of the nineteenth century showed that far-off communities with unstable supply lines could all too soon find themselves in a precarious situation if traffic and communication were halted. The Scottish geographer James Nicol observed that, in 1807, when the Napoleonic Wars cut off the regular supplies of European goods shipped to Greenland, the Danish colonists were 'reduced to the necessity of supporting life by eating small herrings, muscles [*sic*], and seaweed'. In fact, he continues, had the British government not 'generously granted to the Danes every facility of supplying their colonies with provisions' in 1811, the situation would have 'extirpated the Europeans or brought them down to the level of the savages with whom they associated'.[10] If this situation was narrowly avoided in this instance, concerns about 'going native' impinged on writers.

The fear of losing identity was a prime concern in the nineteenth century, when ethnic and national discourses were central pivot points. Hinrich Rink, who served as Royal Inspector of South Greenland, is known for his work with promoting Inuit culture and founding the paper *Atuagagdliutit* to prevent the native Greenlanders from losing their cultural identity. It is therefore not surprising that he also saw the loss of national culture among the medieval Norse settlers as the cause of their downfall. In *Danish Greenland* (1877), Rink argues that the settlers' demise began when 'trade with their fellow-countrymen in Europe' was 'totally discontinued'. Consequently the '[i]solation and privations must necessarily in time have got the better of their national pride' and they were most likely 'incorporat[ed] into the Eskimo nation'.[11] We have in this conjectural account the lineaments of a recurrent anxiety: colonial isolation will lead to the loss of national identity (which included language and religion).

As we have already seen, the deleterious effects of isolation were not only discussed in the abstract but could also be spun to serve contemporary political debate. In an 1837 article from the British magazine *Athenaeum*, the Icelandic scholar Finnur Magnússon is quoted for his opinion that the colony in Greenland perished not only because the sea became filled with ice, but also because of the Danish crown's 'impolitic and arbitrary' decision to introduce a monopoly on trade, which hindered other traders' free access to Greenland's coast. Iceland, a Danish dependency, would probably have suffered a similar fate during the Napoleonic Wars, he continues, had not British merchants flouted a similar ban and supplied the island with 'articles for the existence of its inhabitants'.[12] A criticism of Danish monopoly is here combined with welcoming free trade, for which the British were keen advocates (although free trade became possible in Iceland only with the end to Danish monopoly in 1855).

As mentioned, Hans Egede's *A Description of Greenland* was republished in a second edition in 1818, when Greenland began attracting attention as a result of the Admiralty's Arctic expeditions. However, the danger of colonising these northerly reaches is discussed in the 'Historical Introduction', which an editor added to the new edition. There are multiple concerns about the state of the old colonists in Greenland, who (it is assumed) may still be inhabiting the isolated east coast:

[H]ave they perished by the inclemency of the climate, and the sterility of the soil? or do they still subsist? If they subsist, it must greatly interest our curiosity to learn in what manner they have vanquished the difficulties with which they have had to contend, both from the climate and the soil, and the total privation of all articles of European manufacture ... Have they remained nearly stationary at the point of civilized existence at which their ancestors were placed four centuries ago? or have they entirely degenerated into a savage race, and preserved no memory nor vestige of their original extraction from, and subsequent communication with, the continent of civilized Europe?[13]

A main concern here is how a cooling climate may have resulted in crop failure at the crumbling rim of civilisation. Agriculture was central to Enlightenment narratives about progress, and it was believed to constitute a necessary step on the ladder to civilisation. According to Adam Smith, history was divided into four distinct stages that humankind passes through on the road to civilisation: '1st, the Age of Hunters; 2dly, the Age of Shepherds; 3dly, the Age of Agriculture; and 4thly, the Age of Commerce'.[14] Indeed, it was the cultivation of the soil that had distinguished the European colony in Greenland from the Inuit hunter-gatherers with whom they shared the land. The writer of the 'Historical Introduction' fears, however, that agriculture in Greenland may have been arrested by the cold, and this circumstance would have led the colonists to backslide to a more primitive state of social development.

Another setback is also mentioned: the settlers were cut off from receiving goods from Europe. This predicament also has roots in Enlightenment discourse, which held that modern civilisation was the product of social and commercial interactions, for which the flow of goods was the most prominent expression. With the disruption of such interactions, there was more to lose than just the sweet conveniences of life. In the preface to the Scottish economist Adam Anderson's extensive work on the history of commerce, he lists intellectual 'gratifications', as well as the 'elegance of life', around the world as 'principally communicated by Commerce either primarily or mediately'.[15] That is to say, the idea was that commercial interaction socialises human beings by extending into a non-economic arena: the free market of sociable interactions (*doux commerce*).[16] Thus, when trade was interrupted, societies would struggle to maintain polity and civilisational order. In this optic consumption was central to culture.

The alternative to starvation and death when isolated in a remote colony was to become assimilated by the natives, which meant taking on a new identity instead of the one upheld through the continuous use of European goods and ideas. The trope of 'going native' haunted colonial narratives. The English whaler and explorer William Scoresby Jr was one among many who repeated the belief that the European settlers in Greenland had 'become gradually incorporated with the aborigines'.[17] In a central passage from the account of his survey of Greenland's east coast, he wonders about the circumstances of the settlers, especially their struggle to uphold their Christian beliefs:

What are their present state and situation, – their mental and moral condition? They were a civilized and perhaps intelligent people: To what extent has intercourse admixture with the native Esquimaux barbarized their manners and reduced their mental faculties? They were a Christian people: To what extent has the force of example and incorporation with a heathen nation been productive of demoralization and the loss of the benign influences of Christianity? These are questions which to humanity in and to Christian philanthropy in particular are of deep and intense interest.[18]

Scoresby's questions touch upon well-worn concerns about the loss of faith and national identity when European Christians are plunged into the wild with no contact with civilisation. He was not the only Greenland explorer to express such concerns. George Manby, for example, asks the following question about the 'lost colony': 'Has the pure lamp of faith grown dim and powerless for want of communication with other countries?

Or has it preserved its brightness in the lapse of ages?'[19] August Graah shrinks from the thought that the colonists 'lost what little knowledge they once possessed of God's word' and 'became heathens and adopted the manners and customs of the Esquimaux'.[20] As we saw in the previous chapter, he did not find evidence on his expedition that the Norse settlers had mixed with the Inuit.

To lose one's religion was particularly egregious. We may in this respect remind ourselves of the historian Frederick W. Turner's comment that the mythos of being lost in remote regions often modelled itself on the Christian drama of 'becoming *possessed*' by the wild spirit, whether it is channelled by savage people or the wilderness itself.[21] Indeed, the theory that the settlers had descended to savagery was given substance by Christian missionaries in Greenland, who recorded various Inuit folklore. In fact, Inuit legends aided a fear that the lost settlers had degenerated to the status of the subhuman. The Danish missionary Henrich C. Glahn, who travelled to Holsteinsborg (Sisimiut) in 1763, recounts Inuit tales about the 'Tunnersoit' (i.e. Tunersuit), a name he tells the reader is best translated as 'mountain trolls'. This people (frequent guests in Greenlandic folktales) lived in isolated areas and are said to be incredibly tall and remarkably light-footed, which Glahn concludes must refer to a community of European descendants who had sought refuge from Skraeling violence.[22] A similarly horrific tale is found in Hans Egede Saabye's published diary from Greenland, covering the years 1770 to 1778 (1816; Eng. trans. 1818). Saabye refers to a tradition among the Inuit that there should be 'remains of the ancient Icelanders' on the east coast. The Inuit he had spoken to affirm that 'they had seen tall, bearded men, who were terrible, and, doubtless, man-eaters'.[23]

Cannibalism is a particularly grisly version of 'going native' as accusations of anthropophagy were traditionally levelled at Arctic natives. We see this already in Dionise Settle's account of his voyage with Martin Frobisher in 1577. Settle believes that the natives they encountered were cannibals (presumably because of their predilection for eating raw meat): 'I thinke them rather Anthropophagi, or devourers of mans [sic] flesh then otherwise: for that there is no flesh or fish which they find dead (smell it never so filthily) but they will eate it, as they finde it without any other dressing.'[24] In the nineteenth century, we have Dr John Richardson's account from the overland exploration of Arctic Canada, led by Sir John Franklin, in 1819–22. Richardson accuses the French-speaking Iroquois Michel Teroahauté of having killed and served up 'a portion of the body' of dead fellow travellers.[25] Richardson concludes that Michel's principles were 'unsupported by a belief in the divine truths of Christianity', and from 'his long residence' away from home, he 'seems to have imbibed, or retained, the rules of conduct which the southern Indians prescribe to themselves', which would lead him to cannibalism.[26] Teroahauté is represented as a civilised native corrupted by Indians.

This was tough reading, conveying how quickly the veneer of civilisation could peel off in the Arctic. To European readers, cannibalism was placed at the furthest moral coordinates from civilised life. As Patrick Brantlinger has noted, cannibalism often stood as the epitome of how man could come undone in the wild of colonial spaces.[27] So, not unexpectedly, this spectre was raised time and time again in speculations about the lost settlers in Greenland, but also a transgression taken too far for Europeans. The German mission historian David Crantz, for example, relays several eyewitness accounts from the 1750s and early 1760s about a tribe of 'man-eaters' living in a mountainous area in the north-east who sometimes came down to plunder and destroy villages. Crantz surmises that this people 'may be descendants of the Norwegians, who, protected by their natural barriers, carry on a perpetual war with the savages, in revenge of the ruin of their ancestors'.[28] However, he rejects the rumour that they were 'man-eaters' as fanciful Inuit imaginings. The rejection of cannibalism as a possibility was echoed by Second Secretary of the British Admiralty John Barrow, who asserts in one of his articles that the Inuit legends of 'a tall and barbarous race of men, who live on human flesh' simply reflect a prejudice against what is unknown, a fear that has similarly 'created cannibals on every unknown or uncivilized part of the globe!'[29]

The same refusal to countenance white cannibalism is found in a text for juvenile instruction, *The Lost Greenland; or, Uncle Philip's Conversations with the Children about the Lost Colonies of Greenland* (1840), written by the American educator Francis Lister Hawks. His mouthpiece in the text, Uncle Philip, tells attentive child listeners that a strange people observed on the east coast are most likely 'the descendants of the old Norwegians'.[30] Yet he berates reports that this people should be cannibals. Such rumours are dismissed as the delusions of the Inuit, a 'poor, ignorant people, filled with fear', who believe many untruths and 'teach much nonsense to their children'.[31]

The staunch denial that Europeans could stoop to cannibalism was central to the European cultural self-image. This was so even if cannibalism for survival was sometimes, and unavoidably, a last resort in situations of extreme starvation. Thus, denial was the default response to Dr John Rae's discovery of the last camp of the Franklin expedition (which had set out from Britain in 1845 in search of the Northwest Passage). Based on the find of mutilated bodies and the content of the kettles left in the camp, Rae suggested that the expedition had resorted to eating their dead. The report, which made headlines in late 1854, was vehemently rejected as unthinkable by Charles Dickens in *Household Words* on grounds that anthropophagy would be incompatible with English reason and civilisation.[32]

If cannibalism was generally rejected as inconceivable for Europeans, it is also possible to offer another reason it was disclaimed for the European Greenlanders. To assume that settlers had lost their human dignity would make them undeserving of recovery, and this was, after all, why European merchants and missionaries had initially taken an interest in Greenland. A driving force for early re-colonisation was the belief that there was an enclave of kinsmen who would in principle be susceptible to Protestant instruction.

The Christian Restoration of Greenland

If the demise of Christian Greenland became a paradigm for colonial anxiety, it was also often tied in with a narrative of restoration. It is the idea of Greenland's Christian restoration, as it was given significance in a variety of

English and European texts, which will be the focus in this section. To begin, one should take note of the popularity that books about the progress of the Christian mission in Greenland enjoyed in nineteenth-century Britain. As already mentioned, a new edition of Hans Egede's *A Description of Greenland* (first trans. 1745) was published in 1818, and David Crantz' *The History of Greenland* (first trans. 1767) was retranslated into a more accessible language in 1820. The European importance of Crantz' account of the Moravian mission in Greenland cannot be underestimated and the book is still the object of new studies.[33] In Britain Crantz' account was excerpted in several magazines, periodicals, and promotional pamphlets, but its influence also reached poetic compositions. The poet and hymnodist William Cowper, for example, referred to Crantz' account in the poem 'Hope' (1782), pouring praise on the Moravians for carrying the Word of God to 'the farthest north' and defying the 'rage and rigour of a polar sky' to 'plant successfully sweet Sharon's rose / On icy plains, and in eternal snows'.[34] Cowper's use of *concordia discors* here emphasises the Christian miracle of conversion where nothing but cold, heathen hearts were expected. From a Western perspective Greenland was often seen as one of the coldest and most forbidding places of human habitation, and the savagery of its inhabitants was accordingly believed to be equally absolute. Thus, the advance of Christianity there had great symbolic significance. The Romantic poet Felicia Hemans praised the change Christianity wrought among the Greenlanders in her dramatic sketch 'Scene in the Life of a Moravian Missionary' (1834), based on an incident Crantz had described when an Inuk gave his weapons to a missionary in return for hearing the word of God.[35]

Within the framework of understanding that held Christianity to be a universal religion destined to reach to all ends of the world, Greenland was a particular prize. One theme Crantz conveyed to a Europe-wide readership was that the native Greenlanders were given to all manner of superstition prior to the arrival of missionaries. Yet, he notes, their ideas 'concerning the soul and a future state' indicate 'dim conceptions of religious truth'.[36] The explanation Crantz gives for this is as follows:

> The Greenlanders may also have obtained some information on religious subjects from the old Norwegian Christians, and afterwards have forgotten or altered it according to their own way of thinking especially; as the remnant of the Norwegians were in all probability incorporated with the Aborigines of the country.[37]

The Greenlandic legends summarised in the remainder of the chapter are meant to show how the concepts of Genesis, the Deluge, and the Apocalypse can be found among this 'primitive' people.

Crantz provides proof of Christianity gaining ground in Greenland by including devotional poems composed by Greenlanders. These compositions display the blood-and-wounds theology (*Wundenlitanei*) which characterises the emotional and impassioned devotion that set Moravianism apart from Hans Egede's more measured Lutheranism. (The distinctive vocabulary of Moravian worship was intended to be provocative so that believers would overcome the intellectual defences that could bar them from connecting emotionally with religious truth.) To give just two examples, a Greenlander living in the Moravian settlement at Lichtenfels speaks of how the 'Redeemer's death, his passion, his blood and his wounds ... alone can yield me joy', and a poem by a young Inuit boy informs us that he daily thinks on Christ's 'sufferings, death of wounds' and meditates 'with tears and joys' on the Saviour's 'through-pierced feet'.[38] However, detractors seized upon the corporeality of Moravian rhetoric in these professions of faith as an indication that the Inuit gained (or regained) little understanding of Christianity as the rational system it professes to be. The prolific English scholar and mythographer Jacob Bryant, for example, commented on the Inuit poetry relayed in Crantz' book that it showed Greenlanders were given to unevolved emotionalism and incapable of comprehending an idea of God based on reason and logic. They could therefore be swayed only by a form of emotional idolatry.[39]

Yet the notion that Christianity had enlightened Greenland during its first Scandinavian settlement played a role in the promotion of missionary efforts. The theory that the Greenlanders were particularly predisposed for Christianity was repeated in several pro-missionary publications. An example of this is *The Moravians in Greenland*, a text intended to garner support for the mission which was first published in English in 1830 but issued in several subsequent editions. Most of the work consists of a summary of Crantz' history, but the author includes additional arguments for continuing the missionary efforts in Greenland. One of these is the assertion that the Greenlanders' particular brand of religious superstition in fact prepares them for Christianity. This is because 'a colony of Christian Norwegians in former times settled in Greenland', so that the natives' paganism may be 'the glimmerings of truth which they [the Norwegians] had left behind, and which, though debased and enfeebled, were not quite extinguished'.[40] According to this logic, the missionaries' job was to restore faith among the Inuit, in effect undoing the abject heathenism that had encompassed them.

The claim that the Greenland Inuit carried with them vestiges of Christianity was an object of interest in Europe, and this notion could be converted into sympathy for them, as they were seen as particularly susceptible to the teachings of faith and the benefits of European civilisation. In the following this dynamic will be examined through a cluster of texts related to Azil, a Greenland woman who, at the age of twenty-three, came to Europe in 1827 to be displayed in front of fee-paying audiences.[41] Azil travelled with the Italian showman Signor Paganini, known for exhibiting both animals and people. Paganini wrote a play in four acts to be performed at fairs and courts which dramatises the events of Azil's life. It was later published under the title *Le Avventure di Azil giovane Esquimese del Groenland* (*The Adventures of Azil, a Young Eskimo from Greenland*) in 1837.[42] There is a growing literature on so-called ethnological shows, which deal with the pure exploitation and sometimes contracts between organisers and performers (always with earnings shared unequally to the disadvantage of the performers).[43] I shall not go into this here and instead concentrate on the reference to the Norse inhabitants in the material.

The play tells how Azil's parents, who were out fishing with their baby girl, fell into the hands of Osage Indians.

The parents are killed, but Azil is allowed to live and taken to an area by the Missouri River. There she is later discovered by the explorer and fur trader Wilson Price Hunt, who arranges for her transport to Europe to be shown in Paris together with a number of Osage Indians. In the last act of the play (a strange metadrama in which some of the characters were presumably playing themselves) Azil is given to Paganini, who promises to take good care of her and to keep her for only as long as she agrees to be exhibited.[44] Although Azil acts in the play, and is even given a speaking line, the drama is clearly a Western representation of her history. Central to the play is the Europeans' negotiations over her transport to Europe, and in particular Signor Paganini's kindness in taking her in. In fact, Azil's native Greenland is portrayed as a once orderly society that had descended into unruliness and conflict, which makes Azil's removal to Europe seem like a felicitous escape. In the first act of the play Edumbi, chief of a Greenland tribe, speaks of how rival tribes fish in their waters and hunt in their woods, which is contrasted with a better time when the Danish kings 'Sarno', 'Frodne', and 'Olau' (pseudo-Danish names meant to sound like legendary rulers) and their descendants, who had penetrated into Greenland at a time in the distant past (*da tempo ignoto*) and never violated Eskimo territorial rights.[45]

The memory of Greenland's European history is also important in relation to Azil herself, as is made clear in a pamphlet issued as an advertisement/playbill in the towns Paganini visited (published in Italian, French, German, and Hungarian).[46] The pamphlet narrates Azil's story, but also includes six pages of muddled ethnographic information about the Inuit, their customs, clothing, eating habits, marriage rituals, and so forth. In the 1840 Italian print of the pamphlet, Greenland women are said to be 'almost like ours except some of them have big eyes, big lips, chestnut hair, and a whiter complexion than that of Europeans'.[47] For this, Paganini refers to the British explorer William Parry, who, in the quest for the Northwest Passage, had observed Inuit with elongated faces and white skin. This European appearance is ascribed to a union between natives and the Danish/Scandinavian people.[48] In one version of the pamphlet, Azil is described as having European features: brown hair, chestnut eyebrows, a regular nose, and an oval-shaped face.[49] In a poem Paganini included with this material (rendered in French, German, and Italian) we are told that Azil is living evidence that in the land of 'eternal ice' some souls manage to 'break through the veil of barbarism'.[50] At the heart of the representation is the idea that Azil does not really belong with the present savageness of Greenland – a disjunction we must understand as a natural consequence of her Norse ancestry. Paganini's references to Azil's ethnic heritage defuse the sense of exploitation involved in exhibiting her in Europe – he becomes her benefactor, securing a passage away from savageness to European civilisation which is her spiritual home.

The pamphlet's frontispiece is a drawing of Azil in full sealskin attire and hunting gear, as she would appear to audiences (Figure 5.1). Paganini wanted to show the Greenlandic woman as a spectacle, as he knew well that her exoticism would sell tickets. Yet the accompanying pamphlet prevents a complete 'Othering' of her by

FIGURE 5.1 Illustration from *Le Avventure di Azil giovane Esquimese del Groenland* (1837). Ghent University Library, BIB. ACC.001462/-8. 195.

collapsing boundaries of difference: Azil may come from a strange and primitive Greenland, yet her pale skin, her European heritage, and her conversion to Christianity make her a legitimate object of both sympathy and desire. It is unclear whether the first act of the play, which dramatises the capture and killing of her parents, is based on a story that Azil told herself. There is little attempt to take any real interest in the knowledge Azil would have possessed about world beyond Europe; the emphasis throughout the Paganini material is on what Europeans did to rescue Azil, delivering her into the Christian life she deserves.

It is relevant here to note that we do have first-person accounts from other Inuit who came to Europe. There is the diary of Abraham Ulrikab, who travelled with seven other Inuit from the Moravian mission at Hebron and Nakvak, Labrador, to be exhibited in the showman Carl Hagenbeck's *Völkerschauen* (ethnographic shows) in Germany in 1880. The diary was written in Abraham's native Inuktitut but survives in a German translation, which has been edited by the scholar Hartmut Lutz.[51] Abraham writes about his performance of kayaking and other aquatic tricks, his impression of the gawking crowds, and the noise of German cities, but he also expresses his Christian faith when members of his group start dying of smallpox. Like with Azil, the representation of Abraham's culture was controlled by the European impresario, but Hagenbeck was interested only in promoting the exoticness of the Inuit not in exploring a narrative of their innate potential for Christianity.

Three years earlier, in 1877, Hagenbeck had brought a group of six Greenlanders to Europe for a similar show. Although he was well aware they were Christians, Hagenbeck deliberately downplayed this aspect. In his autobiography he lets on that the selling point of his Arctic menagerie was their primitive lifestyle, 'which was not really very different from that of their ancestors when

Greenland was first *recolonised* by the Scandinavians in the eighteenth century'.[52] Contrary to Paganini, Hagenbeck decided to bracket the influence Christianity has had on the 'Eskimos' both in medieval and recent times because it did not fit his business model.

Nonetheless, the success of Christianity and its civilising energies was the focus in several of the many texts published by missionary and church societies in Britain and the United States. The progress of Christianity in Greenland was often singled out, as can be seen in titles such as *Denmark and Her Missions* (1863), *Lives of Missionaries, Greenland* (1869), and *Amid Greenland Snows; or, The Early History of Arctic Missions* (1892). In some of the texts the paradigm of fall and restoration can be found, often connected with an understanding of Greenland as part of a divine providential history. For example, the book *Greenland Missions* (1831), aimed at the market for children's Sunday reading, concludes with an application of Isaiah 61:4 (on the rebuilding of the temple in Jerusalem) to Egede's restoration of Christianity in Greenland: he was called to 'build the old wastes, to raise up the former desolations, to repair the waste cities, the desolations of many generations'.[53] In a similar vein, the antiquary Edward Charlton noted that the ancient church buildings in Greenland were never 'totally destroyed': they await a 'Christian people' to return 'like the Jews of old, to repair and rebuild the ancient temples of their faith'.[54]

An example of how a fall-and-restoration trope was written into fiction for the popular market is the anonymous novel *The Northern Light: A Tale of Iceland and Greenland in the Eleventh Century* (1860). This book was the seventeenth instalment in a series of historical tales published in Britain to popularise church history. At the end of the dramatised reconstruction of how Christianity spread to the far north in the Middle Ages, the author adds a wistful note: Greenland's supplies from Europe were 'cut off by the interruption of traffic', a catastrophe compounded by 'a sudden increase of ice', which made the colonists 'easy prey to the savage hordes of the Skrællings'.[55]

Christianity is not lost to heathenism for all eternity, however. *The Northern Light* spins on the metaphorical axis of divine illumination. If the luminosity of Christianity was extinguished with the disappearance of the Norse settlers from Greenland's shores, the missions of the eighteenth and nineteenth centuries have rekindled the divine light. To back this up with the evidence of a natural phenomenon, the author claims that the Aurora Borealis has been 'more often seen', and it appears 'much brighter than it used to be in former ages'; it reflects how 'a small body of conscientious and enduring Moravians' are spreading the Gospel to 'the descendants of the Skrællings'.[56] The Catholic author's only misgiving about this restoration of Christianity in the far north is that the Protestant missions lack the 'consistency and effect which Catholicity can only give'.[57]

James Montgomery's Greenland

This fall-and-restoration structure also informs the design of James Montgomery's *Greenland*, to which I will now turn. The Scottish-born poet is today perhaps best known as a popular writer and editor of hymn and psalm collections. The hymn 'Angels from the Realms of Glory', for example, which Montgomery wrote in 1816, won international fame and was even translated into Kalaallisut (by the Danish missionary Knud Kjer) for use in Greenland.[58] Despite the fact that Montgomery's works sold far more copies than many other Romantic-period writers, he is seldom discussed today.[59]

In 1819, the year after the British Admiralty sent two expeditions to the Arctic, Montgomery published *Greenland*, which comprises five cantos of what was intended as an epic in heroic couplets. In the preface to the first edition he is apologetic about bringing it before the public prematurely, leaving readers with an incomplete epic. The reviewer in the *Eclectic Review* commented humorously that Montgomery had decided to 'abandon the half-achieved adventure', so the poem itself became (to the public) the '*lost* Greenland' it was meant to be about.[60]

Montgomery does not reveal in his introduction to the poem why he decided to publish an unfinished epic. Nevertheless, the reviewer of the *British Critic* ventured a guess: Greenland would soon lose its status as 'a topic of fashionable dissertation' when the 'fresher novelty' of the North Pole gripped the public's imagination.[61] Whether this was correct, we cannot know, but book-market statistics of the period show the gamble paid off. An estimated 37,500 copies of the poem were sold, making it one of the bestsellers of the period.[62] Thus, it is strange the poem has not attracted more attention in modern criticism.

The published parts of the poem are essentially a number of episodic segments, or, as a contemporary reviewer put it, 'a loosely floating, incoherent, superb conception of a possible something of which the Poet finds himself unable to give even the outline'.[63] Nonetheless, as all reviewers agreed, Montgomery's verses contain many beautiful and touching scenes. Donald Reiman has written that Montgomery 'may be one candidate for the most *representative* (not the *best*)' Romantic poet, insofar as his writing reflected 'all the central concerns of the Romantic movement'.[64] Certainly Montgomery realised that sublime landscapes, the tragic destruction of a people, and the heroic tribulations of eighteenth-century missionaries pursuing their noble course were subjects suited for treatment in *Greenland*.

The first three cantos focus on the initial Moravian missionaries to Greenland and their struggle to reach Greenland over rough seas. The story arc is here based on a factual ship that sailed to Greenland in 1733 with Matthäus Stach, his cousin Christian Stach, and Christian David, who would set up the mission station of New Herrnhut on the west coast. As is clear from the notes Montgomery adds to the three cantos, he founds the poem on information contained in Crantz' *The History of Greenland*. Moravian missions had Montgomery's interest as he was raised in a Moravian household and educated at the Moravian settlements of Grace Hill, Ireland, and Fulneck, in Yorkshire.

Montgomery's father had missionised for the Moravian church in the West Indies, where both his parents died. In 1809 Montgomery wrote the abolitionist four-part poem *The West Indies*, in which he gives an account of the Moravian mission in this part of the world. This poem was meant to solicit support for Moravian activities, which Montgomery would also actively encourage in *The Iris; or The Sheffield Advertiser*, the paper he edited. Subscriptions to the Moravian mission came in from several Bible societies as a result.[65] Montgomery's *Greenland* was published for Longman, Hurst, Rees, Orme and Brown, the same publisher who would market a second edition of Crantz' *The History of Greenland* a year later, in 1820. The poem may therefore have served a secondary function of soliciting backing for missionary activity, but Montgomery is primarily interested in exploring the larger epic conception of how Christianity would defeat heathen darkness.

In *Greenland* the three cantos on the Moravians' passage across the ocean conclude with the ship reaching a safe harbour on the west coast of Greenland. Montgomery uses the missionaries' arrival as an occasion to redirect his poetic barge and 'Sail up the current of departed time', which means that he turns to describe the loss of Christian Greenland in the following two cantos.[66] After this interlude, Montgomery was evidently planning to return to the progress of the eighteenth-century Moravian missionaries, detailing their commitment to converting the Inuit and thus relieving Greenland from its heathen darkness. These cantos were never written, however. Thus, on a broad thematic level, the finished *Greenland* would have borne a remote structural resemblance to the Italian poet Torquato Tasso's sixteenth-century Christian epic *Jerusalem Delivered*, replacing crusaders with missionaries. (Montgomery would later write about Tasso's epic in the second volume of *Lives of the Most Eminent and Scientific Men of Italy, Spain & Portugal* [1835].)

Montgomery gives multiple explanations for the demise of the first European colony in Greenland: 'War, famine, pestilence, the power of frost / Their woes combining'.[67] Although Inuit violence and the Black Death are both briefly addressed in the poem, it is climate catastrophe (i.e. ice descending upon Greenland's east coast) that commands most space and sympathy in the poem. In one passage we are presented with a scene of 'a beauteous hamlet in the vale' that is crushed by glaciers. The frozen 'turrets', which have accumulated 'through a thousand years', suddenly come tumbling down upon the Norse houses, creating a 'wreck of ice'.[68] This idea was likely inspired by what Montgomery picked up from scientific literature. The *Edinburgh Review*, for example, describes how the Norse settlers may have become 'entombed in ice and snow, as the unhappy citizens of Herculaneum were anciently involved in a dense shower of volcanic ashes'.[69]

In another of Montgomery's scenes, the sea's 'frame of ice, with dire explosion' sends its weight on 'the mingled crowd'.[70] Since no extant records documented how the cooling of Greenland's climate had affected the colony, Montgomery bases this and other scenes on reports of natural disasters that Moravian missionaries had observed in Labrador (as he informs the reader in the notes to *Greenland*). The representation of Norse colonists caught unawares and ambushed by ice alludes to common scientific speculation at the time. The geographer Conrad Malte-Brun, for example, described how a barrage of ice would have come down in torrents on the 'flourishing colony', so that it was 'all at once shut up from the rest of the world'. This was a 'terrible catastrophe', in which 'every thing suddenly perished there … attacked at the same moment with a mortal cold'.[71]

Beyond the individual scenes of devastation, Montgomery also offers a panoramic view of the tragic end to Norse Greenland when he describes how regular sailing routes are discontinued, cutting off the colony's lifeline to Europe: 'Commerce forsakes the' unvoyageable seas, / That year by year with keener rigour freeze', and (applying a mercantile metaphor to the sea freezing over) 'embargoed waves in narrower channels roll'.[72] As we have seen, the cessation of trade was believed to have destroyed the fundament for civilised life in Greenland. Taking advantage of an epic simile, Montgomery metaphorises the world of commercial trade as a large body that becomes sick. The circulation of sea currents is imagined as a global cardiovascular system that 'from the heart of ocean sends the flood / Of living water round the world like blood'. When the climate changes and ice clutters the flow, the amputation of the most northerly extremity is inevitable:

Greenland's pulse shall slow and slower beat,
Till the last spark of genial warmth retreat
And like a palsied limb of Nature's frame,
Greenland be nothing but a place and name.[73]

The allegorical implication of a once green and peaceful Greenland laid waste by ice is also elaborated upon in another metaphorical register: Montgomery invokes the Miltonic theme of the colonists one moment enjoying their 'unlost Paradise', which in the next becomes a 'Paradise for ever lost'.[74]

In this connection it is pertinent to briefly turn to Frederick Rogers Blackley's *The Greenland Minstrel* (1839). Montgomery's *Greenland* seems generally to have pre-empted the market for longer poetic endeavours on the subject, but Blackley, a curate at Rotherham, was one poet who attempted a long, if fragmented, poem about Greenland.[75] In *The Greenland Minstrel* the devastation of climate change is again writ large. Blackley opens his first canto with a description of how the Norse explorers 'first discovered Greenland's distant strands, / Which, varied then, could boast of verdant lands'.[76] In Canto IV ancient Greenland is further imagined as a place of lush vegetation: the Norse inhabitants enjoy '[g]roves and gardens', 'fresh roses', and baths from 'earth's self-opening veins the blood-warm wave'.[77]

The idea of Greenland as a place of significant underground activity (like Iceland) stems from the anecdotal account of a medieval Dominican convent in Greenland (mentioned by both Egede and Crantz), said to be warmed by hot springs from a volcano which provided for gardens with flowers and fruit.[78] However, according to Blackley, this idyll came to an end when 'Nature wrap't in one vast frigid dress / Glories in frightful wildest barrenness'.[79] A frigid wilderness thus took over where once plentiful Norse fields had been – an image that doubles for the Inuit's ungodliness, which darkened Greenland for centuries. However, land is recovered for Christianity when the mission breaks centuries of heathen darkness to shine 'heav'nly radiance on the native's head'.[80]

In Montgomery's *Greenland* fall and restoration is also the fundamental structure meant to organise the poem, although it remains unfulfilled as the poem is incomplete. The cantos dealing with the terrible fall of old Greenland function as historical flashback (analepsis) that puts into perspective the story of Greenland's re-Christianisation through the efforts of the Moravian missionaries into. In fact, Montgomery seems to project onto the history of Greenland a similar idea of divine restoration, which he had pursued in his 1815 poem *The World before the Flood*, whose ten cantos focus on the renewal of the world through devastating destruction.

That the old must give way to new growth also takes centre stage in Montgomery's later proto-Darwinian study of natural life, *The Pelican Island* (1827). He declares the theme of this poem to be 'Time, Life, Death' as 'the world's great actors' that 'wrought / New and amazing changes'.[81] Pelican Island, located in south-eastern Australia, has a significant reef, which Montgomery refers to as an arena where God's universal destruction-renewal scheme is made visible. By what Montgomery calls the 'nice economy of Providence', the early life forms in the ocean are 'overruled' and mummify as coral reef – yet their empty shells become a home for new life.[82] In the same way human history shows us a cycle of destruction and rebuilding: all humankind's '[t]owers, temples, palaces, and sepulchres' will eventually become ruins – even 'Great Babylon was like a wreath of sand / Left by one tide and cancell'd by the next'.[83]

Montgomery understands the fall of Norse Greenland from a similar omniscient perspective of world history. In Canto IV, he speaks of how the 'vigorous race' of Norsemen are replaced by a 'swarthy tribe [of] Skraellings' who sally forth in numbers to populate Greenland by divine will – 'slipt from the hand of Providence'.[84] Why God decided it should be this way cannot be queried. Montgomery refrains from accusing the Norse Greenlanders of sin: the colony's end is simply

God's will and as inscrutable as 'parables', 'symbols', and 'hieroglyphics'.[85]

Montgomery frames the downfall of Christian Greenland as a cultural memento mori that illustrates the transience of all human aspirations. This is epitomised in a literal inscription speaking to us across time, quoted on the title page of the first edition: 'Oft was I weary when I toil'd at thee'.[86] This is the runic inscription found on an oar, which, as Montgomery explains in a note, was 'conjectured to have been brought from East Greenland, a hundred and fifty years after the last ship sailed from Norway for that coast'.[87] For Montgomery, the oar stands as a reminder of the hardworking colonists who, despite the odds, had created a Christian society at a northern outpost, but whose memory is now reduced to flotsam drifting on the sea of time.

Imagining the loss of the Norse colony was a way for Montgomery to reify the poetic notion of human disaster. One may in this connection recall the American novelist John S. Sleeper's essay 'The Lost Colony' (1850), in which he notes that writers have long imagined human demise, 'the last man', in terms of 'beauty', 'sublimity', and 'horror', but that this has always been with 'a remoteness, and indeed an air of improbability about the subject, which robs it of half its force and majesty'. Thus, the historical event of the loss of the Greenland colony would make it 'worthy of being commemorated by the ablest pen'.[88] Montgomery seems already to have grabbed this opportunity to use the event of the 'lost colony' to make concrete philosophical speculations on human history.

In terms of structure, Montgomery forges a link between the fall of Christian Greenland in the fifteenth century and its restoration in the eighteenth with a tale of two ships. In canto five, he relates the story of the Norwegian Andrew, who had been appointed bishop of Greenland, but whose ship never reached its destination (as we have seen in the previous chapter, this story was also picked up by Anna Jane Vardill in 'The Arctic Navigator's Prayer'). In Montgomery's version of the anecdote, Andrew 'sail'd, with hope elate, / For eastern Greenland', but a storm rages and he is 'ensnared by fate'. The scene fades out with the image of the pious Andrew on the deck: 'Now motionless, amidst the icy air, / He breathes from marble lips unutter'd prayer.'[89] Andrew's failure to make his prayers heard in Greenland is brought to completion, however, by the three Moravian missionaries centuries later. Montgomery describes the brethren as standing in the stern of their ship 'with looks inspired / And hearts enkindled with a holier flame / Than ever lit to empire or fame' on their way to let the Gospel ring out in the remote island.[90]

The Moravian missionaries were the first large-scale Protestant missionary movement with activities in North America, Africa, the West Indies, and the Far East. One reason Montgomery chose to focus on the mission in Greenland was undoubtedly that it provided a literary vehicle for illustrating what could be interpreted as a fulfilment of Jesus' commission to his disciples: that they be his witnesses 'unto 'the uttermost part of the earth' (Acts 1:8). Within the framework of fall and restoration, the return of Christianity to the land on the edge of the world could be seen to presage the final victory for faith everywhere.

In 1819, the same year Montgomery's *Greenland* was published, the English vicar Reginald Heber published his famous missionary hymn that begins with the hope that prayers will resound 'From Greenland's icy mountains, / From India's coral strand ... Till each remotest nation / Has learned Messiah's name'.[91] Heber clearly seizes on the metaphoric convenience of casting Greenland as a place on the edge of the world where the cold hearts of the pagans were now being warmed by Christianity. In Blackley's *The Greenland Minstrel*, quoted earlier, we similarly find that the successful progress of Christianity in Greenland is viewed to herald the success of Christianity also in 'more favour'd lands'; so that heathens elsewhere may also gain a 'sense of gratitude to God above'.[92]

This chapter has analysed the paradigmatic tale of losing Western faith, culture, and civilisation in foreign lands. Long before Victorians began to express fears and paranoia over the disintegration of the British Empire and the decline of the white race, Greenland stood as a powerful example of the brittleness of European civilisation when replanted on foreign soil.

The cultural memory of the 'lost' Christian Greenlanders had for centuries invigorated men of religion to seek out Greenland. At the end of the eighteenth century, however, the hope of locating pure descendants of these Europeans faded as it was realised they were not to be found on the east coast. The Inuit therefore became new objects of missionary interest. This chapter has shown that the Inuit were effectively incorporated into the discursive formation of a fall-and-restoration narrative. This was sometimes with the sense that the Christian missions would restore a forgotten faith, because it was believed the old Europeans had either instructed them in matters of religion, or the colonists had mixed with the Inuit. In this perspective the modern missions in Greenland could be seen as activating a dormant sense of Christianity from the pit of forgetfulness.

Narratives of colonial and missionary efforts were ubiquitous in the European book market of the eighteenth and nineteenth centuries. In Britain Montgomery's unfinished but hugely popular *Greenland* was a poetic tribute and commemoration of the Moravian mission in Greenland. Montgomery abstracts scriptural types of a fall-and-restoration mythos and applies it to historical circumstances. Events in Greenland are presented as part of God's providential plan: the flame of religion was extinguished only to give aim and purpose to its rekindling in modern times. One reason *Greenland* enjoyed considerable success in the market was undoubtedly because Greenland had become an object of interest for a Britain in the process of reinventing itself as an Arctic nation after 1818. If no political-imperial dimension is present in Montgomery's poem, the benefit of spreading Christianity is never in doubt.

Later commentators do not always agree with the premise of nineteenth-century Christian triumphalism. When Hans Egede Saabye's missionary account *Journal in Greenland* (1818) was republished in 2009, Aqqaluk Lynge, a prominent Greenlandic politician and member of the United Nations Permanent Forum on Indigenous Issues, wrote in the new foreword that the introduction of Christianity in Greenland had a 'devastating impact'.[93] If missionaries strove 'to help those in need' and did so with compassion, they also contributed to 'exploitation and negative cultural change'.[94] The long-term cultural effects of the Christian mission remains controversial in

Greenland today, but this was not a debate Montgomery could have taken up. Like other religious writers at the time, he saw the history of Greenland as providing obvious rhetorical and symbolic opportunities for the argument that the light of Christianity could shine in even the farthest corners around the globe. If Christianity could be proven to take hold in Greenland, where nothing would grow and people could barely subsist, it could stand as a proving ground for the prospective success of Christian expansionism.

6

The Surpassing Adventures of Allan Gordon

~

This chapter focuses on the novella *The Surpassing Adventures of Allan Gordon* (1837) by James Hogg, today a major figure of Scottish Romanticism.[1] The story is about Allan Gordon, a Scottish ship's boy who spends several years in the Arctic, first drifting on an ice floe in the Greenland Sea, then living with the 'lost colony' in Greenland. Hogg's story is loosely based on *The Life and Strange Surprizing Adventures of Robinson Crusoe* (1719). In fact, the story was meant as 'a mere joke' on the popular novel, as Hogg explains in a letter to his publisher.[2] However, it would be a mistake to read this statement to mean that *Surpassing Adventures* is flippant. Rather, I will suggest, the novella is a dark satire on Daniel Defoe's famous novel, questioning the colonial confidence of the precursor text. Defoe's novel is the archetypal narrative of British colonialism in which the protagonist will confidently assert himself to be 'King, or Emperor over the whole Country which I had Possession of'.[3] In contrast to this, Gordon underperforms, showing himself unable to exert control over his new environment. In this respect it gives narrative form to the colonial anxieties about isolation and succumbing to nature. As we saw in the previous chapter, the 'lost colony' in Greenland became a proxy that made it possible to fix general anxieties of colonialism to a historical example. In line with this, I propose that it is no coincidence that Hogg starts his story as an impossible romance (symbolised by Gordon's semi-amorous relationship with a polar bear) only later to turn it into a gritty chronicle of hardship that ends in the final tragedy of the Greenlanders being devoured by wild animals. In the last section of this chapter I add to the understanding of the 'lost colony' as a mirror for contemporary concerns by arguing that Hogg's story about the foundering colony functions as an analogue to the communities in remote parts of Scotland. It is the environmental and social predicaments of these peripheral communities that Hogg was much concerned with in his other writings.

Hogg's Narrative and Contemporary Contexts

Hogg published under the moniker of the 'Ettrick Shepherd' because most of his youth and early manhood was spent as a shepherd and farmhand. He took care of his own education by immersing himself in reading – before Walter Scott discovered his talent as a writer. Hogg is best known today for his psychological mystery novel *The Private Memoirs and Confessions of a Justified Sinner* (1824), but he published a legacy of poems about the Scottish landscape, as exemplified in the collection *The Mountain Bard* (1807). *Surpassing Adventures* swaps the setting of remote Scotland for Greenland and the Greenland Sea. Nonetheless, the narrator is keen to point out how much the Greenlandic landscape reminds him of Scotland. For example, he likens a Greenland iceberg to North Berwick Law (a conical hill in East Lothian)

(p. 266), other heights remind him of the Grampian Mountains (p. 274), the Arctic light is like a winter twilight in Scotland (p. 266), one hill is like Arthur's Seat (the extinct volcano near Edinburgh) (p. 280), and the phenomenon of 'rime' is what he recognises from the northern parts of Scotland (p. 280).

I shall return to the analogies between Scotland and Greenland, but for the benefit of readers unfamiliar with *Surpassing Adventures* it is useful to begin with a brief outline of the plot. Allan Gordon is a tailor's apprentice from Aberdeenshire. After a violent altercation with his hot-tempered master, Gordon decides to run away and go to sea as a cabin boy. In 1757, he finds himself on board a whaling ship, *Ann Forbes*, bound for the Greenland Sea. The captain is a drunken and conceited Englishman whose ambition is to discover the North Pole. Due to the captain's lack of judgement, the ship is caught in pack ice, which eventually crushes the hulk, leaving Gordon the only survivor. For much of the story, Gordon is drifting on an ice floe between Spitsbergen and Greenland (with a short entry into the Arctic Ocean). Gordon kills a large female polar bear that intrudes into the cabin of the shipwreck where he has been holed up. He learns that the bear had just given birth to a cub, which he decides to nurse. The cub, which Gordon names Nancy, grows up to become of much help to him, catching a surfeit of fish and defending him against other polar bears. Later, Gordon comes upon colonists whose ancestors derived from 'Norgeway' (p. 298). Desperate for new blood, the colonists licence Gordon to take a wife as well as mistresses. However, this arrangement makes Nancy jealous and she runs away. At the end of the story Gordon leads a charge to kill the polar bears that regularly prey on the colonists, thinning out their numbers. This is forestalled, however, by a legion of bears that launch a surprise attack on the settlement. Fortunately, for Gordon, one of the assailant bears turns out to be Nancy, who carries him to safety. Almost all the colonists are devoured but Gordon manages to make his way back to Scotland on a Dutch whaling ship. The story is thus brought to its conclusion.

Hogg's narrative of survival alludes to *Robinson Crusoe* throughout. The relocation of the scene from the warm Pacific to the icy world of the Greenland Sea justifies the ostentatious claim of the title that Gordon's experiences 'surpass' Crusoe's. Stories of shipwrecks in the North Atlantic made popular reading. Two examples are the second volume of *Naufragia, or, Historical Memoirs of Shipwrecks and of the Providential Deliverance of Vessels* (1806), which anthologises several such accounts, while the first volume of the *History of Shipwrecks, and Disasters at Sea from the Most Authentic Sources* (1833) is dedicated to 'Shipwrecks in the Northern and Polar Seas'. Both anthologies include the account of Edward Pellham (or Pelham) entitled *Gods Power and Providence: Shewed, in the Miraculous Preservation and Deliverance of Eight Englishmen, Left by Mischance in Green-land Anno 1630*, published in 1631. Pellham, a gunner's mate, had been left with seven other men on the coast of 'Greenland' (i.e. actually the west coast of Spitsbergen, commonly seen as part of Greenland at the time) for nine months and twelve days. Such survival stories were occasions for rehearsing nationalist sentiment. In his foreword Pellham refers to Willem Barents and Jacob van Heemskerck's ill-fated Dutch expedition of 1596, which saw seventeen men stranded on Novaya Zemlya. Whereas the Dutchmen had beer, wine, bread, coal, and good clothes, Pellham stresses, the English crew had nothing and were forced to hunt to survive. When Cyrus Redding, the editor of the 1833 *History of Shipwrecks, and Disasters at Sea*, compares the Dutch and English ordeals, he makes the assertion that 'every enlightened mind' will see that the Englishmen could fare so well, despite their disadvantages, by dint of their 'strength', 'abler bodies', and 'superior instruction and knowledge'.[4] The ability to survive in the Arctic helped raise the belief in the permanency of British civilisation and its empire.

Against this backdrop of patriotic stories about shipwrecked Englishmen showing their grit, Hogg's story plays on readers' expectations of a heroic, nationalist story of survival. These expectations are manifestly frustrated by a text offering only doubts about the ability to master the Arctic. In particular, Hogg challenges the British self-confidence that dominated public perception prior to the loss of the Franklin Expedition in the mid-1840s. Hogg's satire bites most acerbically in his depiction of the English captain John Hughes, who jeopardises both ship and crew for the blind ambition of reaching the North Pole (pp. 245–8). In fact, Hogg had previously satirised British hubris of reaching the North Pole. In an 1829 verse narrative, Hogg's larger-than-life character Jock M'Pherson tells us that he has already crossed both poles and seen the giants who turn the earth on wheels oiled with 'cans of bear's grease'. It is this (obviously false) knowledge that he will pass on to British polar explorers, 'Barrow, and Parry, and Franklin'.[5] The list of names here refers to Second Secretary of the Admiralty

John Barrow and explorers William Edward Parry and John Franklin, who put British lives at risk to uncover the secrets of the Arctic.

When assessing Hogg's satire on Britain's Arctic ambitions, it is worth briefly drawing attention to the anonymous *Munchausen at the Pole* (1819).[6] Munchausen stories had been published in English since 1785, but this particular offering was a response to the manic post-1818 public interest in Arctic discovery. The narrator, Baron von Munchausen, makes no bones about undertaking a polar journey solely for fame and fortune. On his way to the pole, Munchausen lands on the shores of East Greenland. The crew establish contact with the inhabitants, who present themselves as 'descendants of a colony settled on this coast by Erlfungus from Norway', who had been separated from the home country by 'barriers of ice'.[7] The desperate colonists accept Munchausen as a saviour and he is 'given full sovereignty of East Greenland'.[8] Hogg's story is not as overtly hyperbolical or satirical as this, but it follows a similar trajectory: Gordon is accepted by the Greenland colony and becomes an important man in their community. Unlike Munchausen, who successfully slays monsters on Greenland's fields of ice, Hogg's protagonist must see himself outclassed by ravenous polar bears.

Surpassing Adventures can be read as partly a critique of the overconfident British attitude to Arctic conquest and discovery, upheld by a belief in their own superior maritime knowledge and technology. One may here echo Penny Fielding's observation that Hogg's tale is 'not just a joke about masculinity, but also one about modernity, or at least about a Frankenstein-like overconfidence in the capabilities of an enlightened scientificism'.[9] Certainly, confidence in discovery of the world's farthest reaches was promoted throughout the nineteenth century, although – I will add – contemporary British travel reports contain more than just bravura and national aggrandisement. Nonetheless, even after the national trauma of the failed Franklin Expedition, confidence remained strong. In 1847 *Blackwood's Edinburgh Magazine* (which had helped make Hogg a household name in the 1820s and 1830s) would still cling to the defiant attitude that, when it came to discovery, '[t]he evident design of Providence in placing difficulties before man is, to sharpen his faculties for their mastery'.[10]

The Arctic Wild

To gain an understanding of how Hogg's novella thematises the landscape as an antagonist that must be conquered, it is useful to consider the role that the Greenland Sea plays in the story. Hogg wrote at a time when the Arctic had become a popular subject of Romantic interest. The icy reaches exemplified the absolute wildness of nature in its display of sublime sceneries.[11] Both the Arctic and the Antarctic were locations for well-known Romantic-period narratives invoking sublime experiences: S. T. Coleridge's 'The Rime of the Ancient Mariner' (1798), Mary Shelley's *Frankenstein* (1813), and Edgar Allan Poe's *The Narrative of Arthur Gordon Pym of Nantucket* (1838). In these stories the Polar regions are represented as eerie and mystical climes where supernatural happenings take place and man may come undone. There are also moments of Gothic horror in

Surpassing Adventures. For example, soon after Gordon is shipwrecked off Spitsbergen (p. 248), he kills a huge she-bear that intrudes into the cabin where he is hiding. As the forepart of the bear's dead body hangs out of the cabin window, Gordon hears a strange munching sound which makes him 'more frightened than ever'. He begins to think 'nature was all reversed in that horrible clime' (p. 259). However, as is often the case in Hogg's stories, what seem like strange events can be explained as the narrator's own mind playing tricks on him. On this occasion Gordon discovers that the sound comes from the bear's cub gorging on her mother's loot outside.

The incidents in Hogg's story recall images of Arctic discovery about which the British public could read. A confrontation with a polar bear was one of the striking images connected with the young Horatio Nelson, rumoured to heroically have scared away such a creature on an Arctic expedition in 1773. Robert Southey makes much of this incident in his *The Life of Horatio Nelson* (1813), and it became the subject of Richard Westall's famous painting in 1809, later mass-produced as an engraving by John Landseer.

Hogg also borrows from travel accounts other images of the Arctic as a place of danger. Gordon's first-hand account of his time on an ice floe in the Greenland Sea shows a state of constant phenomenological uncertainty. He soon realises that the high latitude of the Greenland Sea renders time out of joint, as he loses 'all reckoning of months, weeks, or days', and the only means of time-keeping is the increasing length of his beard (p. 257). In the summer season there is also the phenomenon of the midnight sun, which makes it impossible to tell 'one time of the twenty four hours from another' (p. 266).

In their work on the history of Arctic exploration, Charles Officer and Jake Page have noted that the polar region is a place where time zones converge and time loses its meaning, so that space becomes an important dimension.[12] But, for Gordon, even his spatial orientation is perplexed as he experiences strange illusions caused by atmospheric phenomena. For example, he often observes 'hills and glens, with wreaths of snow here and there', but will 'never see them in the same direction again' (p. 267). The inability to make determinate conclusions based on his faculties of sense makes him proclaim that the Arctic is 'a strange unearthly climate' that 'has no congeniality in it with human nature' (p. 267).

Hogg undoubtedly knew the Scottish physicist David Brewster's extended analysis in *Letters on Natural Magic* (1830) concerning the optical illusions and strange fata morganas that confuse and confound the explorer in the Arctic, as Brewster's work was written as a series of letters to Hogg's patron, Walter Scott. It is almost certainly this work that Hogg was thinking of when he prefaces *Surpassing Adventures* with the dedication: 'Humbly and most respectfully inscribed to Sir David Brewster' (p. 241).[13] Hogg uses accounts of the Arctic to paint a picture of the utter strangeness of the place. Hogg is not interested in using these descriptions to aggrandise Gordon's perseverance in this alien climate, however; rather, his conceptual inability to gain control of the environment is a foreboding of how the Arctic will eventually get the better of him.

From Romance to Tragedy

Hogg is consciously using the framework of *Robinson Crusoe* to confront the myth that man can hold dominion over nature. A central theme in Defoe's novel is the remaking of the natural environment, which involves turning the foreign milieu into a liveable habitation that mirrors the structure of Robinson's home country. In the first part of the novella, Hogg plays along with this premise. Hogg steps it up a notch, as Gordon's island is an ice floe drifting in the Greenland Sea. This place belongs in the category Siobhan Carroll has termed an 'atopic space', which is any region 'deemed penetrable but inhospitable', such as the atmosphere, the oceans, and the poles.[14] Yet Gordon goes some way towards modifying the Greenland Sea to make it home. He carves out 'apartments' in his floating iceberg, replete with a fire vent and a pantry. This is an extraordinary feat, of course, and in this part of the narrative there is a conscious play with the idea of romance. Not only does Gordon refer to the iceberg as his 'romantic mountain' (p. 269), but he also imagines that he has a rapport with the Arctic landscape when he shouts into a cavern and is answered by an 'exceedingly romantic voice', as if spoken by the 'spirit of the iceberg' (p. 265). 'Romantic' should here be read in the nineteenth-century sense of 'characteristic of or befitting a romance'.[15] Icebergs had long been objects of fascination and 'formed the foundation of many a romantic tale of the middle ages', as Francis Palgrave, a historian of medieval literature, noted in an 1818 review. Palgrave even claimed that the 'translucent and attractive islands' observed by nineteenth-century Arctic explorers 'remind us at once of the mountain of adamant of Sinbad the Sailor, and of Huon of Bordeaux, and of Duke Ernest of Bavaria', which were well-known stories in medieval tradition (with romance elements).[16]

Gordon certainly idealises his time with Nancy on the iceberg as 'one of such romance, that if I could have been certified that at any future period I should escape to give a relation of it, I would have chosen to remain for the present' (p. 291). This relationship is of an amorous nature. Gordon not only names his companion after his first sweetheart (p. 262), but he also confesses to the reader: 'I loved her sincerely, I might almost say, intensely' (p. 264). When he grooms her it is to make her 'clean as a bride' (p. 288). Gordon and Nancy also sleep in the same bed every night (p. 289). The relationship Gordon develops with Nancy speaks to the eroticisation of colonised space, which is a well-known trope in English writing, as in John Donne's famous analogising of his mistress with America as a 'new-found-land', Richard Hakluyt's discourse on Virginia, or Sir Walter Raleigh's description of Guiana.[17] Is it credible that the icy world can be domesticated when other writers most often depicted it as red in tooth and claw? Hogg seems to undermine the romantic view of the Arctic in a burlesque scene where he lets his protagonist describe promenading on the ice with Nancy as if they were enjoying a stroll on a country road:

I took her paw in my arm, and learned her to walk upright. A pretty couple certainly we were, I dressed like a gentleman in my late captain's holiday clothes, and she walking arm in arm with me, with her short steps, her long taper neck, and unfeasible, long head; there certainly never was any thing more ludicrous. (p. 265)

In this passage Gordon concedes that it is preposterous to impose civilisation and companionship on a polar bear, otherwise depicted in Arctic travel accounts as one of the most dangerous predators. It is therefore hardly surprising that Gordon's endeavours to fit Nancy into the human domain become ever more strained during the course of the novella. For example, it is symbolically significant that she eventually grows so big that her body nearly suffocates Gordon when they sleep in the same bed (p. 307). When Gordon decides to take a wife from among the Norse colonists, Nancy runs away, finally realising her incommensurability with human society. Gordon's attempt at weaning a polar bear from its natural instincts is a romance with the Arctic that is ultimately doomed to fail.

In much of Hogg's work there is an underlying tension between the application of romance and anti-romance.[18] He would sometimes seem to pander to the romantic values he was expected to deliver having branded himself as a Scottish shepherd poet, yet he often also interrogates those same values, engendering a complex irony. In Penny Fielding's words, Hogg often uses the tone of 'ironic pastoral' and includes 'forms of social realism' that 'resist the popular sentimentalising of the rural poor that was common elsewhere in the literature of the period'.[19] When Hogg uses the literary term 'romance' about the Arctic and polar bears in the novella, it sounds a warning bell to the reader: it is as much of an illusion as the strange refractions of landscapes Gordon sees. Not unexpectedly, the romance comes to an end when Gordon comes into contact with the Greenland colonists, which marks the introduction of the 'reality principle' in the story.

The Greenland community is made up of white Europeans, the 'remnant of a colony of Norwegians' who have survived in 'Old Greenland' (p. 300). Having lived in isolation from the surrounding world for centuries, they represent the decidedly unromantic hardship of life that the Arctic offers. If *Surpassing Adventures* concludes with a sudden and brutal devastation of the Norse colony, tragedy seems already unavoidable through the gradual chipping away of civilised life in Greenland. When Gordon first encounters the Norse colony, it is in a sorry state. Most critically, the settlement has suffered regular attacks by polar bears. The colony once counted thousands, but there are now only thirty-one men, ten women, and seven children left, as many colonists have perished.

The colony is a realistic vision of how Arctic Crusoes would have subsisted after centuries of isolation. The colonists still keep the Sabbath and remember to pray, but all their prayers concern hand-to-mouth issues such as finding food and protection against polar bears. Furthermore, they have slackened their morals by allowing every man to take 'handmaidens' to increase the colony's dwindling numbers (pp. 301–2), putting survival above religious strictures. Life in Old Greenland is at subsistence level with the 'repetition' of endless hunting and fishing from 'year to year' (p. 310). The Europeans have been reduced to the primitive life of the Eskimo by eating raw or even frozen fish (p. 307).

This particular piece of information seems to build on the contemporary theory that the ethnonym 'Esquimaux' is translated as 'eaters of raw flesh'.[20] Eating raw meat epitomised the savage, as it was judged to be unsuitable nourishment for civilised people. This distinction comes close to Claude Lévi-Strauss' famous distinction in *Mythologiques* (1964) between 'the raw' and 'the cooked', which is what can roughly be said to separate 'nature' from 'culture'. In *Surpassing Adventures*, Hogg invokes the cultural anxiety of backsliding from civilisation. Greenland is depicted as a wilderness where even the most fundamental Cartesian distinction between animal and man seems to be transgressed. As Gordon realises when he learns how the colonists practically hibernate during the winter months: they are 'little better than the bears lying in a torpid state' (p. 310). Nonetheless the colonists seem oblivious to their sorry reality and pursue the idea of romance: they believe their country to be 'a terrestrial paradise', although Gordon judges the Greenland colony to be 'the bleakest and last abode of living men' (p. 308).

Hogg's novella is an intervention in the debate about the state of the colony in Greenland. Like other British writers, Hogg imagines that the colonists had been forced into destitution behind the wall of ice that prevents any communication with Europe, and thereby cuts them off from civilisation. Unlike in the poetry of Eleanor Anne Porden, however, we no longer find any hope that climate change would again make Greenland a fertile soil. Accounts of ice-filled water from the expeditions led by William Edward Parry (1827), Wilhelm Augustus Graah (1828–30), and John Ross (1829–33) had shown the public that there was no warming of the Arctic.

Hogg's story provides fictional answers to questions mooted at the time about the state of an isolated European settlement in Greenland's hostile climate. With Graah's examination of the east coast, it was becoming increasingly clear that the survival of European colonists in Greenland was unlikely. Hogg offers a solution to the mystery of how the colonists became extinct – which would be shortly before 1764, when a Dutch whaler found Gordon drifting on the sea (p. 241) after having escaped the massacre. As we have seen, it was often pre-sumed that Skraelings had raided the Norse settlements, but Hogg does not apportion blame for genocide on the Inuit. Instead, he recasts the fatal invasion of the Norse settlement as an attack by polar bears.

In *Surpassing Adventures* the bears embody a combi-nation of two regular features that literary historian Rebecca Weaver-Hightower has identified as endemic to the castaway-on-an-island genre: the confrontations with cannibals and dangerous animals that 'carry the island's infectious savagery'.[21] In one of the many nods to *Robinson Crusoe*, Hogg indicates that he wants the bears to fill in for Defoe's cannibals. For example, when Gordon discov-ers what he believes to be human footprints in the snow (only to learn that they have been left by polar bears), it recalls the scene when Crusoe is surprised by a footprint in the sand, which he later discovers belongs to a can-nibal. Usually the castaways in Robinsonades repel both cannibals and dangerous animals, but not so in Hogg's story. If Crusoe successfully ambushes and kills a group of cannibals with the help of Friday, Gordon's attempt at a surprise attack on the polar bears backfires, as they outsmart him. Whereas Crusoe successfully weans his companion, Friday, from the abhorrent practice of can-nibalism, Gordon fails to dampen Nancy's appetite for human flesh and she gleefully assists in the carnage on the Norse colony. Thus the savageness of the Arctic is

eventually reinstated in Hogg's story from its temporary suspension in romance – with an almost vindictive
relish – as the 'white bears' devour the colonists with 'joy
and triumph' while emitting 'growls of voluptuous joy'
(p. 314).

The destruction of the Norse colony and Gordon's
cowardly escape from the carnage stand out in stark
relief against the success of Defoe's protagonist, who
manages to save every one of his fellow men from the
island. If the general narrative drive in Defoe's novel
is to let the forces of civilisation slowly gain the upper
hand over nature, then Hogg insists on the Arctic driving
out human interference. If the colonialism of Robinson
Crusoe is the model against which we are asked to read
the story of Allan Gordon, then the latter offers a decidedly bleak view of man's ability to master and inhabit a
non-European space.

Written during the heyday of Arctic exploration, it is
impossible not to read Hogg's tale as a comment on the
confidence exhibited in public discourse. Ellen Boucher
has analysed how the survival of expeditions and individual explorers in the Arctic became symbolic for the
Victorians as a yardstick for the future 'domination of
a global empire'.[22] There is little hope for such domination in Hogg's story, as the English captain wrecks his
ship, the Greenland colony is on its last legs, and Gordon
fails miserably when it comes to protecting his fellow
men against polar bears. The white carnivores are what
Michael Engelhard has identified as the Arctic's most
recognisable 'icon'.[23] As Sarah Moss notes in a short
commentary on *Surpassing Adventures*, 'Hogg's Norse
Greenlanders die, essentially, of polarisation, fearing and

at last consumed by the frozen shapes that kill'.[24] One might say that Hogg gives the polar bears the role of *genii loci* of Greenland's hostile nature. At least what Gordon learns from the experience is that the Arctic belongs to the bears, the true natives of the Arctic, not the human interlopers.

Greenland As Analogue

We have seen how Greenland and its European colonists became analogues onto which commentators projected contemporary fears of colonial isolation and failure. The argument that I now want to propose is that Hogg analogises in his story the struggling Norse colony with the remote Scottish communities that the metropolitan public often saw as existing beyond the perimeter of modernity. This interpretation gains considerable force when viewed in relation to Hogg's otherwise voluminous output on Scottish matters and his interest in the plight of 'backward' communities, who had not experienced the same degree of progress as the southern part of Britain.

Many of the clues to the analogy are also in the story itself. For example, some of the optical illusions related to high latitudes in the first part of *Surpassing Adventures* are reminiscent of the strange phenomena Hogg elsewhere tells us he had experienced in the hills of Scotland. In the essay 'Nature's Magic Lantern' (1833) Hogg recounts how he once saw a double shadow of himself while walking the Scottish landscape. He would later discuss this vision with Brewster, who accounted for it 'by some law of dioptrical refraction'.[25] At one point in *Strange Adventures*, Gordon is left utterly perplexed at the shape of a figure he sees from the top of his iceberg (p. 274). The figure disappears and no other humans will show themselves for weeks, so it is never known if this sighting is a real person or the transposition of his own image. The description is not unlike the 'airy resemblance' Hogg had observed in the hills of Scotland during 'particular states of the atmosphere'.[26]

The analogy between Greenland and Scotland first becomes apparent in the similarity between the Norse colonists and rural Scots. Gordon realises this when he discovers how easily he can communicate with the Greenland colonists:

> I could not believe my senses that they were not speaking broad Aberdeen, or rather Shetland Scots, the tone and manner were so exactly the same; and yet, when they spoke to me, I could not understand them, though convinced it was a dialect of the same language. (p. 298)

We also learn that the benediction spoken at Gordon's Greenland wedding is remarkably similar to the ceremony as it is performed in Scotland (p. 307). Hogg is referring to the fact that, around AD 800, the Scottish Shetland Islands had been settled by the Norse people, who held sway until the islands were annexed to Scotland in 1471. In fact, Norse control had once extended to much of the Scottish west coast and the Hebrides, for which reason the Scottish antiquary (and Celtophobe) John Pinkerton claimed that the chief families in the Highlands were all 'of Norwegian extract'.[27] As another Scottish antiquary, James Johnstone, averred, it was 'from the Norse & not from the Saxon that the broad Scottish dialect originated'.[28] Hogg's patron and close friend,

Walter Scott, was also interested in the Norse heritage on the periphery of the British Isles. A major theme in his novel *The Pirate* (1822) is the survival of Scandinavian influence in the Shetlands into the early eighteenth century, a culture Scott (to some extent) equates with outmoded superstition and aversion to progress.

Hogg expands on Scotland's connection to the Norse colony when he makes Gordon observe that the Greenland men are 'much like ourselves', only of 'lower stature than Scotsmen', while the women had 'mild simple faces, all of one weather-beaten hue, very like the women of Lewis and Harris' (p. 301). The 'Lewis and Harris', which is mentioned here, refers to the name of a Scottish archipelago in the Outer Hebrides. The comparison to Greenland drawn here is not completely unprecedented. In *Travels in Scotland* (1807) the Rev. James Hall likens the smallish people from the Shetland and Orkney Islands to the short natives that Europeans encountered when they first came to Greenland (this is to support his argument that everything grows smaller in cold climates).[29] Hogg himself had made a note of the harsh climate when visiting Lewis in 1803, observing that waves 'burst into the air as white as snow' on its shores because there was 'no land to break it nearer than North America or Greenland'.[30] The statement that outer Scotland is contiguous to Greenland is transmuted into a symbolic association in *Surpassing Adventures*.

The Highlands and Western Isles were widely recognised at the time as regions of Scotland that embodied backwardness, emerging as 'a counter-exemplar to the patriotic narrative of literary, commercial and agricultural achievement presented by the increasingly prosperous lowland countryside and towns'.[31] With *Surpassing Adventures*, Hogg is not writing a simplistic allegory, but he wants to indicate a similarity between what was imagined to be afflicted colonists in Greenland and the struggling communities in the northernmost reaches of Scotland. The conditions under which remote communities in Britain existed had shocked Hogg, as his published travel letters from three tours of the Highlands and Islands in 1802–4 clearly show. For example, Hogg notes that 'poor people drag on a wretched existence in those distant glens and islands' and that there are 'upwards of ten thousand people subsisting on the dreary and distant Isle of Lewis' whose 'condition cannot be worsed unless they are starved to death'.[32] In *A Shepherd's Guide* (1807) Hogg states that it would be best if the communities living in the non-arable parts of the Highlands could be moved so one could divest 'the wild inhospitable glens and islands of a burden, which nature never intended they should bear. Where thousands of hardy people exist, doing no good either to themselves or others, but merely in order to preserve a wretched existence … and where it can hardly be said, that they even maintain the appearance of civilised life.'[33]

The sense that colonies of people in Britain had ventured too far north, where nature cannot be subjugated, may have drawn Hogg to the history of the colony in far-off Greenland. In fact, Hogg had previously used a literary sleight-of-hand to show how strange and alienating the outer reaches of Scotland could be. In an article published in 1810, in his magazine *The Spy*, Hogg gives an intentionally enigmatic description of a visit to a strange island village, the location of which the speaker only reveals to the reader at the very end. The villagers have a 'savage appearance' and their manners are extraordinarily 'simple and original'. This is partly because their village is 'completely secluded from all communication with the rest of the world during the greatest part of the year', due to 'a tremendous sea breaking upon a most rough and dangerous coast on its Western shore'.[34] At the end of the account, the speaker reveals that it is not, in fact, a colony in a remote Arctic setting, but a scene from the village of Uig, on the Isle of Skye (formerly a Norse possession). One 'could not have believed', Hogg remarks to the astonished reader, that such a community 'yet lingered on the shores of Britain'.[35]

The isolation of the Scottish Isles was also later commented upon by the English novelist Anthony Trollope, who visited St Kilda, a remote island archipelago west of Scotland's Outer Hebrides, in 1878. Employing the same metaphor as Hogg, Trollope observes that the inhabitants were 'excluded from the world, as so many Robinson Crusoes', to which he adds that 'humanity will always desire to restore a Robinson Crusoe back to the community of the world'.[36] When it comes to creating a link between fictional Arctic colonies and actual communities at home, this is also a strategy used by Anna Jane Vardill, whose Arctic prose satire was discussed in Chapter 4. In one of the episodes, entitled 'Extracts from an Arctic Navigator's Journal', Vardill tells the story of explorers who discover 'fair-haired inhabitants' with 'kindred countenances' due to 'the Welsh tradition of Prince Madoc's emigration to North America'.[37] Vardill uses the patently absurd habits and manners of the Arctic colony to make the reader reflect on traditions and customs in Britain. In other words, the purpose of placing a 'British' colony in an alien locality is to expose absurdities at home by creating a prolonged simile in which the subject of satire is described in terms of a different setting. Hogg also points to an ancestral kinship between the visitor and the Arctic community to provoke the reader to see a correlation between the isolated Greenland colonists and conditions at home. However, Hogg's satire is much darker than Vardill's burlesque high jinks; it invites readers to pity the Greenlanders rather than laugh at them.

In *Surpassing Adventures* the analogy between the Greenland colonists and the people in remote regions of Scotland can perhaps usefully be seen as belonging to the intellectual movement in Scottish writing that Murray Pittock has coined *fratriotism*. By this is meant 'the performance of nationality displaced into a reading of the other', which would manifest itself as sympathy for other distressed peoples – whether in the form of cultural or political support – who function as stand-ins for Scottish people.[38] Pittock's discussion is focused on colonial settings and dispossessed nations, but I will argue here that Hogg encodes the failing Greenlanders, whose extinction was regularly the topic of discussion, to serve as a stand-in for Scottish predicaments. He uses their imagined hardships to extrapolate a lesson about the contingencies of life in isolated communities.

To conclude this analysis of *Surpassing Adventures*, we may remind ourselves that Hogg uses the Robinsonade as his literary vehicle. This is significant because *Robinson Crusoe* is one of the founding narratives of colonial storytelling, in fact its prototype. Defoe's story is

commonly understood as an allegory of how civilisation and social order can successfully be transplanted to
remote and isolated parts of the world. Like Defoe's original, Robinsonades usually show us that a coloniser (or
colonisers) can master both the new lands and its inhabitants. As I have argued, Hogg's protagonist falls short
on both counts. Greenland ultimately proves destructive
for the settlers, who are devoured by the polar bears, the
real masters of Greenland. *Surpassing Adventures* was the
first attempt at writing a Robinsonade on ice, predating
both Percy Bolingbroke St John's *The Arctic Crusoe: A
Tale of the Polar Sea* (1868) and William Gordon Stables'
Crusoes of the Frozen North (1901). These tales showed
the pluck and bravery of British heroes while catering
to a public enamoured with tales of Artic travel. In this
company, Hogg's tale is an anomaly because it hits out at
the triumphalist British hopes for mastering the Arctic,
as this chapter has shown.

I have proposed that Hogg's story contains a narrative
doubling: he chose the supposedly struggling colony in
Greenland as an analogue to diminished rural lives in the
far northern corner of Britain. By writing a story about
exploring unknown parts of Greenland, Hogg makes it
possible to give readers an adventure story (with all its
hyperbolic and overblown charms), while also reflecting seriously on communities whose very existence is an
anachronism in the modern world. As we have seen in
previous chapters, seizing on the fate of the Greenland
colonists became a way to mirror contemporary concerns.
Hogg was not the only one to compare Greenland, which
was often perceived as disallowing the inhabitants from
participating in civilisation, to the harsh environment

of northern Scotland. Thomas Babington Macaulay, for example, later suggested that a civilised English traveller to the Highlands would 'endure hardships as great *as if he had sojourned among the Esquimaux* or the Samoyeds'.[39] By transposing a Scottish problem to Greenland, Hogg could avoid the romanticised view of rural Scotland his readers often expected him to deliver.

7

Arctic Adventure Tales
Science and Imperialism

~

In 1878 a writer in *Lippincott's Monthly Magazine* appealed to 'the antiquarian, historian, or even novelist' to take up the mystery of the lost Greenlanders – as there is 'no ghost story like this in literature' – and investigate if they had 'emigrated in a body northwards' and were now 'living at the pole'.[1] The reference to the North Pole reflects the commonly held geophysical theory that the area around the North Pole had several unknown islands and a temperate climate. That the colonists could have escaped from Greenland to higher latitudes was therefore held as a plausible explanation for their disappearance. If the migration of the Norse Greenlanders was long upheld as historical theory, it was an idea ripe for literary exploitation. Indeed, numerous adventure stories about hidden Viking societies were published in the late nineteenth and early twentieth centuries.

It is the aim in the first half of this chapter to introduce the migration theory, including the hypothesis of a navigable sea around the North Pole (often referred to as the Open Polar Sea). I will then examine how fiction writers drew on contemporary geophysical and geoclimatic science to create what I shall coin the 'lost colony' story. In this type of story it is imagined that Greenland settlers had vanished from Greenland to migrate further north, or that Vikings explorers in other ways had explored the polar regions and found a liveable haven there. The literary works in question did not constitute a tight-knit genre, but were a subcategory of the popular 'lost world' / 'lost races' adventure tales, in which explorers come upon a previously unknown world inhabited by a race of people unfamiliar to the outside world. These fiction stories had their heyday between the 1870s and the 1920s.[2]

In adventure fiction of the period, the excitement of exploring unknown reaches and discovering remote peoples often shades into imperialist fantasies of domination and possession. It is this aspect of the 'lost colony' stories which will be addressed in the second half of the chapter. In some of the 'lost colony' stories the colonists are represented as having 'gone native'. Unlike in Hogg's story, however, there is little sympathy for their misfortune; the Norse people function primarily as a foil for a fantasy in which explorers prove themselves the new lords of the Arctic.

As a case study I analyse the American writer Fitzhugh Green's *ZR Wins* (1924), a novel published for the popular market. The story concerns the discovery of the lost Greenland colonists, who now inhabit a secret land in the Arctic. The novel was written with the purpose of canvassing support for Arctic exploration, and it is a good example of how fiction for the popular market could serve as handmaiden of an imperialist programme.

North Atlantic Migrants

Before we examine the 'lost colony' adventure story we must look at the Norse settlers' alleged migration from Greenland. The theory was based on scattered historical clues and spurious ethnological observations. In 1637 Bishop Gísli Oddsson gathered what he considered useful historical notes from documents in the library archives at Skálholt, Iceland, which he submitted to a manuscript. In the entry the bishop writes for the year 1342, he includes the following information: 'The inhabitants of Greenland abandoned the true faith and Christian religion of their own accord and after having laid aside all good customs and true virtues turned towards the people of America.'[3]

This tale of a westward migration and 'going native' cannot be a verbatim transcription of a document written in or shortly after 1342, which the Icelandic bishop found, since the designation 'America' would not have been in use at the time. Perhaps a later scribe, or Gísli himself, is offering a translation for another term such as 'Vinland'. In any case the entry was frequently cited as evidence of the settlers' migration from Greenland, although some commentators reasonably argued that 1342 must be a scribal error for 1432, which would fit better with the known timeline of the colony's demise.[4]

Fast-forwarding to the eighteenth century, the possibility that the European Greenlanders could have migrated elsewhere was raised again by the French Jesuit priest Pierre-François-Xavier de Charlevoix, who was given a royal commission to survey the boundaries of the former French colony of Acadia (which covered parts of eastern Quebec) in the early 1720s. In the third volume of his famous account *Histoire et description generale de La Nouvelle France* (*History and Description of New France*) (1744) he describes the natives he met in Labrador and Newfoundland, noting that they had a distinctively fair complexion as well as blond hair and beards, for which reason he was persuaded that they descended from the Europeans in Greenland.[5] Purely based on Charlevoix' written testimony, the Dano-Norwegian antiquary Erik Pontoppidan conjectured that these Eskimos probably retained 'the ancient Norwegian dialect, such as the Icelanders now speak', and it was only because 'the good father Charlevoix had not so much knowledge of the Norwegian language' that he failed 'to examine whether his supposition were true'.[6] Pontoppidan's armchair speculation shows us not only how such anecdotal information was readily accepted but also how it could be embellished with further inferences.

The theory that the European settlers had found a new home on the American continent was supported by Royal Inspector of South Greenland Hinrich Rink. In his collection of Inuit folklore, *Tales and Traditions of the Eskimo* (1866, Eng. trans. 1875), he relays information received from German missionaries in Labrador about the mysterious Tunit. Rink conjectures that the Tunit might be Norse Greenlanders because they were said to live in stone houses, which would indicate 'ancient settlers of a European race'.[7] The theory that Norse people built these houses found support as late as the 1920s, but this has been abandoned as most researchers believe the Tunit referred to in legend were from the Paleo-Eskimo culture known as the Dorset.[8]

In the late nineteenth century Harvard Professor Eben Norton Horsford presented another theory of migration, addressing what he called the 'unsolved problem' of Norse Greenland's depopulation. Again the disappearance of the Norse colony was explained as a vanishing into 'nativeness'. Horsford argues that the colonists had migrated in substantial numbers to live on the shores of the Charles River in New England, where they intermixed with 'Indian tribes' rumoured to exhibit traces of 'Norse life, ethnological features, and language'.[9] Horsford's claims must be seen in relation to his attempt to provide the continent with a white history. Like other nineteenth-century writers he wanted to link America's roots to Norse forefathers. The focus on the Norse people's Pre-Columbian conquest was based on an argument in favour of ethnic Teutonism. As Edward Watts has recently shown, the argument found considerable traction at the time.[10]

The historical theories of migration and resettlement were worked into tales published for the popular market. In James Otis Kaler's *The Boy Explorers: The Adventures of Two Boys in Alaska* (1895), for example, the San Francisco youths Raymond and Spencer Manning discover Vikings in the interior of Alaska.[11] Kaler's placing of Vikings in Alaska may not be coincidental, I will contend. The United States had acquired Alaska from Russia in 1867, and he enables a reconceptualisation of this new American land as one already heroically conquered (not just bought for money) by America's ancestors. The trend was continued in the Nova Scotia–born author Howard Lewis Dodge's *Attraction of the Compass, or The Blonde Eskimo* (1912), in which a journey up the Yukon River reveals the secret land of Tapond in a volcano-warmed region of Alaska, where the protagonists encounter a population of Norwegian origin.[12] The Canadian-born writer Arthur Stringer places a community of Norse descendants in an undiscovered Alaskan valley in *The Woman Who Couldn't Die* (1929).[13] In Stringer's novel David Law, a Scottish youth, joins a small group of explorers to look for a Norse princess frozen in an ice block a millennium before in an undiscovered Alaskan valley. The gifted Dr Pareso successfully revives the princess, which we may read as an apt metaphor for the desire to recuperate the Viking legacy of the Arctic.

Most important for enabling fiction about Arctic colonies was the notion of an Open Polar Sea theorised to exist north of Greenland. The Open Polar Sea was believed to be surrounded by a ring of ice called the Palaeocrystic Sea where contemporary Arctic explorers often got stuck. In the majority of the 'lost colony' novels Viking descendants inhabit fictional islands with temperate or warm climates. The belief that the North Pole was surrounded by ice-free waters was a chimera dating back to at least the fourteenth century, but most authoritatively depicted from the late sixteenth century on the maps by the influential Flemish cartographer Gerardus Mercator and his successors. Several arguments were offered in support of the Open Polar Sea, including the many months of sustained sunshine during the Arctic summer, a greater depth of the Arctic Ocean preventing the water from freezing over, and the influx of warm currents flowing north between Greenland and Spitsbergen.[14]

One of the most vocal nineteenth-century propagators of the Open Polar Sea was the American adventurer Elisha Kent Kane, who, in concord with other supporters of the theory, held that the climate in the highest northern latitudes was temperate.[15] Arctic explorer Isaac Israel Hayes, who had travelled with Kane, would in 1860 venture out on his own search for an ice-free polar basin, which he later described in his popular travel account *The*

Open Polar Sea: A Narrative of a Voyage of Discovery towards the North Pole (1867).

It is worth noting that the search for this non-existent body of water was made possible partly with the help of the Inuk Hans Hendrik (whose Greenlandic name was Suersaq). Hendrik was hired by both Kane and Hayes as a hunter so the crew would not endure the hunger experienced by previous expeditions. The Open Polar Sea, however, was a Western fantasy with no basis in any Indigenous knowledge of the Arctic. The relatively limited role Hendrik and other Inuit were allowed in the fantasy project is reflected in Hayes' disapproving comments about him and other Inuit throughout his travel accounts.

Fortunately, we have Hendrik's own published account of the travels with Kane and Hayes, which gives us an Inuk's perspective on his important contribution to the expeditions and the haughtiness of his American employers.[16] A criticism Hayes raises against the Inuit is that they kill each other through stealthy ambush or other hidden attacks: they 'have not had ingrafted upon them some of the aggressive customs of the old Norsemen, who, from the ninth to the fourteenth centuries lived, and fought in Southern Greenland'.[17] Evidently Hayes finds something to admire in the old northerners' direct and honest (if bellicose) nature. Aggrandisement of the Norse ancestors was evident in much writing at the time. For instance, it was believed that the Norse Vikings had ably navigated latitudes in the Arctic, even if modern explorers often had to rely on Indigenous people, who had experience with the icy seas.

The theory of a temperate climate around the North Pole encouraged much speculation about the possibility of Norse habitations. For example, in an 1869 article, the geographer Thompson B. Maury surmised that it may be possible within the Arctic Circle to find a 'dwelling upon some of the islands or shores of that sea' where 'some fragment of our race, wafted thither by these mighty currents we have heard of, whose cry of welcome is yet to greet the mariner who finds them'.[18] In 1877 the *Irish Church Advocate* seized on the notion of an open sea north of Greenland as a solution to the mystery of the lost colony: 'If the North Pole be ever reached, there dwelling on the northern frontier of Greenland, the descendants' lost colonists shall be found.'[19]

The scientific speculation about a colony in the Arctic was the premise of a literary tale published just a few years later. The British-American author Frederick Whittaker's short story *The Lost Captain; or, Skipper Jabez Coffin's Cruise to the Open Polar Sea* (1880) is perhaps the earliest Arctic 'lost colony' narrative that makes use of the ice-free North Pole in an adventure story. It became a popular production, printed in several dime novel series between 1880 and 1906. The story includes the discovery of 'remnants of the old Norse colonists that had escaped the treacherous massacre of the fourteenth century' by the Skraelings in Greenland.[20] They fled but found 'a secure haven within the ice-girdle that hid the open polar sea from the world at large'.[21] This body of water is imagined to lie beyond Greenland's Humboldt Glacier and the Smith Sound and is explained to be ice-free because of the sun that shines and heats up the depression in the earth's crust at the top of the world.

The scientific hypothesis on which this story relies was put to good use in several later 'lost colony' narratives.

One may say that the Arctic had been opened as a new space for writers to place lost races. This was in some sense the answer to an increasing sense that the scope for adventure stories was being exhausted. In his best-selling adventure novels, *King Solomon's Mines* (1885), *She* (1886–7), and *Allan Quatermain* (1887), Henry Rider Haggard lets adventure unfold on the African continent, which still had blank spots on the map. However, these places were becoming fewer, not least because of the onward march of European imperialism. In an 1894 article Haggard predicts that the 'ancient mystery of Africa' will soon be fully explored, for which reason one may wonder if 'the romance writers of future generations find a safe and secret place … in which to lay their plots?'[22]

Around the time Haggard posed this question, the biographer Jesse Page provided what came close to an answer in *Amid Greenland Snows, or, The Early History of Arctic Missions* (c.1893): whereas the mystery of Africa is 'shrinking year by year, and the day is not far distant when the flags of the European nations shall wave over every province of the land … the shadowy regions of ice which girdle the North Pole' remain mysteries to be explored.[23] The collusion of geophysical speculation and the idea of a Norse 'lost colony' is discussed next.

'Lost Colony' Fiction

Thomas D. Clareson has observed that the fantastic plots of 'lost race' stories generally stood on the foundation of contemporary popular science that enticed the public.[24] Such is the case with the 'lost colony' narrative. The strategy of encircling fictional lands within real geography is not new to storytelling, of course, as it occurred in ancient Greek texts, where references to the Adriatic would mix with tales of mythical places.[25] In the nineteenth-century 'lost colony' tales, known maps of northern latitudes can be seen to segue into fictional geography. Writers of 'lost colony' fictions often include rather detailed information on travel coordinates and ice formations in the Arctic; and when it comes to placing conjectural lands beyond explored space, writers tether their imaginations to scientific possibility.

The stories would often dovetail with the interest in actual Arctic exploration followed in the press. An example I will mention here exemplifies how these adventure stories appealed to public interest (although it features an Indigenous Polar race rather than descendants of Norsemen). This is *Andrée at the North Pole, with Details of His Fate* (1899), in which the American dime novel writer and lecturer on glaciology Julius Warren Lewis envisages the North Pole as a temperate region placed within the Open Polar Sea. He situates a race of Polar people on an island heated by a combination of the Gulf Stream and volcanic activity.[26]

The novel takes its starting point in a current event: the disappearance of the Swedish explorer Salomon August Andrée, who left to seek the North Pole in a hot air balloon with two companions in July 1897. The three men were not heard from again (the world had to wait until 1930 when it was discovered that the company had perished on White Island, east of Spitsbergen). Lewis wrote his fantasy of Andrée settling in with a 'lost colony' at a time when the expedition could still conceivably be alive. This exploitation of the frenzied media interest in the missing air balloon would hardly be considered ethical today.

Travelling by balloon was a solution for entering the unknown space near the poles, shielded from the world outside by a ring of impenetrable ice. The 1820 novel *Symzonia: A Voyage of Discovery* is a tale about a visit to a utopian society under Antarctica. Reaching it is fraught with danger, however. One of the shipmates initially warns against sailing headlong into ice-filled waters as 'the ice might close upon us and prevent our return to our country', as it once did for the 'colony in Greenland'.[27] Often extraordinary circumstances are needed to break through the ice barriers real-life explorers encountered on their northbound journeys. In Harris Burland's *The Princess Thora* (1904) the combination of a storm and an earthquake takes a ship of explorers through the wall of ice to reveal 'open waters ... as far as the eye could reach'.[28] Burland adds much geographical information to establish a plausible locus for the story. For example, we are told that the temperature rises to 70°F (*c*.21°C) in these regions and an inhabited island with a colony of Europeans is reached around the latitude of 89°.

Another novel that takes its departure in the assumed existence of an 'unfrozen sea' is Albert Sidney Morton's *Beyond the Palaeocrystic Sea* (1895).[29] The story is framed by the discovery in Greenland of a manuscript which contains the diary of Pierre Vacheron from New Orleans. He had come upon Nikiva, a city placed on an island in the Polar Sea, northeast of Smith Sound. The habitation was founded around the year 900 by 'Norse men, those hardy, restless wanderers'.[30] The descendants of these explorers had originally tried to reach Greenland but happened to enter 'open water and there found a current that drove them northward'.[31] The climate on the island is described as having a three-month summer with average temperatures of 60°F (c.16°C).[32] Here, as in many of the 'lost colony' tales, there is an attempt to construct a plausible setting, based on theories of polar climate, as well as oceanographical and geological conjecture. In this way they differ from the science fiction of other tales like Arthur Conan Doyle's *The Lost World* (1912).

William Huntington Wilson's *Rafnaland* (1900) is the story of a Norse people living on warm polar islands, at 89°N 24'W (i.e. only a few miles from the North Pole). Wilson's novel demonstrates that the Open Polar Sea motif was still used for literary purposes at the turn of the century, although the theory had come under pressure after the Norwegian explorer Fridtjof Nansen, on his journey to the North Pole of 1893–5, confirmed that polar ice prevented ships from proceeding north of Franz Josef Land. Rafnaland is made liveable by volcanic activity that heats a series of islands.[33] The geophysical theory of a volcano on the Pole goes back to the Flemish cartographer Gerardus Mercator's depiction of a black rock (*rupes nigra*) placed in the middle of the magnetic North Pole. The idea found its most famous literary manifestation in Jules Verne's two-part novel *Voyages et aventures du capitaine Hatteras* (*The Adventures of Captain Hatteras*) (1864–6), in which, as Terry Harpold has argued, Verne produces 'a sly mixing of fictional and extrafictional orders'.[34]

In a similar way, 'lost colony' fiction often relied on scientific and geographical conjecture to open an imaginative space for alternative history writing on the continued existence of Norsemen/Europeans in the Arctic. In this respect polar lands with an active underground became almost de rigueur in 'lost colony' stories. For this, there was the analogy of the hot springs and volcanic activity known to heat up Iceland, placed just south of the Arctic Circle. In Whittaker's *The Lost Captain*, the migrants from the old Greenland colony now live on geothermally heated islands.[35] In David Lawson Johnstone's *The Paradise of the North: A Story of Discovery and Adventure around the Pole* (1890, illustrated edition 1893) explorers discover the volcanically heated land of Islöken, inhabited by a Norse population who speak a dialect of Icelandic. Islöken has plentiful crops and animals and it is 'ever mild, and occasionally even hot'.[36] Among stories not already mentioned, there are also Viking communities in a temperate land near the pole in Ernest Western's (writing as the narrator Captain E. M'Bride), *Ninety North* (1899), Reginald Wray's (pseudonym of W. B. Home-Gall), *Beyond the Northern Lights: A Tale of Strange Adventure in Unknown Seas* (1903), Fenton Ash's *In Polar Seas: A Romance of Adventure in the Frozen North* (1915–16), Paul Hotspur's *Treasures of the North! A Gripping Romance of Peril & Adventure in the Arctic* (1927), and the anonymous *The Lost Vikings: A Long Yarn of the Arctic Regions* (1928).

Arctic Empire

In 'lost colony' fiction it is imagined that the Norse people were either settlers from Greenland who had migrated to a land near the Pole, or a legion of Vikings who had found a temperate land on one of their indefatigable explorations. In both cases there was a sense that the Norse people had been brave conquerors of the world. Indeed, expansion of the nation is endemic to the adventure novel of the late nineteenth and early twentieth centuries. As Robert T. Tally Jr argues, the popular tales of discovery frequently participate in 'a sort of imperialist project, as they serve to explore, identify, and incorporate foreign spaces and experiences, ineluctably forcing them into the general reservoir of knowledge and power in the metropolitan center'.[37]

In accordance with this, how the Arctic became an imaginative space for imperial thinking will command our attention in the rest of this chapter. I will first show how British and American commentators posited their nation as heir to the Viking adventurers of the past. Then I will discuss the same idea in relation to the textual interactions that took place with the popular readership in adventure fiction. What is legible in the 'lost colony' stories, I argue, is an ideological double inscription: the Scandinavian ancestors are both conquerors of the past who must be admired for their bravery, *and* primitives who must now be ruled/see themselves surpassed by Britain or America as the new discoverers of the Arctic.

In Chapter 5 we saw how British writers were convinced that the mysterious Arctic would be fully explored by British mariners, especially in connection with the resumption of the Admiralty's polar expeditions of 1818. In the course of the nineteenth century this sense of manifest destiny gathered momentum and was sometimes explicitly tied to the notion that British explorers were heirs to the old Scandinavian travellers who had dauntlessly explored the Arctic. An 1859 article in the *Illustrated London News* glosses over the national shame of the failed

Franklin Expedition by praising Sir John Franklin for his explorative bravery, which is 'an instinct that courses in our blood, palpitates in our pulses, and forms one of the main elements of the strength and glory of the nation'.[38] With this effusion of Victorian jingoism, the article claims that courage to venture out was inherited from 'the Sea Kings, our old Danish and Scandinavian ancestors', and it is therefore incumbent upon the British to reveal 'the gloomy secrets of the Arctic and Antarctic Circles'.[39] In 1865 the Royal Navy admiral and Arctic explorer Sherard Osborn proclaimed, with reference to the Norsemen's establishing a 'Scandinavian colony in Greenland', that the colonial impulse and dominion of the seas had 'passed … into England's hands and with it that same daring love of the difficult and unknown which had led the Viking from conquest to conquest'.[40] This illustrates a sense of a blood-based inheritance from the old Scandinavians, whose triumphs England could both claim and reproduce. In these terms the exploration of the polar regions represented a continuity with the past, an ideological imperative, and the nation's ethnic destiny.

The Vikings' widespread conquests around the world are seen as a harbinger for Anglo-American imperialist destiny. In a presidential address to the Royal Geographical Society of 1894, Clements R. Markham claims that Robert Peary's exploration of northern Greenland 'put the finishing touch to the long tale of heroism and constancy'. In fact, the 'romantic story of the Norsemen has been succeeded by the splendid work of Davis and Baffin, followed by the voyages of Ross, Inglefield, Kane, Hayes, Hall, and Nares, and by the sledge journeys of Beaumont and Lockwood'.[41] A history book, published in 1883 for the popular market by the prolific writer W. H. D. Adams, begins with the Norse people colonising Greenland (and discovering America) and continues to celebrate British conquerors such as William Hudson, Francis Drake, and Henry Morgan, in whom 'we find the same broad features of character which marked their forerunners, the Norse vikings, – the same indomitable will, the same restlessness, the same adventurous spirit, the same brilliant daring by Shore and Sea'.[42] Such sentiments hint at the trope of *translatio imperii* – that is, the belief in the transfer of empire, according to which world leadership moved from one people to the next with the dawn of a new age. The Vikings' mantle as conquerors of the Arctic regions was now, by heritage, given over to a new imperial people who spoke English.

In the United States, a rising power, such ideas were echoed and mixed with the idea that America was both established and determined by its heritage of Norse Teutonism. In an 1869 article entitled 'The Ante-Columbian Discovery of the American Continent, by the Northmen', F. Boggild nominates the 'Northman or Scandinavian race' as the stock from which 'the old English (less correctly called Anglo-Saxon) race has sprung'. He adds that 'the very qualities which were so displayed by the daring, adventurous men, who from Iceland and Greenland, went over to this Continent [America]' are the same that have 'raised the Englishmen and Anglo-Americans to the prominent rank they hold among the nations of the earth'.[43]

With respect to American discourses at the turn of the century, the practices of exploration and imperialism were often complementary, if not occasionally mutually constitutive. Although it was of no immediate commercial importance, the North Pole offered an ideal place for the United States to fulfil an expansionist dream and see itself as an imperial power that could compete with the old European empires. In Robert Peary's 1903 address to the National Geographic Society (his primary financier) he appeals to 'patriotism' and 'the obligations of our manifest destiny' when it came to reaching the North Pole.[44] Arctic exploration was not only about international prestige. Peary later proposed that the United States had a legitimate claim to the northern part of Greenland because American explorers, including Kane, Hall, Hayes, and Greely, as well as his own expedition of 1898–1902, had explored and discovered parts of Greenland where no other Western power had been.[45]

The intricate connection between Arctic discovery and new empire is present in many 'lost colony' stories. These were primarily stories supportive of prospective national achievement. In Johnstone's *The Paradise of the North* the fictional Randolph Torrens Expedition comes upon the Norse population living only eighty-three miles from the geographic North Pole. Standing on the very spot that is the magnetic North Pole, one of the expedition members exclaims: 'The whole world, so to speak, is under our feet and, my friends, we are British!'[46]

There is also an imagined taking of the North Pole, this time on behalf of the United States, in William Huntington Wilson's *Rafnaland* (1900). In this novel the Kentuckian protagonist recalls how the colony of Viking descendants helped him to plant the Star-Spangled Banner on the top of the pole: 'my heart beat fast to see the flag of my country waving there' before 'the flag of any other country' would be seen in this spot.[47] This event is a key moment in the novel and is accompanied by a full-page illustration. It is not coincidental that the publication of *Rafnaland* coincided with Peary's efforts to reach the North Pole in 1900. The novel thus capitalised on the intense public interest in polar expedition and hopes of national accomplishment.

If it is generally accepted that the novel, as a form, was an instrument for establishing a national consciousness, as Benedict Anderson would have it, it was also one of the tools for constructing a sense of national aspiration. A novel like *Rafnaland* must be seen, I will argue, as a text that functions as a mediating agent of modern imperial culture and capitalist globalisation. John Rieder has argued that science fiction tales of voyages and encounters emerged as a response to the closing of frontiers when Western imperial expansion had reached maximum extension.[48] If the 'lost colonies' were located in an imagined and yet plausible geography, the stories were nonetheless productive of imperial space, or at least gave a northward direction to imperial conquest by bringing the idea of a temperate Arctic into the orbit of colonisation. The stories also 'whitewash' the Arctic insofar as the idea of an ancestral presence there indirectly challenges Indigenous claims to land.

The idea that future US grandeur lay in the ability to penetrate the northernmost reaches of the world is reflected in the long-running Frank Reade Jr series authored primarily by the Cuban-American writer Luis P. Senarens and published as dime novels towards the end of the nineteenth century. Several of Senarens' patriotic stories included a 'lost race'.[49] The Frank Reade Jr tales

fall under the category of 'Edisonades', a genre closely
related to science fiction in which the mythopoeic power
of technology – that is, Frank's invention of elaborate
vehicles – makes it possible to travel deep into the Arctic.
As historians have made clear, the technology of transportation was crucial for conquering new areas. Daniel
R. Hedrick, for example, speaks specifically of 'steamboat
imperialism' by which ship technology enabled imperialist ventures in Africa and Asia.[50] The trust in shipping
and transportation technology as a gauge of a nation's
greatness is writ large in the Frank Jr. tales.

In *Frank Reade, Jr.'s Electric Ice Boat; or, Lost in the Land
of Crimson Snow* (1893) Frank and his crew undertake
a mission in Greenland to rescue two lost French bal-
loonists. Greenland is here described as a 'strange and
unexplored island' where a medieval rune stone was discovered near Upernavik.[51] This is a reference to the find
of the Kingittorsuaq Stone, uncovered in 1824 at 72°
57'N (i.e. the Norse colony's northern hunting grounds).
Senarens uses this archaeological discovery as a pretext
to tell a story about surviving 'descendants of the Runic
Icelanders, who centuries before had landed in Greenland
with Eric the Red'.[52] The Norsemen are a wild and barbaric people whose skin colour has turned blue over the
years – perhaps symbolising that they have absorbed the
frostiness of their environment. Greenland is represented
as an icy prairie, and the Norse people do little more in
the story than replace the 'red-skinned Indians' Frank
would fight in other stories.

In the story *Latitude 90°, or, Frank Reade, Jr.'s Most
Wonderful Mid-Air Flight* (1896) Frank discovers the
'descendants of Norwegian voyagers', who had become

'Arctic natives'. Their moral degeneration is compounded by a complete lack of communication with the outside world, which has prevented this 'remnant of a once barbaric race' from shaking off their 'warlike and barbarous' nature.[53] This reads like the common colonial anxiety of stasis, which – as we have seen in previous chapters – had been applied in various forms when speculating on the fate of the 'lost colony' of Greenland. Even in the short term, being lost in the Arctic comes with great danger, as is clear from Frank's encounter with a crew of Lascars, Danes, and Swedes, the survivors of a wrecked whaler, who have turned into 'civilized white cannibals' from privation.[54] Such fright scenarios help to create narrative excitement, as Frank, time and time again, must use pluck and inventiveness not to stall his various Arctic aircraft and thereby save his crew from suffering a similar destiny.

Frank, like the progressive nineteenth-century America he represents, must remain in constant forward motion to avoid stagnation, defeat, and moral corruption. The tragic fate of the Norse Greenlanders, unable to return to Europe, is worked into several 'lost colony' stories. In A. S. Morton's novel *Beyond the Palaeocrystic Sea* Vikings on a remote polar island, hidden behind the Arctic barrier of ice, welcome the protagonist, Pierre Vacheron, as their saviour. However, on the last page of the book, Vacheron reflects: 'the ships in which they came have long since rotted, and they have neither the material nor practical knowledge for fashioning or handling others'.[55] What elevates the new Anglo-American Arctic adventurers above their forebears is their global mobility, made possible by technological innovation.

It is also technology that enables domination over other peoples. In two later Frank Reade Jr tales, Frank's crew become involved in a civil war (a common trope in 'lost race' fiction) against competing Norse tribes, making it possible for him to show both fortitude and technical savvy. In *Across the Frozen Sea: Or Frank Reade Jr.'s Electric Snow Cutter* (1894) Frank discovers a temperate region in the Arctic inhabited by Viking descendants with 'flaxen hair and white skin'.[56] Frank wins the day for Eric the Bold and his 'good' Vikings by detonating an electrical bomb in a battle against the men who swear loyalty to Oluf the Cruel.

In *To the End of the Earth in an Air-Ship; or, Frank Reade, Jr.'s Great Mid-Air Flight* (1895), Frank comes upon a Norse people who still adhere to the life and traditions of 'Eric the Red and other Norse heroes and the Vikings'.[57] Frank and crew side with the good Jalmar, whose people are threatened by Harold the Fury's tribe, winning the ensuing battle by dint of his technological know-how. Although Frank, in these stories, intervenes in foreign affairs and directs the course of history in the Arctic, he does not use his superior knowledge to colonial advantage, such as ruling over a people or acquiring new territory for the United States.[58] Nonetheless, the technological progressiveness that Frank represents is securely anchored in American pride in historic firsts. Frank is an entrepreneur who invents the technology required to achieve exploration milestones. The Viking communities in the stories function as foils for Frank: if their pioneering navigation and shipbuilding had led them to explore these remote latitudes, they are now literally stuck, subdued at the frontier they hoped to conquer. The implication is that the mantle of world exploration and empire now belongs to the Americans.

However, one should not draw reductive conclusions about adventure fiction, which is a baggy and ill-defined genre. As critics have noted, even one of the undisputed masters of the genre, Robert Louis Stevenson, may introduce views that disrupt Western idealisations of imperial travel and may present adventurers as cynical mercenaries.[59] Yet imitators sometimes blissfully ignore these aspects. In the same way, not all 'lost colony' fictions were race-based narratives that claimed inherited rights to the Arctic. A critical perspective I will bring up here is the American expatriate writer William Livingston Alden's short story 'Very Cold Truth' (1900). It is an aberrance in terms of the adventure fiction otherwise discussed in this chapter because it is a dark satire on imperialism.

The story's narrator, Martin, is the only survivor from a whaling expedition shipwrecked after the reckless Captain Shattuck separated from the other whalers to explore northern latitudes. The crew arrive at the shores of an unknown ice-free land at the North Pole. This is inhabited by a colony of white people who speak Danish (and thus can communicate with one of the Danish sailors). The colonists have been isolated for generations and have therefore adopted the native habits of Arctic peoples, living in snow huts and eating raw fish and blubber: they have 'gone native'. In this diminished state, they become easy targets for the American captain's imperial desires. He issues orders and they pliantly obey. Subsequently Shattuck uses a racist slur, usually reserved for African slaves, about the once-proud Vikings because of the meekness to which their isolation has apparently reduced them.[60] The 'lost colony' has become so thoroughly nativised that they must be subdued to imperial rule as a matter of course. It is significant that it is the once-proud Norse explorers encountered here and not a native population: this makes the transfer of empire to the nation of America palpably clear.

Yet it is this new sense of aggrandisement that is criticised in the story. Captain Shattuck is described as 'stark mad' with his sense of accomplishment. He places himself on a stone chair carved out of a rock placed at the geographic North Pole and pronounces: 'I take possession of it [the North Pole] in the name of the United States of America in general, and William G. Shattuck in particular.'[61] He then commands his crew to orbit around him like objects in the heavens around 'the centre of the solar system', indicating that the discovery inaugurates a new Copernican re-conception of the world with an American at the epicentre.[62]

The strange ceremony recalls the symbolic acts performed when nations took possession of new land, which were continued on Arctic expeditions in the nineteenth and twentieth centuries.[63] Alden's story has the flavour of Jules Verne's later works, in which the fascination of his early years with science and discovery gives way to a new compulsion to expose greed, capitalism, and destructive ambition.[64] Reaching the North Pole is a hunt for the once-and-for-all, the absolute achievement that only has misery in store for the overachievers – just like Verne's Captain Hatteras, who had sought the North Pole to claim it for Britain but was consumed by madness upon finding it.

Fiction and US Arctic Imperialism

In the 'lost colony' novel that will now be examined as a case study, there is no reticence over colonial activity in the Arctic. The author was the American lieutenant commander and writer Fitzhugh Green (1888–1947). It is relevant first to pay attention to his professional career in the navy and as a writer of popular science articles because he was the last prominent advocate of the belief that Norse Greenlanders could be found in some hidden Arctic land. With Green, we see the permeable boundaries between actual Arctic expedition, imperial imagination, and geophysical speculation on lands and people.

At the age of twenty-five, Green, a Naval Academy graduate who had recently obtained a master's degree in science from Washington University, was commissioned as an ensign on board the *Diana*, with Peary, in 1905–6. On this journey Peary thought he spied a huge island northwest of Ellesmere Island, which was later revealed to be a so-called phantom island (like other non-existent lands that have been proposed to be placed in the Arctic, such as Frisland, Buss, or Bradley Land). However, the dream of finding undiscovered land in the Arctic stayed with Green, as we shall see. A dark shadow was cast over the return trip across the ice of Axel Heiberg Island when Green shot his guide, Puigaattoq, a trusted companion who had previously worked for Robert Peary, Donald Baxter MacMillan, and Knud Rasmussen. Green later explained that the guide had disobeyed orders by deserting him in a snowstorm. The shooting caused considerable consternation in various circles, but Green was never prosecuted.[65]

Green went on to enjoy a distinguished navy career, but also became a prolific writer, authoring several books about travel, including *Arctic Duty* (1917), *Clear the Decks* (1919), and *Peary: The Man Who Refused to Fail* (1926). He also wrote adventure fiction about exploration such as *The Mystery of the Erik* (1923), *Fought for Annapolis* (1925), and *Anchors Aweigh* (1927). Green was furthermore an active contributor on current affairs for a number of journals and magazines, including *American Mercury, Collier's Weekly, Scientific American*, and *International Aeronautics*. In 1923 he published an article in *United States Naval Institute Proceedings* that combined his interest in Arctic exploration with the new possibilities of flight. Green speculated that an air route from Europe to Asia across the North Pole would 'cut their separation from 10,000 miles to 5,000'.[66] This was essentially a revival of the centuries-long search for the Northwest Passage.

As an Arctic explorer himself, Green was excited when the US Bureau of Aeronautics made plans to let the dirigible airship USS *Shenandoah* (ZR-1) fly over the North Pole in the summer of 1924 to collect weather data. The airship suffered damage during a storm on 16 January that year, however, and the expedition was cancelled. In 1923, at a time when it was still thought the flight would go ahead, Green published an article in *Popular Science Monthly*, outlining what he thought the ZR-1 may discover in the Arctic. With reference to his knowledge of Iceland's geology, Green surmised that there may be a volcanically heated landmass in the Polar Sea.[67] In fact, this may be '*a vast continent heated by subterranean fires, and inhabited by descendants of the lost Norwegian colony of Greenland!*'[68] Green's theory was that the colonists, after connections with Norway had discontinued, found a 'land of milk and honey' where their descendants now live 'in dramatic isolation'.[69]

It was still possible to give this kind of speculation a fair hearing since the polar area was not fully explored, but such claims were now mostly reduced to sensationalist conjecture in glossy popular science magazines. Green goes on to propose that the colony could be 'far in advance of our own smug selves in culture, learning, deportment, and social refinement', they may also have mastered 'the secrets of health' and have learned to harness 'natural energy' from the volcanic underground.[70] This shows a clear utopian strain in Green's thinking, which builds on the idea that heated pockets and natural resources existed near the North Pole.

Green's article should be understood against the backdrop of the 1920s, when the United States saw significant social change, fought a diphtheria epidemic, and developed an urgent need for new energy resources. Especially, the problem with providing American society with an efficient solution for energy consumption was a salient issue in what Howard P. Segal has identified as the discourse of 'technological utopianism' – one element of which was the belief that the ability to produce energy and utilise it was the true measure of human progress.[71] Green imagines the Arctic as an epistemology of the future, from which one may learn and gain useful knowledge.

Green's articles were sensationalist and pushed the envelope of believability, but they were always grounded in scientific theory. For example, in an article published in the New York magazine *The Outlook*, in 1923,

Green backs up his idea of an unknown landmass in the Arctic through reference to Rollin A. Harris' book *Arctic Tides* (1911). Harris, who worked for the US Coast and Geodetic Survey, had inferred from observation of currents in the Arctic that a substantial landmass existed in the polar north. Green uses the Harris calculations (later found to have been based on inaccurate evidence) to conjecture that there could be 'a terrestrial oasis somewhere between Alaska and the Pole' to which the Greenland colonists may have migrated for survival when their old home froze over.[72]

When reading Green's article, it becomes immediately clear that the ethnological importance of discovering the isolated colonists is far less important than what their presence will mean for US imperialist ambition. If 'any sort of inhabitants or remains of inhabitants are discovered', Green reflects, then Norway will have a basis for making a claim to the island. Should the hypothetical land be empty and in the vicinity of Canada, Britain may claim it. The question of ownership is important, as the unknown landmass may contain riches like 'the deposit of 32,000,000 tons of coal' recently discovered in Saskatchewan, or the oil 'now flowing within a stone's throw of the Arctic Circle', in which case it would be 'a rich bone to squabble over'.[73]

A note on mining the Arctic for fuel should be inserted here. Green was not the only writer to advocate for an aggressive US policy of exploitation. The Icelandic-American Arctic explorer Vilhjalmur Stefansson, for example, wrote *The Northward Course of Empire* (1922) promoting US imperial expansion into the Arctic to secure a future power supply.[74] As a reference for what may be found, he mentions the successful extraction of coal on the island of Spitsbergen. That the Arctic contained valuable reserves was becoming increasingly clear. In 1923 President Warren G. Harding had designated a large chunk of Alaska as 'Naval Petroleum Reserve 4'. The exploitation of Artic resources by private companies (backed by state actors) is also reflected upon in some of the 'lost colony' novels. In John de Morgan's *Lost in Ice, or, When Adventure Leads* (1914), about the encounter with Norse settlers near the North Pole, the young adventurers Rupert and Edward are captured on their homeward journey and enslaved as workers in a cryolite mine. We learn that 'Russia employed its political exiles in Siberia in mining cryolite, and in Greenland and other northern latitudes', and native peoples are reduced 'to the conditions of slaves in order to toil in the mines'.[75]

Green's articles contain no such compunction about exploitation of Arctic resources, nor is this the case in his 'lost colony' novel, *ZR Wins* (1924), about an airship venturing into the Arctic.[76] With this, Green turned to the domain of fiction, but the motive for writing was the same as in his popular science articles: to whip up public excitement about exploiting the Arctic. In fact, *ZR Wins* is an unapologetic nationalist vision that holds out hope for US imperialist expansion. The novel's protagonist is a US Navy lieutenant, Bliss Eppley, whose airship, the ZR-5 (an imagined future dirigible), competes in a race with Britain, Norway, France, Belgium, and Japan to discover a trade route to Asia across the Arctic. As the plot-spoiling title reveals, the American ZR-5 naturally reaches the North Pole first and thereby cements US technical and aerial superiority.[77]

We are left with little doubt that Eppley is a spokesman for Green. Prior to taking off, Green's literary avatar echoes the idea that the Norse colonists in Greenland may have 'migrated to another happier country to the north and west of Greenland', which Green had floated in *Popular Science Monthly*.[78] Thus, when the Americans' airship drifts off course, the crew come upon an unknown land – a 'polar paradise' – heated by volcanoes. It had originally been discovered by the Norse Greenland colonists, who had visited it every year but kept it a secret from the Norwegian crown because it provided a rich supply of skins, gold, and ivory and they did not want to pay taxes. When the ships from Europe stopped sailing to Greenland, all the colonists decided to migrate to this secret land.[79]

The Norsemen had not turned into savages. The society is utopian with a democratic form of government, an education system, communal division of labour, and pacifist ideals.[80] This is not least because they have access to various forms of energy, and energy was seen as a major civilising force in American discourse of the 1920s. When the new territory is discovered, Eppley immediately raises the possibility of claiming it for the United States. There is sense in this, of course, as the fictional land contains the world's largest helium reserves and there is oil in the ground, which – it is mentioned – the Norsemen do not really need because they have learned to utilise water power and have discovered electricity. Without qualms, Eppley advocates 'the acquisition of such a remarkable colony of people' with the intention of making them US 'dependents'.[81] Yet, as he clarifies, 'we shall not violate the peace and security of the Norse colony: nor shall we permit them to be exploited at the expense of their privacy'.[82] Here was a kinspeople who deserved to maintain their independence but whose territory the United States would exploit for imperial profit.

The attitude expressed in the novel echoes the way in which Denmark wanted to gain access to Greenland's resources by making the colonists (assumed to reside in the country) part of the Danish realm. In fact, Green's fiction story more closely replicates what had been actual US political ambition in terms of acquiring North Atlantic possessions. As mentioned in Chapter 4, an 1867 report suggested to Secretary of State William H. Seward that the ongoing negotiations with Denmark for the purchase of the Danish West Indian islands of St. Thomas and St. John should be extended to Greenland and Iceland. In the report on the profitability of such a purchase, the population of Iceland is discussed as natural dependents of the United States because of their democracy, moral character, and education. The report claims that the Icelanders 'look forward to a glorious future, when a free and enterprising government shall aid them with capital and energy to explore their country's wealth'.[83] In relation to Greenland, the report focuses on potential mineral resources such as coal and cryolite. However, nothing came of these imperialist ambitions as the Senate voted against acquisition of the Danish Virgin Islands due to concerns over recent natural disasters and a developing feud with President Andrew Johnson. Subsequently plans for the purchase of Iceland and Greenland were also dropped.

In Green's novel the patriotic Eppley emphasises the 'commercial and military value' of the new land, both in regard to the 'wealth hidden in its interior' (oil) and the possibility of exerting 'strategical and economic control' of future transpolar air routes.[84] He hopes that air traffic can make a stopover there in the future if refineries could be built to serve as fuelling stations for traffic across the North Pole.[85] In Fenton Ash's *In Polar Seas*, another 'lost colony' story, coal is the major resource that the Vikings extract from the underground with reference to '[Clements] Markham and others [who] have recorded that they found coal in the extreme north'.[86]

In terms of political discourse, supporters of US imperialism in the Artic had proposed the inhabitable shores of Alaska, the Island of Spitsbergen, or other locations as 'busy halfway stations for intercontinental air lines'.[87] For similar reasons Peary argued for acquisition of Greenland in 1916 because it could 'furnish an important North Atlantic naval and aeronautical base'.[88] He was supported in 1920 by General William E. Mitchell, America's leading air strategist, who testified to the Senate on the importance of Greenland as a strategic acquisition. Mitchell continued throughout the 1920s to advocate for the use of the airship USS *Shenandoah* to explore the Arctic and establish military bases on both Greenland and Iceland.[89] This was part of a developing rhetoric about an 'Arctic Mediterranean', which E. C. H Keskitalo has pointed out defined the polar region as an important strategic area of interest for the United States as well as other nations.[90] Green's novel emerges out of a frantic milieu of US imperialist discourse; it is a clear reflection of the necessity of US expansion in the Arctic, which had become part of public awareness.

In *ZR Wins* there is also another way that the steam-heated land will be of advantage: it is to become a US national park with 'streams of tourists that will overrun the place'.[91] This correlates with a burgeoning interest in using the Arctic as an adventure resort. As early as 1893, a broadside with the title *Go North! Greenland's Icy Mountains As a Summer Resort: A Trip to the Arctic Region for Recreation* was issued with the purpose of attracting visitors, sportsmen, and artists on a trip with the SS *Newfoundland*, sailing from New York to Greenland with expert guidance provided by the explorer Frederick Albert Cook.[92] Other Arctic places had already shown their economic potential. By 1890, 5,000 tourists made the trip up the Alaskan waterways every year.[93]

ZR Wins fits a mould of popular writing Martin Green described as 'adventure narrative' that is 'the generic counterpart in literature to empire in politics'.[94] Green's novel may present a fictional and, one may say, fantastical, account of an unknown land in the Arctic, but the fiction is written with a publicist purpose, which is to influence popular opinion and further an agenda of funding the ZR airship programme. The storyline supports this by celebrating the idea of winning prestige and economic return for the United States. Green relies on the template used most effectively by Haggard: a white people is discovered in a secluded and hard-to-get-to place which hides treasure.

ZR Wins, however, deviates from the formula in one important respect. Finding treasure in *King Solomon's Mines*, or Robert L. Stevenson's *Treasure Island* (the story that inspired Haggard) is a question of taking away diamonds and gold, respectively. Importantly, the source of this wealth remains a secret to the world and what is removed from the hidden land is not to be put into general circulation. This convention was also usually adapted in the 'lost colony' novels. In Burland's *The Princess Thora*, for example, the hidden Arctic island of Asturnia is 'rich in mineral and vegetable wealth', which the protagonist, Dr Silex, wants to keep secret from Old World powers and their ravenous imperialism.[95] Dr Silex anticipates colonial annexation attempts by both Britain and the United States, for which reason he threatens, in a letter he writes to a friend at home, that there is enough steel and material for gunpowder in Asturnia to defend the land.[96]

In an essay entitled 'Reading the Future North' Johan Schimanski has pointed to fiction about utopias in the Arctic as congruent with political ideas of a utilisable and exploitable Arctic. However, the modern examples of novels he mentions are predated by the 'lost colony' fiction discussed in this chapter by several decades.[97] In contrast to the colonial sensibilities in recent novels, *ZR Wins* is an unapologetic imperialist fantasy: the polar land will be annexed by the United States and exploited for the benefit of American interests. Green's story paints white ancestors as the first colonisers of an Arctic brimming with resources, morally vindicating Western rights to the Arctic.

To provide a counterbalance to Green's dream of US exploitation of Arctic lands, one may point to *The Inheritors: An Extravagant Story* (1901), a quasi-science fiction story jointly written by Joseph Conrad and Ford Madox Ford (then writing under his actual surname, Hueffer). This is a novel critical of imperial exploitation which uses the Arctic as its example. The plot centres on the Duc de Mersch, an aristocrat who acts as international financier behind 'the Society for the Regeneration of the Arctic Regions' – the promotion of a seemingly philanthropic scheme to open up Greenland to civilisation, including the building of a 'Trans-Greenland Railway'. Duc de Mersch is a character more than a little reminiscent of Leopold II of Belgium, whose similar 'civilisation' programme in Congo Conrad would criticise in *Heart of Darkness*. He seeks to interest the British public in financing this scheme in return for 'an eligible harbour and a strip of coast at one end of the line'; in turn, the British public was 'to be repaid in casks of train-oil and gold and with the consciousness of having aided in letting the light in upon a dark spot of the earth'.[98] Some people realise that the plan is 'neither more nor less than a corporate exploitation of the unhappy Esquimaux', and it is finally exposed for what it is.[99]

To bring the discussion of fiction about Arctic futures to an end, it makes sense to take a short look at early twentieth-century utopian fiction written in Kalaallisut (Greenlandic).[100] The two first novels written in Greenlandic evince progressive ideas about the future of Greenland. In 1914 the priest Mathias Storch published *Sinnattugaq* (*The Dream*), in which the protagonist, Pavia, falls asleep and dreams of Nuuk in the year 2105, where Greenlanders are well educated and have a democracy, and the Danish trade monopoly (in existence since the mid-1770s) has been lifted. The second novel published in Greenlandic was Augustinus 'Augo' Lynge's 1931 *Ukiut 300-nngornerat* (*300 Years After*), which envisions Greenland three centuries after Hans Egede's arrival in

Greenland. We are in the year 2021, when Greenland has become part of the Danish kingdom, but Greenlanders have equal rights with Danes.[101] Nuuk is an important shipping port with shopping facilities, luxury hotels, sheep rearing, and global connections – all for the benefit of the Indigenous Greenlanders. There is also the suggestion that an American scientist has invented a technology for melting the inland ice, which would allow new settlement and perhaps reveal metals hidden underneath.[102] The dream of utilising Greenland is not dissimilar to that which Green sketches out for his imaginary Arctic land, but whereas Green promotes an imperial fantasy for America, Lynge focuses on what will benefit the native Greenlanders.

This chapter started out by examining how 'lost colony' fiction had close rapport with scientific theories and geophysical hypotheses in the construction of its settings. Writers of what I have dubbed 'lost colony' fiction operate within a narrative domain predicated on plausibility, even if the events featured in the novels are clearly fanciful. The 'lost races' encountered in the Arctic were not just made-up natives, as in many other examples of adventure tales, but communities based on historical conjecture about migration – after Greenland had become unliveable or as the result of Viking exploration, which was known to have reached as far as North America centuries before Columbus.

Thus, in some respects, fictions about finding a hidden community in the Arctic were an imaginative prolongation of what was once a real ambition of recovering the 'lost colony'. If the east coast of Greenland had given up its mystery, revealing no hidden settlement of European colonists, there was still a large unexplored

Arctic in which contemporary paradigms of geography would allow Norse settlers to hide. The combination of blank spots on the map and the unwritten pages about the Norse colonists prompted the pleasure of offering closure to remaining mysteries, and this was achieved through the vehicle of fiction.

Yet solving the mystery of what lay behind the Arctic rim of ice also prompted new speculation. In some 'lost colony' stories, we see the dream of empire projected into the Arctic when Western powers had partitioned most other world territories. Both Britain and America were major players in jockeying for empire, and they also became competitors in the race to the North Pole. For both British and American writers, the accepted blood-line of Anglo-American ethnicity – all the way back to the Vikings – became an explanation for why these two nations were destined to conquer the Arctic. The old Greenland settlement was a cultural memory that provided a transit between past and present.

However, the Viking communities encountered in the stories are often represented as teetering between kinship and alterity. Like it was believed to have been the case with the Greenland settlers, the Vikings are often shown as isolated, which has led them to culturally deteriorate. This is symbolically important as it enables the trope of *translatio imperii*: the imbrication of the past with explorers from present Britain or America shows that the legacy of the past is transferred to a new nation in accordance with the inexorable course of empire. As we see it with particular emphasis in the Frank Reade Jr tales, it is not least the deft mobility of American-invented maritime and aerial machinery that qualifies the nation as a new world leader. If imperial fantasies are clearly criticised in some texts (with a precedent in Jules Verne's late tales), in Green's *ZR Wins*, the propagandist function of encouraging investment in the future glory of the United States is central to the textual interchange with the reader.

By the late 1920s, the scientific possibility that had kept the 'lost colony' fiction afloat was all but drying up. Just a few years after Green published his novel on 9 May 1926, an American pilot, Richard Evelyn Byrd Jr, flew from Spitsbergen over the Arctic Ocean in the tri-motor monoplane *Josephine Ford*. Hard on the heels of this flyover, on 11–12 May, Roald Amundsen and fifteen other men crossed from Spitsbergen to Alaska in the airship *Norge*. Neither expedition sighted any unknown land. This rendered void the speculations about a 'lost colony' in the Arctic which Green entertained in his popular science articles. Green represents the last gasp of scientific and antiquarian paradigms that were becoming outmoded. As is often the case, the death of a belief system is frequently foreshadowed by a fervent defence of the faith.

8

Vanished Settlers
A Return to New Beginnings

~

In an 1847 article for the *Dublin Review* the historian
Edward Charlton expresses excitement about the possibility that an Arctic expedition may find the European
Greenlanders who had been 'cut off for the last four
hundred years from all intercourse with the civilized
world'.[1] He imagines that it would make for 'a singular
and an interesting scene' when you have 'the first meeting between the polished and advanced citizens of our
present Europe, and the rude uncivilized Northman,
retaining unchanged the habits and idea of the fifteenth
century'.[2] In fact, several such meetings did take place, if
only imaginatively in adventure novels. The purpose of
this chapter is to examine a dimension of the 'lost colony' fiction by which the colony's primordiality is represented as a boon to the traveller. The Norse colonists
may be backward, but they are also seen to embody the
ethnic strength and vigour of the Teutonic race. In some
important respects, this runs counter to the more impe-
rious attitude adopted in some representations, as we saw
in the previous chapter. That there were different uses
of the Viking past need not send us into a methodolog-
ical spin, as it is well known that representations of the
Old North were continually reshaped to serve a variety of ideological purposes. It is for this reason Annette

Kolodny has aptly referred to nineteenth-century appropriations as the 'plastic Viking'.[3]

This chapter will analyse Arctic 'lost colony' stories that either directly or indirectly draw inspiration from the cultural memory of the settlement in Greenland. The fictional colonies are often represented as self-contained white communities that have escaped the vicissitudes of world history. Therefore, they could afford readers with a salutary alternative to contemporary social decline. The adventurer finds himself (and it is invariably a 'he') in an invigorating milieu from which he may learn something now lost to his own world. My argument is that this meta-narrative, inscribed in many of the popular tales, must be understood against the backdrop of their cultural contexts. Thus, the chapter will interrogate how the time-worn legend of the isolated colony was harnessed to reflect public debates, on both sides of the Atlantic, about race, immigration, and the effeminising effects of modernity.

In the last subsection of this chapter I will discuss the discovery of the so-called Blond Eskimos near Victoria Island, which became a press sensation that put a final twist in the long tale of looking for Greenland's vanished settlers. The purported discovery of what had happened to the beleaguered settlers disrupted the imagination of uncorrupted white colonies and brought back the old idea that the European colony had mixed with the native Inuit in order to survive. The 'Blond Eskimo' sensation is relevant also in terms of adventure fiction, and it has not previously been examined how mixed-blood characters made their way into the pages of stories for the popular market. Again, fiction stories can function as reflections and refractions of wider cultural discourses, and the stories coincided with an emergent recognition of the Inuit for their survival skills in the Arctic.

Isolated Worlds: Utopia and Arctic Colonies

Stuart Hall has noted that popular entertainment, especially 'the male-dominated world of imperial adventure' often found in nineteenth-century fiction, can speak with a 'grammar of race'.[4] Race is certainly important in the 'lost colony' tales discussed in this section, not so much in terms of degrading non-white people, but rather in relation to how the tales create nostalgia for a past with only white people.

We have seen in previous chapters how the segregation of the Greenland colony from European civilisation was overwhelmingly assessed as negative. Yet, in the course of the nineteenth century, other voices were heard. In his seminal work on *European Colonies* (1834) John Howison entertains the thought that the Greenland settlers might be living in a haven as their isolation would mean that they have remained unaffected by the revolutionary unrest and the wars that had plagued late eighteenth- and early nineteenth-century Europe:

Had East Greenland been a fertile country, and capable of subsisting upon her own resources, her separation from the rest of the world by the closure of the ice would have been the happiest event in her history; because she was in this way protected from the evils of foreign intrusion and social refinement, and from the machinations of those self-styled philanthropists, and religious and political reformers, whom Europe has produced in such numbers within these few centuries past, and who have in general spent their idle hours in contriving how they could best sow dissension between their fellow creatures.[5]

Howison posits the colony as a remote satellite of European civilisation that had escaped the wars, the encroaching softness of over-civilised life, as well as the social dissension sown by so-called progressive philosophers who insisted that the common people should be allowed 'religious and political speculations' rather than limiting themselves to their 'daily toil'.[6] In other words, the Greenland settlers' simple life spoke to a sense of agrarian idyll shorn of modern political freethinking. In what is akin to a Burkean rejection of social revolution, the distance from the degenerative forces of change is welcomed as a positive.

Another optimistic view of isolation, but with a different political spin, was espoused by the Arctic explorer Isaac Israel Hayes. He cherished the thought of the Norse Greenlanders living independently of European governments, making it possible to exist 'quite unmolested by the outside world'. If settlers survived, they would be like 'a fragment thrown off from a revolving wheel by centrifugal force'.[7] Because the colonists were 'undisturbed by wars and rumours of wars', they could be 'as happy as any people need wish to be'.[8] The idealisation of the isolated colony that is found in both this and Howison's statement is a fantasy of a community shielded from the iniquities visited upon the Western world.

Indeed, as the century progressed, colonies that were detached from the waning centre were sometimes imagined to be conservatories of old and uncorrupted values.

For example, in *Oceana; or, England and Her Colonies* (1886), the preeminent historian James Anthony Froude speaks of the British colonies as 'other Englands ... where the race is thriving with all its ancient characteristics'.[9] Such an idealisation of the *colony* as not subjected to the corruption of modernity is visible in the stories produced for the popular market that I will discuss here.

To take just a couple of examples of how ideas of preservation are reflected in fiction, we may first consider William Huntington Wilson's *Rafnaland* (1900), a story of the young John Heath Howard, who discovers a series of Polar islands warmed by volcanic activity inhabited by descendants of Norsemen. In an echo of the Puritan pilgrims who had fled religious persecution in England, these Norsemen wanted to flee to Greenland to avoid the injunction to worship the 'White Christ' in Iceland, but a storm threw them off course, so they ended up in an undiscovered part of the Arctic. Jack Bechdolt's *The Lost Vikings* (1931) is a story of a colony of Vikings who have made their way from Greenland to a hidden geyser-heated valley somewhere north of Point Barrow (Nuvuk). The colony protects their old ways and the religion of Odin to the extent that they forbid anyone to leave to tell the outside world about their existence.[10] Thus, the quest to leave is a central part of the plot in this book about the adventurous Barrow brothers and their Eskimo friend, Ooganik.

Prominent in many of the tales is the idea that isolation has enabled the community of unmixed racial strength. This fantasy owes something to the well-known Greek myth of Hyperboreans, a race of giant people said to live beyond the North Wind, supposedly untouched by the ravages of old age and disease. Michael Bravo has shown how the ideas of a hyperborean Eden near the North Pole continued to impact nineteenth- and twentieth-century culture, including references in the occult practices of Madam Blavatsky.[11] Moreover, elements of the hyperborean myth also made it into nineteenth-century novels, where we often see a metaphorical connection between the unpolluted whiteness of ice and racial purity.[12] The fictional travel account *Symzonia* (1820), for example, is the story of the American Adam Seaborn, who finds a secret land in a cavity at the South Pole. When comparing his own Caucasian complexion to the supremely pale Symzonians, he comes to the realisation that 'I was not a white man.'[13]

In the American author P. Fishe Reed's *Beyond the Snow* (1873) the protagonist discovers the warm land of Nordlichtschein, located in the vicinity of the North Pole and inhabited by an incredibly tall people with pale blue eyes, white hair, and a skin 'so pure and white that the fairest baby would seem mulatto in comparison'.[14] Many of these hyperborean fantasies are also visions of utopian societies. For this reason, Heidi Hansson has coined the term *Arctopia* for novels that create 'a kind of dream-time' embodying 'primitivism as well as future potential' by offering an alternative to 'modern life' by imagining an isolated world hidden in the far north.[15]

The key dynamism here is the way the hidden world is distanced from the decay and degeneration outside. Not unexpectedly, in a nineteenth century obsessed with race, many such stories focus on racial hygiene. In Henry Clay Fairman's *The Third World: A Tale of Love and Strange Adventure* (1895), for example, the narrator informs us that a race living under the North Pole had come to 'possess what no other race can boast – pure blood' by virtue of being '[i]solated from mankind'.[16] In John O. Green's *The Ke Whonkus People* (1890), a Canadian navigator discovers a temperate land north of Grinnell Land. The people there have developed a healthy system of socialism, free public schools, tax exemptions for the poor, and equal rights. The social utopia is mirrored in their physical bodies, which are 'symmetrical in form and handsome in features with well shaped [*sic*] heads, according to phrenological rules'.[17]

A racist spin on white superiority was later pursued in the German pulp writer Paul Alfred Müller's series *Jan Mayen, Der Herr der Atomkraft* (*Jan Mayen, Master of Atomic Power*) (1936–8). In one storyline Mayen enters through a tunnel placed in Greenland to the Hollow Earth, where he learns that his destiny is to lead the Aryan race into the future. With the help of a solar mirror, he plans to turn Greenland into fertile, arable farmland, as well as raise Atlantis from the sea.[18] Advocacy for eugenics – and non-whites depicted as willingly subdued – links the series to the promotion of Aryan ideology in Germany at the time.

Already in 1918 the German occultist Rudolf von Sebottendorff had established the Thule Gesellschaft (Thule Society), a group of Aryan patriots who referred to 'Ultima Thule' as the capital of Hyperborea, in which a tall, blond, and blue-eyed race with special psychic powers once lived. This occultist mythology was later incorporated as a strand of Nazi ideology.[19] However, it would be a mistake to use this very particular political racism anachronistically to say something about romance novels published by British and American authors in the nineteenth century. It does indicate, however, that the myth of a people living in isolation at the North Pole was paradigmatically encoded with an idea of racial purity, which could then be given quite a wide range of ideological accents.

The 'lost colony' tales imagine a community of Viking forefathers who have remained pure by having no communication with the outside world, rather than superhuman races. The stories follow the familiar template of other 'lost race' adventure fiction, which has been described in several studies: travellers from a first-world nation (Britain, United States, or Australia) come to an uncharted part of the globe that can only be reached through considerable effort and faced with great danger they discover a hidden culture, which is often an ancient white civilisation.[20] This standard plot may be seen as underpinned by anti-modernist sentiment.

In a general overview of 'lost race' fiction, Marionne Cronin has argued that its appeal resides in the fact that it redresses the perceived consequences of modern life by allowing the visitor to enter 'an othered space that exists outside the boundaries of the modern, civilized, everyday world'.[21] Angela Poon, in her analysis of Henry Rider Haggard's *Alan Quartermain* (1884–5), argues that the fantasy of communities in isolation is born out of a desire to preserve racial integrity against enervating forces in the author's contemporary world.[22] This is why Haggard's eponymous protagonist wants to shut off the white-skinned Zulu-Vendis colony from the outside world.

It is relevant to add here that Haggard's strong and heroic Zulu-Vendis warriors share surprisingly many characteristics with the Vikings that he would celebrate in *Eric Brighteyes* (1890), his now seldom-read novel about tenth-century Icelandic Vikings, whom he calls 'our Norse forefathers'.[23] What sets the Arctic 'lost colony' narratives apart from the mould of fantasies about hidden white civilisations in Africa or elsewhere is the often clear indication that the Viking societies are the ancestral forefathers to the Anglo-American visitors who come to their world. In David Lawson Johnstone's *The Paradise of the North* (1892), for example, the English discoverer Godfrey Oliphant confidently asserts that the exploration of 'far-off Arctic land' will lead to the discovery of 'a race kindred to our own'.[24] Later, when Oliphant and his expedition first encounter a representative of a people living near the North Pole, it is a magnificent warrior who gives the onlookers a sense of 'the old Saxon or Norse conquerors of early Britain come to life'.[25]

The Arctic 'lost colony' stories share some traits in common with the myth of the superhuman Hyperborean races in nineteenth-century utopian fiction. One prevalent theme is that the Norse colonists have retained the physical excellence of the race as an effect of preserving an untainted gene pool. We see this trope in Frederick Whittaker's *The Lost Captain; or, Skipper Jabez Coffin's Cruise to the Open Polar Sea* (1880), in which the New Englander Reuben Macy discovers descendants of the 'old Norsemen that once held all Greenland'.[26] In their new abode, a volcano-heated place near the North Pole, they live 'without the advantages of civilization' and have therefore 'stood still for six centuries'.[27] But this isolation is not unequivocally a bad thing, for, as Macy and the other explorers recognise, the Norsemen are 'our ancestors', who have retained 'an absolute purity of race'.[28] In the story it is clear the old Greenlanders have preserved a primordial strength and physique, by dint of not intermixing with other races and not having surrendered to the sedate living of modern societies. In fact, Reuben does not remember ever to have met 'such glorious figures, physically, in his life' with their 'gigantic stature' and 'huge muscular limbs that told of a vigorous, outdoor life'. The old Greenlanders are paragons of racial purity:

They were all white men, the whitest Reuben had ever seen, with bright, golden hair and fierce, blue eyes. There was not a dark face or figure among them, and not a man but had the muscles of an athlete.[29]

The women are 'beautiful', 'tall and finely molded, far above the average stature of American women' with 'proud, regular features, high foreheads, straight noses', and 'firm, resolute chins'.[30] The American visitors' ancestral link to the Norsemen is pointed out at several junctures in the story. For example, it is noted that the Old Norse language is 'very much the same as English' and not unlike the way American 'country folks talk' today.[31] In this way the story stages a meeting with an ethnic past that invites speculation on what contemporary Americans have lost. The Greenlanders' strength is aggrandised in a nostalgia for a simple, active life that has vanished with urbanisation and industrialisation.

Isolation is the operative term for 'lost race' literature, and the hidden polar lands are like the secluded literary islands that Niall Sreenan describes as places where ideas of purity are often played out. The island allows 'a type of imagined biological independence which is no longer available to humanity after Darwin'.[32] For an Arctic island story in which the inhabitants have escaped the enervating racial degeneration of the outside world, we may turn to the Scottish author William Gordon Stables' tale *The City at the Pole* (1906).

The title of the novel refers to the island of Astragaard, near the North Pole, where a Viking civilisation resides. An ancestral link to these colonists is clearly indicated as the Astragaard people possess 'the indomitable spirit', which is 'the heirloom of all the Saxon race, whether British or German'.[33] The Norse people have benefitted to a higher degree than their kin because of their isolation: they have an unusually long life span made possible by operating the eugenic policy that 'the sick and the mad and the deformed' are banished to subterranean dwellings where they slave 'for the great and the good'.[34] This could be read as dehumanising, but such dehumanising practices, presented as a form of racial hygiene, are consistent with those of a Viking community which traditionally thrived on the use of thralls.

There is another reason the eugenic policy could be read as harshly utopian rather than dystopian. Besides writing fiction, Stables produced an extensive range of health guides that Hilary Marland has described as dovetailing with 'eugenicist ideas and language' regularly found 'in the build-up of anxieties about race, nation and Empire at the turn of the century'.[35] Stables' Viking colony is a fantasy of a secluded and self-determining civilisation that refuses to let itself be compromised by decline, and the colony's isolation and ability to keep eugenic measures in place yields positive results. Thus, the 'city at the pole' is a thought experiment about an alternative society that may be primitive but also, in some respects, like the proverbial City on a Hill: a beacon of hope for a failing world.

The hidden Arctic was a convenient location for alternative social worlds. This was not least because scientific hypotheses allowed for the existence of unknown land-masses and a temperate climate near the North Pole. Furthermore, Viking ancestors were known to have inhabited the Arctic. That their community may still exist in uncorrupted form because of their isolation was clearly an allure to writers who sympathised with eugenic ideas. A major driver behind the eugenics movement was the belief that modern societies were degenerating.

The cultural desire to speculate on the societal boon of distilling Viking heritage from the general degener-ative human pollution of inheritance can also be seen in other British fiction at the time. An example I will mention here is Charles Wicksteed Armstrong's first novel, *The Yorl of the Northmen; or The Fate of the English Race* (1892), in which the narrator is granted a vision of England a hundred years in the future. A feudal colony of Englishmen and Scandinavians has been established in northern England (roughly the area of the old Danelaw). Through their segregation from the rest of England, they have cultivated sound health and robust bodily strength via stringent eugenic policies.

In the preface, Armstrong explains that the novel is a reaction to the sorry contemporary state of the nation: 'We must regain some of the hardiness, the bodily har-diness of our long-ago forefathers.' He continues: '[t]he Vikings' blood must again be stirred', because 'it is our physical degeneracy, our bodily effeminacy, which is dragging us down'.[36] Like Stables, Armstrong pursued eugenic policies outside of literary narrative. For example, in his 1933 article 'A Eugenic Colony: A Proposal for South America' he proposes a colonial English settlement that could fulfil the hopes of cultivating a pure and pristine community away from the waning centre.[37] Here, Armstrong expresses unalloyed faith in colonial isolation as holding the potential for cultural and racial revival.

To make use of Umberto Eco's taxonomy of fictional worlds, the Arctic 'lost colony' narratives most often take up a position between the *utopia*, a 'possible world' that exists in 'a place that would normally be inaccessible', and the *uchronia*, a story of 'what would have happened if what really did happen had happened differently'.[38] The stories can be read as speculation on counterfactual history: What would have happened to the race if it had lived free of the vitiating changes? What is imagined in such stories is not a historical past, but what Nadia Khouri in her analysis of 'lost race' fiction calls 'a nevermore which does not seem to have totally vanished'; it reflects the realisation at the end of the nineteenth century that 'history is not a constructive dynamo fueled by a sense of progress and achievement'.[39] In other words, 'lost race' fiction insulates a part of the past at the cost of removing the larger narratives of historical change.[40]

The tales of Viking colonies in polar regions draw something from the memory of the isolated Greenland settlement and uses this memory to promote a fantasy of a purity of body and culture. They speculate on what could be if the world had been unpolluted by foreign blood. An example of this is the British author Harris Burland's *The Princess Thora* (1904), which tells the story of a colony of Normans (here replacing Vikings for their direct descendants, the Norman dukes) discovered in a hidden Arctic location.

The Normans had fled from Henry I's brutal invasion of the Duchy of Normandy in 1105 to start a new life. After first reaching Greenland, their ship broke through the ice barrier and came upon the volcanically heated land of Asturnia, near the North Pole. Living in perfect isolation for centuries, 'the best blood of Normandy' has been able to flow unadulterated, for which reason the Normans have attained an impressive physique and a constitution that is 'strong, noble-minded and intelligent'.[41] Their main representative in the novel, Sir Thule de Brie, is 'beautifully moulded as the statue of a Greek God', and his '[e]very limb was perfect in proportion and symmetry, every muscle was hard as steel, and showed clear cut under his smooth white skin'.[42] The Normans' preservation of supreme physical form goes hand in hand with the conservation of the chivalric code that was the prevailing norm in the high medieval world they left behind. So, despite bearing the mark of medieval men of 'rough natures', they have maintained 'a vein of chivalry that would have disgraced Sir Launcelot himself'.[43]

Burland's novel remains a celebration of chivalric values rather than an attack on them, as is the case in Mark Twain's earlier satire, *A Connecticut Yankee in King Arthur's Court* (1889). In the last chapter, 'The Better Life', the protagonist, Dr Silex, relishes the thought that he will enlighten Asturnia with 'those new ideas and discoveries that have benefitted the human race'.[44] Such sifting of the best of Western knowledge to a country 'rich in mineral and vegetable wealth' has the potential to create an ideal society. Thus, in this tale, past manners are seen as a better starting point for achieving utopia than the present, but it is recognised that the past needs improvement.

Most of the 'lost colony' stories are not about a protagonist changing them for the better, rather authors represent the Norse colony as a snapshot of past ethnic vigour and values from which the visitor may learn. It is through the experience of the visitors that readers are invited to diagnose what is wrong with their present society. In relation to the broader 'lost race' category of stories, Bradley Deane argues that the narratives promote an 'empowering fantasy' of 'passionate masculine authenticity' that takes the form of a 'relapse into barbarism' by letting the civilised explorers fight in simple, brutal, native battles.[45]

This exertion of masculinity has redemptive potential because it offers the possibility of the protagonist to uncover his 'true' identity, thereby providing a corrective to civilisational degeneracy. For a clear-cut example of how Vikings were particularly suitable as a historical reference in this respect, we may choose *In Polar Seas: A Romance of Adventure in Polar Seas* (1915–16) by Fenton Ash (the British writer Francis Henry Atkins).[46] Here, adventurers discover a heated 'green land' near the pole with a population of Norsemen. Once this colony is found the story proceeds primarily as a series of swordfights and wrestling matches, in which the protagonist, Hugh Arnold, is pitted against the Vikings or the half-human Borghen. On several occasions we are told how much the crew of adventurers 'enjoy' the fighting they face time and time again.

The Norse world even acts as a catalyst for the crew's Eskimo companion, Amaki. If we are presented with the common prejudice that 'Eskimos are not by nature a fighting race', we soon learn that 'all was changed' after immersion in Viking culture.[47] Eskimo companions to Western adventurers is a feature in several stories, reflecting a growing recognition of Indigenous helpers in Arctic exploration, to which I will return at the end of the chapter. Having dealt with some British fiction stories, I will now discuss some North American examples in relation to their cultural context.

Norse America

A premise in the Arctic 'lost colony' novels is that isolation has sheltered the Norse people from the West's slow but inevitable collapse. The myth of cultural decline gained sway at the end of the nineteenth century. Warning bells were sounded in Bénédict Morel's studies of psychiatry, Cesare Lombroso's works on criminology, and Max Nordau's statements on the wayward decadence of culture.

In nineteenth-century America whiteness became an ethnic touchstone for a definition of American identity in response to perceived threats of immigration and inter-mixing. According to Betsy L. Nies, the secluded colonies discovered in Edgar Rice Burroughs' adventure novels and Tarzan books 'reflect the anxieties of eugenicists in very explicit form'.[48] Among white races that appear in adventure fiction, Vikings had a particular appeal. The foundation for this was laid by the Danish antiquarian Carl Christian Rafn, who argued in a series of publications (*Antiquitates Americanae* [1837], *Discovery of North America in the Tenth Century* [1838], and *Supplement to the Antiquitates Americanae* [1841]) that the Norse Greenlanders had sailed to America and established permanent colonies there. As evidence, Rafn pointed to the round Newport Tower in Rhode Island, which he claimed was a Christian place of worship in what would have been one of the chief parishes of the Norse colony, based on its similarity to round buildings found in Greenland and Denmark.[49] The Newport Tower is known today to be the ruins of a mid-seventeenth-century windmill, but Rafn's theory was generally accepted at the time, as was his claim of a permanent Norse settlement (rather than the Greenland settlers just setting up camp for the hunting season).

Norse heritage became cultural capital in an increasingly racially conscious nineteenth-century America. There was also the widely reported 1843 find of arrows in California, 'resembling in all respects those used by the ancient Greenlanders', which added fuel to the notion that North America had been thoroughly Norse – a claim that is now discredited.[50] In an 1849 review of the slew of recent books about the Norse conquest of America, James Elliot Cabot could proclaim that '[w]e may confidently assert, that the modern New England character has in it more of the Norse than the Saxon'.[51] The idea of a pre-Columbus Norse America was reflected in two novels by Ottilie A. Liljencrantz', recounting a story of Norse Greenlanders establishing a successful colony in Vinland: *The Thrall of Leif the Lucky* (1902) and the children's book *The Vinland Champions* (1904). In the latter much of the action takes place in Greenland, from where ships sail out to America. There was general interest in America's Scandinavian roots, as several studies of nineteenth-century literary fiction have shown.[52]

Precisely how Greenland played an important role in this reconstruction of America's Norse identity warrants further critical attention. Rasmus B. Anderson, a Wisconsin professor of Scandinavian languages, published *America not Discovered by Columbus* (1874, rev. ed. 1877), in which he gives an account of how the Norsemen were the true discoverers of America and had trafficked regularly between America and Greenland.[53] The focus on America as part of a Norse empire before Columbus could sometimes shade into what Douglas Hunter has dubbed 'White Tribism', which was the attempt to circumscribe the importance of Native Americans and claim America's foundation for a white European past.[54]

No hidden colony of white Scandinavians was ever found in the Arctic. However, Dimitrios Kassis has analysed travelogues of nineteenth-century American travellers who visited the Nordic countries and found the ancestral glory they longed for at home. They came back with near-utopian descriptions of how the Scandinavians had maintained their full vigour; there was a 'systematic portrayal of the Nordic stock as extremely masculine'.[55] The reports of travels to a racially unmixed Scandinavia, also seen as partially segregated from mainland Europe, supported an American discourse of 'Anglo-Saxonism, Nordicism and eugenics that occupied an integral part of the American national discourse at the close of the nineteenth century'.[56] The adventure story's voyages to isolated Arctic islands is the fictional (and fantastical) counterpart to these real-life travel accounts.

The preservation of racial purity provides many advantages, as is made clear in one the most popular of the 'lost colony' novels, the American author Robert Ames Bennet's *Thyra: A Romance of the Polar Pit* (1901), the story of a party of explorers who crash their balloon near the North Pole. Under the icy surface they discover the Runefolk – descendants of Jarl Biorn – who left Norway in the early tenth century. The explorers note that the population appear 'perfect in health and physique, and bright with intelligence', and not a single 'stupid or evil face' could be found among them.[57] Isolated from the outside world the Runefolk have avoided racial pollution and created a utopian society of 'pure out and out democracy and Christianity'.[58]

The veneration for Norse culture, its democratic *Thing* (assembly), the masculine code of honour, and so forth would combine with an anti-modernist ideology in the United States which worked to aggrandise the roots of white America. Particularly relevant in the present connection is the antiquary Thomas E. Pickett's thesis *The Quest for a Lost Race* (1907). Pickett holds that the English-speaking people were the heirs to the 'daring, crafty, and indomitable race' of the Scandinavians, whose descendants still shape 'the political destinies of men' around the world.[59] However, he laments that this racial legacy has been vitiated by the insidious 'softness' of modern culture. To save society, Pickett therefore calls for a revival of Americans' 'puissant racial force' that is at risk of becoming 'dissipated and lost' in the present.[60] The 'lost race' of Pickett's title refers to the racial impulse that has been buried within the American nation – that is, their forgotten Norse strength.

The Viking cultures we find in the pages of literary adventure stories can be seen as the exteriorisation of what Pickett and others believed had been foreclosed and forgotten in modern man. The modern visitors confronted with the Viking colonies of the past find their heritage rejuvenated. Through the challenges of duel and combat, which is the order of the day in the Viking world, they must quickly learn to measure up to the living embodiments of the racial past. To pick an example of how this worked in practice, we may turn again to the American author William Huntington Wilson's *Rafnaland* (1900).

Rafnaland is the story of a young Kentuckian, John Heath Howard, whose air balloon crashes in a warm region near the North Pole. There he finds a contingent of Norsemen who teach him the forgotten arts of hand-to-hand combat, chivalry, and hunting. Much of the middle part of the novel is concerned with Howard being trained in *holmgang* (a Norse duel). Finally, he excels in such skills and wins axe and knife battles against the novel's antagonist, Thorkel. After Howard has proven his worth, the Norsemen want to crown him as their king. He honourably declines this but accepts marriage to Princess Astrid, whose heart he has won. By rewarding Howard with both high social acclaim and love, the novel becomes an eroticised hunt for primordial masculinity.

The battles in Rafnaland are fictional, but Wilson also wrote fiction about contemporary war in the short story 'The Return of the Sergeant', published in the widely circulated *Harper's Weekly* in the same year as *Rafnaland*.[61] This is a story about the recent Spanish–American War. It concerns an African American bellboy who steals a white officer's uniform and pretends to have fought heroically in Cuba. However, this fraud is eventually exposed. In what is a fairly unambiguous literary expression of white anxiety, Wilson's purpose with the story is to deflate the mythic figure of the black war hero. In this context it is difficult not to read *Rafnaland* as a call to white America to reassert its self-perceived inherent strength and heroic legacy as a badge of honour.

In the wider cultural discourse of the early twentieth century, one thing that was said to weaken America was the mixing of blood. The outspoken American eugenicist Madison Grant saw the danger of immigration from Southern and Eastern Europe as diluting America's Nordic legacy, claiming that 'the amount of Nordic blood in each nation is a very fair measure of its strength in war and standing in civilization'.[62] The 'lost colony' stories should not be seen as direct extensions of such ideology, but narratives often thematise the purity of the Norse bloodline, as we shall now see.

Purity and Pollution

In the majority of 'lost colony' novels the Arctic is devoid of any native population. However, when Indigenous peoples are present, they are segregated from the Norse community and make up a subordinate section of society. In Johnstone's *The Paradise of the North*, for example, Norse speakers are the aristocracy while a native people who speak a different tongue (presumably an Inuit language) have been enslaved as peasants on vassal farms.[63] In Wilson's *Rafnaland* a colonial theme is also briefly touched upon: it is mentioned that a 'strange race of people ... short of stature, with dark skins, and their hair and eyes were black' serve the Norsemen as thralls.[64] The necessary separation from native populations is even more pronounced in stories about imaginary Norse colonies outside of the relatively empty Arctic.

South America sets the scene for the dime-story *An Amazonian Queen* (1907) about a bold adventurer, Nick Carter, who comes across a race of Amazons in the South American Andes.[65] South America is not a random location; the Prussian explorer and polymath Alexander von Humboldt had famously proposed that Vikings had established colonies in Brazil.[66] In the story, the beautiful queen and the rest of the aristocracy communicate in ancient Norse – a language they have inherited from the original conquerors – while the populace, descended from the enslaved natives, speak an Indian tongue.

James W. Jackson's adventure novel *A Queen of Amazonia* (1928) also takes place in Brazil, where the explorer Raymond Lester finds himself among a people of Norse descent (the Vertaens) who face rebellion from the subjugated Quechua-speaking Sayans.[67] Racial clashes ensue and the Norse Viking army is defeated, but only because they are outnumbered three to one. Lester and his comrades narrowly escape with the white queen, Cettys. It is tempting to see the Norse colony defeated by natives in this story as a deliberate parallel to the cultural myth of the Skraelings invading the settlements in Greenland, but racial enmity is a standard trope in the adventure fiction written by Haggard and his imitators.

If natives can be a threat to the colony, a greater danger in some stories is racial mixing. In Bennet's *Thyra: A Romance of the Polar Pit*, the ideal order of Viking society is threatened by a rival, heathen Norse tribe who live under the rule of monarchy and practice human sacrifice. These enemies are allied with an ape-like race of Dwergers, with whom they have intermixed. Although Dwergers are mythical creatures known from Germanic folklore, the story presents a thinly veiled fear of miscegenation as the cause of pollution to body and mind, as well as to the health of religion and order. Bennet was otherwise known as a writer of Westerns, in which it is often the Indians who constitute danger on the frontier. In Fitzhugh Green's *ZR Wins* the antagonist in the hidden land of Norsemen is also of suspect ethnic heritage: a 'half-breed' and a 'throwback' with 'an admixture of Eskimo blood', which dates back to the time the Norsemen were mixing with natives in Greenland.[68]

Racial intermixing becomes a central theme in Ralph Milne Farley's *The Radio Flyers* (1929).[69] The aviators Eric Redmond and Angus Selkirk crash their plane in the Arctic and drift on an ice floe into a land under the crust of the earth. The land is inhabited by a race ruled by a descendant of the last bishop of Greenland. Eric becomes enamoured with the chief's daughter, Helga, after rescuing her from the violent enemy (Skraelings, or 'Innuits', as they call themselves).[70] Angus falls in love with Astroo, a Skraeling princess who is unusually white-skinned. Despite her acceptable exterior, Eric is nonetheless compelled to admonish his friend that Astroo's 'children may revert to the ancestral type'. Angus risks becoming 'the father of a lot of yellow brats like those we saw in the settlement at Disco Bay'.[71] It is eventually revealed that Astroo is of Norse blood and is really called Astrid (a good

Scandinavian name). As soon as this comedy of errors is resolved, Angus and Eric can both settle down to a happy life with their respective wives in their new world.

Racial mixing is also seen to undermine Norse strength in Arthur A. Nelson's cult novel *Wings of Danger* (1915), which focuses on the discovery of the hidden Viking colony in East Africa. Alan Severn leads a group of English adventurers who find the hidden kingdom of Valkyria, in which the inhabitants are primarily mulattos due to the Norsemen intermixing with the local population. In this whirlpool of races the royal family is now struggling, vitiated by impurity. On first seeing the nearly seven-foot-tall King Fágu, the narrator observes:

> He was white – or nearly white; but the lips were thick, and somewhere in the dark veins which stood out like cords upon the bloated face there was an unmistakable hint of the pollution of a lower race ... Clearly, the royal caste, or as it was known, 'the Mohanza' had tried and failed to keep the blood pure through the long centuries of miscegenation which had finally absorbed and swallowed up the Norse conquerors, leaving only the shadow of their former greatness behind them in their warlike customs and in the heritage of their magnificent physiques.[72]

In a plot device borrowed from Haggard, it transpires that King Fágu is a usurper, and the English explorers help install the rightful heir, Ingulf, on the throne. Since the Norse race has been diluted over the generations, it is incumbent upon the English, who are representatives of the greatest modern 'white' empire in the world, to intervene and restore the rightful order, which happens to further 'the cause of Cecil Rhodes' and Queen Victoria.[73]

Nelson's novel is an unashamed representation of the belief that the white race was the first conquerors of the world, which in turn would legitimise imperialism as a liberation of Africa from the darkness into which it had fallen. Michael F. Robinson provides an excellent discussion of this cultural paradigm in *The Lost White Tribe: Explorers, Scientists, and the Theory That Changed a Continent*.[74] This work is an investigation of the role played by the Hamitic hypothesis, which was the scripturally based theory that Aryan ancestors had conquered the world and now could perhaps be found in isolated pockets. According to Robinson, the theory of ancient white conquest played a significant role in justifying empire. As part of his discussion, Robinson includes a short reference to the sensation of 'blond Eskimos' in the Arctic.[75] This discovery falls somewhat outside of his main thesis, however, because a possible intermixing of Inuit with Norsemen would be an event much younger than the biblical Aryan migration he otherwise examines. However, the sensation of the 'Blond Eskimos' is of central interest in the present book, and the traction the discovery gained in the 1920s will therefore be discussed in the remainder of the chapter.

Blond Eskimos

As we have seen, speculation that the Greenland settlers had been defeated and subsequently mixed with the Inuit can be traced back to the early seventeenth century. The theory was given a remarkable new lease of life when the Canadian-born American explorer and ethnologist Vilhjalmur Stefansson made a splash in the press with the claim that he had discovered 'Blond Eskimos', ostensibly the descendants of the Norse colonists. Stefansson had met the Danish whaler and trader Christian Klengenberg, who told him that the 'Copper Eskimos' (named so because of their extensive use of copper tools), living on the south-western coast of Victoria Island, Canada, were unusually fair. This intrigued Stefansson, and on a 1912 mission, mainly sponsored by the American Museum of Natural History, he sought out the Copper Eskimos. The account *My Life with the Eskimo* (1913) reads like an adventure story, in which Stefansson narrates how he found the group (many of whom had never seen Europeans before) and spent a year with them.[76] He describes the appearance of this community to be 'like Europeans', which he took as evidence that he had come upon the 'solution of one of the historical tragedies of the past'.[77] The history he reconstructed was that the Norse colonists had abandoned Greenland to escape hardship and migrated to Victoria Island where they blended with natives.[78] Stefansson had studied anthropology, briefly at Harvard and later, more intensively, at Grand Forks, North Dakota. He therefore took time to measure the Copper Inuit's facial index (once used as a denominative scale for determining race) and came to 97, which was the same range as Europeans or peoples of mixed European–Inuit ancestry, whereas pure Inuit generally scored above 100.[79]

To the physiological evidence, Stefansson added that he had heard one of their songs with 'a rhythm resembling that of the ancient Norse scaldic poems'.[80] Although the Copper Eskimos would have had contact with Europeans since the late eighteenth century, these would only have been sporadic encounters. Thus, Stefansson concludes that intermixing with the Scandinavian colony in Greenland 'furnishes not only an explanation, but the only explanation'.[81] This was not what he had expected to find, at least not if we consider a 1906 article in which he held that 'the Icelandic colony in Greenland was destroyed by the Eskimo rather than assimilated with them'.[82]

Upon his return from northern Canada, Stefansson gave an interview to the *Seattle Daily Times*. On 9 September 1912, the paper ran the headline 'American Explorer Discovers Lost Tribe of Whites, Descendants of Leif Ericson', describing the discovery of 'a lost tribe of 1,000 white people' as ranking next in importance to 'the discovery of the lost tribes of Israel'.[83] Understandably, the story made front page news in an array of American newspapers with headlines such as 'American Explorer Discovers Lost Tribe of Whites, Descendants of Lief [*sic*] Eriksen', and 'Finder of New Race Returns ... Tells of Blond Eskimos. Believes They Descend from Scandinavian Glory', and the story subsequently made news around the world.[84] However, the term 'Blond Eskimos', which stuck in the popular imagination, is inaccurate: Stefansson did not claim that the Copper Eskimos were blond, only that they had red-brownish hair and beards, as opposed to the black hair of other Inuit.

Stefansson's claims were backed up by the US army officer and polar explorer Adolphus Greely, who compiled travellers' accounts of 'white' Eskimos dating back to the seventeenth century, which he published in *National Geographic*. The reports included accounts from witnesses such as Hans Egede, John Franklin, and W. A. Graah, as well as Hinrich Rink's retelling of a tale from the Eskimo language about fair-haired people at Cape Farewell.[85] One could object, of course, that the wide geographical spread of the sightings Greely listed, in effect, undermined Greely's argument insofar as the list seemed to show that 'white' traits occur naturally in Inuit populations. In fact, one of the detractors of the Norse-blood theory was the Greenlandic–Danish polar explorer and anthropologist Knud Rasmussen, who spent considerable time studying the Copper Eskimos in 1923–4. In the book, *Intellectual Culture of the Copper Eskimos*, he states unequivocally that the 'special types [Blond Eskimos] are due to purely biological conditions that are quite accidental'.[86]

Stefansson's claims about the Copper Inuit were tested in 2003 by the geneticist Agnar Helgason and anthropologist Gísli Pálsson, who compared DNA from 100 Victoria Island Inuit with DNA from Iceland, producing no match.[87] A later study of more than 10 per cent of the adult population in Greenland also found no physical evidence of Norse genes (although later European influence could be traced in 80 per cent of the population sample).[88] Thus, Stefansson was wrong, but the lack of scientific counterevidence in the early twentieth century made the theory believable.

The modern anthropologist John Steckley has written one of the most insightful accounts of the 'Blond Eskimo' sensation; one of his conclusions about what motivated interest in the discovery needs qualification, however. Steckley sees the popularity of the 'Blond Eskimo' as based on a 'racist notion that Europeans and their culture are indomitable', an idea that 'Arctic survival capacity developed through hundreds of years of Inuit cultural innovation could readily be equalled by Westerners within a short time'.[89] If a racial bias was undoubtedly present in much writing at the time, it seems that Stefansson himself thought the Eurocentric Norse colonists came to the realisation that Indigenous knowledge of the Arctic was superior to their own. In an article, Stefansson reflected on the 'Blond Eskimo' phenomenon, claiming that 'the fundamental superiority of European blood is only a European self-glorification'; the isolated Norse Greenlanders had 'slowly gone Eskimo in customs', in recognition of the fact that their survival could only be secured by mixing with the Eskimos 'through marriage'.[90]

A question that has not been asked about Stefansson's discovery is what it meant for adventure fiction. Prior to the media splash, blond Eskimos were a rarity in fiction stories, as the predilection was for representing colonies of 'pure' ancestors in Arctic hideaways. However, the British-American writer John de Morgan includes a mixed-race population in *The Strange Adventures of Two New York Boys in the Realm of the Polar North* (serialised in *Golden Hours*, 1890). This is the story of Rupert Godfrey and Edward Somers, who sail on a whaler to the Arctic and eventually manage to move up along the Greenland coast to a warm biosphere near the Pole. There they encounter 'Eskimos' who speak a quaint Scandinavian language and believe in Thor and the Norse gods, revealing a past intermixing of races in Greenland. These Scandinavian Eskimos are 'tall and slender, with oval faces, very different to the squat figures and stupid, expressionless faces of the

Western Eskimos, or the Siberian Aborigines'.[91] After the buzz caused by Stefansson's discovery, an opportunity to capitalise on the sensation led to a republication of John de Morgan's story, as it had now gained unsuspected topicality. The nearly twenty-five-year-old story was reissued in book form under the new title *Lost in the Ice; or Where Adventure Leads* (1914).

Other authors who wrote for the juvenile market were also quick to jump on the extraordinary discovery. The American author Howard Lewis Dodge had published his 'lost colony' adventure tale *Attraction of the Compass: A Romance of the North* in 1912 – that is, just before the 'Blond Eskimo' sensation broke. However, in the slipstream of the huge press interest in Stefansson's discovery, he slightly revised the book and reissued it under the new title *Attraction of the Compass, or The Blonde Eskimo* (1916).[92] The novel features a Norse civilisation that has survived in a volcano-warmed region of Alaska. The chief of the Norse people is Eric, a 'pure Norwegian, a descendant of a band of pirates who lived in the day of Eric the Red'. However, we also learn that 'part of his tribe were mixed with Eskimo, as well as other nationalities'.[93] There is also talk of several 'uncivilized tribes of blond Eskimos' elsewhere in Alaska.[94] There had been no mention of 'Blonde Eskimos' in the 1912 edition, so this was added to capitalise on the sensation. Despite the introduction of mixed-blood natives into the narrative of the second edition, the central premise of the narrative remains intact: the princely Eric's offspring will remain unadulterated 'white', as he marries one of the explorers, Minna, a blonde Scandinavian girl, and thereby safeguards the purity of the royal Norse bloodline.

The Heroic Inuit?

At the time when the 'Blond Eskimo' sensation made headlines, the evaluation of the Eskimo was undergoing a change. David Thomas Murphy has detailed how nineteenth- and twentieth-century German writers developed a complex view of the Inuit as braver and more honourable than other natives.[95] However, Murphy's claim that German perspectives contrast with pundits of 'English-language literature', who were given to 'tut-tutting' the Inuit for their lack of hygiene and sexual decorum, does not quite stand up to scrutiny.[96] The English journalist James Greenwood, to give just one example, tells us that the inclusion of the 'Esquimaux' in his *Curiosities of Savage Life* (1863–4) was made only reluctantly. The reason for this was that the 'Esquimaux' had 'adopted civilization' as far as is possible in the Arctic, the best proof of which was that 'Europeans cast among them' within 'a single generation become thoroughly Esquimaux in their habits, not by preference, but by sheer compulsion'.[97] This was another statement against Eurocentric arrogance when it came to Artic survival.

Francis Spufford has identified Arctic exploration with a 'national tradition of endurance' in Britain, and Michael F. Robinson, in relation to the American media, refers to the North as 'the coldest crucible' where men could prove their worth.[98] But, it is important to note, successful exploration could not entirely depend on Western courage. In the course of the nineteenth century, it was increasingly accepted that successful discovery of high northern latitudes was dependent upon emulating Inuit techniques: kayaking, hunting, and fishing with few tools, as well as harnessing native knowledge on making warm clothing and shelters. For example, Janice Cavell has shown that the Scottish explorer John Rae, who searched for the lost Franklin Expedition, would purposefully adopt Inuit ways as a means to survive the cold.[99] In a paper read to the Royal Geographic Society of London in 1859, F. L. McClintock reflected on the Franklin crew's failure to survive the Arctic and that Europeans would have done well to 'adapt themselves to native habits'.[100]

To return to adventure fiction, we may ask in what ways such realisation percolated into the consciousness of authors? Robert G. David has shown that Victorian juvenile fiction books about Arctic exploration often show the Inuit as strong, hardy, and courageous, although authors were not able to shake traditional reservations about perceived Inuit savagery in other areas (such as hygiene and manners).[101] As a case study in how the adventure tale responded to the re-evaluation of the 'Eskimo', I will take up for discussion the American author Samuel Scoville Jr's *The Boy Scouts in the North* (1919–20), one of the several serialised stories he wrote about the Argonauts (the young scouts Will, Joe, and Fred).[102] The story posits an Eskimo character as a positive model of bravery, and does so by referring to Stefansson's 'Blond Eskimo' discovery. Thus, the infusion of Norse blood is the trope that legitimises the heroism of his character.

Scoville sends his boy scouts on an adventure to upper Alaska in search of a valuable blue pearl. The scouts hire Eskimo hunters to guide them on their journey (as was also the custom on actual expeditions). One of the guides is Saanak, described as having a head 'like that of an Eskimo', yet he is incredibly tall, and instead of brown eyes and black hair, he has blue eyes and a gold-en-red beard. Because of his unusual demeanour, he is described as resembling 'Eric the Red come back to earth again'.[103] We are given the following backstory on his racial provenance:

Saanak was one of the blond Eskimos from Victoria Island far away in the frozen North. A thousand years ago, Eric the Red sailed from Iceland and discovered Greenland. There he founded a colony which flourished on the southwestern coast of Greenland until the black death in the fourteenth century swept the shipping of the world from off the seas and the colony was lost for a hundred years. When it was found again, the people had disappeared, merged in Eskimo tribes which wandered up until they settled on Victoria Island.[104]

Victoria Island is, of course, a direct reference to where Stefansson had discovered the Copper Inuit. Saanak shows his Norse origins in his belief in Scandinavian mythology. More importantly, he is an unusually brave individual known to have singlehandedly killed a whale. He shows his courage on several occasions, even when he takes a fatal arrow to the chest, and he is the object of much admiration throughout the story. As a mixed-blood descendant of the Greenland colonists, Saanak remains a liminal character, regarded as a stranger by other Eskimos, but, to the young scouts, he is the embodiment of heroic virtues that they cannot find in the civilised world of tea and tennis at home.

Shari M. Huhndorf has written lucidly about the often-puzzling inclusion of Indians as models to be emulated in the early American scout movement. This included the donning of feather headdresses, sleeping in tipis, and practicing archery.[105] In US mythology, the non-white Indians may be enemies, but they also represented a stage of the country's past that could be harnessed to rejuvenate what was increasingly viewed as a degenerate modern America. It goes without saying that such Indigenous role models were not always appreciated by conservative commentators. With the character of Saanak, Scoville eschews some of the anticipated scepticism against representing a heroic native by borrowing Stefansson's 'Blond Eskimo' who, after all, has Norse blood coursing through his veins.

After Saanak's valiant death, the young scouts meet various trials in the Siberian Arctic, which tests their mettle. Saanak has shown the way for how one can deal with challenges of the Arctic. Eventually, the scouts are found worthy of entering the secret place of Goreloi, a warm haven on one of the distant Alaskan islands where the scouts acquire the blue pearl that was the goal of their mission. When the American boys return with the pearl on the doorstep of their financier, Jim Donegan, their act of 'going native' is still visible: they are 'brown and burned and swarthy from sun and wind' and dressed in Inuit attire.[106] This spectacle puts a fright in the butler, who opens the door, because he mistakes them for Eskimos. However, they are soon washed and given new clothes. In summary, Scoville's adventure tale projects an ideal of American boys who learn to become Arctic survivors by adapting native skills. Yet they can easily be re-assimilated as heroes in the national space, as they would never truly 'go native'; it only takes a hot shower to wash off the savageness.

To conclude, we have seen how the settlement in Greenland was used as an example, if only hypothetically, of a colony that had avoided the turbulence of nine-teenth-century unrest and the cultural corrosion of modernity. I have argued in this chapter that we see a conjunction between 'lost colony' tales and an imping-ing sense of cultural and civilisational malaise. The old Scandinavians were seen as ancestors of the modern Anglo-Saxon nations. Thus, the fictional adventurer in the stories may discover a strange world of medieval cul-ture, but it is also a process of realising that the strange or uncanny is a remembering of the adventurer's own past. The representation of Norse colonists, who had upheld a colony in the Arctic, provided narratives of permanence at a time when culture at home was seen to be regressing. Although the 'lost colony' is seldom represented as a per-fect society, it contains a recognition of the past's desir-ability and may compel the reader to value those elements of history that must be recuperated and brought back for the good of society now and in the future.

That manly adventures in far-off locations had an invigorating effect is, of course, common in the popular fiction that piggy-backed on the success of Henry Rider Haggard's novels. However, the literary motor behind the plots featuring isolated Norse communities in the Arctic was fuelled by (and frequently referred to) the memory of the colony in Greenland. In several examples the concept of a remote and isolated Arctic colony was instrumental-ised as nostalgia for autochthonous whiteness.

Stefansson's discovery of 'Blond Eskimos' rekindled the old hope that the mystery of the Greenland colony's fate could be solved. As it is the premise for the discus-sion in this chapter that adventure fiction did not exist in a vacuum, it is perhaps not surprising that the 'Blond

Eskimo' also made it into the pages of popular books. The fictional accounts were helped by the growing cultural capital that Eskimo skills and resilience gained in the early twentieth century, but the mixed-race hero was too unstable a proposition to have long-lasting purchase. This was perhaps not least because it robbed the 'lost colony' of its most important fantasy: the unadulterated preservation of an unmixed whiteness. The fictional stories of Arctic colonies had a long run, propelled by an extended fin-de-siècle sense of cultural decay. However, towards the end of the 1920s, narratives about Norse survivors at the very end of the world began to wane in popularity. One reason for this was that its underlying template of 'lost race' fiction began to feel trite, collapsing under the weight of its own success. Second, the advances in Arctic mapping also narrowed the space for imaginative hideouts for hidden colonies.

CONCLUSION

The chapters in this book have examined how the memory of the colony 'at the end of the world' became an enduring reference point in the Western imagination. I will now summarise the key findings and offer a final synthesis of the central ideas. The Norse colony in Greenland was remembered as a *lieu de mémoire* – a cultural heritage proudly seen as an extension of Christian Europe, marking an outpost of civilisation and the success of colonisation. Its loss was seen as an amputation. In the centuries after communication was discontinued, Greenland took on an important role in the collective memory of the West and the idea of 'Greenland' as a land of wealth and violence was constructed through an array of historiographical, scientific, and popular texts. In this way Greenland was more than a geographical entity; it became a conceptual space.

The general direction of the chapters has tracked a movement from real to fictional space: from expeditions that ventured out to find the vanished settlers to searches that take place in literary texts. If the former were unsuccessful, the latter made the goal achievable. If real-life adventurers had long had a burning desire to discover how the colonists had managed in isolation, and commentators reflected on this same question in numerous articles and books, it is no surprise that fictional adventurers were given the opportunity to assess the state of the colony and weigh it up against 'civilisation' at home. The conclusions reached in fictional texts were not univocal but varied according to whether 'civilisation' at home was seen as commendable or in need of reform. This observation puts emphasis on a point that has been repeated several times in this book: an undiscovered 'Greenland' at the periphery of the known world was created as a series of projections from the centre. Throughout, I have traced the chain of tropes and themes related to Greenland and its settlers, which in many cases can be seen to transcend time periods and national borders, creating a textual loop. Yet, as I hope to have shown, tropes become significant within specific historical contexts. Sometimes we see accents shift over time, other times the mystery of Greenland's vanished settlers accumulated new meanings.

The belief that descendants of the original settlers were still alive cast a powerful spell over Europe for centuries. The pleas to help them maintain their Christian faith are found in the first documents that speak of a 'lost' Greenland. However, at this time in the fifteenth century, the settlements were probably already deserted. Nonetheless the hope of remaking Greenland as a Christian land – a light that would shine against the dark at the farthest frontier of the known world – was a hope not easily extinguished despite the lack of any significant life signs. The hope was underpinned by the myth that the settlers needed to be rescued from the clutches of the pagan Skraelings. However, it was eventually the Skraelings' ancestors, the Inuit, who the missionaries would find. That restoration would come to fruition was given some hope in the belief that the Inuit were in some way descendants of the Norse population. It was eventually through readjustment that the imagined providential drama of restoration could be maintained: commentators tied the idea of re-establishing Christianity to the *land* in the north rather than to a particular ethnic community.

For the Inuit, perception of Greenland was created organically through interaction with the physical environment (as was also the case for the Norse settlers). However, prior to Danish colonisation in 1721, the European image of Greenland was based on a narrow band of books whose information subsequently swelled into numerous commentaries and surveys. European texts perpetuated legends of riches, which in turn encouraged imperial desire. Greenland became a contested territory. There were concrete disputes over access to fishing grounds and trading, but notions of other more sensational riches were also projected onto the unknown land in the north. Even after Greenland was once again observed with European eyes, a trust in bookish tradition often continued to take precedence over first-hand observations. Even stories of the past told by the Inuit were recast to make them fit what Europeans thought they already knew. The realisation that Greenland neither had a surviving European colony nor riches was a long-drawn-out process. Only gradually would surveys, hard won by rigorous field study (often significantly helped by Indigenous guides), retire old knowledge.

Cultivating memories of the past can be driven by national and geopolitical motivations, as the growing field of memory studies has made us aware. From the perspective of the Danish crown, an essential component in memorialising the Greenland settlers was to assimilate them as ethnically and politically Danish. This would guarantee rights to Greenland through the axiom that habitation of land amounted to ownership. The chapters have shown that the intense efforts of claiming or seeking out the existence of the Greenland settlers, in some measure, were linked with the rhythm of rival nations making incursions into the Arctic.

A central point raised in the present study is that making claims to Greenland often required demonstrating knowledge about it: collecting, selecting, and disseminating information about the old colonials, and I have chosen to end my tracing of the twists and turns of the settler legends in the 1920s because by this time belief in a 'lost colony' hidden in Greenland or the wider Arctic became scientifically untenable – as a consequence, the uncharted space for literary imagination also diminished. But the Norse colony was not forgotten and remained a reference with political potency. It makes sense here to provide an afterword that briefly considers the legal settlement reached over Greenland. This is because the ruling took into account some of the arguments examined in this book.

In 1933 the Permanent Court of International Justice ruled in favour of Denmark in the dispute with Norway over possession of Greenland. In the ruling we see how the performative action of speaking, asserting possession in words just as much as in action, carried judicial weight. First let us examine some background on what led to the dispute. After the Kiel Treaty of 1814, Denmark was forced to cede Norway to Sweden, but not its dependencies of Greenland, the Faroe Islands, and Iceland.

Norway's union with Sweden was dissolved in 1905 and therefore Norway was also capable of controlling its own foreign policy. Since Greenland had for a time in the Middle Ages been under the Norwegian crown, the claim was made that Greenland should be returned to a now-independent Norway.

There was an extended lead-up to the dispute. First of all, Norwegian activity in east Greenland intensified in the early twentieth century, including several hunting and scientific expeditions. Norway's minister of foreign affairs, Nils Claus Ihlen, issued a declaration on 22 July 1919 stating that Denmark's claims to sovereignty over the whole of Greenland would not be accepted. In 1920 the Danish government managed to obtain formal recognition of its sovereignty over Greenland from France, Italy, Japan, and (reluctantly) Great Britain.[1] Only the Norwegian government did not sign any declaration but held that Denmark only had rights to the areas that were effectively settled – that is, populated areas on the west coast between 60° and 73°. The establishment of a Norwegian telegraph station in Myggbukta (now part of Northeast Greenland National Park) in 1922 was a decisive move. Generally, the 1920s saw an increase in Norwegian research expeditions with several over-winterings and the construction of semi-permanent cabins, which could be interpreted as taking possession of the east coast. In the period between 1908 and 1931 Norwegian trappers put up more than eighty buildings.[2] On 27 June 1931, five Norwegian hunters together with the meteorologist Hallvard Devold (who was carrying out research in Greenland) hoisted their flag at Mackenzie Bay in north-eastern Greenland at 73° 26'N.

The following month, the east coast between Carlsberg Fjord and Bessel Fjord (extending from latitude 71° 30′N to 75° 40′N) was given the name 'Eirik Raudes Land' [Erik the Red's Land] and claimed in the name of the Norwegian king Haakon VII. The name was a misnomer in the sense that Erik the Red had landed on the west coast of the island.

Denmark took the case to the Permanent Court of International Justice in The Hague. The legal dispute was concluded with the Court's judgment on 5 April 1933, granting full sovereignty over all of Greenland to Denmark.[3] The Court ruled that the kings of Norway held dominion over the whole of Greenland (not just the area of the medieval settlements), for which reason the island could not be territorially segmented. It was established that Greenland had come under Danish rule when the crowns were united in 1380. When Frederick VI was forced to cede Norway to Sweden in 1814, it was expressly mentioned in the treaty that the dependencies of Greenland, Iceland, and the Faroe Islands were not included in the surrendering of land rights.[4] It was therefore decided that Denmark was the rightful owner of all of Greenland.

In relation to the material examined in this book, it is worth noting that the judgment of the international tribunal relied on the consideration of sagas and various documents from the age of exploration. Among the evidence presented as proof that Greenland belonged to the Danish crown was the seventeenth-century explorer Godske Lindenov's reference to 'our country Greenland' in 1605, and Christian IV, who spoke of the Inuit kidnapped on that occasion as 'our subjects'. The tribunal also considered the language of the royal concession given to certain citizens of Copenhagen in 1636 for trading with 'our poor people, our subjects and inhabitants' in Greenland.[5] The tribunal found that the use of possessive pronouns was deemed crucial for understanding the political mindset at the time. In fact, it may be possible to analyse the tribunal's logic behind interpreting such pronouncements as akin to performative speech acts (to borrow J. L. Austin's terminology). The counter-case with which Norwegians responded to the Danish lawsuit had highlighted the fact that Danish attempts to find the colonists were unsuccessful and that there was therefore no continuous occupation of land.[6] Yet the tribunal construed the attempts as showing in themselves a commitment to ownership. To sum up, if Denmark did not have a physical presence in Greenland, the will and ability to speak of Greenland in possessive terms helped to constitute a de facto possession. The Danes were seen to never have lowered their voice, even after ships no longer sailed to Greenland on a regular basis.

The judgment was the termination of numerous wrangles over Greenland reaching back centuries. The ruling took for granted that the law of ownership could only be decided between nations subject to international law. So, although it was generally assumed that the Inuit had driven out the old Norse settlers with violence (as discussed in Chapter 1), this was not considered a conquest of territory since '[t]he principle does not apply in a case where a settlement has been established in a distant country and its inhabitants are massacred by the aboriginal population'.[7] In effect, the Inuit were disenfranchised; their voices were not heard or considered of any legal consequence.

Nonetheless, opinion about the court case was uttered in Kalaallisut, the native language of Greenland. Karen Langgård has examined the Greenlandic paper *Atuagagdliutit* from around the time of the trial, providing insight into the Greenlanders' perspective.[8] She notes how the editor, Kristoffer Lynge, uses the possessive case when speaking about Greenland, and the dispute between Denmark and Norway is referred to in terms of two nations fighting over 'our country'.[9] Thus, Greenlanders did not renounce ownership of their country, even if they recognised Denmark as the ruling colonial power.[10] The discussions in the paper reveal that the Greenlanders did not generally welcome Norway as a new coloniser, but at the same time they wanted the Danes to treat them with more respect and they hoped for a more extensive opening up of the country to international trade.[11] Other unrecorded (and perhaps divergent) opinions may have existed at the time, of course.

Britain was another European power that vied for Arctic possession. In a letter dated 20 May 1920, Lord Curzon informed Denmark that recognition of Danish sovereignty was on the condition that Greenland should be granted to the British Empire in the event Denmark wanted to dispose of the territory.[12] As I have discussed in this book, English explorers had landed in Greenland already in the late sixteenth century. At the dawn of Britain's new era of Arctic exploration in the early nineteenth century, British discourse about Greenland gathered momentum. Several commentators discussed the possibility of reaching and potentially exploiting the east coast. This was a discussion driven by the cultural (but factually erroneous) memory of a thriving Norse colony there. At this time British colonialism had progressed sufficiently for writers to use the case of the Greenland settlers to articulate concerns about contemporary communities cut off from material and spiritual ties with European metropoles. I have shown how the legend of Greenland's vanished settlers became a prism for expressing such anxieties. James Hogg's *Surpassing Adventures of Allan Gordon* is a fictional story reflective of these same concerns. The adventure narrative about a Scottish boy who encounters the 'lost colony' in Greenland serves as a good segue to the second part of the study since it shows how the reference to the European settlers became over-determined: it was possible to reconfigure and re-actualise them as a mirror held up to contemporary society.

In the latter half of the nineteenth century, when the hope of finding descendants of the Greenland settlers began to fade, the coordinates for rediscovering the vanished settlers were moved further afield to the unexplored reaches of the Arctic. Geological theory held that temperate conditions and geyser-heated pockets could be found near the North Pole. It is one of the central arguments in Chapter 7 that scientific theorising and ethnological speculation allowed the legend to linger. Scientific speculation opened up a fictional space for what I have dubbed 'lost colony' narratives. The adventure stories I have analysed do not constitute a genre in their own right; yet they share enough common traits that we can discuss them as a group. The trend in some of these tales was to express confidence in the ascendency of Britain or America as the new masters of the Arctic. Fitzhugh Green's novel *ZR Wins* is a particularly apposite example of this, which is essentially an updated version of the old belief that the Greenland settlers could be found to be in possession of valuable resources ready to be exploited. Just as Green does so explicitly (and literally in his non-fictional articles), writers of 'lost colony' tales can often be seen to nod towards the cultural memory of the Norse people having ventured out to explore the North Atlantic and settle in Greenland. So, compared to the glut of 'lost race' tales published for the popular market, the Arctic tales had an edge by working on the (false) assumption that there was a theoretical possibility that Norse colonies could exist near the Pole.

If the reasons for seeking out the vanished settlers were manifold, the idea that the Vikings were Anglo-American ancestors fostered several literary fantasies of their vigorous and sanguinary virtues. These fantasies could be employed to offset the feeling of cultural decay increasingly felt in the Anglo-American world towards the end of the nineteenth century. So, if ships had once set sails with the hope that white gold would grace the explorers' view of Greenland, fictional adventurers were now dispatched to discover the glory of ancestral whiteness. When fiction writers populated the Arctic with miraculously surviving settlers, they were not speaking about another people: they were speaking about themselves.

In the fictional stories about the vanished Greenlanders or other Viking settlers, the past is not cordoned off but preserved, so that it can be reconfigured as relevant to the present. The fictional visitor who reaches the lost Viking community is an intruder from the present who may wonder about the backwardness of the isolated world; yet the visitor is simultaneously exposed to the scrutiny of the past and will recognise the shortcomings of the present. Violence, which was seen as a threat to the life and well-being of colonial settlers, re-emerges as a prominent theme in these adventure stories. Violence was now a remedy that was welcomed as an antidote to a modernity weighed down by a sense of cultural weakness and racial degeneration. The legend of the vanished settlers of Greenland has continually gained new topicality over the centuries. What characterises the quest for finding these settlers, whether in real terms (by the employment of ships) or in fictional texts, is the pursuit for a part of oneself that has been lost. The symbolic drama of reconciliation remained present and powerful across the centuries.

NOTES

Introduction

1. Lévi-Strauss, *Structural Anthropology*, 203–6.
2. See Depledge, *Britain and the Arctic*, 13–34.
3. Conan Doyle, *Dangerous Work*, 319–25.
4. Ibid., 325.
5. Ibid.
6. Snelling, *Polar Regions of the Western Continent Explored*, 59.
7. Waller, 'Connecting Atlantic and Pacific'.

Prologue

1. Dussel, *Invention of the Americas*.
2. Jesch, *Viking Diaspora*.
3. For a discussion of the different dates in various manuscripts, see Helgason, 'Introduction', 19.
4. Nedkvitne, *Norse Greenland*, 32–5.
5. O'Gorman, *Invention of America*, 45.
6. Cited in Seaver, '"Pygmies" of the Far North', 70.
7. Diamond, *Collapse*, 235.
8. Strauch, *Mittelalterliches Nordisches Recht Bis 1500*, 273.
9. See Boulhosa, *Icelanders and the Kings of Norway*.
10. Marcus, 'The Greenland Trade-Route', 77.
11. '*Lögmannsannáll*, Year *1410*', in Storm, *Islandske Annaler indtil 1578*, 289–90.
12. Nedkvitne, *Norse Greenland*, 162–4.

13. Egede and Egede, *Continuation af Hans Egedes Relationer fra Grønland, samt Niels Egede*, 268.

14. For this debate, see Sines, *Norse in the North Atlantic*, 79.

15. Gad, *History of Greenland*, 1:159; Seaver, *Frozen Echo*, 167–70, 179–80.

16. Seaver, *Frozen Echo*, 178–9; Plank, *Atlantic Wars*, 206.

17. Þórhallsson and Kristinsson, 'Iceland's External Affairs from 1400 to the Reformation', 117–19.

18. Nordtop-Madson, 'The Cultural Identity of the Late Greenland Norse'.

19. See Fagan, *The Great Warming*, 93–4; Dugmore, Keller, and McGovern, 'Norse Greenland Settlement', 12–36; and Diamond, *Collapse*, 266–7 (Norse Greenland's demise is discussed extensively on 248–76).

20. There are many studies of the cooling in the Subarctic. For an extensive account containing references to earlier research, see Cussans, 'Biometry and Climate Change in Norse Greenland'.

21. Marcus, 'The Greenland Trade-Route', 77.

22. For a summary, see Pringle, 'Death in Norse Greenland'.

23. See, for example, Jackson, Arneborg, Dugmore et al. 'Disequilibrium, Adaptation, and the Norse Settlement of Greenland', and Arneborg, 'Norse Greenland'.

24. Gordon, *Introduction to Old Norse*, 218.

25. See Gulløv, 'Inuit–European Interaction in Greenland', 903; Darwent and Darwent, 'Scales of Violence across the North American Arctic', 192–3.

26. Gulløv, 'Nature of Contact between Native Greenlanders and Norse'; and Arneborg, 'Cultural Borders', 41–6.

27. See Star, Barrett, Gondek, and Boessenkool, 'Ancient DNA Reveals the Chronology of Walrus Ivory Trade from Norse Greenland', 9152–7.

28. See, for example, Frei, Coutu, Smiarowski et al., 'Was It for Walrus?'.

29. See Barrett, Boessenkool, Kneale, O'Connell, and Star, 'Ecological Globalisation, Serial Depletion and the Medieval Trade of Walrus Rostra'.
30. Diamond, 'Why Do Societies Collapse?'.
31. Lynnerup, 'Endperiod Demographics of the Greenland Norse'.
32. McGhee, *Last Imaginary Place*, 97.

1 Land of Wealth and Violence

1. 'Gardar' is a transliteration of the Norse Garðar. For the report, see Jónsson, *Grönlandia eller historie om Grønland*, 57–65.
2. For a summary of this opinion, see Seaver, *Frozen Echo*, 91.
3. The language of the oldest manuscript is Old Norwegian as it sounded during the mid-fourteenth century. A modern edition with comments is Bárdarson, *Det gamle Grønlands beskrivelse*, henceforth cited as *DGB*. For an English translation, see Mathers, 'A Fourteenth-Century Description of Greenland'.
4. *DGB*, 31.
5. *DGB*, 8.
6. 'A Treatise of Iver Boty, a Gronlander', in Purchas, *Purchas His Pilgrimes*, 163.
7. For a general overview of what has been called the 'trans-national turn' in memory studies, see Erll and Rigney, *Cultural Memory Studies after the Transnational Turn*, and Bond and Rapson, *Transcultural Turn*.
8. *DGB*, 20.
9. Quinn, 'Newfoundland in the Consciousness of Europe', 9.
10. Fuller, 'Images of English Origins in Newfoundland and Roanoke'. Nonetheless, some eulogies were published,

most notably Sir William Vaughan's *Cambriensis Caroleia* (1625) and Robert Hayman's *Quodlibets, Latterly Come from New Britaniola* (1628).

11. See Seaver, *Frozen Echo*, 225.

12. See commentary in Valkendorf, 'Om de af Erkesbiskop Erik Walkendorff'.

13. Hamre, *Erkebiskop Erik Valkendorf*, 47–53.

14. Valkendorf, 'Om de af Erkesbiskop Erik Walkendorff', 492–3.

15. See Seaver, *Last Vikings*, 186–9.

16. For unknown reasons, the text did not appear in print until 1688, when it was published in an Icelandic translation by Einar Eyjólfsson. The importance of Arngrímur's work should not be underestimated, however, as other antiquaries scoured the manuscript for knowledge about Greenland's resources and its colonial past.

17. Jónsson, *Gronlandia*, 232.

18. The Northwest Passage did not exist at the time. Only between 1903 and 1906 did the Norwegian explorer Roald Amundsen successfully navigate such a route. In fact, the journey was not completed in a single season until 1944, but it is becoming a possibility in the twenty-first century due to climate change.

19. Major, *Voyages of the Venetian Brothers*, 20–1.

20. Fuller, *Remembering the Early Modern Voyage*, 23.

21. For Frobisher's failed expedition and its aftermath, see Dunlap, *On the Edge*, 85–6.

22. Best, *A True Discourse of the Late Voyages of Discoverie*, 2.

23. See Settle, 'Second Voyage of Master Martin Frobisher', 227.

24. Hall, 'A Report to King Christian IV of Denmark', 10.

25. King Christian IV, Letter of Instruction, 15–17.

26. Gatonby, 'An Account of the English Expedition to Greenland', 105.

27. Ellis, 'In Praise of Maister Martine Frobisher'.
28. Ibid.
29. For an examination of this trope, see Bartosik-Velez, *Legacy of Christopher Columbus in the Americas*, especially 18–20, 38–52.
30. Naipaul, *Loss of El Dorado*, 38.
31. Rørdam, *Klavs Christoffersen Lyskanders Levned*, 37.
32. An English translation appeared in Churchill's *Collection of Voyages and Travels* (first published 1704), which went through four eighteenth-century editions. In 1855 the Hakluyt Society published an English translation of the text in *A Collection of Documents of Spitzbergen and Greenland*. Since La Peyrère had summarised the Danish captain Jens Munk's *Navigatio septentrionalis* in *Relation du Groenland*, the German translation of Munk's diary (1650) excerpted La Peyrère's work for the introduction. The English version of Munk's text (1650, 1704, 1732, and 1744) was based on the German edition and thus also included the passages from *Relation du Groenland*. An abbreviated Dutch version of both Munk's and La Peyrère's texts was published in 1663 and 1685.
33. For Le Vayer's statements on this topic, see Gabriel, 'Periegisis and Skepticis', 161–2.
34. La Peyrère, *Relation du Groenland*, 11.
35. Ibid., 2: *Les perils, qui se rencontrent dans cette Navigation … de m'informer tout à loisir de la route que je devois prendre, pour trouver cette Terre Septentrionale.*
36. *DGB*, 32.
37. Mathers, 'A Fourteenth-Century Description of Greenland', 77.
38. For La Peyrère's account of Greenland's riches, see *Relation du Groenland*, 52–62.
39. See Popkin, *Isaac La Peyrère*, 10–11.

40. La Peyrère, *Relation du Groenland*, 4. Although the identity of 'M. Rets' has long been a mystery, Peder Reedtz is clearly mentioned in relation to *Relation du Groenland* in the letters La Peyrère writes to Ole Worm on 26 September 1647 and 22 March 1648. See Worm, *Breve til og fra Ole Worm*, 3:280, 306.

41. La Peyrère acknowledges in his correspondence that Worm had made available most of the material for the book; see Worm, *Breve til og fra Ole Worm*, 3:280, 306.

42. La Peyrère, *Relation du Groenland*, 72–82.

43. Ibid., 53–5.

44. La Peyrère, 'Kaert von Groen-Land'.

45. For this tradition, see Ísleifsson, 'Islands on the Edge', 53.

46. 'Beschrijvingh van Groenlandt', 28.

47. Ogilby, *America*, 663.

48. La Peyrère, *Relation du Groenland*, 204–5.

49. Ogilby, *America*, 663.

50. *DGB*, 29.

51. *DGB*, 29.

52. *DGB*, 30.

53. See the anonymous 'Historical Introduction' in Egede, *A Description of Greenland*, xxxiii.

54. Seaver, *Frozen Echo*, 108–9.

55. The passage is quoted in full in Storm, 'Den Danske Geograf Claudius Clavus eller Nicolaus Niger', 143.

56. Nansen, *In Northern Mists*, 85.

57. Petersen, 'Claudius Clavus Niger', 54. Perhaps somewhat counter-intuitively, Petersen's conclusion is that Clavus does after all refer to the Karelians.

58. Jensen, 'Denmark and the Crusades', 150–8.

59. See letter from Pope Nicholas V to the bishops of Skaalholt and Hólar, 20 September 1448, in Unger and Huitfeldt, *Diplomatarium Norvegicum*, 554–6.

60. See Seaver, *Frozen Echo*, 176.

61. I find support for the interpretation that the writer of the letter sees the attackers as Skraelings in Gad, *History of Greenland*, 1:157–8.
62. For an extended discussion of this passage, see Kolodny, *In Search of First Contact*, 57–60.
63. See Seaver, *Frozen Echo*, 175.
64. See letter from Pope Alexander VI, 23 October 1492, in *Diplomatarium Groenlandicum*, 3. For an English translation of the document, see Enterline, *Erikson, Eskimos, and Columbus*, 210–11.
65. *Diplomatarium Groenlandicum*, 3.
66. For a recent discussion of Olaus' image in the context of North Atlantic conflict, see Plank, *Atlantic Wars*, 3–7.
67. See Seaver, '"Pygmies" of the Far North', 85.
68. See Freist, 'Lost in Time and Space?'.
69. Egede, *A Description of Greenland*, 11–12.
70. Ibid.
71. O'Gorman, *A History of the Roman Catholic Church in the United States*, 11.
72. Shahan, 'Miscellaneous Studies', 427.
73. See especially Arneborg, 'Norse Greenland', 268.
74. Nedkvitne, *Norse Greenland*, 327–77, especially 340.
75. The methodology is explained in Davis, 'Decentering History', 190. In terms of the Arctic, Michael Bravo has significantly contributed to redressing the balance between Inuit and Western perspectives. See, for example, 'Indigenous Evangelical Voyaging' and 'The Postcolonial Arctic'. See also Karen Routledge's *Do You See Ice?*
76. Pratt, *Imperial Eyes*, 8.
77. Citation from Poul's diary, in Egede and Egede, *Continuation af Hans Egedes Relationer fra Grønland, samt Niels Egede*, 37.
78. Egede, *A Description of Greenland*, 12.
79. Nørlund, *Viking Settlers in Greenland*, 139.

80. Sonne, *Worldviews of the Greenlanders*, 180–2; Thisted, 'Narrative Expectations', 274; Arneborg, 'Contacts between Eskimos and Norsemen in Greenland'.

81. Egede, *Relationer fra Grønland 1721–36*, 65: *de Vilde selv negter dette aldeelis iche, naar som vi hafver sagt, at de ere de afdøde Norskes Børn.*

82. Egede, *A Description of Greenland*, 23.

83. Porter, *Inconstant Savage*, 480.

84. Egede, *A Description of Greenland*, 10.

85. Arneborg, 'Kulturmødet mellem nordboere og eskimoer i Grønland', 50–96.

86. Egede, *Efterretninger om Grönland*, 33.

87. Egede, *A Description of Greenland*, 12.

88. Tonkin, *Narrating Our Pasts*, 38, 52.

89. Arneborg, 'Aqissiaq og nordboerne', 217.

90. Goffart, 'Did the Distant Past Impinge on the Invasion-Age Germans?', 24.

91. Liebeschuertz, 'Debate about the Ethnogenesis of the Germanic Tribes', 345.

92. Comeau, 'Stories of Taqilituq & Ipirvik', 16–17.

93. See Stevenson, 'Ethical Injunction to Remember', and several of the other essays in the collection.

94. Rink writes 'Tunnit'. An older Kalaallisut form of the same ethnonym was Torngit.

95. Steckley and Cummins, *Full Circle*, 42.

96. For Aron's tales and illustrations, see Thisted, *'Således skriver jeg'*, 1:94–9.

97. Ibid., 1:101.

98. See Knuth, *K'avdlunâtsianik*, 24.

99. The letter is transcribed in Knuth, *K'avdlunâtsianik*, 84.

100. For a summary of Inuit perspectives on legend, see also Thisted, 'Greenlandic Perspectives', 798–804.

101. Thisted, 'Narrative Expectations', 274–7.

102. For a general consideration of Indigenous collective memory as counter-memory, see Michael Rothberg's discussion in 'Remembering Back', especially 370.

103. Richards, *Unending Frontier*.

2 Greenland and Discourses of Possession

1. On the Zeno map Greenland was placed 20° too far to the west and 6° too far north. Among the fictitious islands plotted in, 'Freeseland' was at the right latitude for this misidentification.

2. Best, *A True Discourse of the Late Voyages of Discoverie*, 47.

3. Ibid., 9.

4. Ibid., 10.

5. Ibid.

6. For the suggestion that the objects derived from the Norse colony, see Di Robilant, *Irresistible North*, 178. A well-informed assessment of Best's information in relation to European trade along Arctic whaling routes in the sixteenth century is Seaver, 'A Very common and usuall trade', 19.

7. See open letter from Frederik II to James Alday, 21 May 1579, in *Diplomatarium Groenlandicum*, 8.

8. Letter from Fredrik II to Elizabeth I, 15 August 1582, in *Diplomatarium Groenlandicum*, 11.

9. See MacMillan, *Sovereignty and Possession in the English New World*, 53–64; Knight, 'Arctic Arthur', especially 61–2.

10. Zeiders, 'Conjuring History'.

11. Dee, *Private Diary of Dr. John Dee*, 4.

12. Spradlin, 'GOD ne'er Brings to pass Such Things for Nought'. For a discussion of the use and confusion of place names in the manuscript tradition concerning

British legendary figures settling in the north, see Gwyn A. Williams' seminal study *Madoc*, 58, 60–1, 64.

13. See Truett, 'Borderlands and Lost Worlds of Early America', 303.

14. See Sanders, *Wales, the Welsh and the Making of America*, 1–30.

15. Schröter, *Allgemeine Geschichte der Länder und Völker von Amerika*, 2:652–3.

16. Richards, *Unending Frontier*, 592–3, 597.

17. Craciun, *Writing Arctic Disaster*, 205.

18. Cited in Gosch, *Danish Arctic Expeditions*, 1:xx–xi.

19. Fuller, *Remembering the Early Modern Voyage*, 16.

20. *C. C. Lyschanders digtning 1579–1623*, 2 vols, ed. Flemming Lundgren-Nielsen (Copenhagen: Det Danske Sprog- og Litteraturselskab, 1989), vol. 1, ll. 3499–3509. Henceforth, citations are indicated by line numbers in the text.

21. Hall, 'Another Account of the Danish Expedition to Greenland', 34.

22. See Gosch, *Danish Arctic Explorations*, map I, facing 1:18.

23. Stevens, 'Leviticus Thinking'.

24. Jónsson, *Gronlandia*, 267.

25. Ibid.

26. Beyer, *Om Norgis Rige*, 63.

27. Lyschander, 'Til Læseren': *Gvds Rige, oc saa voris Danske Mact / Motte spredis til Værdens Ende*. All references to Lyschander's *Chronica* are to the edition *C. C. Lyschanders digtning 1579–1623*, ed. Flemming Lundgren-Nielsen (Copenhagen: Det Danske Sprog- og Litteraturselskab, 1989), vol. 1, and will henceforth be cited by line numbers in the text. My translation.

28. See Letter of Instruction, 18 April 1605, translated in Gosch, *Danish Arctic Expeditions*, 1:xxvi.

29. Refdahl to Frederik IV, 17 March 1721, *Diplomatarium Groenlandicum*, 68–9.

30. The Bergen Company, Public Notice, 3 March (signed 7 February) 1723, *Diplomatarium Groenlandicum*, 95.
31. Foucault, *Security, Territory, Population*, 122.
32. See Elden, 'How Should We Do the History of Territory?'.
33. Seed, *Ceremonies of Possession in Europe's Conquest of the New World*, 16–31.
34. For a nuanced account of colonial techniques of governance in Greenland, and how strict colonial rule mixed with respect for traditional Inuit ways of life, see Rud, *Colonialism in Greenland*.
35. Blefken, *Islandia sive populorum et mirabilium quae in ea insula reperiuntur accuratior description*, 58–71.
36. Gad, *History of Greenland*, 1:187.
37. Capel, *Norden, Oder Zu Wasser und Lande im Eise und Snee*, 181–2.
38. See Egede (who expresses scepticism about the story's validity), *A Description of Greenland*, 20, and Crantz, *History of Greenland*, 1:244.
39. Gad, *History of Greenland*, 1:237–8. For an assessment of European trade along Arctic whaling routes in the sixteenth century, see Seaver, 'A Very common and usuall trade'.
40. Engelhard, *Ice Bear*, 40–1.
41. Olesen, 'Vor och Cronens Land', 89.
42. See Wood-Donnelly, *Performing Arctic Sovereignty*, especially 9–22, 52–5, and 111–22.
43. Nicol, 'Denmark–Norway: Eastern Greenland', 146.
44. See James Hall's report on the 1605 voyage in *Purchas His Pilgrimes*, 820.
45. Shoemaker, 'A Typology of Colonialism'.
46. Vaughan, 'Historical Survey of the European Whaling Industry', 126–7.
47. Naja Mikkelsen, Antoon Kuijpers, Sofia Ribeiro et al. 'European Trading, Whaling and Climate History of

West Greenland Documented by Historical Records, Drones and Marine Sediments', *GEUS: Geological Survey of Denmark and Greenland Bulletin* 41 (2018): 67–70, at 67–8.

48. Resen, *Groenlandia*.
49. Ibid., 157.
50. Lyotard, *Libidinal Economy*, 198.
51. Resen, *Groenlandia*, 158.
52. Ibid., 156–60.
53. MacMillan, *Sovereignty and Possession in the English New World*, 136–40.
54. Transcript of the manuscript is available in Vídalín, *Den Tredie Part*, citation on 70.
55. Ibid., 47–8.
56. Ibid., 60.
57. Ibid., 74.
58. See Belmessous, 'Assimilation and Racialism in Seventeenth- and Eighteenth-Century French Colonial Policy'.
59. Vídalín, *Den Tredie Part*, 58; see also 72.
60. Pagden, *Burdens of Empire*, especially 120–52.
61. In the following I summarise Thormod Torfæus' letter to Christian V from 18 January 1683, in *Diplomatarium Groenlandicum*, 22–4.
62. Gad, *History of Greenland*, 1:317.
63. Jensson, '*Hypothesis Islandica*', 47.
64. Ilsøe, 'Historisk censur i Danmark indtil Holberg'.
65. Torfæus, *Gronlandia Antiqua*, 41–3.
66. Letter from Torfæus to Ditlev Vibe, 5 September 1704, cited in Wallin, *Vulkantiden*, 31.
67. La Peyrère, *Relation du Groenland*, 204–5.
68. *English Atlas*, 10.
69. *An Account of Several Late Voyages & Discoveries*, 188.
70. Pinkerton, *Modern Geography*, 409.

71. See Torfæus' Danish translation, *Det gamle Grønland*, 213–16.

72. Letter from Hans Egede to Frederik IV, 4 June 1720, in *Diplomatarium Groenlandicum*, 60–1.

73. Ibid.

74. Crull, *A Supplement to Mr. Samuel Puffendorf's Introduction to the History of Europe*, xiv.

75. Ibid., 671–3, citation on 673.

76. Ibid., 663.

77. Ibid., 679.

78. For an analysis of how eighteenth-century writers were often open about their bias in their dedication to patrons and and did not shy away from adopting celebratory tones, see Black, *Charting the Past*, especially 33.

79. Elkin, *A View of the Greenland Trade and Whale Fishery*.

80. Mauricius, *Naleesing over Groenland*. The five Discourses in the book are dated October–December 1740 and have separate pagination.

81. Ibid. Letter dated 23 October 1740 (inserted between Discourses I and II): *de pretenfie van eigendom over Groen land ... gants ongegrond is*.

82. Mauricius, *Naleesing*, letter dated 7 October 1740, prefaced to Discourse 1.

83. Ibid. (Discourse I), 11.

84. Ibid. (Discourse I), 3.

85. Ibid. (Discourse II), 4.

86. Ibid. (Discourse III), 5.

87. Mortensen, 'Before Historical "Sources" and Literary "Texts"', 9–10.

88. Mauricius, *Naleesing* (Discourse V), 13.

89. Hann, *Beschryving van de straat Davids benevens des zelven inwooners zede gestalte en gewoonte misgaders hunne visvangst en andere handelingen*, 5–6.

90. Ibid., 25.

91. Ibid.
92. Wallace, 'Norse in Newfoundland'.
93. Mauricius, *Naleesing* (Discourse I), 5.
94. Rose, *Property and Persuasion*, 15.

3 Beyond the Horizon

1. See, for example, Rud, *Colonialism in Greenland*, and the collections of essays edited by Ole Høiris in *Grønland*. See also Naum and Nordin, *Scandinavian Colonialism and the Rise of Modernity*.
2. Tyssot de Patot, *Voyage de Groenland*. The German translation, published in Leyden in 1721, is *Der Robinson Crusoe dritter und vierter Theil, oder Lustrige und seltsame Lebens-Beschreibung Peter von Mesange, worinnen er seine Reise nach Grönland & a. beschreibet*. A modern English translation by Brian Stableford is available in *The Strange Voyages of Jacques Massé and Pierre de Mesange*.
3. Tyssot de Patot, *Voyage de Groenland*, 1:36.
4. For these suggestions of influence, see Atkinson, *Extraordinary Voyage in French Literature*, 109–10.
5. See Tyssot de Patot, *Voyage de Groenland*, 1:92.
6. Elliott, *The Old World and the New*; Lach, *Asia in the Making of Europe*; and Quinn, 'New Geographical Horizons'.
7. Egede, *Omstændelig og udførlig Relation*, 2.
8. All references to this work are from Egede, *A Description of Greenland*. The reference to 'Old Greenland' in Egede's original Danish title is to distinguish what we now know as Greenland from Spitsbergen, which was often given the name 'New Greenland'. Egede uses the name 'New Greenland' about Spitsbergen; see *A Description of Greenland*, 37.
9. Egede, *A Description of Greenland*, 5–6, 12, and 38–9.

10. Ibid., 113.

11. Ibid., 114.

12. Ibid.

13. Egede, *A Description of Greenland*, 165–78; see also his *Relationer fra Grønland*, 36–7.

14. Egede, *Relationer fra Grønland*, 36–7.

15. For an assessment, see Kleivan, 'European Contacts with Greenland', 135.

16. Egede, *Relationer fra Grønland*, 65.

17. Egede, *A Description of Greenland*, 183–4.

18. Giesecke, *On the Norwegian Settlements on the Eastern Coast of Greenland*, 7.

19. Egede, *A Description of Greenland*, 197.

20. Ibid., 197.

21. For a recent study, see Fenton, *Old Canaan in a New World*.

22. Egede, *A Description of Greenland*, 10.

23. Holberg, epistle 350, from *Epistler*, digitised as part of *Ludvig Holbergs Skrifter*.

24. See Traeger, 'Poq og Qiperoq'.

25. Thrush, in *Indigenous London*, 115–18, describes how military officer George Cartwright transported five Canadian Inuit to London in 1772 and analyses their impressions with respect to Inuit conceptions and perspectives. See also Routledge, *Do You See Ice?*

26. Bielke, *Relation om Grønland*. Henceforth line numbers will be cited in brackets.

27. On the kidnapping and transportation of Inuit to Denmark, and an attempt to see these events from the perspective of the Greenlanders, one should consult Harbsmeier, 'Bodies and Voices from Ultima Thule'.

28. For a discussion of Grotius' monogenetic theory, see Livingstone, 'Geographical Inquiry', especially 95–102.

29. La Peyrère, *Relation du Groenland*, 48, 273–7.

30. For this suggestion, see Livingstone, 'Geographical Inquiry', 95–102.
31. La Peyrère, *Relation du Groenland*, 203.
32. Olearius, *Voyages and Travells of the Ambassadors*, 52–3.
33. Greenblatt, *Marvelous Possessions*.
34. Egede, *A Description of Greenland*, 41.
35. Ibid., 46.
36. Grafton, 'Introduction', 5.
37. David Cranz' work was published under the name 'Crantz' in English. By convention, I will use the anglicised form.
38. Crantz, *History of Greenland*, 1:253.
39. Egede, *A Description of Greenland*, 62–3.
40. Ibid., 47–8.
41. Stephen Parmenius' Latin letter to Richard Hakluyt, 6 August 1583, translated in *The New Found Land of Stephen Parmenius*, 171.
42. Ibid., 173.
43. Egede, *A Description of Greenland*, 42.
44. Lutz, 'Introduction', 3.
45. Egede, *A Description of Greenland*, 23.
46. Ibid., 41.
47. Ibid., 42.
48. Ibid.
49. Ibid., 45.
50. Sørensen, *Denmark–Greenland in the Twentieth Century*, 36.
51. Archaeological finds show that the medieval colonists, helped by a warmer medieval climate, grew barley; see Gulløv, 'Norse Agriculture in Greenland?'.
52. Moss, *Frozen Ship*, 44.
53. Bravo, 'Mission Gardens Natural History and Global Expansion, 1720–1820'.

54. Paars' Report to Frederik IV, 13 July 1729, in *Diplomatarium Groenlandicum*, 187–8.

55. Ibid., 189.

56. Egede, *A Description of Greenland*, 43.

57. Ibid., 222.

58. Ibid., 217.

59. Ibid., 218.

60. Ibid.

61. For the exegesis of Genesis in relation to the cultivation of wastelands, see for comparison Harrison, 'Fill the Earth and Subdue It'.

62. Hayes, *Land of Desolation*, 41.

63. Ibid., 23.

64. Ibid., 39.

65. Egede, *Relationer fra Grønland*, 65.

66. Egede, *A Description of Greenland*, 14–27.

67. Egede, *Nova Delineatio Grønlandiæ Antiqvæ*.

68. Egede writes of forests on the east coast in *Relationer fra Grønland*, 32.

69. In fact, the station was set alight twice, in 1725 and 1731, as Dutch whalers and traders did not like the competition.

70. See the facsimile in Kejlbo, 'Nova Delineatio Grønlandiæ Antiquæ', 53–4.

71. Bowen, 'A Map of Old Greenland, or Øster Bygd & Wester Bygd, Agreeable to Egede's Late Description of Greenland', in *A Complete System of Geography*, 2:inserted between pp. 760 and 761.

72. Ibid., 6.

73. Egede, *A Description of Greenland*, 38–40.

74. See in particular Trap, 'The Cartography of Greenland', especially 157–9.

75. Lennox, *Homelands and Empires*, 212–62.

76. For the tradition, see Unger, *Ships on Maps*.

77. Letter from the Bergen Company to the Greenland Council, 19 April 1723, *Diplomatarium Groenlandicum*, 97–8.

78. See Egede, *Relationer fra Grønland*, 87–8; Gad, *History of Greenland*, 2:42–3.

79. The Bergen Company's Instructions to Hans Fæster, 21 April 1724, in *Diplomatarium Groenlandicum*, 113–15.

80. Frederik IV's instructions to C. E. Paars, 7 May 1728, in *Diplomatarium Groenlandicum*, 158.

81. Paars' Report to Frederik IV, 13 July, in *Diplomatarium Groenlandicum*, 186.

82. See Bobé, *Hans Egede*, 178.

83. Lindenberg, 'Oplysninger om officerer i Grønlandsfarten 1721–1971', 88.

84. Mathias Jochimsen's report from Godthaab to Privy Councillor Løvenørn from 1732, printed in *Minerva*, 3 (July 1788), 31–4. See also letter from Egede to the Navy General Commissariat, 13 June 1733, *Diplomatarium Groenlandicum*, 222.

85. Jochimsen's report, 71–3.

86. Wesley, 'On the Spread of the Gospel', 288.

87. Ibid.

88. Letter from the Bergen Company to Frederik IV, 16 December 1721, *Diplomatarium Groenlandicum*, 83. See also Egede, *Relationer fra Grønland*, 11, 24, 25, and 35.

89. Gosden, *Archaeology and Colonialism*, 82.

90. Rasch, 'Betænkning om Handelen og Missionen paa Grønland 1747', 86.

91. Ibid., 88.

92. Ibid., 88–9.

93. Walløe, *Peder Olsen Walløes dagbøger fra hans rejser i Grønland 1739–53*.

94. Egede, *A Description of Greenland*, 38.

95. Bobé, 'Early Exploration of Greenland', 33.

96. Egede, *Rejsebeskrivelse til Øster-Grønlands Opdagelse 1786–87.*
97. Eggers, 'Om Grønlands Østerbygds sande Belligenhed'.
98. See, for example, the review of C. C. Zahrtmann's 'Remarks on the Voyages to the Northern Hemisphere', 102; and 'W. R.', review of August Graah's *Narrative of an Expedition to the East Coast of Greenland*, 165.

4 1818

1. 'Polar Regions', 13.
2. See Wheatley, 'The Arctic in the *Quarterly Review*'.
3. [John Barrow], 'Polar Ice'. The publication of the *Quarterly Review* was lagging at this time, so the imprint does not correspond to the actual date of publication. Although the review was published anonymously, it is generally recognised as one of the pieces Barrow contributed to the journal. For the number of copies sold of the issue, see Cutmore, '*Quarterly Review*, Volume 18, Number 35'.
4. [John Barrow], 'Polar Ice', 202.
5. See Potter, *Arctic Spectacles*, 49–51.
6. Bravo, 'Anti-anthropology of Highlanders and Islanders'.
7. Ross, *A Voyage of Discovery*, 1:169.
8. I owe the information on the publication figure to Adriana Craciun, who lists several print runs for Arctic publications at the time; see *Writing Arctic Disaster*, 249, note 55.
9. Barrow, *Chronological History*, 364–5.
10. Ibid., 13.
11. See the anonymous 'Historical Introduction', in Egede, *A Description of Greenland*, ix.
12. Ibid., x–xi.

13. News for Tuesday 30, *Royal Magazine* (November 1750): 467. The same news item was also conveyed in *The London Magazine*, *Gentleman's Magazine*, and *The Scots Magazine*.
14. Malthe Brun [Conrad Malte-Brun], 'On the Expeditions to the North Pole', 282.
15. This signature was first identified by Donald H. Reiman in *'Christobell, or, The Case of the Sequel Preemptive'*, and has since been generally accepted.
16. Vardill, 'The Arctic Navigator's Prayer', 62.
17. Ibid., 61 note.
18. Ibid., 61.
19. Review of 'Account of the Expedition to Baffin's Bay under Captain Ross and Lieutenant Parry', 151.
20. 'V' [Anna Jane Vardill], 'Extracts from an Arctic Navigator's Journal', 196. This was the second instalment of the three-part satire.
21. Ibid.
22. 'V' [Anna Jane Vardill], 'Origin of an Arctic Colony', 390.
23. *Patriot*, 8.
24. Johnston, *Mariner*, 45–6.
25. Barrow, *Chronological History*, 13.
26. See, for example, Lambert and Lester, 'Geographies of Colonial Philanthropy', 322.
27. Ibid.
28. Wilton, 'Polar Ice', 85.
29. Ibid.
30. Ibid., 93.
31. Marshall, 'Wilton, Charles Pleydell'.
32. Vardill, 'To the Authoress of the Arctic Expeditions'.
33. Review of Porden's *Arctic Expeditions*, 250.
34. Porden, *Arctic Expeditions*. Verse lines will be cited by number in the text.
35. Ibid., 5.

36. Ibid., 9 note.
37. Hill, *White Horizon*, 81.
38. For this critical paradigm, see Hyndman, 'Mind the Gap'.
39. Richardson, 'Women, Philanthropy, and Imperialism'.
40. Ibid., 204–6.
41. For an analysis of the context for Porden's poem, see Cavell, 'Miss Porden, Mrs. Franklin, and the Arctic Expeditions'; and Johns-Putra, 'Historicizing the Networks of Ecology and Culture'.
42. Porden, *Veils*, notes on 27–30. For Porden's use of Knight's theories, see Lidwell-Durnin, 'Inevitable Decay'.
43. Bravo, 'Geographies of Exploration and Improvement', 521–2.
44. Drayton, *Nature's Government*, xv.
45. *Extracts from the Kongs-Skugg-Sio*, 10. Contemporary book catalogues indicate the translation was made by the Norwich scholar Anna Gurney.
46. [Francis Palgrave], review of Hans Egede Saabye's *Brudstykker af en Dagbok*, 485.
47. For a mention of marble deposits, see Egede, *A Description of Greenland*, 48–9.
48. [Francis Palgrave], review of Hans Egede Saabye's *Brudstykker af en Dagbok*, 485.
49. See 'List of Specimens of the Rocks Brought from the Eastern Coast of Greenland with Geognostical Memoranda by Professor Jameson', in Scoresby, *Journal of a Voyage*, 399–409.
50. O'Reilly, *Greenland*, 243.
51. Adriana Craciun, in her excellent article 'What Is an Explorer?', 33, makes a passing reference to this aspect.
52. In fact, O'Reilly includes a damning assessment of what he calls Barrow's 'utopian paper-built plan of sailing to the north pole [*sic*]', a project he asserts must be abandoned as it would be impossible to penetrate the ice-crowded

waters (243). In return, O'Reilly's book received unusually harsh treatment in the *Quarterly Review* by the anonymous reviewer (Barrow), who accused O'Reilly of producing a work written only 'to gratify the eager appetite' of the public for books on the Arctic and thereby 'put money in his purse'. See the review of O'Reilly's *Greenland*, 208.

53. O'Reilly, *Greenland*, 216.
54. Ibid., 287.
55. Ibid., 269–70.
56. Ibid., 275–6.
57. Ibid., 270.
58. For a discussion of the declining British whale trade and its contribution to the domestic economy after the Napoleonic Wars, see Jackson, *British Whale Trade*, 105–28.
59. Cited in Barr, 'Harpoon Guns', 305.
60. Cited in ibid.
61. Cited in ibid.
62. Manby, *Journal of a Voyage to Greenland*, 97.
63. Manby, *Reflections and Observations*, 12.
64. Bentham, *Principles of Penal Law*, 492–8.
65. Manby, *Reflections and Observations*, 12.
66. Ibid., 13.
67. Godwin, *Enquiry Concerning Political Justice*, 2:757.
68. Pelham, *God's Power and Providence*, 10.
69. 'From the Baltimore American'.
70. Manby, *Hints for Improving the Criminal Law*, 4 note.
71. Ibid., 4.
72. Ibid., 4.
73. Ibid., 3.
74. Frederik IV to the poor law authorities, 5 April 1728, in *Diplomatarium Groenlandicum*, 153.

75. Bobé, *Hans Egede*, 141; and Toft, 'Erfaringer', 70.
76. Manby, *Hints for Improving the Criminal Law*, 4.
77. See Morris, *Convicts and Colonies*, 5–6.
78. Peirce, *A Report on the Resources of Iceland and Greenland*, 51.
79. Ibid., 49.
80. Ibid., 51.
81. Scoresby, *Journal of a Voyage*, 337–8.
82. Ibid., 184.
83. Review of Graah, *Undersögelses-Rejse*, 84.
84. Baught, 'Seapower and Science'.
85. 'Legal Status', PCIJ Series A/B, 35.
86. Graah, *Narrative*, x.
87. I quote the English translation: Graah, *Narrative*, 13.
88. 'Groenland: Découverte d'un colonie chrétienne'; 'Die alte norwegische Colonie in Grönland; 'Notice regarding the Lost Greenland'.
89. 'Miscellaneous Scientific Proceedings on the Continent'.
90. 'Greenland', in *Encyclopaedia Americana*, 51.
91. Graah, *Undersøgelses-Reise til Østkysten af Grønland*, 119; Graah, *Narrative*, 173–4.
92. Review of Graah's 'A Voyage to the East Coast', 515.
93. For research into the Arctic craze in public print, see Cavell, *Tracing the Connected Narrative*. See also Keighren, Withers, and Bell, *Travels into Print*, especially 45–52.
94. Pickford, 'Travel Writing and Translation', 84.
95. Graah, *Narrative*, 90 note.
96. Ibid., 'The Editor', 'Preface', a2.
97. Review of Graah's 'A Voyage to the East Coast', 516.
98. For a summary, see Winsor, *'Pre-Columbian Exploration'*, 109.
99. Rafn, 'Sinerissap inuinik sujugdlernik ilisimassaussut ilait'.

100. 'Legal Status', PCIJ Series A/B, 35.
101. See Markham, *Threshold of the Unknown Region*, 144–7.

5 Greenland's Fall and Restoration

1. See, for example, McCorristine, *Spectral Arctic*, and Bowers, 'Haunted Ice'. Specifically in relation to Greenland, Maike Schmidt uses imagology to analyse eighteenth-century German texts (travelogues, philosophy, and fiction) in *Grönland*.
2. Hase, *History of the Christian Church*, 510.
3. Craciun, *Writing Arctic Disaster*.
4. Torgovnick, *Gone Native*. Specific colonial vulnerabilities are also discussed by Linda Colley in *Captives* and exemplified with a specific focus by Mark Condos in *Insecurity State*.
5. Howison, *European Colonies*, 2:189–91.
6. Ibid., 2:192.
7. Ibid., 2:194.
8. Ibid.
9. Ibid., 2:197.
10. Nicol, *Historical and Descriptive Account*, 285.
11. Rink, *Danish Greenland*, 25.
12. Review of *Antiquarian Miscellany*.
13. See 'Historical Introduction', in Egede, *A Description of Greenland*.
14. Quoted in Meek, *Social Science and the Ignoble Savage*, 117.
15. Anderson, *Historical and Chronological Deduction*, vii.
16. For an analysis of this dynamic in Enlightenment thought, see Gordon, 'The Dematerialization Principle'.
17. Scoresby, *Journal of a Voyage*, 338.
18. Ibid., xxv–xxvi.
19. Manby, *Hints for Improving the Criminal Law*, 4.
20. Graah, *Narrative*, 6.

21. Turner, *Beyond Geography*, 236.
22. Glahn, *Missionær i Grønland*, 69–71.
23. Saabye, *Greenland*, 117.
24. Settle, 'Second Voyage of Master Martin Frobisher', 227.
25. See 'Dr. Richardson's Narrative', in Franklin, *Narrative of a Journey*, 2:332.
26. Ibid., 2:344.
27. For Patrick Brantlinger's study of nineteenth-century cannibalistic lore, see *Taming Cannibals*, especially 65–85.
28. Crantz, *History of Greenland*1:246–7.
29. [John Barrow], 'Polar Ice and Northern Passage into the Pacific', 210.
30. [Francis Lister Hawks], *Lost Greenland*, 56. Hawks wrote several titles under the pen name 'Uncle Philip' for Harper's Boys' and Girls' Library imprint series.
31. Ibid., 57.
32. Dickens, 'Lost Arctic Voyagers', 362–5, 387–93. For a detailed discussion of the media commotion caused by Rae's discovery, see Hill, *White Horizon*, 113–50.
33. See Jensz and Petterson, *Legacies of David Cranz's 'Historie von Grönland'*.
34. Cowper, *Poems*, 164.
35. Hemans, 'Indian's Revenge'.
36. Crantz, *History of Greenland*, 1:188.
37. Ibid.
38. Crantz, *History of Greenland*, 2:225–6, 228.
39. Bryant, *Treatise upon the Authenticity of the Scriptures*, 16–18.
40. *Moravians in Greenland*, 48.
41. The scholarship on Azil is sparse. Francesca Bertino has made some headway in her article 'Exhibition of Otherness'. However, this has regrettably not been followed up by further critical studies.
42. Paganini, *Le Avventure di Azil*.

43. See, for example, Blanchard, Bancel, Boetsch, Deroo, and Lemaire, *Human Zoos*.
44. Ibid., 45.
45. Ibid., 4.
46. See Bertino, 'Exhibition of Otherness', 8, note.
47. Paganini, *Dettagli*, 4: *quasi come i nostril, eccettuatene alcune, fra esse che hanno gli occhi grandi, le labbra grosse, i capelli castagni ed il colorito più bianco di quello degli Europei.*
48. Paganini, *Dettagli*, 5: *Il Capitano CARRY [sic] ha veduto sopra la costa della Greonlandia degli Esquimaudi i di cui lineamenti allungati gli fecero credere che vi sia stata qualche unione fra queste orde selvaggie e la razza dei Danesi e Scandinavi.* For William Parry's description, see *Journal of a Second Voyage*, 493.
49. This information from the earliest version of the pamphlet is cited in Bertino, 'Exhibition of Otherness', 10.
50. Paganini, *Dettagli*, p. 16: *Qualch'alma giuuse a rompere / Delle barbarie il velo.* This line also appears in the German version, but not in the French.
51. Lutz, *Diary of Abraham Ulrikab*.
52. Hagenbeck, *Beasts and Men*, 39. My emphasis.
53. *Greenland Missions*, 45. Most of the book consists of excerpts from Crantz' *History of Greenland*.
54. Charlton, review of *Grönlands historiske Mindesmærker*, 74.
55. *Northern Light*, 115.
56. Ibid., 116.
57. Ibid.
58. See 'Ivngertose isuanit', in *Tuksiautit: julesiutit*, 27–9.
59. In terms of modern critical attention, see, however, Lansdown, *Literature and Truth*, 96–116; and Sangster, *Living As an Author*, 69–75. Neither discusses Montgomery's most famous poem.
60. Review of Montgomery's *Greenland*, *Eclectic Review*, 215.

61. Review of Montgomery's *Greenland*, *British Critic*, 212.

62. St Clair, *Reading Nation in the Romantic Period*, 218, see also 619.

63. Review of Montgomery's *Greenland*, *Eclectic Review*, 215.

64. Reiman, 'Introduction', viii.

65. Hutton, *History of the Moravian Church*, 454.

66. Montgomery, *Greenland, and Other Poems*, 67.

67. Ibid., 82.

68. Ibid., 93, 97.

69. Citation from John Leslie, 'Polar Ice and a North-West Passage'.

70. Ibid., 104.

71. Malthe Brun [Conrad Malte-Brun], 'On the Expeditions to the North Pole', 282. See also the findings of Giesecke, *On the Norwegian Settlements*, 6.

72. Montgomery, *Greenland, and Other Poems*, 82.

73. Ibid., 109–10.

74. Ibid., 82.

75. Blackley, *Greenland Minstrel*. Acknowledging the source of his inspiration, Blackley sent a copy of his poem to a reportedly appreciative Montgomery: see Newsam and Holland, *Poets of Yorkshire*, 188–9.

76. Blackley, *Greenland Minstrel*, 5.

77. Ibid., 76.

78. Egede, *A Description of Greenland*, 21–2; Crantz, *History of Greenland*, 1:244.

79. Blackley, *Greenland Minstrel*, 5.

80. Ibid., 108.

81. Montgomery, *Pelican Island and Other Poems*, 1.

82. Ibid., 28.

83. Ibid., 30–1.

84. Ibid., 82–3.

85. Ibid., 89. Egyptian hieroglyphics were indecipherable in the West until 1822 when Jean-François Champollion

deciphered them. Cf. Montgomery's *West Indies*, 47: 'Through all the glory of his works we trace / The hidings of his counsel and his face; / Nature and time and change and fate fulfil / Unknown, unknowing his mysterious will; / Mercies and judgments mark him every hour / Supreme in grace and infinite in power'.

86. Montgomery, *Greenland, and Other Poems*, title page.
87. Ibid., see note 68.
88. Sleeper, 'Lost Colony', 222.
89. Ibid., 118–20.
90. Ibid., 2.
91. Heber wrote the hymn for the Society for the Propagation of the Gospel in Foreign Parts, a Church of England missionary organisation active in the British Atlantic world, and he was himself appointed the bishop of Calcutta in 1823. See Richards, *Imperialism and Music*, 386–7.
92. Blackley, *Greenland Minstrel*, 114.
93. Lynge, 'Introduction', 14.
94. Ibid., 17.

6 The Surpassing Adventures of Allan Gordon

1. All citations from *Surpassing Adventures of Allan Gordon* will be from the version published in *Tales and Sketches by the Ettrick Shepherd*, vol. 1 (Glasgow: Blackie & Son, 1837) and will henceforth be referenced by page number in the text. Hogg died in 1835; the novella was published posthumously.
2. Letter from Hogg to Blackie & Son, 25 March 1834, in Hughes, *Collected Letters of James Hogg*, 209.
3. Defoe, *Life and Strange Surprizing Adventures of Robinson Crusoe*, 151.
4. Redding, *History of Shipwrecks*, 1:114.
5. Hogg, 'P and Q', 694.

6. *Munchausen at the Pole*, 29. Michael Bravo includes a fine contextualising reading of the Munchausen satire in *North Pole*, 152–5.

7. Ibid., 29.

8. Ibid., 30.

9. Fielding, 'No Pole nor Pillar', 52.

10. Review of Jukes, *Narrative of the Surveying Voyage*, 516.

11. The 'Arctic sublime' was an aesthetic vogue that became a category in its own right during the Romantic period. As a topic, it was first examined in Chauncey C. Loomis' seminal article 'The Arctic Sublime'. For an update on this subject, see Robert W. Rix, 'The Arctic Sublime', in *The Cambridge Companion to the Romantic Sublime*, ed. Cian Duffy (forthcoming).

12. Officer and Page, *A Fabulous Kingdom*, 3.

13. Hogg furthermore acknowledges Brewster's influence by making use of his theory of an Open Polar Sea. At one point Gordon's ice floe drifts into this mythical ice-free water (which does not exist) before he is again carried south by a rapid current (pp. 272–6). See Brewster, 'Observations on the Mean Temperature of the Globe'.

14. Carroll, *An Empire of Air and Water*, 7.

15. 'Romantic, adj. and n'. 2a. *OED Online*, Oxford University Press, December 2019. www.oed.com/view/Entry/167122.

16. [Francis Palgrave], review of Hans Egede Saabye, 493.

17. For a discussion of erotic metaphors in colonial rhetoric, see Carey, 'Spenser, Purchas, and the Poetics of Colonial Settlement'.

18. As an illustration of how Hogg yokes together romance and anti-romance (or the ironic), his 1822 novel *Three Perils of Man* is often mentioned as an example. See, for example, Douglas Gifford's 'Introduction' in Hogg, *Three Perils of Man*, xiv–xxv.

19. Fielding, 'James Hogg', 66.

20. For a contemporary etymological explanation, see O'Reilly, *Greenland*, 58 and 60.
21. Weaver-Hightower, *Empire Islands*, especially 94 and 144.
22. Boucher, 'Arctic Mysteries and Imperial Ambitions', 47.
23. Engelhard, *Ice Bear*.
24. Moss, 'Romanticism on Ice'.
25. Hogg, 'Nature's Magic Lantern', 356.
26. Ibid., 360.
27. Pinkerton, *An Inquiry into the History of Scotland*, 1:350.
28. Johnstone, *Lodbrokar Quida*, 101.
29. Hall, *Travels in Scotland*, 2:598.
30. Hogg, *A Tour in the Highlands in 1803*, 109.
31. Deans, 'Pastoral Optimism', 135.
32. Hogg, *Highland Tours*, 77.
33. Hogg, *Shepherd's Guide*, 295. Hogg advocated that communities in the Highlands should be moved away from areas of non-arable lands, which could then be turned into large-scale sheep farming. For an analysis of Hogg's modernisation project, see Deans, 'Pastoral Optimism'.
34. Hogg, *The Spy*.
35. Ibid.
36. Trollope, *How the 'Mastiffs' Went to Iceland*, 6.
37. 'V' [Anna Jane Vardill], 'Extracts from an Arctic Navigator's Journal', 196.
38. Pittock, *Scottish and Irish Romanticism*, 235–58.
39. Macaulay, *History of England from the Accession of James II*, 3:239. Italics in the original.

7 Arctic Adventure Tales

1. R. H. D., 'Lost Colony'.
2. For a fairly exhaustive list of 'lost world' / 'lost races' stories, see Teitler, *By the World Forgot*.

3. Rafn and Magnússon, *Grönlands historiske mindesmærker*, 459: *Groenlandiæ incolæ a vera fide et religione christiana sponte sua defecerunt, et repudiatis omnibus honestis moribus et veris virtutibus ad Americæ populos se converterunt.*

4. See, for example, Maurer, 'Geschichte der Entdeckung Ostgrönlands', 235 note.

5. Charlevoix, *Histoire et description generale de La Nouvelle France*, 179: ... *je suis persuadé qu'ils sont originaires du Groenland.*

6. Pontoppidan, *Natural History of Norway*, 234.

7. Rink, *Tales and Traditions of the Eskimo*, 469–70.

8. For a summary and debunking of the Norse theory, see Therkel, 'Norse Ruins in Labrador?'.

9. Horsford, *Defenses of Norumbega*, 83.

10. Watts, *Colonizing the Past*, especially 162–210.

11. Harry Prentice [pseudonym for James Otis Kaler], *Boy Explorers*.

12. Dodge, *Attraction of the Compass*.

13. Stringer, *Woman Who Couldn't Die*.

14. Carter, 'The Sea Fryseth Not', 237.

15. Craciun, 'Frozen Ocean', 696.

16. See Hendrik, *Memoirs of Hans Hendrik*.

17. Hayes, *Open Polar Sea*, 116.

18. Maury, 'Gateways to the Pole', 537.

19. A. F. L., 'Church in Greenland III', 61.

20. Whittaker, *Lost Captain*, 15.

21. Ibid., 14.

22. Haggard, 'Elephant Smashing and Lion Shooting' (1894), quoted in Belk, *Empires of Print*, 73.

23. Page, *Amid Greenland Snows*, 11–12.

24. Clareson, 'Lost Lands, Lost Races'.

25. See Westphal, *Geocriticism*, 80–3.

26. Leon Lewis [Julius Warren Lewis], *Andrée at the North Pole*, 169.

27. Seaborn [pseudonym], *Symzonia*, 38.
28. Burland, *Princess Thora*, 137.
29. Morton, *Beyond the Palaeocrystic Sea*, 14.
30. Ibid., 38.
31. Ibid., 263.
32. Ibid., 44.
33. Wilson, *Rafnaland*, 68–70.
34. Harpold, 'Verne's Cartographies', 20. Verne's several Arctic tales were well researched as he read and copied various travel accounts of Arctic exploration, see Riffenburgh, 'Jules Verne and the Conquest of the Polar Regions'.
35. Whittaker, *Lost Captain*, 14.
36. Johnstone, *Paradise of the North*, 80.
37. Tally, *Topophrenia*, 130.
38. 'History of Arctic Adventure', 316.
39. Ibid., 317.
40. Osborn, *Stray Leaves from an Arctic Journal*, 149–50.
41. Markham, 'Promotion of Further Discovery in the Arctic', 328.
42. Adams, *Shore and Sea*, vi.
43. Boggild, 'Ante-Columbian Discovery of the American Continent'. Originally printed in the *New Orleans Sunday Times*.
44. Peary, 'Value of Arctic Exploration', 436.
45. Berry, 'Monroe Doctrine and the Governance of Greenland's Security', 108–9.
46. Johnstone, *Paradise of the North*, 238.
47. Wilson, *Rafnaland*, 69.
48. Rieder, *Colonialism and the Emergence of Science Fiction*.
49. For the full list of Frank Reade Jr 'lost race' stories, see Williams, *Gears and God*, 13 note.
50. Headrick, *Power over Peoples*, 177–225.
51. Noname, *Frank Reade, Jr.'s Electric Ice Boat* (part I), 6, 9.
52. Ibid., 13.

53. Noname, *Latitude 90°*, 11.
54. Noname, *Frank Reade, Jr.'s Electric Ice Boat* (part 2), 3–4.
55. Morton, *Beyond the Palaeocrystic Sea*, 264.
56. Noname, *Across the Frozen Sea*, 10.
57. Noname, *To the End of the Earth in an Air-Ship*, 12.
58. For the anti-imperialist ideology in the Frank Reade Jr stories, see Williams, *Gears and God*, 45–61.
59. For a recent reading of Stevenson as a writer who criticised the imperialist ideology of the adventure novel, see Elleray, *Victorian Coral Islands of Empire*.
60. Ibid., 256.
61. Alden, 'Very Cold Truth', 254.
62. Ibid., 256.
63. See Wood-Donnelly, *Performing Arctic Sovereignty*, 32.
64. Chesneaux, *Political and Social Ideas of Jules Verne*, 41–68.
65. For a recent account of the shooting, see Solberg, *Arctic Mirage*, 55–68.
66. Green, 'Across the Pole by Plane', 937.
67. Ibid., 31.
68. Green, 'Will the ZR-1 Discover a Polar Paradise?', 29.
69. Ibid., 31.
70. Ibid.
71. Segal, *Technological Utopianism in American Culture*.
72. Green, 'Over the Top of the World', 682.
73. Ibid., 682–3.
74. Stefansson, *Northward Course of Empire*, especially 13–18.
75. De Morgan, *Lost in Ice*, 100.
76. Green, *ZR Wins*.
77. An airship to the North Pole is also part of the plot in another 'lost race' novel, Edgar Rice Burroughs, *Tarzan at the Earth's Core* (1930), which features the construction of the O-220 dirigible.
78. Green, *ZR Wins*, 5.
79. Ibid., 149–50.

80. Ibid., 156.
81. Green, *ZR Wins*, 179.
82. Ibid., 269.
83. Peirce, *Report on the Resources of Iceland and Greenland*, 22.
84. Green, *ZR Wins*, 179.
85. Ibid., 209.
86. Ash, *In Polar Seas*, 46.
87. See, for example, the anonymous article 'Blazing the Trail for Polar Airlines'.
88. Quoted in Emmerson, *Future History of the Arctic*, 105.
89. See ibid.
90. E. C. H Keskitalo analyses the rhetoric of the Arctic in terms of its strategic and resource-orientated use in *Negotiating the Arctic*; see page 34 for the definition of the 'Arctic Mediterranean'.
91. Green, *ZR Wins*, 220.
92. *Go North!*
93. Lee, 'Tourism and Taste Cultures', 267–8.
94. Green, *Dreams of Adventure*, 37.
95. Burland, *Princess Thora*, 358.
96. Ibid., 358–60.
97. Schimanski, 'Reading the Future North'.
98. Hueffer and Conrad, *The Inheritors*, 45–6.
99. Ibid., 121.
100. For an analysis of these books, see Berthelsen, 'Greenlandic Literature', 341–2.
101. Lynge, *Trehundrede år efter*, 98.
102. Ibid., 30.

8 Vanished Settlers

1. Charlton, Review of Magnussen and Rafn's *Grönlands historiske Mindesmærker*, 74.
2. Ibid.

3. Annette Kolodny refers to the frequently conflicting uses of the Vikings in a nineteenth-century American context. See *In Search of First Contact*, especially 204–12. For the diversity of British appropriations, see Wawn, *The Vikings and the Victorians*.

4. Hall, 'Whites of Their Eyes'.

5. Howison, *European Colonies*, 2:198.

6. Ibid., 2:199.

7. Hayes, *Land of Desolation*, 51.

8. Ibid., 54.

9. Froude, *Oceana*, 17.

10. Bechdolt, *Lost Vikings*.

11. Bravo, *North Pole*, especially 136–47.

12. Cf. Jen Hill, who notes how nineteenth-century discourse on polar exploration 'draws comparison between Arctic purity and racial whiteness'; see *White Horizon*, 8.

13. Seaborn [Pseudonym], *Symzonia*, 110.

14. Fishe, *Beyond the Snow*, 23.

15. Hansson, 'Arctopias', 70.

16. Fairman, *Third World*, 91.

17. Ibid. Greene, *Ke Whonkus People*, 102.

18. Müller published the series under the pseudonym Freder van Holk. For Jan Mayen's Greenland adventures, see Galle, *Sun Koh*, 288–9.

19. For a scholarly treatment of these myths, see Godwin, *Arktos*, 47–62.

20. See Rieder, *Colonialism and the Emergence of Science Fiction*, especially 22–3 and 52–3; Hanson, 'Lost among White Others'; and Dixon, *Writing the Colonial Adventure*.

21. Cronin, 'Technological Heroes', 59.

22. Poon, *Enacting Englishness in the Victorian Period*, 139 and 145.

23. Haggard, *Eric Brighteyes*, x.

24. Johnstone, *Paradise of the North*, 158.

25. Ibid., 153.
26. Whittaker, *Lost Captain*, 14.
27. Ibid., 14.
28. Ibid., 14, 15.
29. Ibid., 14.
30. Ibid., 16.
31. Whittaker, *Lost Captain*, 15, 16.
32. Sreenan, 'Dreaming of Islands', 268.
33. Stables, *The City at the Pole*, 95.
34. Ibid., 197.
35. Marland, '"Bicycle-Face" and "Lawn Tennis" Girls', 78–9.
36. Armstrong, *Yorl of the Northmen*, viii.
37. Armstrong, 'A Eugenic Colony'.
38. Eco, 'Science Fiction and the Art of Conjecture'.
39. Khouri, 'Lost Worlds and the Revenge of Realism', 171–2.
40. Ibid., 178.
41. Burland, *Princess Thora*, 358.
42. Ibid., 108.
43. Ibid., 122.
44. Ibid., 358.
45. Deane, *Masculinity and the New Imperialism*, 47–69, quotations on 149.
46. Ash, *In Polar Seas*.
47. Ibid. (February 5, 1916): 43–4.
48. Nies, *Eugenic Fantasies*, 37.
49. Rafn, *Supplement to Antiquitates Americanæ*, especially 19.
50. 'Antiquarian Researches'.
51. Cabot, 'Discovery of America by the Norsemen', 189.
52. See Kolodny, *In Search of First Contact*; Barnes, *Viking America*; and Thurin, *American Discovery of the Norse*.
53. Anderson, *America Not Discovered by Columbus*, especially 58–92.

54. See Hunter, *Place of Stone*, 130–53.
55. Kassis, *American Travellers in Scandinavia*, 87.
56. Ibid., 1.
57. Bennett, *Thyra*, 67.
58. Ibid., 84.
59. Pickett, *Quest for a Lost Race*, 40.
60. Ibid.
61. Wilson, 'Return of the Sergeant'.
62. Grant, *Passing of the Great Race*, 175.
63. Johnstone, *Paradise of the North*, 165–6, 174, 176, and 181.
64. Wilson, *Rafnaland*, 93–4.
65. *An Amazonian Queen*.
66. In the early nineteenth century Alexander von Humboldt associated the Mayan culture hero Votan with Odin/Woden of Norse mythology. See Humboldt's *Views of the Cordilleras and Monuments*, especially 92, 173–5. Dubious archaeological discoveries were later made in Bahia, Brazil: purportedly Scandinavian tools and an object inscribed with Runic characters. For this, see 'Antiquarian Researches' and 'Eskimos of Greenland'.
67. Jackson, *Queen of Amazonia*.
68. Green, *ZR Wins*, 167.
69. Ralph Milne Farley, *The Radio Flyers* was originally serialised in *Argosy-All-Story* (1929), 11 May–8 June 1929. References here are to the reprint in *Famous Fantastic Classics* no. 2 (San Bernardino, CA: Borgo Press, 1975), 20–131. Farley was a pseudonym of Roger Sherman Hoar, a senator for the state of Massachusetts.
70. Ibid., 79.
71. Ibid., 91.
72. Nelson, *Wings of Danger*, 274.
73. Ibid., 397.
74. Robinson, *Lost White Tribe*, 103.
75. Ibid., 162–9.

76. In fact, his contact with them was much more limited, see Damas, 'Journey at the Threshold', 130–2.
77. Stefansson, *My Life with the Eskimo*, 192.
78. Ibid., 200.
79. Ibid., 195.
80. Ibid., 186. The famous ethnologist Edward Burnett Tylor had in the study 'Old Scandinavian Civilisation among the Modern Esquimaux' claimed that the songs as well as customs and dress of Greenland Inuit showed clear signs of influence from close contact with the Norse colony, but he does not mention intermarriage as the cause.
81. Ibid., 200.
82. Stefansson, 'Icelandic Colony in Greenland', 270.
83. Stefansson later denounced the information contained in the article as highly inaccurate reporting; see his 'My Quest in the North', 4.
84. Levere, *Science and the Canadian Arctic*, 387. See also John Steckley's *White Lies about the Inuit*, especially 77–102.
85. Greely, 'Origin of Stefansson's Blonde Eskimo'.
86. Rasmussen, *Intellectual Culture of the Copper Eskimos*, 75.
87. See Pálsson, 'Genomic Anthropology'.
88. Moltke, Fumagalli, Korneliussen et al., 'Uncovering the Genetic History'.
89. Steckley, *White Lies about the Inuit*, 77–102, citation on 101.
90. Stefansson, 'Republic of Greenland', 264.
91. De Morgan, *Lost in Ice*, 67.
92. Dodge, *Attraction of the Compass: A Romance of the North*; *Attraction of the Compass, or, The Blonde Eskimo*.
93. Dodge, *Attraction of the Compass, or, The Blonde Eskimo*, 201.
94. Ibid., 191.
95. Murphy, *German Exploration of the Polar World*, 164–75.
96. Ibid., 165.

97. Greenwood, *Curiosities of Savage Life*, 1:416–17.
98. Spufford, *I May Be Some Time*, 54; Robinson, *Coldest Crucible*.
99. Cavell, 'Going Native in the North', 33.
100. McClintock, 'Discoveries by the Late Expedition', 12.
101. David, *The Arctic in the British Imagination*, 207–10.
102. Scoville, *Boy Scouts*. A book version was published in 1920.
103. Ibid., 810.
104. Ibid., 624.
105. Huhndorf, *Going Native*, 72–4.
106. Scoville, *Boy Scouts*, 1119.

Conclusion

1. See June debates in US Congress, *Congressional Record*, 7683–4.
2. Skarstein, *'Erik the Red's Land'*.
3. Justice Dionisio Anzilotti's dissenting opinion, which was enclosed with the judgment, is the subject of Cavell, 'Historical Evidence and the Eastern Greenland Case'.
4. 'Legal Status', *Geographical Journal*.
5. 'Legal Status', PCIJ Series A/B, 27–8.
6. Ibid., 27.
7. Ibid., 47. For considerations on this issue in relation to Greenland's Indigenous population, see Green and Dickason, *Law of Nations and the New World*, 85–90.
8. Langgård, 'Greenlandic Attitudes towards Norwegians and Danes'.
9. Ibid., 65.
10. Ibid., 60–1.
11. Ibid.
12. Kaarsted, *Great Britain and Denmark 1914–1920*, 130.

BIBLIOGRAPHY*

A. F. L. 'The Church in Greenland III', *Irish Church Advocate* 40, no. 475 (March 1877): 60–2.

An Account of Several Late Voyages & Discoveries ... towards Nova Zembla, Greenland or Spitsberg, Groynland or Engrondland. London: Sam. Smith and Benj. Walford, 1694.

Adams, William Henry Davenport. *Shore and Sea; Or, Stories of Great Vikings and Sea-Captains.* London: Hodder & Stoughton, 1883.

Alden, W. L. 'Very Cold Truth', *Idler* 11 (February 1897): 252–8.

'Die alte norwegische Colonie in Grönland wieder aufgefunden', *Dinglers polytechnisches Journal* (October 1831): 237.

An Amazonian Queen, or, Nick Carter Becomes a Gladiator. New York: Street & Smith, 1907.

Anderson, Adam. *An Historical and Chronological Deduction of the Origin of Commerce, from the Earliest Accounts*, rev ed. London: J. Robson et al. [1764] 1787.

Anderson, Rasmus B. *America Not Discovered by Columbus*, rev. ed. Chicago, IL: S. C. Griggs and Company, 1877.

'Antiquarian Researches', *Gentleman's Magazine* 173 (May 1843): 521.

Armstrong, Charles Wicksteed. 'A Eugenic Colony: A Proposal for South America', *Eugenics Review* new series 6, no. 2 (1933): 91–7.

Armstrong, Charles Wicksteed. *The Yorl of the Northmen; or, The Fate of the English Race Being the Romance of a Monarchical Utopia.* London: Reeves and Turner, 1892.

---

* For Icelandic names, entries are ordered in accordance with Icelandic alphabetical practice.

Arneborg, Jette. 'Aqissiaq og nordboerne', *Tidsskriftet Grønland* 6 (1990): 213–19.

Arneborg, Jette. 'Contacts between Eskimo and Norsemen in Greenland: A Review of the Evidence'. In *Beretning fra tolvte tværfaglige vikingesymposium*, edited by Else Roesdahl and Preben Sørensen Meulengracht, 23–36. Aarhus: Hikuin, 1993.

Arneborg, Jette. 'Cultural Borders: Reflections on Norse–Eskimo Interaction'. In *Fifty Years of Arctic Research: Anthropological Studies from Greenland to Siberia*, edited by Rolf Gilberg and Hans Christian Gulløv, 41–6. Copenhagen: National Museum of Denmark, 1997.

Arneborg, Jette. 'Kulturmødet mellem nordboere og eskimoer i Grønland. Vurderet i norrønt perspektiv'. PhD thesis, University of Copenhagen (1991).

Arneborg, Jette. 'Norse Greenland: Research into Abandonment'. In *Medieval Archaeology in Scandinavia and Beyond: History, Trends and Tomorrow*, edited by Mette Svart Kristiansen, Else Roesdahl, and James Graham-Campbell, 257–71. Aarhus: Aarhus University Press, 2015.

Ash, Fenton. *In Polar Seas: A Romance of Adventure in Polar Seas*, serialised in *Nelson Lee Library*, nos. 19–37 (1915–16). Digital version at www.friardale.co.uk/ESB/Nelson%20Lee.htm.

Atkinson, Geoffroy. *The Extraordinary Voyage in French Literature from 1700 to 1720*. Paris: Édoard Champion, 1922.

Baldur Þórhallsson and Þorsteinn Kristinsson, 'Iceland's External Affairs from 1400 to the Reformation: Anglo-German Economic and Societal Shelter in a Danish Political Vacuum', *Icelandic Review of Politics and Administration* 9, no. 1 (2013): 113–37.

Bárdarson Ívar., *Det gamle Grønlands Beskrivelse*, edited by Finnur Jónsson. Copenhagen: Levin & Munksgaard, 1930.

Bárdarson Ívar., 'A Treatise of Iver Boty, a Gronlander'. In *Hakluytus Posthumus or, Purchas His Pilgrimes Contayning a History of the World in Sea Voyages and Lande Travells by*

Englishmen and Others, vol. 13, 163–71. Cambridge: Cambridge University Press, 2014.

Barnes, Geraldine. *Viking America: The First Millennium.* Cambridge: D. S. Brewer, 2001.

Barr, William. 'Harpoon Guns, the Lost Greenland Settlement, and Penal Colonies: George Manby's Arctic Obsession', *Polar Record* 37 (2001): 291–314.

Barrett, James H., Sanne Boessenkool, Catherine J. Kneale, Tamsin C. O'Connell, and Bastiaan Star, 'Ecological Globalisation, Serial Depletion and the Medieval Trade of Walrus Rostra', *Quaternary Science Reviews* 229 (2020). https://doi.org/10.1016/j.quascirev.2019.106122.

Barrow, John. *A Chronological History of Voyages into the Arctic Regions ... from the Earliest Periods of Scandinavian Navigation, to the Departure of the Recent Expeditions.* London: John Murray, 1818.

Barrow, John. '"On the Polar Ice and Northern Passage into the Pacific", a Review of Edward Chappel's *Narrative of a Voyage to Hudson's Bay*', *Quarterly Review* 18, no. 35 (October 1817): 199–223.

Barrow, John. 'Review of O'Reilly's *Greenland, the Adjacent Seas*', *Quarterly Review* 19, no. 37 (April 1818): 208–14.

Bartosik-Velez, Elise. *The Legacy of Christopher Columbus in the Americas: New Nations and a Transatlantic Discourse of Empire.* Nashville, TN: Vanderbilt University Press, 2014.

Baught, Daniel A. 'Seapower and Science: The Motives for Pacific Exploration'. In *Background to Discovery: Pacific Exploration from Dampier to Cook*, edited by Derek Howse, 1–55. Berkeley: University of California Press, 1990.

Bechdolt, Jack. *The Lost Vikings.* New York: Cosmopolitan Book Corporation, 1931.

Belk, Patrick Scott. *Empires of Print: Adventure Fiction in the Magazines, 1899–1919.* London: Routledge, 2017.

Belmessous, Saliha. 'Assimilation and Racialism in Seventeenth- and Eighteenth-Century French Colonial Policy', *American Historical Review* 110, no. 2 (2005): 322–49.

Bennett, Robert Ames. *Thyra: A Romance of the Polar Pit*. New York: Henry Holt and Company, 1901.

Bentham, Jeremy. *Panopticon; or, The Inspection-House: Containing the Idea of a New Principle of Construction*. London: T. Payne, 1791.

Bentham, Jeremy. *The Principles of Penal Law. In Works: Part II*. Edinburgh: William Tait, 1838.

Berry, Dawn Alexandrea. 'The Monroe Doctrine and the Governance of Greenland's Security'. In *Governing the North American Arctic: Sovereignty, Security, and Institutions*, edited by Dawn Alexandrea Berry, Nigel Bowles, and Halbert Jones, 103–26. Houndmills: Palgrave Macmillan, 2016.

Berthelsen, Christian. 'Greenlandic Literature: Its Traditions, Changes, and Trends', *Arctic Anthropology* 23, no. 1/2 (1986): 339–45.

Bertino, Francesca. 'The Exhibition of Otherness: The Travels of an Eskimo and Her Impresario in France, Italy and the Habsburg Empire in the First Half of the 19th Century', *Cromohs: Cyber Review of Modern Historiography* 18 (2013): 1–22. https://doi.org/10.13128/Cromohs-14114.

'Beschrijvingh van Groenlandt'. In *Drie voyagien gedaen na Groenlandt*, 28. Amsterdam: Gillis Joosten Saeghman, 1663?.

Best, George. *A True Discourse of the Late Voyages of Discoverie*. London: Henry Bynnyman, 1578.

Beyer, Absalon Pedersön. *Om Norgis Rige*. Bergen: F. Beyers, [1567] 1928.

Bielke, Jens. *Relation om Grønland: & Ennlystig disceptaz*, edited by Flemming Lundgreen-Nielsen. Copenhagen: Reitzel, 1990.

Black, Jeremy. *Charting the Past: The Historical Worlds of Eighteenth-Century England*. Bloomington, IN: Indiana University Press, 2018.

Blackley, Frederick Rogers. *The Greenland Minstrel: A Poem in Six Cantos. With an Introductory Narrative.* London: Simpkin and Marshall, 1839.

Blanchard, Pascal, Nicolas Bancel, Gilles Boetsch, Eric Deroo, and Sandrine Lemaire, eds. *Human Zoos: Science and Spectacle in the Age of Colonial Empires.* Liverpool: Liverpool University Press, 2008.

'Blazing the Trail for Polar Airlines', *Popular Science Monthly* (July 1923): 27.

Blefken, Dithmar. *Islandia sive populorum et mirabilium quae in ea insula reperiuntur accuratior description: Cui de Gronlandia sub sinem quædam adjecta.* Lugduni Batavorum: Henrici ab Haestens, 1607.

Blome, Richard. *A Geographical Description of the Four Parts of the World: Taken from the Notes & Workes of the Famous Monsieur Sanson, Geographer of the French King, and Other Eminent Travellers and Authors.* London: Printed for R. Blome, 1670.

Bobé, Louis, ed. *Diplomatarium Groenlandicum 1492–1814: Aktstykker og Breve til Oplysning om Grønlands Besejling, Kolonisation og Missionering.* Copenhagen: C. A. Reitzel, 1936.

Bobé, Louis. 'Early Exploration of Greenland'. In *Greenland*, vol. 1, edited by Martin Vahl, Georg Carl Amdrup, Louis Bobé, and Adolf Severin Jensen, 1–36. Copenhagen: C. A. Reitzel, 1928.

Bobé, Louis. *Hans Egede, Grønlands Missionær og Kolonisator.* Copenhagen: C. A. Reitzel, 1944.

Boggild, F. 'The Ante-Columbian Discovery of the American Continent, by the Northmen', *Historical Magazine* new series 5, no. 3 (March 1869): 170–8.

Bond, Lucy and Jessica Rapson. *The Transcultural Turn: Interrogating Memory between and beyond Borders.* Berlin: De Gruyter, 2014.

Boucher, Ellen. 'Arctic Mysteries and Imperial Ambitions: The Hunt for Sir John Franklin and the Victorian Culture of Survival', *Journal of Modern History* 90 (2018): 40–75.

Boulhosa, Patricia Pires. *Icelanders and the Kings of Norway: Mediaeval Sagas and Legal Texts.* Leiden: Brill, 2005.

Bowen, Emanuel. *A Complete System of Geography: Being a Description of all the Countries, Islands, Cities, Chief Towns, Harbours, Lakes, and Rivers, Mountains, Mines, &c. of the Known World*, 2 vols. London: William Innys et al., 1747.

Bowers, Katherine. 'Haunted Ice, Fearful Sounds, and the Arctic Sublime: Exploring Nineteenth-Century Polar Gothic Space', *Gothic Studies* 19, no. 2 (2017): 71–84.

Brantlinger, Patrick. *Rule of Darkness: British Literature and Imperialism, 1830–1914.* Ithaca, NY: Cornell University Press, 1988.

Brantlinger, Patrick. *Taming Cannibals: Race and the Victorians.* Ithaca, NY: Cornell University Press, 2011.

Bravo, Michael. 'The Anti-anthropology of Highlanders and Islanders', *Studies in History and Philosophy of Science Part A* 29, no. 3 (1998): 369–89.

Bravo, Michael. 'Geographies of Exploration and Improvement: William Scoresby and Arctic Whaling, 1782–1822', *Journal of Historical Geography* 32, no. 3 (2006): 512–38.

Bravo, Michael. 'Indigenous Evangelical Voyaging: Authorship and Perspective'. In *Curious Encounters: Voyaging, Collecting, and Making Knowledge in the Long Eighteenth Century*, edited by Adriana Craciun and Mary Terrall, 71–112. Toronto, ON: University of Toronto Press, 2019.

Bravo, Michael. 'Mission Gardens Natural History and Global Expansion, 1720–1820'. In *Colonial Botany: Science, Commerce, and Politics in the Early Modern World*, edited by Londa Schiebinger and Claudia Swan, 49–65. Philadelphia: University of Pennsylvania Press, 2007.

Bravo, Michael. *North Pole: Nature and Culture.* London: Reaktion Books, 2019.

Bravo, Michael. 'The Postcolonial Arctic', *Moving Worlds: A Journal of Transcultural Writings* 15 (2015): 93–111.

Bravo, Michael and Sverker Sörlin, eds. *Narrating the Arctic: A Cultural History of Nordic Scientific Practices*. Canton, MA: Science History Publications, 2002.

Brewster, David. 'Observations on the Mean Temperature of the Globe', *Transactions of the Royal Society of Edinburgh* 9 (1823): 201–25.

Bryant, Jacob. *A Treatise upon the Authenticity of the Scriptures, and the Truth of the Christian Religion*, 2nd ed. London: T. Cadell and P. Elmsly, 1792.

Burland, Harris. *The Princess Thora*. Boston, MA: Little, Brown, and Company, 1904.

Cabot, James Elliot. 'Discovery of America by the Norsemen', *Massachusetts Quarterly Review* 6 (March 1849): 189–215.

Capel, Rudolph. *Norden, Oder Zu Wasser und Lande im Eise und Snee*. Hamburg: Johann Nanmann, 1678.

Carey, Daniel. 'Spenser, Purchas, and the Poetics of Colonial Settlement'. In *Studies in Settler Colonialism: Politics, Identity and Culture*, edited by Fiona Bateman and Lionel Pilkington, 28–46. Houndmills: Palgrave Macmillan, 2011.

Carroll, Siobhan. *An Empire of Air and Water: Uncolonizable Space in the British Imagination, 1750–1850*. Philadelphia: University of Pennsylvania Press, 2015.

Carter, Christopher. '"The Sea Fryseth Not." Science and the Open Polar Sea in the Nineteenth Century', *Earth Science History* 32, no. 2 (2013): 235–51.

Cavell, Janice. 'Going Native in the North: Reconsidering British Attitudes during the Franklin Search, 1848–1859', *Polar Record* 45, no. 232 (2009): 25–35.

Cavell, Janice. 'Historical Evidence and the Eastern Greenland Case', *Arctic* 61, no. 4 (2008): 433–41.

Cavell, Janice. 'Miss Porden, Mrs. Franklin, and the Arctic Expeditions: Eleanor Anne Porden and the Construction of Arctic Heroism (1818–25)'. In *Arctic Exploration in the Nineteenth Century: Discovering the Northwest Passage*, edited by Frédéric Regard, 79–94. London: Pickering & Chatto, 2013.

Cavell, Janice. *Tracing the Connected Narrative: Arctic Exploration in British Print Culture, 1818–1860*. Toronto: University of Toronto Press, 2008.

Charlevoix, Pierre-Francois-Xavier de. *Histoire et description generale de La Nouvelle France*, 6 vols. Paris: Rollin, 1744.

Charlton, Edward. Review of F. Magnussen and C. C. Rafn's *Grönlands historiske Mindesmærker*, *Dublin Review*, 27 (September 1849): 35–74.

Chesneaux, Jean. *The Political and Social Ideas of Jules Verne*, translated by Thomas Wikeley. London: Thames and Hudson, 1972.

King Christian IV. 'Letter of Instruction, 6 May 1607'. In *Diplomatarium Groenlandicum 1492–1814: Aktstykker og Breve til Oplysning om Grønlands Besejling, Kolonisation og Missionering*, edited by Louis Bobé, 1–19. Copenhagen: C. A. Reitzel, 1936.

Clareson, Thomas D. 'Lost Lands, Lost Races: A Pagan Princess of Their Very Own', *Journal of Popular Culture* 8, no. 4 (1975): 714–23.

Clarke, Richard H. 'America Discovered and Christianized in the Tenth and Eleventh Centuries', *American Catholic Quarterly Review* 13 (1888): 211–37.

Clayton, Daniel. 'Imperial Geographies'. In *A Companion to Cultural Geography*, edited by James Duncan, Nuala C. Johnson, and Richard H. Schein, 449–68. Oxford: Blackwell, 2004.

Colley, Linda. *Captives: Britain, Empire, and the World, 1600–1850*. New York: Anchor Books, 2004.

Comeau, Robert. 'The Stories of Taqilituq & Ipirvik'. In *Nilliajut: Inuit Perspectives on the Northwest Passage, Shipping and Marine Issues*, 16–25. Ottawa, ON: Inuit Tapiriit Kanatami, 2017.

Conan Doyle, Arthur. *Dangerous Work: Diary of an Arctic Adventure*, edited by Jon Lellenberg and Daniel Stashower. Chicago, IL: University of Chicago Press, 2012.

Condos, Mark. *The Insecurity State: Punjab and the Making of Colonial Power in British India*. Cambridge: Cambridge University Press, 2017.

Cowper, William. *Poems*. London: J. Johnson, 1782.

Craciun, Adriana. 'The Frozen Ocean', *PMLA* 125, no. 3 (2010): 693–702.

Craciun, Adriana. 'What Is an Explorer?', *Eighteenth-Century Studies* 45, no. 1 (2011): 29–51.

Craciun, Adriana. *Writing Arctic Disaster: Authorship and Exploration*. Cambridge: Cambridge University Press, 2016.

Crantz, David. *The History of Greenland: Including an Account of the Mission Carried on by the United Brethren in that Country*, 2 vols. London: Longman, Rees, Orme, and Brown, 1820.

Cronin, Marionne. 'Technological Heroes: Images of the Arctic in the Age of Polar Aviation'. In *Northscapes: History, Technology, and the Making of Northern Environments*, edited by Dolly Jørgensen and Sverker Sörlin, 57–81. Vancouver: University of British Columbia Press, 2013.

Crull, Joducus. *A Supplement to Mr. Samuel Puffendorf's Introduction to the History of Europe*, 2nd ed. London: W. Taylor, 1710.

Cussans, Julia E. M. 'Biometry and Climate Change in Norse Greenland: The Effect of Climate on the Size and Shape of Domestic Animals'. In *Climate Change and Human Responses: A Zooarchaeological Perspective*, edited by Gregory Monks, 197–218. Dordrecht: Springer, 2017.

Cutmore, Jonathan, ed. '*Quarterly Review*, Volume 18, Number 35', *Quarterly Review Archive*, in *Romantic Circles*. https://romantic-circles.org/reference/qr/index/35.html.

Damas, David. 'Journey at the Threshold: Knud Rasmussen's Study of the Copper Eskimos, 1923–24', *Études Inuit Studies* 12, no. 1/2 (1988): 129–49.

Darwent, John and Christyann M. Darwent. 'Scales of Violence across the North American Arctic'. In *Violence and*

Warfare among Hunter-Gatherers, edited by Mark W. Allen and Terry L. Jones, 182–203. London: Routledge, 2014.

David, Robert G. *The Arctic in the British Imagination 1818–1914.* Manchester: Manchester University Press, 2000.

Davis, John. *The Voyages and Works of John Davis, the Navigator.* London: Hakluyt Society, 1880.

Davis, Natalie Zemon. 'Decentering History: Local Stories and Cultural Crossings in a Global World', *History and Theory* 50, no. 2 (2011): 188–202.

De Morgan, John. *Lost in Ice, or, When Adventure Leads.* New York: Street and Smith, 1914.

Deane, Bradley. *Masculinity and the New Imperialism: Rewriting Manhood in British Popular Literature, 1870–1914.* Cambridge: Cambridge University Press, 2014.

Deans, Alex. 'Pastoral Optimism at Enlightenment's Frontier: James Hogg's Highland Journeys'. In *Cultures of Improvement in Scottish Romanticism, 1707–1840,* edited by Alex Benchimol and Gerard Lee McKeever, 132–51. New York: Routledge, 2018.

Dee, John. *The Private Diary of Dr. John Dee, and the Catalogue of His Library Manuscripts,* edited by James O. Halliwell. London: Camden Society, 1842.

Defoe, Daniel. *The Life and Strange Surprizing Adventures of Robinson Crusoe.* London: W. Taylor, 1719.

Depledge, Duncan. *Britain and the Arctic.* Cham: Palgrave Macmillan, 2018.

Diamond, Jared. *Collapse: How Societies Choose to Fail or Succeed,* rev. ed. New York: Penguin, 2011.

Diamond, Jared. 'Why Do Societies Collapse?', TED Talk video 2003. www.ted.com/talks/jared_diamond_on_why_societies_collapse?language=en.

Dickens, Charles. 'The Lost Arctic Voyagers', *Household Words* (2 and 9 December 1854): 362–5, 387–93.

Di Robilant, Andrea. *Irresistible North: From Venice to Greenland on the Trail of the Zen Brothers.* New York: Alfred A. Knopf, 2011.

'Divers other Voyages to Greenland, with Letters of those which were there employed, communicated to mee by Master William Heley'. In Samuel Purchas' *Hakluytus Posthumus or, Purchas His Pilgrimes*, vol. 14, 91–108. Cambridge: Cambridge University Press, 2014.

Dixon, Robert. *Writing the Colonial Adventure: Race, Gender and Nation in Anglo-Australian Popular Fiction, 1875–1914.* Cambridge: Cambridge University Press, 1995.

Dodge, Howard Lewis. *Attraction of the Compass: A Romance of the North.* Long Beach, CA: Dove & Courtney, 1912.

Dodge, Howard Lewis. *Attraction of the Compass; or, The Blonde Eskimo; A Romance of the North, Based upon Facts of a Personal Experience.* 2nd ed. Long Beach, CA: Seaside Printing Company, 1916.

Drayton, Richard. *Nature's Government: Science, Imperial Britain, and the 'Improvement' of the World.* New Haven, CT: Yale University Press, 2000.

Dugmore, Andrew J., Christian Keller, and Thomas H. McGovern, 'Norse Greenland Settlement: Reflections on Climate Change, Trade, and the Contrasting Fates of Human Settlements in the North Atlantic Islands', *Arctic Anthropology* 44, no. 1 (2007): 12–36.

Dunlap, Thomas R. *On the Edge: Mapping North America's Coasts.* Oxford: Oxford University Press, 2012.

Dussel, Enrique *The Invention of the Americas: Eclipse of the Other and the Myth of Modernity*, translated by Michael D. Barber. New York: Continuum, 1995.

Eco, Umberto. 'Science Fiction and the Art of Conjecture', *TLS* 4257 (2 November 1984): 1257–8.

Egede, Christian Thestrup. *Rejsebeskrivelse til Øster-Grønlands Opdagelse 1786–87.* Copenhagen, n.p. 1789.

Egede, Hans. *A Description of Greenland*. London: T. and J. Allman, 1818.

Egede, Hans. *Nova Delineatio Grønlandiæ Antiqvæ*, in the Royal Danish Library, digital collections. www5.kb.dk/maps/kortsa/2012/jul/kortatlas/object67502/da.

Egede, Hans. *Omstændelig og udførlig Relation, angaaende den Grønlandske Missions Begyndelse og Forsættelse*. Copenhagen: J. C. Groth, 1738.

Egede, Hans. *Relationer fra Grønland 1721–36 og Det gamle Grønlands ny Perlustration 1741, Meddelser fra Grønland* vol. 54, edited by Louis Bobé. Copenhagen: Kommisionen for Ledelsen af de Geologiske og Geografiske Undersøgelser i Grønland, 1925.

Egede, Poul. *Efterretninger om Grönland uddragne af en Journal helden fra 1721 til 1788*. Copenhagen: Hans Christopher Schrøder, 1788.

Egede, Poul and Niels Egede. *Continuation af Hans Egedes Relationer fra Grønland, samt Niels Egede: Beskrivelse over Grønland*, edited by H. Ostermann. Copenhagen: C. A. Reitzel, 1939.

Eggers, Heinrich Peter von. 'Om Grønlands Østerbygds sande Belligenhed', *Det kongelige danske Landhuusholdings-Selskabs Skrifter* 4 (1792): 239–320.

Elden, Stuart. 'How Should We Do the History of Territory?' *Territory, Politics, Governance* 1, no. 1 (2013): 5–20.

Elkin, Henry. *A View of the Greenland Trade and Whale Fishery, with the National and Private Advantages Thereof*, 2nd ed. London: Edward Symon, 1725.

Elleray, Michelle. *Victorian Coral Islands of Empire, Mission, and the Boys' Adventure Novel*. New York: Routledge, 2020.

Elliott, J. H. *The Old World and the New: 1492–1650*. Cambridge: Cambridge University Press, 1970.

Ellis, Thomas. 'In Praise of Maister Martine Frobisher'. In *A True Report of the Third and Last Voyage into Meta Incognita:*

Ahieued by the Worthie Capteine, M. Martine Frobisher Esquire. London: Thomas Dawson, 1578.

Emmerson, Charles. *The Future History of the Arctic.* New York: Public Affairs, 2010.

Engelhard, Michael. *Ice Bear: The Cultural History of an Arctic Icon.* Seattle: University of Washington Press, 2016.

The English Atlas, vol. 1. Oxford: Moses Pitt, 1680.

Enterline, James Robert. *Erikson, Eskimos, and Columbus: Medieval European Knowledge of America.* Baltimore, MD: Johns Hopkins University Press, 2002.

Erll, Astrid and Ann Rigney, eds. *Cultural Memory Studies after the Transnational Turn*, special edition of *Memory Studies* 11, no. 3 (2018).

'The Eskimos of Greenland', *Spectator* (11 August 1894): 24.

Fagan, Brian. *The Great Warming: Climate Change and the Rise and Fall of Civilizations.* New York: Bloomsbury, 2008.

Fairman, Henry Clay. *The Third World: A Tale of Love and Strange Adventure.* Atlanta, GA: Third World, 1895.

Farley, Ralph Milne. *The Radio Flyers.* In *Famous Fantastic Classics*, vol. 2, 20–131. San Bernardino, CA: Borgo Press, 1975.

Fenton, Elizabeth. *Old Canaan in a New World: Native Americans and the Lost Tribes of Israel.* New York: New York University Press, 2020.

Fielding, Penny. 'James Hogg'. In *The Oxford Encyclopedia of British Literature*, edited by David Scott Kastan, vol. 1, 66–99. Oxford: Oxford University Press, 2006.

Fielding, Penny. '"No Pole nor Pillar": Imagining the Arctic with James Hogg', *Studies in Hogg and His World* 9 (1998): 45–63.

Fishe, P. Reed. *Beyond the Snow: Being a History of Trim's Adventures in Nordlichtschein.* Chicago, IL: Lakeside Press, 1873.

Foucault, Michel. *Security, Territory, Population: Lectures at the College de France, 1977–78*, edited by Michael Senellart, translated by Graham Burchell. Basingstoke: Palgrave Macmillan, 2007.

Franklin, John. *Narrative of a Journey to the Shores of the Polar Sea*, 2 vols. London: John Murray, 1823.

Frei, Karin M., Ashley N. Coutu, Konrad Smiarowski et al., 'Was It for Walrus? Viking Age Settlement and Medieval Walrus Ivory Trade in Iceland and Greenland', *World Archaeology* 47, no. 3 (2015): 439–66.

Freist, Dagmar. 'Lost in Time and Space? Glocal Memoryscapes in the Early Modern World'. In *Memory before Modernity Practices of Memory in Early Modern Europe*, edited by Erika Kuijpers, 203–22. Leiden: Brill, 2013.

'From the Baltimore American', *Christian Journal, and Literary Register* 13, no. 10 (October 1829): 317.

Froude, James Anthony. *Oceana; or, England and Her Colonies*. London: Longmans, Green and Company, 1886.

Fuller, Mary C. 'Images of English Origins in Newfoundland and Roanoke'. In *Decentring the Renaissance: Canada and Europe in Multidisciplinary History 1500–1700*, edited by Germaine Warkentin and Carolyn Podruchny, 141–58. Toronto, ON: University of Toronto Press, 2001.

Fuller, Mary C. *Remembering the Early Modern Voyage: English Narratives in the Age of European Expansion*. New York: Palgrave, 2008.

Gabriel, Frédéric. 'Periegisis and Skepticis: La Peyrère, Geographer'. In *Skepticism in the Modern Age: Building on the Work of Richard Popkin*, edited by José Maia Neto, Gianni Paganini, and John Christian Laursen, 159–70. Leiden: Brill, 2009.

Gad, Finn. *The History of Greenland*, 3 vols. London: C. Hurst & Company, 1970–3.

Galle, Heinz J. *Sun Koh, der Erbe von Atlantis und andere deutsche Supermänner. Paul Alfred Müller alias Lok Myler alias Freder van Holk: Leben und Werk*. Zürich: SSI-Media, 2003.

Gatonby, John. 'An Account of the English Expedition to Greenland, under the Command of Captain James Hall, in 1612'. In *Danish Arctic Expeditions*, edited by C. C. A. Gosch, 2 vols., 1:82–119. London: Printed for the Hakluyt Society, 1897.

Giesecke, Carl Ludwig. *On the Norwegian Settlements on the Eastern Coast of Greenland, Or Osterbygd, and Their Situation*. Dublin: Royal Irish Academy, 1824.

Gifford, Douglas. 'Introduction'. In *Three Perils of Man*, edited by James Hogg, vii–xl. Edinburgh: Canongate Books, 1996.

Gísli Pálsson. 'Genomic Anthropology: Coming in from the Cold?', *Current Anthropology* 49, no. 4 (2008): 545–68.

Glahn, Henrich C. *Missionær i Grønland Henric Christopher Glahns Dagbøger for Aarene 1783–84, 1766–67 og 1767–68*, edited by H. Osterman. Copenhagen: Gad, 1921.

Go North! Greenland's Icy Mountains As a Summer Resort under the Direction of Dr. F. A. Cook. Brooklyn, NY: n.p., 1893.

Godwin, Joscelyn. *Arktos: The Polar Myth in Science, Symbolism, and Nazi Survival*. Kempton, IL: Adventures Unlimited Press, 1996.

Godwin, William. *An Enquiry Concerning Political Justice, and Its Influence on General Virtue and Happiness*, 2 vols. London: G. G. J. and J. Robinson, 1793.

Goffart, Walter. 'Did the Distant Past Impinge on the Invasion-Age Germans?'. In *On Barbarian Identity: Critical Approaches to Ethnicity in the Early Middle Ages*, edited by Andrew Gillet, 21–37. Turnhout: Brepols, 2002.

Gordon, Daniel. 'The Dematerialization Principle: Sociability, Money and Music in the Eighteenth Century', *Historical Reflections / Réflexions Historiques* 31, no. 1 (2005): 71–92.

Gordon, E. V. *An Introduction to Old Norse*, rev. by A. R. Taylor, 2nd ed. Oxford: Clarendon, 1957.

Gosch, C. C. A. *Danish Arctic Expeditions, 1605 to 1620*, 2 vols. London: Printed for the Hakluyt Society, 1897.

Gosden, Chris. *Archaeology and Colonialism: Cultural Contact from 5000 BC to the Present*. Cambridge: Cambridge University Press, 2004.

Graah, Wilhelm August. *Narrative of an Expedition to the East Coast of Greenland, Sent by Order of the King of Denmark, in Search of the Lost Colonies*. London: John W. Parker, 1837.

Graah, Wilhelm August. *Undersøgelses-Reise til Østkysten af Grønland*. Copenhagen: Quist, 1832.

Grafton, Anthony. 'Introduction'. In *New Worlds, Ancient Texts: The Power of Tradition and the Shock of Discovery*, edited by Anthony Grafton with April Shelford and Nancy Siraisi, 1–10. Cambridge, MA: Belknap Press, 1992.

Grant, Madison. *The Passing of the Great Race, or The Racial Basis of European History*. New York: Charles Scribner's Sons, 1916.

Greely, A. W. 'The Origin of Stefansson's Blonde Eskimo', *National Geographic* (December 1912): 1225–38.

Green, Fitzhugh. 'Across the Pole by Plane', *United States Naval Institute Proceedings* 49 (June 1923): 937–48.

Green, Fitzhugh. 'Over the Top of the World', *Outlook* (December 1923): 681–3.

Green, Fitzhugh. 'Will the ZR-1 Discover a Polar Paradise?', *Popular Science Monthly* (December 1923): 29–31.

Green, Fitzhugh. *ZR Wins*. New York: Appleton, 1924.

Green, Leslie C. and Olive Patricia Dickason. *The Law of Nations and the New World*. Edmonton: University of Alberta Press, 1989.

Green, Martin. *Dreams of Adventure, Deeds of Empire*. London: Routledge and Kegan Paul, 1980.

Greenblatt, Stephen. *Marvelous Possessions: The Wonder of the New World*. Chicago, IL: University of Chicago Press, 2008.

Greene, John O. *The Ke Whonkus People: A Story of the North Pole Country*. Indianapolis, IN: Vincent [1890].

'Greenland'. In *Encyclopaedia Americana*, new ed., 51–3. Philadelphia, PA: Lea & Blanchard, 1849.

Greenland Missions: With Biographical Sketches of Some of the Principal Converts, 2nd ed. Dublin: Religious Tract and Book Society for Ireland, 1831.

Greenwood, James. *Curiosities of Savage Life*, 2 vols. London: S. O. Beeton, 1863–4.

'Groenland – Découverte d'un colonie chrétienne', *Archives du Christianisme au XIXe siècle* (October 1830): 527.

Gulløv, Hans Christian, ed. *Grønlands forhistorie*. Copenhagen: Gyldendal, 2004.

Gulløv, Hans Christian. 'Inuit–European Interaction in Greenland'. In *The Oxford Handbook of the Prehistoric Arctic*, edited by T. Max Friesen and Owen K. Mason, 897–914. Oxford: Oxford University Press, 2018.

Gulløv, Hans Christian. 'The Nature of Contact between Native Greenlanders and Norse', *Journal of the North Atlantic* 1, no. 1 (2008): 16–24.

Gulløv, Hans Christian. 'Norse Agriculture in Greenland? Farming in a Remote Medieval Landscape'. In *Agrarian Technology in the Medieval Landscape*, edited by Jan Klápště, 237–45. Turnhout: Brepols, 2016.

[Gurney, Anna]. *Extracts from the Kongs-Skugg-Sio; or, Speculum Regale*. Norwich: Stevenson, Matchett & Company, 1817.

Hagenbeck, Carl. *Beasts and Men: Being Carl Hagenbeck's Experiences for Half a Century among Wild Animals*, translated by Hugh S. R. Elliot and A. G. Thacker. London: Longmans, Green, and Company, 1912.

Haggard, H. Rider. *Eric Brighteyes*. London: Longmans, Green & Company, 1895.

Hall, James. 'Another Account of the Danish Expedition to Greenland ... 1605'. In *Danish Arctic Expeditions*, edited by

C. C. A. Gosch, 2 vols., 1:237–45. London: Printed for the Hakluyt Society, 1897.

Hall, James. Report on the 1605 voyage. In *Purchas His Pilgrimes, part 3, in fiue books The First Part*, edited by Samuel Purchas, 814–21. London: Henrie Fetherstone, 1625.

Hall, James. 'A Report to King Christian IV of Denmark on the Danish Expedition to Greenland, under the command of Captain John Cunningham, in 1605'. In *Danish Arctic Expeditions*, edited by C. C. A. Gosch, 2 vols., 1:1–19. London: Printed for the Hakluyt Society, 1897.

Hall, James. *Travels in Scotland, by an Unusual Route, with a Trip to the Orkneys and Hebrides*, 2 vols. London: J. Johnson, 1807.

Hall, Stuart. 'The Whites of Their Eyes: Racist Ideologies and the Media'. In *Silver Linings: Some Strategies for the Eighties*, edited by George Bridges and Rosalind Brunt, 28–52. London: Lawrence and Wishart, 1981.

Hamre, Lars. *Erkebiskop Erik Valkendorf. Trekk av hans liv og virke*. Oslo: J. Grieg, 1943.

Hann, Lourens Feykes. *Beschryving van de straat Davids benevens des zelven inwooners zede gestalte en gewoonte misgaders hunne visvangst en andere handelingen*. Amsterdam: Gerard van Keulen, 1720.

Hanson, Carter F. 'Lost among White Others: Late-Victorian Lost Race Novels for Boys', *Nineteenth-Century Contexts* 23, no. 4 (2002): 497–527.

Hansson, Heidi. 'Arctopias: The Arctic As No Place and New Place in Fiction'. In *The New Arctic*, edited by Birgitta Evengård, Joan Nymand Larsen, and Øyvind Paasche. Cham: Springer 2015.

Harbsmeier, Michael. 'Bodies and Voices from Ultima Thule: Inuit Explorations of the Kablunat from Christian IV to Knud Rasmussen'. In *Narrating the Arctic: A Cultural History of Nordic Scientific Practices*, edited by Michael Bravo and

Sverker Sörlin, 33–71. Canton, MA: Science History Publications, 2002.

Harkin, Michael E. 'Performing Paradox: Narrativity and the Lost Colony of Roanoke'. In *Myth and Memory: Rethinking Stories of Indigenous–European Contact*, edited by John Sutton Lutz, 103–17. Vancouver: University of British Columbia Press, 2008.

Harpold, Terry. 'Verne's Cartographies', *Science Fiction Studies* 32, no. 95 (2005): 18–42.

Harrison, Peter.' "Fill the Earth and Subdue It": Biblical Warrants for Colonization in Seventeenth Century England', *Journal of Religious History* 29 (2005): 3–24.

Hase, Karl August von. *A History of the Christian Church*, translated by Charles Edward Blumenthal and C. P. Wing. London: Trubner & Company, 1855.

[Hawks, Francis Lister]. *The Lost Greenland; or, Uncle Philip's Conversations with the Children about the Lost Colonies of Greenland*. New York: Harper and Brothers, 1840.

Hayes, Isaac Israel. *The Land of Desolation: A Personal Narrative of Adventure in Greenland*. London: Sampson Low, Marston, Low, and Searle, 1871.

Hayes, Isaac Israel. *The Open Polar Sea: A Narrative of a Voyage of Discovery towards the North Pole*. London: Sampson, Low, Son, and Marston, 1867.

Headrick, Daniel R. *Power over Peoples: Technology, Environments, and Western Imperialism, 1400 to the Present*. Princeton, NJ: Princeton University Press, 2010.

Hemans, Felicia. 'The Indian's Revenge', *Blackwood's Edinburgh Magazine* 35 (April 1834): 504–7.

Hendrik, Hans. *Memoirs of Hans Hendrik, the Arctic Traveller: Serving under Kane, Hayes, Hall and Nares, 1853–1876*, translated by Hinrich Rink. London: Trubner & Company, 1878.

Hill, Jen. *White Horizon: The Arctic in the Nineteenth-Century British Imagination*. Albany, NY: State University of New York Press, 2008.

Hindsberger, Mogens. *Den grønlandske kristendomsopfattelse fra Hans Egede til vore dage*. Copenhagen: Museum Tusculanum, 2007.

'Historical Introduction'. In Hans Egede, *A Description of Greenland*, i–xci. London: T. and J. Allman, 1818.

'The History of Arctic Adventure', *Illustrated London News* 35 (1 October 1859): 316–17.

Hogg, James. *The Collected Letters of James Hogg: Volume 3, 1832 to 1835*, edited by Gillian Hughes. Edinburgh: Edinburgh University Press, 2008.

Hogg, James. *Highland Tours: The Ettrick Shepherd's Travels in the Scottish Highlands and Western Isles in 1802, 1803 and 1804*, edited by William F. Laughlan. Hawick: Byways, 1981.

Hogg, James. 'Nature's Magic Lantern'. In *Tales and Sketches by the Ettrick Shepherd*, vol. 4, 352–66. Edinburgh: Blackie & Son, 1837.

Hogg, James. 'The P and Q; or The Adventures of Jock M'Pherson', *Blackwood's Magazine* 26 (October 1829): 693–5.

Hogg, James. *The Shepherd's Guide: Being a Practical Treatise on the Diseases of Sheep ... with Observations on the Most Suitable Farm-stocking for the Various Climates of this Country*. Edinburgh: A. Constable, 1807.

Hogg, James. *The Spy* 4 (22 September 1810): 32.

Hogg, James. Surpassing Adventures of Allan Gordon, in *Tales and Sketches by the Ettrick Shepherd*, vol. 1, 241–316. Glasgow: Blackie & Son, 1837.

Hogg, James. *A Tour in the Highlands in 1803: A Series of Letters ... Reprinted from The Scottish Review*. London: Alexander Gardner, 1888.

Holberg, Ludvig. *Epistler,* in *Ludvig Holbergs Skrifter.* http://holbergsskrifter.dk/holberg-public/view?docId=adm/main.xml.

Horsford, Eben Norton. *The Defenses of Norumbega.* Boston, MA: Houghton, Mifflin, 1891.

Howison, John. *European Colonies, in Various Parts of the World: Viewed in Their Social, Moral and Physical Condition,* 2 vols. London: Richard Bentley, 1834.

Hueffer, Ford Madox and Joseph Conrad. *The Inheritors: An Extravagant Story.* Boston, MA: Gregg Press, 1976.

Huggan, Graham. 'Introduction: Unscrambling the Arctic'. In *Postcolonial Perspectives on the European High North: Unscrambling the Arctic,* edited by Graham Huggan and Lars Jensen, 1–30. London: Palgrave Macmillan, 2016.

Huhndorf, Shari M. *Going Native: Indians in the American Cultural Imagination.* Ithaca, NY: Cornell University Press, 2001.

Humboldt, Alexander von. *Views of the Cordilleras and Monuments of the Indigenous Peoples of the Americas: A Critical Edition,* edited by Vera M. Kutzinski and Ottmar Ette, translated by J. R. Poynter. Chicago, IL: University of Chicago Press, 2012.

Hunter, Douglas. *The Place of Stone: Dighton Rock and the Erasure of America's Indigenous Past.* Chapel Hill: University of North Carolina, 2017.

Hutton, J. E. *History of the Moravian Church.* London: Moravian Publication Office, 1909.

Hyndman, Jennifer. 'Mind the Gap: Bridging Feminist and Political Geography through Geopolitics', *Political Geography* 23, no. 3 (2004): 307–22.

Høiris, Ole, ed. *Grønland: En refleksiv udfordring. Mission, kolonisation og udforskning.* Aarhus: Aarhus Universitetsforlag, 2009.

Ilsøe, Harald. 'Historisk censur i Danmark indtil Holberg', *Fund og Forskning i Det Kongelige Biblioteks Samlinger* 20, no. 1 (1973): 45–70.

Ísleifsson Sumarliði R., 'Islands on the Edge: Medieval and Early Modern National Images of Iceland and Greenland'. In *Iceland and Images of the North*, edited by Sumarliði R. Ísleifsson. Québec, QC: Presses de l'Université du Québec, 2011.

Jackson, Gordon. *The British Whale Trade*. Oxford: Oxford University Press, 2005.

Jackson, James W. *A Queen of Amazonia*. London: Henry Walker, 1928.

Jackson, Rowan, Jette Arneborg, Andrew Dugmore et al. 'Disequilibrium, Adaptation, and the Norse Settlement of Greenland', *Human Ecology* 46, no. 5 (2018): 665–84.

Jensen, Janus Møller. 'Denmark and the Crusades 1400–1650', PhD thesis, University of Southern Denmark (2005).

Jensson, Gottskálk. 'Hypothesis Islandica, or Concerning the Initially Supportive but Ultimately Subversive Impact of the Rediscovery of Medieval Icelandic Literature on the Evaluation of Saxo Grammaticus as a Historical Authority during the Heyday of Danish Antiquarianism'. In *Boreas Rising: Antiquarianism and National Narratives in 17th- and 18th-Century Scandinavia*, edited by Bernd Roling and Bernhard Schirg, 13–60. Berlin: De Gruyter, 2019.

Jensz, Felicity. '"A Collection of Absurdities": Reception of Two English Versions of Cranz's Book in Britain, 1767 and 1820'. In *Legacies of David Cranz's 'Historie von Grönland' (1765)*, edited by Felicity Jensz and Christina Petterson, 71–92. Cham: Palgrave Macmillan, 2020.

Jesch, Judith. *The Viking Diaspora*. Abingdon: Routledge, 2015.

Jochimsen, Mathias. 'Report from Godthaab to Privy Councilor Løvenørn from 1732', *Minerva* 3 (July 1788): 18–78.

Johns-Putra, Adeline G. 'Historicizing the Networks of Ecology and Culture: Eleanor Anne Porden and Nineteenth-Century

Climate Change', *ISLE: Interdisciplinary Studies in Literature and Environment* 22, no. 1 (2015): 27–46.

Johnston, Archibald. *The Mariner: A Poem in Two Cantos*. Philadelphia, PA: Edward Earle, 1818.

Johnstone, David Lawson. *The Paradise of the North: A Story of Discovery and Adventure around the Pole*. London: W. and R. Chambers, 1892.

Johnstone, James. *Lodbrokar Quida; or the Death-Song of Lodbroc*. Copenhagen: Bonnier, 1813.

Jón Helgason, 'Introduction'. In Arngrímur Jónsson, *Gronlandia 1688*, 5–38. Copenhagen: Einar Munksgaard, 1942.

Jónsson, Arngrímur. 'Gronlandia'. In *Bibliotheca Arnamagnæana: Arngrimi Jonae opera*, edited by Jón Helgason, 227–67. Copenhagen: E. Munksgaard, 1941.

Jónsson, Arngrímur. *Grönlandia eller historie om Grønland*, translated by Andreas Bussæus. Copenhagen: H. H. Rotmer, 1732.

Kaarsted, Tage. *Great Britain and Denmark 1914–1920*. Odense: Odense University Press, 1979.

Kassis, Dimitrios. *American Travellers in Scandinavia*. Cambridge: Cambridge Scholars, 2016.

Keighren, Innes M., Charles W. J. Withers, and Bill Bell. *Travels into Print: Exploration, Writing, and Publishing with John Murray, 1773–1859*. Chicago, IL: University of Chicago Press, 2015.

Kejlbo, Ib Rønne. 'Nova Delineatio Grønlandiæ Antiquæ. Et hidtil ukendt Hans Egede kort erhvervet til Det Kongelig Biblioteks samling', *Fund og Forskning* 21 (1974): 47–66.

Keskitalo, E. C. H. *Negotiating the Arctic: The Construction of an International Region*. London: Routledge, 2004.

Khouri, Nadia. 'Lost Worlds and the Revenge of Realism', *Science Fiction Studies* 10, no. 2 (1983): 170–90.

Kleivan, Inge. 'European Contacts with Greenland As Reflected in the Place-Names'. In *Language Contact across the*

North Atlantic, edited by P. Sture Ureland and Iain Clarkson, 125–51. Tubingen: Niemeyer, 1996.

Knight, Stephen. 'The Arctic Arthur', *Arthuriana* 21, no. 2 (2011): 59–89.

Knuth, Eigil. *K'avdlunâtsianik Nordboer og Skrællinger. The Norsemen and the Skraelings*, translated by Jens Poulsen and Clive Bayliss. Nuuk: Kalâtdlit-nunâle nak'iterisitsissarfik, 1968.

Kolodny, Annette. *In Search of First Contact: The Vikings of Vinland, the Peoples of the Dawnland, and the Anglo-American Anxiety of Discovery*. Durham, NC: Duke University Press, 2012.

La Peyrère, Isaac. 'Kaert von Groen-Land'. In *Ausführliche Beschreibung des Theils bewohnt, Theils unbewohnt, so genannten Grönlands*. Nürnberg: Verlegung Christof Riegels, 1679.

La Peyrère, Isaac. *Relation du Groenland*. Paris: Augustin Courbe, 1647.

Lach, Donald. *Asia in the Making of Europe*, vol. 2. Chicago, IL: University of Chicago Press, 1970.

Lambert, David and Alan Lester. 'Geographies of Colonial Philanthropy', *Progress in Human Geography* 28, no. 3 (2004): 320–41.

Langgård, Karen. 'Greenlandic Attitudes towards Norwegians and Danes from Nansen's Icecap Crossing to the 1933 World Court Verdict in The Hague', *Études Inuit/Inuit Studies* 38, no. 1/2 (2014): 53–71.

Lansdown, Richard. *Literature and Truth: Imaginative Writing As a Medium for Ideas*. Leiden: Brill, 2018.

Latour, Bruno. *Science in Action*. Cambridge, MA: Harvard University Press, 1987.

Lee, Molly. 'Tourism and Taste Cultures: Collecting Native Art in Alaska at the Turn of the Twentieth Century'. In *Unpacking Culture: Art and Commodity in Colonial and Postcolonial Worlds*, edited by Ruth B. Phillips and Christopher B. Steiner, 267–81. Berkeley: University of California Press, 1999.

'The Legal Status of Eastern Greenland', *Geographical Journal* 82, no. 2 (1933): 151–6.

'Legal Status of Eastern Greenland', PCIJ Series A/B, no. 53, 22–147. https://jusmundi.com/en/document/decision/en-legal-status-of-eastern-greenland-judgment-wednesday-5th-april-1933.

Lennox, Jeffers. *Homelands and Empires: Indigenous Spaces, Imperial Fictions, and Competition.* Toronto: University of Toronto Press, 2017.

Leslie, John. 'Polar Ice and a North-West Passage', *Edinburgh Review* 30 (June 1818): 1–58.

Levere, Trevor H. *Science and the Canadian Arctic: A Century of Exploration, 1818–1918.* Cambridge: Cambridge University Press, 1993.

Lévi-Strauss, Claude. *Structural Anthropology*, translated by Claire Jacobson. London: Penguin, 1968.

Lewis, Leon [Julius Warren Lewis]. *Andrée at the North Pole, with Details of His Fate.* New York: G. W. Dillingham Company, 1899.

Lidwell-Durnin, John. 'Inevitable Decay: Debates over Climate, Food Security, and Plant Heredity in Nineteenth-Century Britain', *Journal of the History of Biology* 52, no. 2 (2019): 271–92.

Liebeschuertz, Wolf. 'The Debate about the Ethnogenesis of the Germanic Tribes'. In *From Rome to Constantinople: Studies in Honour of Averil Cameron*, edited by Hagit Amirav and Robert Barend ter Haar Romeney, 341–55. Leuven: Peeters, 2007.

Lindenberg, N. 'Oplysninger om officerer i Grønlandsfarten 1721–1971', unpublished manuscript in the archives of the Royal Greenland Trading Department (1971).

Livingstone, David N. 'Geographical Inquiry, Rational Religion, and Moral Philosophy: Enlightenment Discourses on the Human Condition'. In *Geography and Enlightenment*, edited by David N. Livingstone and Charles W. J. Withers, 93–124. Chicago, IL: University of Chicago Press, 1999.

Lloyd, H. E. 'Preface'. In Hans Egede Saabye, *Greenland: Being Extracts from a Journal Kept in that Country in the Years 1770 to 1778*, translated by H. E. Lloyd, iii–v. London: Boosey and Sons, 1818.

Loomis, Chauncey C. 'The Arctic Sublime'. In *Nature and the Victorian Imagination*, edited by U. C. Knoepflmacher and G. B. Tennyson, 95–112. Berkeley: University of California Press, 1977.

Lutz, Hartmut, ed. and trans. *The Diary of Abraham Ulrikab: Text and Context*. Ottawa: University of Ottawa Press, 2005.

Lutz, John Sutton. 'Introduction: Myth Understandings; or First Contact, Over and Over Again'. In *Myths and Memory: Stories of Indigenous–European Contact*, edited by John Sutton Lutz, 1–14. Vancouver: University of British Columbia Press, 2007.

Lynge, Aqqaluk. 'Introduction', in Hans Egede Saabye, *Journal in Greenland, Being Extracts from a Journal Kept in That Country in the Years 1770 to 1778*, 11–22. Hanover: IPI Press, 2009.

Lynge, Augo. *Trehundrede år efter ...*, translated by Trine Graversen and Kirsten Thisted. Nuuk: Atuakkiorfik, 1989.

Lynnerup, Niels. 'Endperiod Demographics of the Greenland Norse', *Journal of the North Atlantic* 7 (2014): 18–24.

Lyotard, Jean-François. *Libidinal Economy*, translated by Iain Hamilton Grant. London: Continuum, 2004.

Lyschander, Claus Christoffersen. *Den Gronlandske Chronica*. In C. C. Lyschanders digtning 1579–1623, 2 vols., edited by Flemming Lundgren-Nielsen, 1:129–262. Copenhagen: Det Danske Sprog- og Litteraturselskab, 1989.

Macaulay, Thomas Babington. *The History of England from the Accession of James II*, 5 vols. Philadelphia, PA: J. B. Lippincott, 1868.

MacMillan, Ken. *Sovereignty and Possession in the English New World: The Legal Foundations of Empire, 1576–1640.* Cambridge: Cambridge University Press, 2006.

Major, Richard Henry. *The Voyages of the Venetian Brothers, Nicolò and Antonio Zeno, to the Northern Seas in the XIVth Century: Comprising the Latest Known Accounts of the Lost Colony of Greenland; and of the Northmen in America before Columbus.* Abingdon: Routledge, [1873] 2016.

Malthe Brun [Malte-Brun, Conrad]. 'On the Expeditions to the North Pole', *Philosophical Magazine and Journal* 51, no. 240 (1818): 279–86.

Manby, George W. *Hints for Improving the Criminal Law by the Enactment of Secondary Punishments with Suggestions for the Settlement of a New Convict Colony.* n.p., 1831.

Manby, George W. *Journal of a Voyage to Greenland, in the Year 1821.* London: G. and W. B. Whittaker, 1822.

Manby, George W. *Reflections and Observations upon the Probability of Recovering Lost Greenland.* Yarmouth: W. Megey, 1829.

Marcus, G. J. 'The Greenland Trade-Route', *Economic History Review*, n.s. 7, no. 1 (1954): 71–80.

Markham, Clements R. 'The Promotion of Further Discovery in the Arctic and the Antarctic Regions', in *Miscellaneous Documents of the House of Representatives for the Third Session of the Fifty-Third Congress 1894–95*, 317–41. Washington, DC: US Government Printing Office, 1895.

Markham, Clements R. *The Threshold of the Unknown Region.* London: Sampson, Low, Marston, Low, & Searle, 1873.

Marland, Hilary. '"Bicycle-Face" and "Lawn Tennis" Girls', *Media History* 25, no. 1 (2019): 70–84.

Marshall, Herbert. 'Wilton, Charles Pleydell (1795–1859)', *Australian Dictionary of Biography.* https://adb.anu.edu.au/biography/wilton-charles-pleydell-2807/text4009.

Mathers, Derek. 'A Fourteenth-Century Description of Greenland', *Saga-Book* 33 (2009): 67–94.

Mathiassen, Therkel. 'Norse Ruins in Labrador?', *American Anthropologist* 304 (Oct.–Dec. 1928): 569–79.

Maurer, Konrad. 'Geschichte der Entdeckung Ostgrönlands'. In *Die zweite deutsche Nordpolarfahrt in den Jahren 1869 und 1870*, vol. 1, 201–89. Leipzig: Brockhaus, 1874.

Mauricius, Jan Jacob. *Naleesing over Groenland voor de historie van den Noorweeschen Erik* [Hamburg: 1741?].

Maury, T. B. 'The Gateways to the Pole', *Putnam's Magazine of Literature, Science, Art, and National Interests* 4, no. 81 (November 1869): 521–37.

McClintock, F. L. 'Discoveries by the Late Expedition in Search of Sir John Franklin and His Party', *Proceedings of the Royal Geographical Society of London* 4, no. 1 (1859–60): 2–14.

McCorristine, Shane. *The Spectral Arctic: A History of Dreams and Ghosts in Polar Exploration.* London: UCL Press, 2018.

McGhee, Robert. *The Last Imaginary Place: A Human History of the Arctic World.* Oxford: Oxford University Press, 2006.

Meek, Ronald L. *Social Science and the Ignoble Savage.* Cambridge: Cambridge University Press, 1976.

Mikkelsen, Naja, Antoon Kuijpers, Sofia Ribeiro et al. 'European Trading, Whaling and Climate History of West Greenland Documented by Historical Records, Drones and Marine Sediments', *GEUS: Geological Survey of Denmark and Greenland Bulletin* 41 (2018): 67–70.

'Miscellaneous Scientific Proceedings on the Continent', *Journal of the Royal Institution of Great Britain* (December 1831): 174.

Moltke, Ida, Matteo Fumagalli, Thorfinn S. Korneliussen et al. 'Uncovering the Genetic History of the Present-Day Greenlandic Population', *American Journal of Human Genetics* 96, no. 1 (2015): 54–69.

Montgomery, James. *Greenland, and Other Poems*. London: Longman, Hurst, Rees, Orme, and Brown, 1819.

Montgomery, James. *The Pelican Island and Other Poems*. London: Longman, Rees, Orme, Brown, and Green, 1828.

The Moravians in Greenland, 3rd ed. Edinburgh: William Oliphant and Son, 1839.

Morris, George Sculthorpe. *Convicts and Colonies: Thoughts on Transportation & Colonization*. London: Hope and Company, 1853.

Mortensen, Lars Boje. 'Before Historical "Sources" and Literary "Texts": The Presentation of Saga Literature in Tormod Torfæus' *Historia rerum Norwegicarum* (1711)', *Renæssanceforum* 5 (2008): 1–14. www.njrs.dk/rf_5_2008.htm.

Morton, A. S. *Beyond the Palaeocrystic Sea, or The Legend of Halfjord*. Chicago, IL: Privately printed, 1895.

Moss, Sarah. *The Frozen Ship: The Histories and Tales of Polar Exploration*. New York: Blue Bridge, 2006.

Moss, Sarah. 'Romanticism on Ice: Coleridge, Hogg and the Eighteenth-Century Missions to Greenland', *Romanticism on the Net* 45 (2007). https://id.erudit.org/iderudit/015816ar.

Munchausen at the Pole: Or The Surprising and Wonderful Adventures of a Voyage of Discovery: Consisting of Some of the Most Marvellous Exploits Ever Performed by Man. London: J. Johnston, 1819.

Murphy, David Thomas. *German Exploration of the Polar World: A History, 1870–1940*. Lincoln: University of Nebraska Press, 2002.

Naipaul, V. S. *The Loss of El Dorado: A History*. New York: Alfred A. Knopf, 1970.

Nansen, Fridtjof. *In Northern Mists: Arctic Exploration in Early Times*, vol. 2. Cambridge: Cambridge University Press, [1911] 2014.

Naum, Magdalena and Jonas M. Nordin. *Scandinavian Colonialism and the Rise of Modernity: Small Time Agents in a Global Arena*. New York: Springer, 2013.

Nedkvitne, Arnved. *Norse Greenland: Viking Peasants in the Arctic*. Abingdon: Routledge, 2019.

Nelson, Arthur A. *Wings of Danger: A Novel*. New York: Robert M. McBride & Company, 1915.

'News', *Royal Magazine, or, Quarterly Bee* (November 1750): 467.

Newsam, William Cartwright and John Holland. *The Poets of Yorkshire*. London: Groombridge and Sons, 1845.

Nicol, Heather N. 'Denmark–Norway: Eastern Greenland'. In *Border Disputes: A Global Encyclopedia*, 3 vols., edited by Emmanuel Brunet-Jailly, 1:143–53. Santa Barbara, CA: ABC Clio, 2015.

Nicol, James. *Historical and Descriptive Account of Iceland, Greenland, and the Faroe Islands*, 2nd ed. Edinburgh: Oliver & Boyd, 1841.

Nies, Betsy L. *Eugenic Fantasies: Racial Ideology in the Literature and Popular Culture of the 1920s*. New York: Routledge, 2002.

Noname, *Across the Frozen Sea: or Frank Reade, Jr.'s Electric Snow Cutter* 4, no. 83. New York: Frank Tousey, 1894.

Noname, *To the End of the Earth in an Air-Ship; or, Frank Reade, Jr.'s Great Mid-Air Flight* 5, no. 111. New York: Frank Tousey, 1895.

Noname, *Frank Reade, Jr.'s Electric Ice Boat, or, Lost in the Land of Crimson Snow* (part I) 3, no. 61. New York: Frank Tousey, 1893.

Noname, *Frank Reade, Jr.'s Electric Ice Boat, or, Lost in the Land of Crimson Snow* (part II) 3, no. 61. New York: Frank Tousey, 1893.

Noname, *Latitude 90°, or, Frank Reade, Jr.'s Most Wonderful Mid-Air Flight* 5, no. 125. New York: Frank Tousey, 1896.

Nordtop-Madson, M. A. 'The Cultural Identity of the Late Greenland Norse'. In *Identities and Cultural Contacts in the Arctic: Proceedings from a Conference at the Danish National Museum, Copenhagen. November 30 to December 3, 1999*, edited by E. Martin Appelt, Joel Berglund and Hans Christian Gulløv, 55–60. Copenhagen: Danish National Museum, 2000.

Nørlund, Poul. *Viking Settlers in Greenland and Their Descendants during Five Hundred Years*. Copenhagen: G. E. C. Gad, 1936.

The Northern Light: A Tale of Iceland and Greenland in the Eleventh Century. London: John Henry and James Parker, 1860.

'Notice regarding the Lost Greenland', *Edinburgh Philosophical* (January–March 1831): 187.

O'Connor, J. P. 'Bernard O'Reilly: Genius or Rogue?', *Irish Naturalists' Journal* 21, no. 9 (1985): 379–84.

OED Online, Oxford University Press, December 2019. www .oed.com/view/Entry/167122.

Officer, Charles and Jake Page. *A Fabulous Kingdom. The Exploration of the Arctic*, 2nd ed. Oxford: Oxford University Press, 2012.

Ogilby, John. *America: Being the Latest, and Most Accurate Description of the New World*. London: Printed by the author, 1671.

O'Gorman, Edmundo. *The Invention of America an Inquiry into the Historical Nature of the New World and the Meaning of Its History*. Bloomington: Indiana University Press, 1961.

O'Gorman, Thomas. *A History of the Roman Catholic Church in the United States*. New York: Christian Literature Company, 1895.

Olearius, Adam. *The Voyages and Travells of the Ambassadors Sent by Frederick, Duke of Holstein, to the Great Duke of Muscovy and the King of Persia*. London: John Starkey and Thomas Basset, 1669.

Olesen, Simon Mølholm. "'Vor och Cronens Land'": Dansk-Norske Forestillinger om Retten til Grønland, ca. 1550–1700', *Temp – Tidsskrift for Historie* 10, no. 19 (2019): 71–101.

O'Reilly, Bernard. *Greenland, the Adjacent Seas, and the North-West Passage to the Pacific Ocean: Illustrated in a Voyage to Davis's Strait, during the Summer of 1817*. London: Baldwin, Cradock, and Joy, 1818.

Osborn, Sherard. *Stray Leaves from an Arctic Journal: or, Eighteen Months in the Polar Regions, in search of Sir J. Franklin's Expedition, in the Years 1850–51*, new ed. Edinburgh: Blackwood, 1865.

Paganini, Signor. *Le Avventure di Azil giovane Esquimese del Groenland*. Udine: Vendrame, 1837.

Paganini, Signor. *Dettagli sopra la giovine Esquimaude giunta in Francia il 27 Juglio 1827*. Cremona: C. Manini, 1840.

Pagden, Anthony. *The Burdens of Empire: 1539 to the Present*. Cambridge: Cambridge University Press, 2015.

Page, Jesse. *Amid Greenland Snows, or, The Early History of Arctic Missions*. New York: Fleming H. Revel, c.1893.

[Palgrave, Francis]. Review of Hans Egede Saabye's *Brudstykker af en Dagbok*, *Quarterly Review* 18, no. 36 (January 1818): 480–96.

Parmenius, Stephen. *The New Found Land of Stephen Parmenius*, edited and translated by David B. Quinn and Neil M. Cheshire. Toronto: Toronto University Press, 1972.

Parry, William. *Journal of a Second Voyage for the Discovery of a North-West Passage from the Atlantic to the Pacific: Performed in the Years 1821–22–23*. London: John Murray, 1824.

The Patriot: A Poem. Edinburgh: Printed for the Author, 1804.

Peary, Robert. 'The Value of Arctic Exploration', *National Geographic Magazine* 14 (December 1903): 429–36.

Peirce, Benjamin Mills. *A Report on the Resources of Iceland and Greenland*. Washington, DC: US Government Printing Office, 1868.

Pelham, Edward. *God's Power and Providence*. London: J. Partridge, 1631.

Petersen, Robert. 'Claudius Clavus Niger om den danske geograf og kartograf Claus Claussøn Swart og hans formodede rejse til Grønland i 1420'rne eller 1430'rne'. *Grønland* 57, no. 1 (2009): 42–57.

Pickett, Thomas E. *The Quest for a Lost Race*. Louisville, KY: John P. Morton & Company, 1907.

Pickford, Susan. 'Travel Writing and Translation'. In *Handbook of British Travel Writing*, edited by Barbara Schaff, 79–94. Berlin: Walter de Gruyter, 2020.

Pinkerton, John. *An Inquiry into the History of Scotland Preceding the Reign of Malcolm III. Or the Year 1056, Including the Authentic History of that Period*, 2 vols. London: John Nichols, 1789.

Pinkerton, John. *Modern Geography: A Description of the Empires, Kingdoms, States, and Colonies*, vol. 2. London: T. Cadell and W. Davies, 1811.

Pittock, Murray. *Scottish and Irish Romanticism*. Oxford: Oxford University Press, 2008.

Plank, Geoffrey. *Atlantic Wars: From the Fifteenth Century to the Age of Revolution*. Oxford: Oxford University Press, 2020.

'Polar Regions', in *The Edinburgh Encyclopaedia*, 18 vols., vol. 17, 1–40. Edinburgh: Blackwood, 1830.

Pontoppidan, Erik. *The Natural History of Norway ... Translated from the Danish Original*. London: A. Linde, 1755.

Poon, Angela. *Enacting Englishness in the Victorian Period*. Aldershot: Ashgate, 2008.

Popkin, Richard H. *Isaac La Peyrère (1596–1676): His Life, Work and Influence*. Leiden: Brill, 1987.

Porden, Eleanor Anne. *The Arctic Expeditions: A Poem*. London: John Murray, 1818.

Porden, Eleanor Anne. *The Veils, or The Triumph of Constancy: A Poem.* London: John Murray, 1815.

Porter, H. C. *The Inconstant Savage: England and the North American Indians, 1500–1660.* London: Duckworth, 1979.

Potter, Russell A. *Arctic Spectacles: The Frozen North in Visual Culture, 1818–1875.* Seattle: University of Washington Press, 2007.

Pratt, Mary Louise. *Imperial Eyes: Travel Writing and Transculturation.* London: Routledge, 1992.

Prentice, Harry [James Otis Kaler]. *The Boy Explorers, or, The Adventures of Two Boys in Alaska.* New York: A. L. Burt, 1895.

Pringle, Heather. 'Death in Norse Greenland', *Science* 275, no. 5302 (1997): 924–6.

Quinn, D. B. 'New Geographical Horizons: Literature'. In *First Images of America: The Impact of the New World on the Old*, edited by F. Chiappelli, 2:635–58. Berkeley: University of California Press, 1976.

Quinn, D. B. 'Newfoundland in the Consciousness of Europe in the Sixteenth and Early Seventeenth Centuries'. In *Early European Settlement and Exploitation in Atlantic Canada*, edited by G. M. Story, 9–30. St. Johns, Newfoundland: Memorial University of Newfoundland, 1982.

R. H. D. 'A Lost Colony', *Lippincott's Magazine of Popular Literature and Science* 22 (August 1878): 252–4.

Rafn, Carl Christian. 'Sinerissap inuinik sujugdlernik ilisimassaussut ilait', *Atuagagdliutit* (February 1864): 354–68.

Rafn, Carl Christian. *Supplement to Antiquitates Americanæ.* Copenhagen: Secretary's Office of the Society, 1841.

Rafn, Carl Christian and Finnur Magnússon, eds. *Grönlands historiske mindesmærker*, vol. 3. Copenhagen: Kongelige Nordiske Oldskrifts-Selskab, 1845.

Rasch, Niels Axelsen. 'Betænkning om Handelen og Missionen paa Grønland 1747'. In *Meddelelser no. 51: Bidrag til*

Grønlands Beskrivelse Forfattet av Nordmenn før 1814, 65–108. Oslo: Jacob Dybwad, 1942.

Rasmussen, Knud. *Intellectual Culture of the Copper Eskimos.* Copenhagen: Gyldendalske Boghandel, 1932.

Redding, Cyrus. *History of Shipwrecks, and Disasters at Sea from the Most Authentic Sources*, 2 vols. London: Whittaker, Treacher, & Company, 1833.

Reiman, Donald H. '*Christobell*, or, *The Case of the Sequel Pre-emptive*', *Wordsworth Circle* 6, no. 4 (1975): 283–9.

Reiman, Donald H. 'Introduction', in James Montgomery, *The West Indies*, v–x. New York: Garland, 1979.

Resen, Peder Hansen. *Groenlandia*, translated by J. Kisbye Møller. Copenhagen: Det Grønlandske Selskab, 1987.

Richards, Jeffrey. *Imperialism and Music: Britain 1876–1953.* Manchester: Manchester University Press, 2001.

Richards, John F. *The Unending Frontier: An Environmental History of the Early Modern World.* Berkeley CA: University of California Press, 2003.

Richardson, Sarah. 'Women, Philanthropy, and Imperialism in Early Nineteenth-Century Britain'. In *Burden or Benefit? Imperial Benevolence and Its Legacies*, edited by Helen Gilbert and Chris Tiffin, 90–102. Bloomington IN: Indiana University Press, 2008.

Rieder, John. *Colonialism and the Emergence of Science Fiction.* Middletown, CT: Wesleyan University Press, 2008.

Riffenburgh, Beau. 'Jules Verne and the Conquest of the Polar Regions', *Polar Record* 27, no. 162 (1991): 237–40.

Riffenburgh, Beau. *The Myth of the Explorer: The Press, Sensationalism, and Geographical Discovery.* Oxford: Oxford University Press, 1994.

Rink, Henry [Hinrich]. *Danish Greenland, Its People and Its Products.* London: H. S. King & Company, 1877.

Rink, Hinrich. *Tales and Traditions of the Eskimo, with a Sketch of Their Habits, Religion, Language and Other Peculiarities.* Edinburgh: W. Blackwood and Sons, 1875.

Rix, Robert W. 'Romancing Scandinavia: Relocating Chivalry and Romance in Eighteenth-Century Britain', *European Romantic Review* 20, no. 1 (2009): 3–20.

Robinson, Michael F. *The Coldest Crucible: Arctic Exploration and American Culture.* Chicago, IL: University of Chicago Press, 2006.

Robinson, Michael F. *The Lost White Tribe: Explorers, Scientists, and the Theory That Changed a Continent.* Oxford: Oxford University Press, 2016.

Rørdam, Holger F. *Klavs Christoffersen Lyskanders Levned: Samt hans Bog om danske Skribenter.* Copenhagen: Forlaget af Samfundet til den danske Litteraturs Fremme, 1868.

Rose, Carol. *Property and Persuasion: Essays on the History, Theory, and Rhetoric of Ownership.* Boulder, CO: Westview Press, 1994.

Ross, John. *A Voyage of Discovery … for the Purpose of Exploring Baffin's Bay, and Enquiring into the Probability of a North-West Passage,* 2 vols. London: Longman, Hurst, Rees, Orme, and Brown, 1819.

Rothberg, Michael. 'Remembering Back: Cultural Memory, Colonial Legacies, and Postcolonial Studies'. In *The Oxford Handbook of Postcolonial Studies,* edited by Graham Huggan, 359–79. Oxford: Oxford University Press, 2013.

Routledge, Karen. *Do You See Ice? Inuit and Americans at Home and Away.* Chicago, IL: University of Chicago Press, 2018.

Rud, Søren. *Colonialism in Greenland: Tradition, Governance and Legacy.* Cham: Palgrave, 2017.

Saabye, Hans Egede. *Brudstykker af en dagbog, holden i Grønland i aarene 1770–1778.* Odense: S. Hempel, 1816.

Saabye, Hans Egede. *Greenland: Being Extracts from a Journal Kept in that Country in the Years 1770 to 1778*, translated by H. E. Lloyd. London: Boosey and Sons, 1818.

Sanders, Vivienne. *Wales, the Welsh and the Making of America*. Cardiff: University of Wales Press, 2021.

Sangster, Matthew. *Living As an Author in the Romantic Period*. Cham: Palgrave Macmillan, 2021.

Schimanski, Johan. 'Reading the Future North'. In *Future North: The Changing Arctic Landscapes*, edited by Janike Kampevold Larsen and Peter Hemmersam, 16–25. London: Routledge, 2004.

Schmidt, Maike. *Grönland – Wo Nacht und Kälte wohnt: eine imagologische Analyse des Grönland-Diskurses im 18. Jahrhundert*. Gottingen: V&R Unipress, 2011.

Schröter, Johann Friedrich. *Allgemeine Geschichte der Länder und Völker von Amerika*, 2 vols. Halle: Justinus Gebauer, 1753.

Scoresby, William Jr. *Journal of a Voyage to the Northern Whale-Fishery: Including Researches and Discoveries on the Eastern Coast of West Greenland*. Edinburgh: Constable, 1823.

Scoville, Samuel Jr. *The Boy Scouts in the North; or, The Blue Pearl*, in *St. Nicholas Magazine* (November 1919–October 1920).

Seaborn, Adam [pseudonym]. *Symzonia: Voyage of Discovery*. New York: J. Seymour, 1820.

Seaver, Kirsten A. 'Desirable Teeth: The Medieval Trade in Arctic and African ivory', *Journal of Global History* 4, no. 2 (2009): 271–92.

Seaver, Kirsten A. *The Frozen Echo: Greenland and the Exploration of North America, ca. A.D. 1000–1500*. Stanford, CA: Stanford University Press, 1996.

Seaver, Kirsten A. *The Last Vikings: The Epic Story of the Great Norse Voyages*. London: I. B. Tauris 2010.

Seaver, Kirsten A. '"Pygmies" of the Far North', *Journal of World History* 19, no. 1 (2008), 63–87.

Seaver, Kirsten A. "'A Very common and usuall trade": The Relationship between Cartographic Perception and Fishing in the Davis Strait circa 1500–1550', *British Library Journal* 22, no. 1 (1996): 1–26.

Seed, Patricia. *Ceremonies of Possession in Europe's Conquest of the New World, 1492–1640*. New York: Cambridge University Press, 1997.

Segal, Howard P. *Technological Utopianism in American Culture: Twentieth Anniversary Edition*. Syracuse, NY: Syracuse University Press, 2005.

Settle, Dionise. "The second Voyage of Master Martin Frobisher'. In Richard Hakluyt, *The Principal Navigations Voyages Traffiques and Discoveries of the English Nation*, vol. 7, 211–30. Cambridge: Cambridge University Press, [1904] 2014.

Shahan, Thomas J. 'Miscellaneous Studies', *Catholic University Bulletin* 1, no. 3 (July 1895): 411–51.

Shoemaker, Nancy. 'A Typology of Colonialism', *Perspectives on History* 53, no. 7 (2015). www.historians.org/publications-and-directories/perspectives-on-history/october-2015/a-typology-of-colonialism.

Sines, Ryan. *Norse in the North Atlantic*. Lanham, MD: Hamilton Books, 2020.

Skarstein, Frode. '*Erik the Red's Land*: The Land That Never Was', *Polar Research* 25, no. 2 (2006): 173–9.

Sleeper, John S. 'The Lost Colony', in *The Boston Book: Being Specimens of Metropolitan Literature*, vol. 4, 218–22. Boston, MA: Ticknor, Reed and Fields, 1850.

Snelling, William Joseph. *The Polar Regions of the Western Continent Explored*. Boston, MA: W. W. Reed, 1831.

Solberg, Winton U. *Arctic Mirage: The 1913–1920 Expedition in Search of Crocker Land*. Jefferson, NC: McFarland, 2019.

Sonne, Birgitte. *Worldviews of the Greenlanders: An Inuit Arctic Perspective*. Fairbanks: University of Alaska Press, 2017.

Sørensen, Axel Kjær. *Denmark–Greenland in the Twentieth Century*. Copenhagen: Commission for Scientific Research in Greenland Press, 2006.

Sorenson, John L. and Martin H. Raish, eds. *Pre-Columbian Contact with the Americas across the Oceans: An Annotated Bibliography*, 2nd rev. ed., 2 vols. Provo, UT: Research Press, 1996.

Southey, Robert. *Joan of Arc: An Epic Poem*. Bristol: Joseph Cottle, 1796.

Spradlin, Derrick. '"GOD ne'er Brings to pass Such Things for Nought": Empire and Prince Madoc of Wales in Eighteenth-Century America', *Early American Literature* 44, no. 1 (2009): 39–70.

Spufford, Francis. *I May Be Some Time: Ice and the English Imagination*. New York: St. Martin's Press, 1997.

Sreenan, Niall. 'Dreaming of Islands: Individuality and Utopian Desire in Post-Darwinian Literature', *Island Studies Journal* 12, no. 2 (2017): 267–80.

St Clair, William. *The Reading Nation in the Romantic Period*. Cambridge: Cambridge University Press, 2007.

Stables, William Gordon. *The City at the Pole*. London: James Nisbet & Company, 1906.

Stables, William Gordon. *To Greenland and the Pole*. London: Blackie and Son, 1895.

Star, Bastiaan, James H. Barrett, Agata T. Gondek, and Sanne Boessenkool. 'Ancient DNA Reveals the Chronology of Walrus Ivory Trade from Norse Greenland', *Proceedings: Biological Sciences* 285, no. 1884 (2018). https://doi.org/10.1098/rspb.2018.0978.

Steckley, John L. *White Lies about the Inuit*. Peterborough, ON: Broadview Press, 2008.

Steckley, John L. and Bryan David Cummins. *Full Circle: Canada's First Nations*. Toronto, ON: Prentice Hall, 2001.

Strauch, Dieter. *Mittelalterliches Nordisches Recht Bis 1500: Eine Quellenkunde*. Berlin: De Gruyter, 2011.

Stefansson, Vilhjalmur. 'The Icelandic Colony in Greenland', *American Anthropologist* new series 8, no. 2 (1906): 262–70.

Stefansson, Vilhjalmur. *My Life with the Eskimo*. New York: Macmillan, 1913.

Stefansson, Vilhjalmur. 'My Quest in the North', *Harper's Monthly Magazine* 126 (December 1912): 4–13, 512–22.

Stefansson, Vilhjalmur. *The Northward Course of Empire*. New York: Harcourt, Brace and Company, 1922.

Stefansson, Vilhjalmur. 'The Republic of Greenland', *Forum* 80, no. 2 (August 1928): 250–66.

Stevens, Paul. '"Leviticus Thinking" and the Rhetoric of Early Modern Colonialism', *Criticism* 35, no. 3 (1993): 441–61.

Stevenson, Lisa. 'The Ethical Injunction to Remember'. In *Critical Inuit Studies: An Anthology of Contemporary Arctic Ethnography*, edited by Pamela Stern and Lisa Stevenson, 168–86. Lincoln: University of Nebraska Press, 2006.

Storm, Gustav. 'Den Danske Geograf Claudius Clavus eller Nicolaus Niger', *Ymer* 9 (1889): 129–46.

Storm, Gustav, ed. *Islandske Annaler indtil 1578*. Christiania: Grøndahl & Søns Bogtrykkeri, 1888.

Stringer, Arthur. *The Woman Who Couldn't Die*. Indianapolis, IN: Bobbs-Merrill Company, 1929.

Tally, Robert T., Jr. *Topophrenia: Place, Narrative, and the Spatial Imagination*. Bloomington: Indiana University Press, 2019.

Teitler, Stuart. *By the World Forgot: Towards a Bibliography of Lost Race Fiction from 1800*. London: Ferret Fantasy, 2013.

Thisted, Kirsten. 'Greenlandic Perspectives', *Handbook of Pre-modern Nordic Memory Studies*, vol. 2, edited by Jürg Glauser, Pernille Hermann, and Stephen A. Mitchell, 798–804. Berlin: De Gruyter, 2019.

Thisted, Kirsten. 'On Narrative Expectations: Greenlandic Oral Traditions about the Cultural Encounter between Inuit and Norsemen', *Scandinavian Studies* 73, no. 3 (2001): 253–96.

Thisted, Kirsten, ed. '*Således skriver jeg, Aron*': *Samlede fortællinger og illustrationer af Aron fra Kangeq*, 2 vols. Nuuk: Atuakkiorfik, 1999.

Thrush, Coll. *Indigenous London: Native Travelers at the Heart of Empire*. New Haven, CT: Yale University Press, 2016.

Thurin, Erik Ingvar. *The American Discovery of the Norse: An Episode in Nineteenth-Century American Literature*. Lewisburg, PA: Bucknell University Press, 1999.

Toft, Peter A. 'Erfaringer, ekspansion og konsolidering 1721–82'. In *Grønland. Den arktiske koloni*, edited by Hans Christian Gulløv, 46–107. Copenhagen: Gad, 2017.

Tonkin, Elizabeth. *Narrating Our Pasts: The Social Construction of Oral History*. Cambridge: Cambridge University Press, 1992.

Torfæus, Thormod. *Det gamle Grønland*. Oslo: A. W. Brøggers Boktrykkeris, 1927.

Torfæus, Thormod. *Gronlandia Antiqua, seu Veteris Gronlandiæ Descriptio*. Copenhagen: ex Typographéo Regiæ Majest. & Univerts., 1706.

Torgovnick, Marianna. *Gone Native: Savage Intellects, Modern Lives*. Chicago, IL: University of Chicago Press, 1990.

Traeger, Vera. 'Poq og Qiperoq: To eskimoportrætter', *M/S Museet for Søfarts årbog* 51 (2017): 117–44.

Trap, F. H., 'The Cartography of Greenland'. In *Greenland*, vol. 1, edited by M. Vahl et al., 137–79. Copenhagen: C. A. Reitzel, 1928.

Trollope, Anthony. *How the 'Mastiffs' Went to Iceland*. London: Virtue and Company, 1878.

Truett, Samuel. 'The Borderlands and Lost Worlds of Early America'. In *Contested Space of Early America*, edited by Juliana Barr and Edward Countryman, 301–24. Philadelphia, PA: University of Pennsylvania Press, 2014.

Tuksiautit: julesiutit, translated by Knud Kjer. Copenhagen: Farritius de Tengnage-Ikut Nakrittareit, 1831.

Turner, Frederick W. *Beyond Geography: The Western Spirit against the Wilderness*, rev. ed. New Brunswick, NJ: Rutgers University Press, 1992.

Turner, Jack. 'The Wild and The Self'. In *The Rediscovery of the Wild*, edited by Peter H. Kahn and Patricia H. Hasbach, 27–50. Cambridge, MA: MIT Press, 2013.

Tylor, Edward Burnett. 'Old Scandinavian Civilisation among the Modern Esquimaux', *Journal of the Anthropological Institute of Great Britain and Ireland* 13 (1884): 348–57.

Tyssot de Patot, Simon. *The Strange Voyages of Jacques Massé and Pierre de Mesange*, edited and translated by Brian Stableford. Encino, CA: Black Coat Press, 2015.

Tyssot le Patot, Simon. *La vie, les aventures, & les voyage de Groenland du Révérend Père Cordelier Pierre de Mésange. Avec une Relation bien circonstanciée de l'origine de l'histoire, des mœurs, & du Paradis des Habitans du Pole Arctique ... de l'origine de l'histoire, des moeurs, et du paradis des habitans du Pole Arctique*, 2 vols. Amsterdam: D'Etienne Roger, 1720.

Unger, Carl R. and H. J. Huitfeldt. *Diplomatarium Norvegicum*, vol. 6. Christiania: Malling, 1863.

Unger, Richard W. *Ships on Maps: Pictures of Power in Renaissance Europe*. Houndmills: Palgrave Macmillan, 2010.

US Congress. *Congressional Record: Proceedings and Debates of the 76th Congress, Third Session*, vol. 86, part 7. Washington: US Government Printing Office, 1940.

Valkendorf, Erik. 'Blandede optegnelser'. In *Grönlands Historiske Mindesmærker*, vol. 3, edited by Finn Magnusen and Carl Christian Rafn, 490–3. Copenhagen: Det Kongelige Nordiske Oldskrift-Selskab, 1845.

Valkendorf, Erik. 'Om de af Erkesbiskop Erik Walkendorff (henved 1516) samlede eller meddelte Efterretninger om Grönland'. *Grönlands Historiske Mindesmærker*, vol. 3, edited by Finn Magnusen and Carl Christian Rafn, 495–504.

Copenhagen: Det Kongelige Nordiske Oldskrift-Selskab, 1845.

Vardill, Anna Jane. 'The Arctic Navigator's Prayer', *European Magazine* 74 (July 1818): 61–2.

Vardill, Anna Jane. 'To the Authoress of the Arctic Expeditions'. Attic Chest Project. https://attic.vardill.org/season-10/meeting-94/arctic.

'V' [Vardill, Anna Jane]. 'Extracts from an Arctic Navigator's Journal', *European Magazine* 74 (September 1818): 193–7.

'V' [Vardill, Anna Jane]. 'Origin of an Arctic Colony', *European Magazine* 74 (November 1818): 385–90.

Vaughan, Richard. 'Historical Survey of the European Whaling Industry'. In *Arctic Whaling: Proceedings of the International Symposium Arctic Whaling, February 1983*, edited by H. K. Jacob, K. Snoeijing, and R. Vaughan, 121–79. [Groningen]: Arctic Centre, University of Groningen, 1984.

Vídalín, Thorkelsson Arngrímur. *Den Tredie Part af Det saa kaldede Gamle og Nye Grønlands Beskrivelse.* Copenhagen: Det Grønlandske Selskab, 1971.

Wade, Peter. *Race: An Introduction.* Cambridge: Cambridge University Press, 2015.

Wallace, Birgitta. 'The Norse in Newfoundland: L'Anse aux Meadows and Vinland', *Newfoundland Studies* 19, 1 (2003), 5–43.

Waller, Nicole. 'Connecting Atlantic and Pacific: Theorizing the Arctic', *Atlantic Studies* 15, no. 2 (2018): 256–78.

Wallin, Hans-Jørgen Weihe. *Vulkantiden: Historikeren Tormod Torfæus (1636–1719), livshistorie og reiser.* Stavanger: Hertervig Akademisk, 2015.

Walløe, Peder Olsen. *Peder Olsen Walløes dagbøger fra hans rejser i Grønland 1739–53*, edited by Louis Bobé. Copenhagen: Det Grønlandske Selskab, 1927.

Wamsley, Douglas W. 'Tales of the Far North: Dr William Gordon Stables and the Arctic Adventure Story in the Late Victorian Era', *Polar Record* 54, no. 4 (2018): 245–54.

Warkentin, Germaine, and Carolyn Podruchny, eds. *Decentring the Renaissance: Canada and Europe in Multidisciplinary History 1500–1700*. Toronto: University of Toronto Press, 2001.

Watts, Edward. *Colonizing the Past: Mythmaking and Pre-Columbian Whites in Nineteenth-Century American Writing*. Charlottesville, VA: University of Virginia Press, 2020.

Wawn, Andrew. *The Vikings and the Victorians: Inventing the Old North in Nineteenth-Century Britain*. Cambridge: D. S. Brewer, 2000.

Weaver-Hightower, Rebecca. *Empire Islands: Castaways, Cannibals, and Fantasies of Conquest*. Minneapolis, MN University of Minnesota Press, 2007.

Wesley, John. 'On the Spread of the Gospel'. In *The Works of the Rev. John Wesley*, vol. 6, 281–90. New York: J. J, Harper, 1826.

Westphal, Bertrand. *Geocriticism: Real and Fictional Spaces*, translated by Robert T. Tally Jr. New York: Palgrave Macmillan, 2011.

Wheatley, Kim. 'The Arctic in the *Quarterly Review*', *European Romantic Review* 20, no. 4 (2009): 465–90.

Whittaker, Fred. *The Lost Captain; or, Skipper Jabez Coffin's Cruise to the Open Polar Sea*, in *Beadle's Half-Dime Library* 8, no. 159. New York: Beadle and Adams, 1880.

Williams, Gwyn A. *Madoc: The Making of a Myth*. Oxford: Oxford University Press, 1987.

Williams, Nathaniel. *Gears and God: Technocratic Fiction, Faith, and Empire in Mark Twain's America*. Tuscaloosa:, AL University of Alabama Press, 2018.

Williams, Robert A. Jr. *Savage Anxieties: The Invention of Western Civilization*. Basingstoke: Palgrave, 2012.

Wilson, William Huntington. *Rafnaland: The Strange Story of John Heath Howard*. New York: Harper & Brothers, 1900.

Wilson, William Huntington. 'The Return of the Sergeant', *Harper's Weekly* 44 (September 1900): 872–4.

Wilton, Pleydell. 'The Polar Ice'. In *Geology and Other Poems*. London: J. Hatchard, 1818.

Winsor, Justin. *'Pre-Columbian Exploration'*. In *Narrative and Critical History of America*, edited by Justin Winsor, 59–116. Boston, MA: Mifflin and Company, 1889.

Wood-Donnelly, Corine. *Performing Arctic Sovereignty: Policy and Visual Narratives*. London: Routledge, 2019.

Worm, Ole. *Breve til og fra Ole Worm*, 3 vols., translated by H. D. Schepelern. Copenhagen: Munksgaard, 1965–8.

Zeiders, Blaire. 'Conjuring History: The Premodern Origins and Post-truth Legacy of John Dee's *Brytanici Imperii Limites'*, *Journal of Medieval and Early Modern Studies* 49, no. 2 (2019): 377–401.

Anonymous Reviews in Periodicals (chronologically ordered)

Review of Eleanor Anne Porden's *Arctic Expeditions, Anti-Jacobin Review and Protestant Advocate* 54 (April 1818): 250–2.

Review of 'Account of the Expedition to Baffin's Bay under Captain Ross and Lieutenant Parry Drawn up from Captain Ross's Account of the Voyage and Other Sources of Information', *Edinburgh Philosophical Journal* (June 1819): 150–9.

Review of James Montgomery's *Greenland, British Critic* (August 1819): 211–18.

Review of James Montgomery's *Greenland, Eclectic Review* 12 (September 1819): 210–28.

Review of Graah's 'A Voyage to the East Coast', *Foreign Quarterly Review* 12, no. 24 (1833): 515–16.

Review of C. C. Zahrtmann's 'Remarks on the Voyages to the Northern Hemisphere', *Journal of the Royal Geographic Society of London* 5 (1835): 102–37.

Review [by 'W. R'.] of August Graah's *Narrative of an Expedition to the East Coast of Greenland, London and Westminster Review* 27 (July 1837): 139–65.

Review of Antiquarian Miscellany 1, 2, & 3, Copenhagen 1832–6, *Athenaeum: Journal of Literature, Science, and the Fine Arts* no. 512 (August 1837): 595–8.

Review of Graah, *Undersögelses-Rejse, North British Review*, 6 (November 1845): 77–95.

Review of J. B. Jukes, *Narrative of the Surveying Voyage, in Blackwood's Edinburgh Magazine* (November 1847): 515–33.

INDEX